AN INTRODUCTION TO TH  M

AN INTRODUCTION TO THE ENGLISH LEGAL SYSTEM

Fourth Edition

MARTIN PARTINGTON

OXFORD
UNIVERSITY PRESS

OXFORD
UNIVERSITY PRESS

Great Clarendon Street, Oxford OX2 6DP

Oxford University Press is a department of the University of Oxford.
It furthers the University's objective of excellence in research, scholarship,
and education by publishing worldwide in

Oxford New York

Auckland Cape Town Dar es Salaam Hong Kong Karachi
Kuala Lumpur Madrid Melbourne Mexico City Nairobi
New Delhi Shanghai Taipei Toronto

With offices in

Argentina Austria Brazil Chile Czech Republic France Greece
Guatemala Hungary Italy Japan Poland Portugal Singapore
South Korea Switzerland Thailand Turkey Ukraine Vietnam

Oxford is a registered trade mark of Oxford University Press
in the UK and in certain other countries

Published in the United States
by Oxford University Press Inc., New York

© Martin Partington 2008

The moral rights of the author have been asserted

Crown copyright material is reproduced under Class Licence
Number C01P0000148 with the permission of OPSI
and the Queen's Printer for Scotland

Database right Oxford University Press (maker)

First edition 2000
Second edition 2003
Reprinted 2004
Third edition 2006
Fourth edition 2008

British Library Cataloguing in Publication Data

Data available

Library of Congress Cataloging in Publication Data
Partington, Martin.
An introduction to the English legal system / Martin Partington.— 4th ed.
   p. cm.
Includes bibliographical references and index.
ISBN-13: 978-0-19-923810-1 (alk. paper)
1. Law—Great Britain.   I. Title.
KD661.P37 2008
349.42—dc22   2008003357

Typeset by Newgen Imaging Systems (P) Ltd., Chennai, India
Printed in Great Britain
on acid-free paper by
Ashford Colour Press, Gosport, Hampshire

ISBN 978-0-19-923810-1

1 3 5 7 9 10 8 6 4 2

Foreword

I am delighted to have been asked to write this foreword to the fourth edition of Professor Partington's *Introduction to the English Legal System*.

I believe strongly that there needs to be much greater public understanding of law and the legal system. Public legal education is a vital component of modern citizenship. This was an issue I was anxious to promote while I was chair of the Civil Justice Council. I fully support the ambitions of the Ministry of Justice to promote public legal education.

Public legal education cannot happen without appropriate educational materials being available. Much legal writing is, of necessity, rather heavy going and daunting for the non-specialist. But there is also a very important place for introductory books which, while not going into every last detail, can engage the non-specialist reader.

In my view, Martin Partington has succeeded admirably in providing a text which both explains things clearly, and encourages the reader to think about the enormous changes currently affecting the legal system. He has been able to draw on his experience not only as a teacher of law, but also as law reformer and contributor to the work of many important committees.

I wish the new edition every success.

Phillips of Worth Matravers
Lord Chief Justice of England and Wales

Preface to the fourth edition

It is only two years since I completed the third edition of this book. Despite this relatively short time, there has been an enormous amount of change, which is reflected in the text. The whole book has been revised and updated. Among the most significant changes have been:

- publication of a consultation paper on the Governance of Britain, raising issues about the possibility of a written constitution and a British Bill of Rights (Chapter 2);
- creation of the Ministry of Justice to replace the Department of Constitutional Affairs (which had in turn replaced the Lord Chancellor's Department) (Chapter 4);
- appointment of the first Lord Chancellor who is a member of the House of Commons (Chapter 4);
- creation of the new Judicial Appointments Commission (Chapter 4);
- reshaping of the responsibility for criminal justice, resulting from the transfer of functions from the Home Office to the Ministry of Justice (Chapter 5);
- passing of legislation to underpin the creation of the new Tribunals Service (Chapter 6);
- proposals for radical reform of Child Support and the creation of a new Child Maintenance and Enforcement Commission (Chapter 7);
- development of plans for the creation of a new Supreme Court (Chapter 8);
- bringing into effect proposals for creation of a new Legal Services Board and other mechanisms to regulate the legal professions and others who provide legal services (Chapter 9); and
- further proposals for the reform of legal aid (Chapter 10).

The aims of the book remain the same—to provide all those coming new to the study of law, whether at A-level, degree level, or postgraduate conversion level, with an overview of the context within which law is made and practised in England and Wales; to provide a text that is as approachable as possible; and, more generally, to create a resource for those teaching citizenship in schools which can inform and encourage a key part of the National Curriculum.

The importance of better public understanding of law and legal institutions can hardly be overstated. Indeed, since the last edition of this book was published, the Government has recognized this through the establishment of the Taskforce on Public Legal Education and Support, chaired by Professor Dame Hazel Genn, DBE. (See Chapter 1) I hope this book will make a contribution to this better understanding.

The increasing amount of material available on the internet is reflected in the large number of websites cited in the text. All these sites have been successfully accessed during the period this new edition was being prepared (September–October 2007). More detailed descriptions and other suggestions for further reading are available on the book's Online Resource Centre at www.oxfordtextbooks.co.uk/orc/partington4e/. Information about new sites which you find interesting but which are not mentioned in the text may be fed back to me through the ORC. Similarly please let me know through the ORC of links that no longer work.

Since completing the third edition, my appointment as special consultant to the Law Commission has come to an end. So too has my appointment as research adviser to Lord Justice Carnwath, Senior President of the new Tribunals Service. During the period I was a member of the Public Legal Education Taskforce, mentioned above. As with previous editions, I emphasize that I write here in a purely personal capacity. None of the official bodies with which I am or have been associated is to be taken as agreeing with what I have written here.

As always, my debt to my family, friends, and colleagues is enormous. I am particularly grateful to the Lord Chief Justice for agreeing to write the foreword to this fourth edition. At the risk of offending others, I would like to offer special thanks to two people who have helped clarify ideas or provided new insight: Robert Musgrove, the indefatigable chief executive of the Civil Justice Council, whose work behind the scenes for the development of the civil justice system is tireless; and Michael Napier, CBE, QC, whose work promoting pro bono legal work is an inspiration to all who work in the English Legal System. At Oxford University Press, Melanie Jackson has presided over the preparation of this edition with her usual tact and courtesy. I thank her and others involved in the production of this book. I am also most grateful to the anonymous referees who, as part of OUP procedures, commented on the strengths and weaknesses of the third edition. While I may not have fully incorporated their comments, they all provoked thought and reflection. I remain responsible for all errors and omissions.

Bristol, 22 October 2007

Preface to the first edition

The original proposal that I should write this book came from Professor Peter Cane when he, with Professor Jane Stapleton, were editors of the Clarendon Law Series, published by Oxford University Press. Though it has now been decided that the book should not appear in that series, I have nonetheless adhered to my initial instructions. These were that the book should: be genuinely introductory; be around 200 pages long; be relatively uncluttered by footnotes; be accessible to the more general reader; but at the same time offer an approach to thinking about the English legal system and its place in society not found elsewhere. With these strictures in mind, this book has been written particularly for those coming to the study of law for the first time. I also hope that others, keen to look behind the magical veil that all too often shrouds the legal system and its actors in mystery, will find the book of interest. It is, in short, intended for all those interested in the phenomenon of law and the important role it plays in the ordering of our society but without any detailed knowledge of it.

Over the last thirty or so years, I have been associated with a wide range of bodies and institutions, from whom I have learned much and who have helped to inform my ideas about the English legal system and the forces that shape it. They include, at different stages, and for different lengths of time: the Hillfields Advice Centre in Coventry; the Legal Action Group; the Training Committee of the Institute of Housing; the Management Committees of Citizens' Advice Bureaux in Coventry, Paddington and Uxbridge; the Education Committee of the Law Society; the Lord Chancellor's Advisory Committee on Legal Aid; the Independent Tribunal Service for Social Security Appeal Tribunals; the Judicial Studies Board (both the main Board and its Tribunals Committee); the Council on Tribunals; the Civil Justice Council (and its sub-committee on Alternative Dispute Resolution); the Committee of Heads of University Law Schools; the Socio-Legal Studies Association; and the Socio-Legal Research Users' Forum. I am grateful to the numerous friends and colleagues from all these bodies—too numerous to list here—for their generosity of spirit, enthusiasm, and sheer hard work in the development of the practices and institutions of law in England.

I also thank my colleagues at Bristol for their support, in particular Rebecca Bailey-Harris, David Cowan, Gwynn Davies, Clare Lewis, Donald Nicolson, Stratos Konstadinidis, and Andrew Sanders. I am grateful to successive generations of students at Bristol, and before then Brunel, Universities to whom I offered instruction in English Legal System and English Legal Methods for their critical responses to what I have had to say. I have been particularly fortunate that, as part of the writing process, I was able to deliver early versions of this text as introductory lectures to first year students at the University of Bristol; and to discuss them in an informal 'reading group'. They helped me determine important questions of structure and content. I am most grateful to all those who offered their comments. However, I remain wholly responsible for what follows.

My editor at Oxford University Press, Michaela Coulthard, has been a model of tolerance as I have failed to meet a variety of deadlines.

I am not sure that my children Adam and Hannah have ever been particularly conscious of what I do in my professional life. Nonetheless I am grateful to both for allowing me to share some of my initial thoughts about this book with them. They were particularly encouraging at times when encouragement was needed. As always I am especially indebted to Daphne for her insistence that I retain a sense of balance in my life.

I have sought to bring the text up to date to the date shown below.

Bristol, 27 April 2000

Guide to the Online Resource Centre

www.oxfordtextbooks.co.uk/orc/partington4e/

The online Resource Centre that accompanies this book provides students and lecturers with ready-to-use teaching and learning materials. These resources are free of charge and are designed to maximise the learning experience.

Student resources

Updates
An indispensable resource allowing you to access changes and developments in the law that have occurred since the publication of the book. These are added to the website as and when they arise and are organised by chapter, enabling you to easily identify which material has been superseded or supplemented.

> **Reform of legal aid**
>
> Controversy over the reform of legal aid continues unabated. Continuing stories in the media about the collapse of legal aid. been expanding – and on civil legal aid, which has been contra *Implementing Legal Reform: Government response to the Con* 220607.htm). This is an issue on which there will be continuing

Web links and further reading
A selection of annotated web links and texts for further reading allow you to easily research those topics that are of particular interest.

> **Criminal trials**
>
> www.dca.gov.uk/procedurerules/criminalpr_committee.htm
> This is the site of the Criminal Procedure Rules Committee, es
>
> www.hmcourts-service.gov.uk/onlineservices/xhibit/index.htm
> Site of the new electronic information system, Xhibit, which pro
> system. It has been on trial for a number of years; national roll

Multiple choice questions
The best way to enforce your understanding of the English legal system is through frequent and cumulative revision. As such, a bank of self-marking multiple-choice questions has been provided for each chapter of the text, and includes instant feedback on your answers, and cross-references to the textbook, to assist with independent self-study.

> **Question 01**
>
> Who is the head of the judiciary?
>
> ○ a) The Lord Chancellor
> ○ b) The Master of the Rolls

Crosswords
Key legal definitions are presented in an interactive crossword format, allowing you to test your knowledge.

Additional questions

Focusing on the issues raised in the first chapter, the author provides a number of questions relating to the grandeur that surrounds the legal system, encouraging you to consider the role and the impact this has on both the legal profession and the public.

Additional questions

This is an experimental part of the site designed to encourage
The sites here offer some photographic or other forms of imag
photos of the interiors of courts in England, as photography is

Much of the legal system is surrounded by grandeur – grand b

Flashcard glossary

A series of interactive flashcards containing key terms and concepts have been provided to test your understanding of legal terminology before exams.

PREVIOUS   FLIP CARD   NEXT

Sentencing

Lecturer resources

Password protected to ensure only lecturers can access these resources, each registration is personally checked to ensure the security of the site.

Registering is easy: click on the 'Lecturer Resources' on the Online Resource Centre, complete a simple registration form which allows you to choose your own password, and access will be granted within 72 hours (subject to verification).

Customisable PowerPoint presentations

For each chapter there is a corresponding lecture presentation provided in PowerPoint. Each presentation lists the main points for discussion and is easily downloadable for customisation and use in lectures and seminars.

The legislative process

- Points to note
  - the pre-legislative stages: Green Papers and White papers
  - Bills published in advance for consultation
  - Private Members' Bills - distinct from

Seminar ideas

A list of suggested topics to cover in seminars to encourage students to reflect upon their reading and to consider the challenges and controversies faced by the English legal system.

Seminar ideas: tips and techniques o

The Newspaper exercise

Legal skills

Images of law

Discussion Questions

Author commentary on role of the discussion questions posed in the book and how these can be used so as to encourage students to fully consider the role of the legal system in society.

Guidance on how to use discussion

The book was written primarily for students to read without the
contains a set of multiple choice questions which students car

In those institutions where there is teaching of the issues cons
for discussion.

Outline contents

Contents

PART II THE INSTITUTIONAL FRAMEWORK

PART III THE DELIVERY AND FUNDING OF LEGAL SERVICES

List of boxes

INTRODUCTION

1

'Knowledge', themes, and structure

Introductory

This book aims to provide an introductory account of the English legal system, how it has developed in recent years, and how it may develop in future. I want readers to think about the legal system and to question the extent to which it is fit for purpose. I want readers to see the links between the legal system and some of the most difficult issues facing the modern world. For example, where should the balance be struck between the need to protect civil liberties, and the government's need to take action to reduce risks associated with terrorism?

The book is primarily about the *English* legal system (which includes for most practical purposes the legal system in Wales). There is a quite different system in Scotland and a rather different system in Northern Ireland. There are times when it is not sensible to refer just to 'England'—thus the phrases 'Great Britain' or 'United Kingdom' are used where they seem more appropriate. Nonetheless, the focus of the book is on the English legal system.

This does not mean that the book is exclusively about institutions located in England and Wales. The English legal system is subject to important external factors, in particular the law and institutions of the European Union and Council of Europe.

Many who study law in England come from other countries. I hope that readers from overseas can both learn from the issues discussed here, and relate the questions raised to the situation in their home countries. Are the legal systems with which they may be more familiar fitted to their purpose? Are there lessons to be learned from the English experience? And, turning these questions around, what should the English be learning from experience elsewhere?

'Knowledge'

Images and pre-conceptions

Even readers of an introductory work on law come to it with a good deal of 'knowledge' of law, shaped by what they have read or heard in the media. However much of what appears in the media about law is, at best misleading, at worst quite wrong. It is therefore not surprising that most people's prior knowledge of law is incomplete. Interestingly, the importance of the general public being able to find out more about how law and the legal system work—one of the themes which underpins this book— has recently been recognized by government, following publication—in July 2007—of the report of the Taskforce on Public Legal Education, *Developing Capable Citizens: the role of Public Legal Education.*

There are at least five images of law which I suggest readers of this book may have, but which are incorrect or misleading, and which any programme of public legal education should address.

The scope of the legal system

First, most media discussion of law and the legal system concentrates on what happens in criminal trial courts. This is understandable. It is there that the murders and other serious criminal cases (such as theft or fraud) are dealt with. The perception of the central place of the criminal justice system is reinforced by endless television plays and films which draw on the inherent drama of the criminal trial.

But such a view is far too narrow. First, as discussed in Chapter 5, the vast majority of key criminal justice decisions are taken not in courts, but elsewhere, e.g. in the police station or by the parole board. Secondly, focusing on the criminal trial ignores the existence of other equally important parts of the English legal system—the *civil justice, administrative justice,* and *family justice* systems considered in Chapters 6 to 8.

Providers of legal services

Media treatment of the question who provides legal services, focuses—again understandably—on professionally qualified lawyers. Again this is too narrow. As shown in Chapter 9 (and part of Chapter 7), many others provide legal services to the public.

In addition, media descriptions of lawyers are often very unflattering. Some regard them as cynical parasites, willing to undertake any task for which a client is willing to pay—the 'hired gun' model of the lawyer. Others note the salaries lawyers are paid, which promotes the 'fat cat' image of the lawyer. Some portray lawyers as using their legal training and professional status to enhance their earnings by creating a mystique around the law which prevents ordinary people from making effective use of law—the lawyer as 'freemason'. There may also be perceptions about the education, class background, gender, or ethnicity of lawyers which arise from media coverage. While there may be *some* truth in some of these perceptions, a more detailed look provides a picture that is both more complex and more interesting.

Resistance to change

The media can portray the law and the legal system as old-fashioned and backward looking. The Victorian architecture of law's landmark buildings, such as the Old Bailey or the Royal Courts of Justice in London, reflect a bygone age, as do the robes and dress that lawyers adopt, particularly when appearing in court. This may lead to a more general impression of resistance to change.[1]

Many who practise law do resist change. It is disturbing and unsettling. But for many, change is what prevents life becoming boring. The last thirty or so years have witnessed a large number of changes in law and legal process, many of which have been very dramatic. Indeed the number of changes needed to bring this fourth edition up-to-date suggests that the pace of change is, if anything, increasing. Another of the themes explored in this book relates to the forces for change—the *dynamism*—within the law and the legal system.

In Chapter 4 we consider the contribution of government to the pressure for change. Throughout the work, we note numerous examples of how practice and procedure have changed in recent years. Implicit in this discussion is a more important question: should those who work in the legal system be more willing to proclaim change as an important part of our legal culture than has happened in the past?

Inefficiency, expense, and delay

The media often suggest that legal proceedings suffer from inordinate delay and expense. This is a perception that has driven much current debate about reform of the civil justice system, discussed in Chapter 8. It underlies many of the other changes made to the justice system. However, before concluding that the whole of the system is dogged by inefficiency, delay, and expense, we again need to consider the evidence carefully and ask how far popular images reflect the whole truth about the English legal system. We also need to ask whether pressure for greater speed and efficiency can sometimes act against the interests of justice.

Miscarriages of justice

A final issue which dominates media treatment of law relates to miscarriages of justice. This may suggest that there are serious, even structural, defects with the legal system that result in these miscarriages. There is no doubt that from time to time things do go seriously wrong. Cases are improperly investigated, or inadequately presented in court, or inexpertly handled by the trial judge, or insufficiently considered on appeal. It is right that the media draw attention to them.

But miscarriages of justice also demonstrate another side to the English legal system. Whatever the difficulties, there are those within the system willing to challenge decisions that have not been arrived at by due process of law. Many of those arguing that miscarriages of justice have occurred are themselves lawyers. Miscarriages of justice may lead some to perceive the legal system as a system in crisis. Paradoxically, though, they may also be a source of reassurance, that the system and those who work

---

[1] On the specific question of court dress, the Lord Chief Justice announced on 12 July 2007 that, from 1 January 2008, judges in civil and family courts will wear a simple gown over their ordinary working clothes; robes and wigs will no longer be worn. The Bar Council is currently running a consultation on the dress lawyers should wear when they appear in court.

within it are sufficiently independent and robust to challenge those who have made mistakes.

The primary purpose of this book is to provide a general overview of the framework within which the law of England (and Wales) is made and practised, which will illuminate and where necessary alter such initial images and pre-conceptions. Where there is truth in those images and pre-conceptions, particularly negative ones, I hope readers can learn from the fact that not everything is perfect and reflect on what may need to be changed. Where images of law and the legal system are unfair, I hope they become better informed.

Themes

Although an introductory book, it seeks to address themes inadequately considered in other books with the same or similar titles.

- First, many current accounts of the English legal system are rather 'practitioner-driven'; they focus primarily on those parts of the system in which professionally qualified lawyers practise their law. Here a more holistic approach is taken, designed to introduce the reader to a wider range of activities and functions often ignored elsewhere.

- Secondly, other introductory accounts are somewhat descriptive and 'static' in nature, providing a snapshot of the system at the moment of writing. As already suggested, the English legal system is considerably more dynamic and more responsive to change than is often realized. A recurring theme will be on change and the forces that have shaped and are shaping the English legal system. At the same time, questions are raised about the extent to which particular changes are desirable or should be resisted.

- Thirdly, the English legal system is often portrayed as something distinct from the British system of government. Indeed one of the important claims made for law and its practice is that it is 'independent' of government. Yet the government of the country is based in law; the institutions of law derive their power and authority from the system of government. Understanding the constitutional function of the English legal system and the relationship of the legal system to other branches of government is therefore another theme underpinning the discussion in this work.

- Finally, the assertion is often made that 'we have the best system of justice in the world'. It may be a good system, indeed a very good system. But this conclusion should be arrived at on the basis of evidence, not mere assertion. This book is intended to provide a basis for thinking critically about the institutions and practices of the law and contemplating change where inadequacy or inefficiency is demonstrated to exist.

Structure

Having considered the images and pre-conceptions which those coming new to the study of law may have; and having set out the themes that underlie the book, the structure of the book is as follows:

Part I consists of two chapters that discuss the social functions of law and the legitimacy of law. Chapter 2 considers the roles which law plays in the regulation of modern society. Chapter 3 considers how law is made, who makes it, where they get the authority for making it, whether the processes currently used for making law should be changed and, if so, how.

Part II considers the institutional framework within which law is developed and practised. The discussion opens, in Chapter 4, with an account of the role of government in shaping the institutions and practice of law. Chapters 5 to 8 look in turn at the four legal systems which, for the purpose of this account, comprise the English legal system: the *Criminal Justice* system; the *Administrative Justice* system; the *Family Justice* system; and the *Civil and Commercial Justice* system. In each chapter there is consideration not only of formal legal institutions such as courts, but also informal or other processes that do not catch the public eye (and indeed which are often not properly understood by professional lawyers) but which form an essential part of the framework of the English legal system seen in the round.

Part III looks at the personnel of the law, and the tasks they perform in delivering legal services. Chapter 9 considers the role not only of those professionally qualified to practise law, but others who play a part in the workings of the legal system, including adjudicators and jurists. Chapter 10 reflects on how the provision of legal services is paid for.

Finally, a short concluding chapter asks whether the English legal system is in fact fit for the purposes it is required to perform. Is the English legal system 'the best in the world' in need of little or no change? Or is the system simply not delivering what is required of it, and thus in need of fundamental change? If changes are needed, what are they? What are the forces likely to render change difficult, if not impossible?

Questions for reflection and discussion

1. To what extent do you share the images and pre-conceptions set out in this chapter?
2. What other images of law do you have?
3. How have you acquired your knowledge about law?

A useful exercise, to see the extent to which law affects our lives, often without realizing it, is to read any daily newspaper carefully from cover to cover. Ask yourself: which items deal with some aspect of the practice of law, the making of law, the resolution of disputes? Consider not just home news pages or specialist law pages, but the whole paper, including the international pages, the business pages, and the sports pages. You will be surprised how many stories have a legal dimension to them.

4. Have you, or any member of your family, had any personal experience of going to law? If so, what did you learn about the legal system as a result?

5. How would you seek to engage mass media interest in law and the legal system?

6. Has anyone you know undertaken jury service? What did they think of the experience?

Further reading

BAILEY, S., GUNN, M., ORMEROD, D., and CHING, J., *Smith, Bailey and Gunn on The Modern English Legal System* (4th edn., London, Sweet and Maxwell, 2002)

BANKOWSKI, Z., and MUNGHAM, G., *Images of Law* (London, Routledge and Kegan Paul, 1976)

COWNIE, F., BRADNEY, A., and BURTON, M., *English Legal System in Context* (4th edn., London, Oxford University Press, 2007)

JACONELLI, J., *Open Justice: A Critique of the Public Trial* (Oxford, Oxford University Press, 2002)

MACHURA, S., and ROBSON, P. (eds), *Law and Film: Representing Law in Movies* (Oxford, Blackwell, 2001)

PODGORECKI, A., *et al.*, *Knowledge and Opinion about Law* (London, Martin Robertson, 1973)

SLAPPER, G., and KELLY, D., *The English Legal System* (8th rev. edn., London, Cavendish, 2006)

WARD, R., and WRAGG, A., *Walker and Walker's English Legal System* (9th edn., London, LexisNexisUK, 2005) (10th edn. forthcoming March 2008)

ZANDER, M., *Cases and Materials on the English Legal System* (10th edn., Cambridge, Cambridge University Press, 2007)

—— *A Matter of Justice: The Legal System in Ferment* (London, Tauris, 1988)

—— *The State of Justice* (London, Sweet & Maxwell, 2000)

Websites

http://www.bailii.org/ *(Electronic library of legal materials, with links to other world materials)*

http://www.kent.ac.uk/lawlinks/ *(Legal information on the internet)*

http://www.venables.co.uk/ *(Privately run gateway to information about law and solicitors)*

http://www.intute.ac.uk/socialsciences/law/ *(Social sciences information gateway, material on law)*

http://www.coe.int/DefaultEN.asp *(Council of Europe portal)*

http://eur-lex.europa.eu/en/index.htm *(European Union legal portal)*

http://www.justice.gov.uk/ *(Ministry of Justice home page)*

http://www.pleas.org.uk/index.html *(Public Legal Education Taskforce Report)*

http://www.berr.gov.uk/consumers/index.html *(Confident consumers website)*

PART I

LAW, SOCIETY, AND AUTHORITY

This Part considers, first, what functions law plays in the way in which society is ordered (Chapter 2). Secondly, it asks what are the sources of authority from which those who make law base their claim to have the power to make law (Chapter 3).

2

Law and society: the purposes and functions of law

Introduction

One aim of this book is to enable readers to understand the institutional framework within which rules of law are made and used; it does not analyse specific rules of law, for example, 'what is the legal definition of murder' or 'when is a contract legally binding'. Nonetheless, it is hard to make any sense of that framework without at least some indication of what the rules of law are to which the framework of the English legal system applies and, in particular, what the *social purpose* or *social function* of those rules of law is. In considering this, I draw a distinction between the macro and the micro functions of law. The macro functions of law are those that relate to the general role law plays in the running and ordering of society. The micro functions—which derive from those macro functions—relate to more specific uses to which law is put. The distinction becomes clearer as the discussion proceeds.

The macro functions of law: law and orders

If one asks: what is the role of law in society? a common response would be 'to maintain order'. Much public debate and political rhetoric links law and order. There are two problems with this response.

First it is extremely ambiguous. There is no single concept of order, but rather a variety of orders in relation to which the law may play a role. These include:

- public order;
- political order;
- social order;
- economic order;
- international order; and
- moral order.

Second, the relationship between law and each of these types of order is extremely complex. The ability of law to shape these different orders is not unconstrained, but is itself shaped by wider political and social forces. The law is not a neutral force which contributes to the organization of society, but which is otherwise detached from that society. The relationship between law and orders in any given society cannot be understood without an understanding of the political, social, and economic ideologies that underpin that society. The role law plays in one society differs from that which it plays in another.

The ambiguities surrounding the concept of order, and the complexity of the relationship between law and orders are considered further in the following paragraphs.

Law and public order

Many argue that a—possibly the—primary function of law is the *preservation of public order*. But maintaining public order is not exclusively a task for law; many other factors such as pressure from family or friends or work colleagues play an important part. Nonetheless the fact that law sets the boundaries of acceptable behaviour and prescribes sanctions for breaches of those boundaries (which is in essence the function of criminal law) makes a significant contribution to preserving public order.

The preservation of public order, however, immediately raises another but not necessarily consistent function for law: the *protection of civil liberties and human rights*. The ability of people to argue freely about their beliefs is an important aspect of life in a democratic society. Limits may need to be set to the freedom of individuals to advance unpopular views, for example, those that are obscene or defamatory or which incite racial or religious hatred. Nevertheless, within those limits, freedoms of speech and thought must be protected by law.

Until recently, the British had no formal statement of human rights, comparable to the Bill of Rights enshrined in the constitution of the United States of America. Rather they relied on long-standing principles of law allowing people to indicate dissent, for example, by peaceful demonstrations or marches. Since October 2000, when the Human Rights Act 1998 came into effect, a more formal code of human rights has applied in the United Kingdom. Protection of human rights and civil liberties can therefore be identified as another function of the law. But it is not always consistent with the aim of preserving public order. There are occasions when the preservation of public order results in restrictions on civil liberties. Conversely, the protection of civil liberty on occasion limits the ability of public authorities to control public order.

In highly repressive societies, the function of law in preserving public order may become so dominant that the effect is the destruction of civil liberties and other fundamental freedoms. In more tolerant societies where dissent is permitted, there must be a balance. There is always sharp debate about the extent to which law's function is to preserve public order, as opposed to protecting other rights and freedoms. *Liberty, Justice,* and other pressure groups which seek to defend civil liberty may not always persuade governments to change their minds on proposals relating to the development of law. But their ability to challenge and criticize is fundamental to supporting a democratic system based on the rule of law. The law's function in relation to the maintenance of public order is, thus, highly contingent upon the nature of the society in which law operates.

Law and political order

Another primary function of law is to underpin the political order of the country—the constitutional function of law. In this respect, the United Kingdom is something of an oddity. It is one of a very few countries that does not have a written constitution. Indeed many important practices within the British Constitution derive from unwritten 'conventions', rather than from written rules of law. (*See below, Box 3.1.*) Some crucial aspects about the way the system of government is organized in the United Kingdom fall outside the scope of law altogether, being based more in political theory than in legal rules. In view of this, some may think that support for constitutional arrangements should not be regarded as one of the macro functions of law.

Nevertheless, despite the lack of a written constitution, it is appropriate to include this topic here. It emphasizes the fact that, although the United Kingdom has no written constitution, a great deal of fundamental law regulates the way in which our political system operates. Indeed the programme of constitutional reform being advanced by the present Labour government, and further developed in the recent Green Paper on the Governance of Britain,[1] suggests that we may be witnessing the birth of a legally based constitutional settlement. So many aspects of our constitutional arrangements are either now enshrined in law or shortly will be.

To give some examples:

- British membership of the European Union, recognized in such fundamental statutes as the European Communities Act 1972 and as amended to take account of changes to the European Treaties, has, among other things, set limits to the legislative power—the sovereignty—of the British Parliament;

- The Scotland Act 1998 and the Wales Act 1998 (supplemented by the Government of Wales Act 2006) both provide for devolution of powers from the government in London to, respectively, the Scottish Parliament and the Welsh Assembly. This provides a new legal framework for the regulation of the relationship between the government in London, and governments in Edinburgh and Cardiff;

- The Human Rights Act 1998 has significantly affected the practice of government. Legislation must be compliant with the provisions of the European Convention on Human Rights which are incorporated in that Act;[2]

---

[1] http://www.justice.gov.uk/publications/governanceofbritain.htm.

[2] For information about recent developments under the Human Rights Act see http://www.justice.gov.uk/guidance/humanrights.htm.

- laws relating to official secrecy and freedom of information[3] determine the extent to which governments can operate openly or in secret. This is another example of the use of fundamental law to support constitutional arrangements;
- if there is reform of the House of Lords—a process whose outcome is still uncertain[4]—this will only be achieved by Act of Parliament. This will form another part of British constitutional law;
- many other examples can be given: the detailed law relating to the running of elections; or the law regulating the relationship between central and local government.[5]

Given this rapidly growing body of law, some now argue that the British should take the last step and adopt a written constitution, which would codify into a single legislative measure all these constitutional provisions.[6]

Law and social order

Law also contributes to a country's 'social order'. Defining the nature of social order is extremely complex and an issue on which there are wide differences of opinion. However, it is clear that in the United Kingdom, as in many other countries in the Western democratic tradition, there are substantial differences between individuals. These may arise from differences of ability, or differences of income or wealth, or differences of birth or class. These differences are reflected in many rules of law, in particular those that define concepts of property and contract. The present social order and the law that supports that social order have the effect of protecting the rights of those with property and the economic power to enter and enforce contractual arrangements. Much criminal law also seeks to protect property rights. On this analysis, the relationship between law and social order may be seen as conservative, in the sense that it seeks to conserve established social arrangements.

As with the role of law in relation to public order, there are other ways of thinking about the relationship between law and social order. Many assert that a fundamental purpose of law today is to promote a more dynamic social order, designed to ensure that society is not locked into historic structures which sustain inequality, but is based on principles of equality and the prevention of social exclusion.

How to attack inequality is the subject of fierce debate. Some argue that equality can be achieved only if there is a complete removal of the differences between people—so

---

[3] The Freedom of Information Act 2000 came into effect in 2005. For information on the Act, see www.dca.gov.uk/foi/index.htm.

[4] For background material, see www.dca.gov.uk/constitution/holref/holrefindex.htm.

[5] Political Parties, Elections and Referendums Act 2000, the Local Government Act 2000 and the Electoral Administration Act 2006. For general information on elections, including trials of new voting methods, see http://www.justice.gov.uk/guidance/elections.htm.

[6] The Constitution Unit at University College London is taking a lead in this debate. See www.ucl.ac.uk/constitution-unit/.

that, for example, everyone in employment receives more or less equal pay, that there is equality in the amounts of wealth capable of being held by individuals, and so on. Others take the view that equality in this sense is neither the right nor a sensible way to promote a new social order. They argue that the focus should be on *equality of opportunity*, for example, in the provision of education or health care or work opportunities.

Many modern rules of law have the promotion of equality of opportunity as a prime objective. Both within the United Kingdom and more broadly in the European Union, there is law designed to combat discrimination based on grounds of gender, ethnicity and race, disability or age. This is driven not by simplistic notions of political correctness but by the very practical belief that the collective good of nations is enhanced by ensuring that all citizens can play a full part in the economic and social life of those nations. To give a simple example, if women are excluded from the workforce, 50 per cent of available talent is thereby excluded.

Box 2.1   Time for change

New anti-discriminatory measures

Reflecting the present government's commitment to increasing equality of opportunity, there is currently a great deal of change affecting both the institutional framework which works against discriminatory behaviour and in the law which underpins that work.

Following the passing of the Equality Act 2006, a new Commission for Equality and Human Rights has been established, which started work on 1 October 2007. It brings together three existing agencies—the Commission for Racial Equality, the Equal Opportunities Commission, and the Disability Rights Commission. The advantages of having a single body include the fact that it can bring together experts on equality issues; be a single source of information; be a single point of contact for individuals, business, and those working in government and the voluntary sector; help avoid disputes (thus preventing costly litigation) by promoting awareness of equality issues; and enable discrimination to be tackled in a holistic way. The work of the new Commission is informed by the results of the Equality Review, led by Trevor Phillips, which reported in March 2007. It set out his analysis of the causes of persistent discrimination and inequality in this country.

As regards the legal framework, the government established a Discrimination Law Review in 2005. Following the work of the review, in June 2007, the government published proposals for a new single piece of anti-discrimination legislation. The consultation period on these proposals ended in September 2007; further developments are expected in the near future.

Further information can be found at the following websites:
http://archive.cabinetoffice.gov.uk/equalitiesreview/
http://www.communities.gov.uk/documents/corporate/doc/322984.doc

In addition to specific anti-discrimination legislation, a great deal of public policy is directed to devising social, welfare and educational policies which seek to assist in the creation of a new social order. Law gives legitimacy to those policies. There is nothing new about this. Since the development of the Welfare State in the middle of the nineteenth century, it has been argued that it is right that governments should seek, to varying degrees, to promote equality. The law clearly has had and continues to have a central part to play in these developments.

The mere fact that policies are developed and enshrined in Acts of Parliament does not mean that a new social order is thereby automatically created. The evidence is that in modern Britain there remain very marked inequalities—whether based on class, education, employment, health, or other life opportunities. While there may be aspirations towards equality, the social reality is that equality—however defined—has not yet been fully realized.

The claim that law has a role in the promotion of equality is one that is frequently made, and can thus be included as one of the macro functions of law. However the part played by law in maintaining the existing social order may be said to be in conflict with its function in promoting greater equality. This leads some to argue that law has another, more political, function of supporting the status quo against other ways of promoting social order. As with the tension between the preservation of public order and the protection of human rights, there are tensions between the role of law in the preservation of the existing social order and its role in the promotion of a new social order.

Similarly, claims are made that a function of law is to promote social justice. The extent to which law and the legal system, by themselves, can deliver social justice is limited. Social justice is more a political concept than a legal one. Law may be able to support steps taken to achieve social justice and thus promote a new social order; but it would be unrealistic to claim that law can achieve this in isolation from other non-legal factors which underpin modern society.

Even if the ability of law directly to foster social justice or equality is limited, there is nevertheless an important claim for law: that it does have a role to play in protecting the weak against the powerful. This became a very important function for law as the concept of the Welfare State developed, not just in the United Kingdom but across the developed world.

Law and economic order

The relationship between law and economic order raises matters similar to those considered in the relationship between law and social order. The dominant economic philosophy in the United Kingdom, indeed throughout the Western world, is market capitalism.[7] Here, a very important function of law has lain in the recognition

---

[7] Differences between different models of capitalism—e.g. the North American model, the European model, or the Japanese model—are not considered here. But it should not be assumed that the operation of capitalist systems is the same in all countries.

of rights in private property, whether in land or other forms of security. It is in law that definitions of ownership rights in property are found. The law provides procedures for the transfer of these ownership rights from one person to another. The law enables different property rights (e.g. tenancy or trust) to co-exist in the same piece of property. And the law provides mechanisms for the enforcement of those rights. The notions of property developed in law have, historically, assisted in the development of this economic framework and continue to sustain it.

Similar arguments can be made in relation to contract. The recognition of the principle of the legally enforceable bargain (contract), breaches of which can be pursued and enforced through the courts, has been an essential tool in the development of the modern market capitalist economy. As with its function in the maintenance of the social order, law can also be seen as instrumental in the creation and underpinning of the economic order.

Nevertheless, there are other ways in which law is now used to regulate the economic order. It has long been recognized that there are socially desirable outcomes which market economies are bad at delivering. Operating factories or machinery with proper regard for health and safety is one example. A great deal of modern law focuses on the creation of regulatory frameworks within which capitalist entrepreneurs must operate. These are justified on the grounds that they fill the gaps left by market failure.

Similarly, it has long been recognized that untrammelled capitalist activity contains its own contradictions. There is an inexorable tendency for capitalists to accumulate market position, and if possible dominate that position through the exercise of monopoly power. However, the shift from competition to monopoly poses a fundamental threat to the operation of the market. Thus legal mechanisms are used to promote competition and to limit the development of monopolistic positions.

There is also an inevitable tendency for those with greater bargaining power to seek through contract to impose their wishes on parties with weaker bargaining positions. A great deal of modern law is designed to level the playing field. Thus a vast body of consumer law is designed to soften the binding nature of contractual relationships by giving rights to consumers in situations where the bargaining power between the supplier of goods or services and the consumer of those goods or services is regarded as unequal. For example, there are legal requirements that those who sell insurance policies or other expensive financial products must allow the purchaser a 'cooling-off period' within which she may change her mind. Housing law regulates the relationship between landlords and tenants. Employment law regulates the relationship between employer and employee. More generally there are measures enabling the consumer to challenge terms in contracts thought to be 'unfair'.

Here again, as with law and public order and law and social order, in relation to the economic order the law performs functions that are to a degree in conflict. Law has helped to legitimate the tools essential to the commercial context within which market capitalism is able to flourish. At the same time law is used to limit the excesses of market behaviour that can arise from unregulated operation of market capitalism.

Law and international order

Another function for law is support for international order. This is an extremely complex and controversial subject not considered in detail here. Some argue that there is really no such thing as international law; rather that maintenance of international order is sustained by international relations and diplomatic pressure. But in many respects, international bodies and politicians like to point to legal authority for what they are trying to achieve. For example:

- recent incursions by the United Nations into the world's trouble-spots have been justified in part by reference to the legal framework of the United Nations Charter and its executive bodies, in particular the role of the Security Council;[8]

- attempts to deal with 'crimes against humanity'—a particular curse of the modern age—are being made through a special War Crimes Tribunal which has been established by the UN and which sits in the Hague and elsewhere;

- in other areas, such as the regulation of world trade or the protection of the environment, the regulation of the use of the sea, or space, there is an increasing tendency not only to enter treaties—which historically was common practice—but also to create special institutions and mechanisms for enforcement like courts or tribunals, which are independent of particular national governments;

- the conduct of war has long been subject to international legal constraints, for example the Geneva Convention on the treatment of prisoners of war. Similarly other constraints on behaviour in war and other situations of conflict, such as the prevention of torture, have been prescribed in instruments of international law; and

- one of the most pressing of current social issues, the protection of those seeking asylum in one country because of a well-founded fear of persecution in another, is essentially shaped by principles of international law.

These are important and controversial issues. Even though the focus of this work is on the rather more parochial subject of the 'English legal system', we cannot ignore the global context in which countries now operate. It has been argued that, following the collapse of communism, a 'new world order' has emerged. Legal instruments and institutions play a significant part in its development; this wider dimension of the role of law should not be forgotten.

Law and moral order

Another macro function of law is to provide support for the moral ordering of society. This is also extremely controversial. Some theorists argue that there should be little, if any, distinction between law and morality; that the law should clearly and deliberately

---

[8] Much of the controversy about the war in Iraq arose from arguments that any hostility against Iraq should be properly justified in international law.

mirror those issues of morality which people think 'ought' to inform the way we should behave. Others seek to draw a clear distinction between law and morality. They argue that the mere fact that many people believe that certain forms of behaviour or activity are morally wrong (for example engaging in homosexual activity) should not mean that they should be defined as unlawful.

There are clear dangers and considerable difficulties in seeking to equate law and morality, not least because of the problems of determining what the common morality is on any given issue. Nevertheless many rules of law are founded on a moral view of society. Perhaps the clearest example is the moral imperative not to kill people, reflected in rules of criminal law which outlaw such activity.

In general it may be suggested that rules of criminal law which reflect some common morality, however defined, may be more acceptable and effective in regulating behaviour than those rules which do not. For example, there may well be behaviours which many would regard as undesirable—dressing shabbily or drinking cheap alcohol in the streets—but which should not of themselves be defined as criminal. Conversely, there may be rules of criminal law, for example not exceeding speed limits, which many do not regard as particularly morally repugnant, but which should nevertheless be defined as criminal.[9]

In a different context, much of the law which seeks to regulate relationships between individuals is also based in concepts of morality, for example the law relating to marriage. Here is another context in which law provides at least some support for the moral order, a function reinforced by the protection of family life under Article 8 of the European Convention on Human Rights.

Related to the relationship between law and moral order is the relationship between *law and religious order*. Despite the apparent decline in religious belief in England, there are still many who argue that religion—both formal and informal—remains an important facet of society at large. However, and in contrast with discussion about the relationship between law and morality, it is not now often argued that law should be directly supportive of religion. Indeed many would argue, whether in general principle or because of their own religious (or anti-religious) beliefs, that law should *not* be used to support the religious order. Questions of spirituality and religious belief should fall within that private sphere of activity in which the law should not intervene.

Nevertheless, the historical role played by religion in the development of modern England cannot be wholly ignored. At its most basic, our calendar and major festivals are firmly based in the Christian tradition, rather than that of other religious

---

[9] Historically this has often happened. For example many of the criminal offences that 200 or 300 years ago might have led to draconian punishments such as transportation or even the death penalty now seem very trivial, and are either not criminal at all or dealt with much less severely. Today many argue that a less criminal approach to the use of soft drugs might not only lead to more equitable treatment of drug users, as compared with those who use alcohol or nicotine, but also lead to reductions in other forms of criminality resulting from the need for drug users to obtain the money to buy their drugs. On the other hand, there are powerful political arguments that any relaxation in the government's approach to drug use would send 'the wrong signal' to the community at large.

groupings. There are a number of legal privileges that attach exclusively to the Church of England; there are others that apply to religious groups more generally. There remains a specific law against blasphemy which effectively applies only to the Christian religion. Thus it is arguable, though not often seen in this light, that present-day law still plays a residual part in the support of religious order, in particular the Christian religious order.

This is controversial, not least because of the rise in a number of countries of various forms of religious fundamentalism. These are often accompanied by degrees of intolerance towards others that are quite unacceptable in a modern pluralistic society. Indeed it may be the case that, in order to protect social pluralism, the law should be used more to protect the ability of those of different religious beliefs to hold and practise their religion, another issue embraced in the European Convention on Human Rights (Article 9).

Other macro functions

In addition to the ways in which law may interact with the maintenance of and challenges to different types of order, law also has a number of other macro functions.

The resolution of social problems

The response of politicians and their officials to many of the issues perceived as social problems is to create more laws seeking to regulate the behaviour complained against. This is the expected political response. Only rarely do politicians concede that there may be enough law, and that what is needed is better understanding of or enforcement of existing law. Even more rarely are politicians willing to accept that a possible solution to a problem might be to repeal existing rules of law or to develop the law in such a way as to 'decriminalize' the activity in question. Their mindset assumes that a function of law is 'to solve social problems'. Indeed whole careers are devoted to the promotion of legislation allegedly designed to address particular social issues—even if, as often happens, there is already perfectly satisfactory law already available, or where changing the law is not really a solution to the problem.

One obvious consequence of creating legal provisions to solve social problems is that people—ever mindful of their own self-interest—respond to new legal frameworks in ways not predicted by the law-makers. A hidden but often inevitable consequence of using law to solve social problems is, therefore, that the very process of creating new law results not in the solution of existing social problems but rather in the creation of new social problems. The process of dealing with one issue leads to the creation of another, which in turn has to be 'solved' later.

The regulation of human relationships

Another important function of law is the regulation of the nature and extent of human relationships. The definition of and the formalities relating to the creation of marriage are determined by legal rules, often supplementing different religious rules. Law provides a framework for the distribution of assets on the breakdown of marriage. The law is also currently being developed in relation to the regulation and underpinning of other long-term relationships—both heterosexual and homosexual—where persons have not gone through the formalities of marriage. Law sets boundaries to the scope of sexual relationships, prescribing for example the minimum age of sexual consent, and making certain sexual relationships within the 'prohibited degrees of consanguinity' (incest and other close relationships) unlawful. The law also sets down a framework for the treatment of children and other family members.

The educative or ideological function of law

A further function of law, almost irrespective of its impact in particular cases, is an educative one; it contributes to the shaping of the 'ideology' of a nation. To give a simple if significant example, there is no doubt that attitudes to drinking and driving have changed dramatically over the last twenty-five years. In part this is the result of powerful advertising, demonstrating the devastating impact that drink-drive accidents can have on victims and their families. But the change in attitude has also been the result of changes in the law contributing to a climate of opinion in which drinking and driving is no longer regarded as socially acceptable behaviour.

Another example is law, mentioned above, outlawing various forms of discrimination. When such laws come into effect, those who argue for their introduction often accept that the law does not, on its own, alter the attitudes of mind that lead to the discriminatory behaviours which result in the creation of those laws. However, those who have sponsored such laws see them as not only creating certain legal rights which may be enforceable by individuals, but also sending a more general educative signal to members of society at large that discriminatory behaviour is not acceptable.

More generally, countries that embrace the principle of the rule of law are, in effect, asserting that powers of officials of the state must be limited and that the individual citizen should have both the right and the opportunity to challenge decisions where they are thought to be wrong or in some respect unfair.

The decision by the British government to introduce the Human Rights Act, incorporating the European Convention on Human Rights directly into English law, is another example of legislation that not only creates legal rights which individuals may seek to enforce through the courts, but which also sends an important educative signal about the limits within which people, particularly those who work within government, must behave. In this sense, therefore, another macro function of law relates to the education of the public's social attitudes and responsibilities.

Micro functions of law

Turning from the 'macro' to the 'micro' level involves consideration of rather more specific functions for law, many of which derive from the 'macro' functions identified above. A number of examples are offered; this does not purport to be a comprehensive list. The reader is invited to think of other functions not identified here. In addition, the reader may be able to think of other examples to illustrate the particular functions which have been identified.

Defining the limits of acceptable behaviour

Most people have at least some awareness of the *criminal law*. A major objective of this branch of the law is to prescribe the limits of socially acceptable behaviour. The criminal law prohibits many kinds of activity about which there would be widespread agreement, such as murder and violent crime. It also outlaws a wide range of other activities about which there may be more debate, such as the use of particular types of drugs. The following points may be made in this context.

- Not all behaviour which may be regarded by many as undesirable is characterized in legal terms as criminal. Thus there is no law preventing a person over the age of 18 from drinking alcohol. However, where the consequences of that conduct may impinge on others the law often steps in. There is a strict law which makes it unlawful for persons who have been drinking alcohol to drive.

- Human conduct is regulated in many ways in addition to the use of law. Codes of morality, religious principles, pressures of friends and family all constrain the ways in which people behave.

- Different countries set the boundaries of their criminal law in different places: what is criminal in one country is not necessarily criminal in another.[10] Although there is a great deal of commonality between different bodies of criminal law, in important respects the boundaries of criminal law are *culturally determined*, set by the demands of the specific society. There are particularly important distinctions in societies with different religious traditions or moral backgrounds: laws applying in Islamic countries are in many respects quite different from those in countries founded on the Judaeo-Christian tradition.

- The boundaries of the criminal law are *dynamic*. Activity which has historically been regarded as criminal is not necessarily regarded as criminal for ever. The prohibition of alcohol in the United States during the 1920s is a good example.

---

[10] This has the important practical consequence that, if a person commits a criminal act in one country and flees to another country where that act is not criminal, this is often the basis for successfully resisting extradition proceedings—official proceedings to bring the alleged miscreant back for trial to the country where the original act took place.

The use of law to regulate human behaviour is not exclusively through the criminal law. Areas of *civil law* also seek to do this. For example, if a party to a contract breaks that contract, rules of law allow the party affected to claim compensation from the person in breach. The law of negligence prescribes situations in which a person who has negligently injured another has to compensate that other for the injury. In short, law defines the scope of obligations that exist between individuals and provides remedies for breach of those obligations. Although the objective of civil law is not to punish an offender, in the sense used in considering criminal law, it is nevertheless the case that rules of civil law indicate that a contract cannot be breached with impunity, nor can one person act negligently in relation to another. In this sense, the rules of civil law also send the message that certain types of behaviour are unacceptable or undesirable.

Defining the consequences of certain forms of behaviour

Law does not simply define forms of behaviour which are unacceptable. It also prescribes consequences. In the case of criminal law, these are the punishments that attach to a finding of guilt. Similarly in the area of civil law, law prescribes the remedies that the person affected by a breach of contract or a negligent act may obtain from the perpetrator.

In some situations the same facts may generate a variety of legal consequences. For example, a road accident may be caused by a person driving a car carelessly or recklessly. This may result in the police seeking to get that person prosecuted through the criminal courts; if found guilty this may result in the imposition of a fine or even imprisonment. If the accident causes damage to another, that other person may seek compensation by bringing an action for damages in negligence against the driver. The driver may argue that the accident occurred because her car was improperly serviced, and may therefore bring an action for breach of contract against the garage. Three different legal consequences have arisen from the same incident.

Defining processes for the transaction of business and other activities

A rather different function of law is to define procedures by which certain transactions must be carried out. Some of these are quite straightforward, such as those relating to the making of simple contracts. In other cases, particularly where there is concern to prevent fraud, considerable formality may be required. Many of these relate to transactions dealing with the transfer of property rights. For example, the process of buying and selling houses is subject to a number of formal legal requirements, known collectively as the rules of conveyancing. There are detailed rules relating to the creation of leases. There are special rules for the creation of wills. Similarly, there are detailed requirements for the creation of trusts or settlements of property.

One of the problems with prescribing formal requirements is that, whatever the law states, in practice people attempt to carry out these transactions in ignorance of the rules. The law then has to develop supplementary principles to prevent injustice occurring, notwithstanding the existence of procedural irregularity. Many of the principles of the law of equity have developed in response to this problem.

Creating regulatory frameworks

A great deal of law seeks to regulate those who provide services to the public. For example, substantial bodies of law regulate the activities of solicitors, doctors, architects, nurses, or estate agents. There is a vast regulatory framework designed to control the activities of those who provide financial services to the public to prevent fraud and other breaches of trust. A consequence of the privatization of formerly nationalized industries has been to create an extensive body of law designed to regulate the activities of companies now in the private sector (such as telecommunications, utilities, and transport) including the promotion of competition and the regulation of prices. And specific areas of economic activity are subject to the most detailed legal regulation designed to promote standards and give the consumer value for money. The regulation of the housing market through housing law is a prime example.

A different form of regulatory law, but one that has been in existence for many years, is planning law regulating the use to which land can be put in this country. Law which seeks to regulate industry in order to protect the environment is another example. In this context, the law operates at an international as well as a national level.

Regulatory law also serves another purpose. It defines the categories of persons able to make representations to government about a particular policy or decision. For example, again in the context of planning law, the relevant law determines who may challenge decisions of the planning authorities and who may appear to make their case at any public inquiry resulting from a planning decision.

Giving authority to agents of the state to take actions against citizens

Another function of law is to give power to state officials to take action against members of the public. There are numerous examples: the powers of the police to stop, search, question, arrest, and caution members of the public is one; the power of doctors to detain in mental hospitals those diagnosed as suffering from acute mental illness is another; the power of social workers to remove children from families where they are thought to be at risk and to place them in the care of the local authorities a third. Similarly, agents of both central and local government are given power to take money away from members of the public through taxation.

A rather different example is the power given to government and other agencies of the state to acquire land compulsorily in the public interest.

Preventing the abuse of power by officials

In contrast to the last head, much law is designed to prevent abuses of power by public servants. For example, the police are required to operate within a framework of powers prescribed by the Police and Criminal Evidence Act 1984, which limits their powers of arrest, search, and questioning.

The essence of administrative law, considered further in Chapter 6, relates to the importance of officials acting within a framework of law which prescribes their power; not allowing officials to use discretionary powers in an abusive way; and giving people the opportunity to take advantage of certain procedural safeguards—for example a right to a hearing—before adverse decisions about them are taken. These are further examples of rules of law setting boundaries to the power of state officials.

Giving power/authority to officials to assist the public

The law also sets down a vast range of requirements for agencies of the state to provide services or other goods to the public. At the most general level, all public expenditure has to be legitimated by special Acts of Parliament known as Appropriation Acts. These give general authority for the expenditure of public money on the whole range of programmes run by government.

More specific bodies of law deal with the details. Social security law is one example, setting out as it does the entitlements to social security benefits which have been created by government. Many other examples could be given: entitlement to free education is one, free treatment within the National Health Service another. All these activities, of the social security, education, and health authorities, are underpinned by detailed legal frameworks.

Prescribing procedures for the use of law

In addition to prescribing procedures for conducting different types of transaction, there is another important body of law—procedural law—which seeks to control the ways in which courts and other adjudicative bodies operate. This body of law may set limits to the evidence that can be brought in different types of cases. It also prescribes the way in which different types of proceedings, whether in the courts or other forums, are to be conducted.

Conclusion: law and society

It is not claimed here that these examples of the macro and micro functions of law in society are exhaustive. Readers should ask themselves whether there are other functions for law and whether they should be regarded as macro or micro in character.

There is indeed a huge literature on the relationship of law and society of which the foregoing is only a very limited summary. However a number of points can be noted.

(1) All the functions of law, whether macro or micro, are *contingent* upon the stage in the development of that society and the pressures and challenges facing that society. While many of these functions of law are common to very many societies, others are not.

(2) The laws that exist and the ways in which they are used are dependent on the ideology and politics of the particular country. For example, current notions of social justice and equality in the United Kingdom have developed in the light of particular socio-political and economic theories. They will change in the future. The list of functions proposed here should not therefore be regarded as set in concrete; it reflects broader changes in the social and political ideas and ideals of that society.

(3) The functions of law are by no means always consistent with each other: preservation of social order may on occasion be in sharp conflict with the function of protecting civil liberties; the role of law in advancing equality or social justice may be in conflict with its role in supporting current social and economic orders.

(4) It should be remembered that there are still activities which are not currently the subject of legal regulation. Governments frequently claim that they are seeking to limit the encroachment of law. Interestingly, however, when a new technology arrives which actually enables activities to occur outside conventional regulatory frameworks—the internet is a good current example—politicians and others quickly become agitated.

(5) There are many mechanisms, outside law, which are used to regulate and alter people's behaviour. Much of the practice of economics is based on the assumption that, if financial incentives are right, behaviours change. An interesting example is the proposal that problems of global pollution and global warming must be tackled not just by laws saying what should or should not be done, but also by getting financial incentives right—higher taxes paid by those who pollute, for example.

(6) More fundamentally, there are significant issues about the way in which we order our society which are either not touched on at all by law or only in relatively insignificant ways. For example, one of the major social issues of our time relates to the extent to which groups in the community are excluded from the mainstream of social life, whether through lack of money or other material resources such as housing. To be sure, there are legislative provisions relating to the provision of social security benefits or to the provision of accommodation to the homeless. But the entitlements contained in these bodies of law are not absolute but are highly contingent on legal tests being met. Those claiming benefits or access to housing have a substantial list of conditions that they must satisfy before they will be helped. The fact that the rhetoric of law employs concepts such as liberty or justice does not mean that substantive law actually delivers social justice to all citizens of the United Kingdom.

(7) Perhaps the most important point to stress is that although the discussion has, perhaps, been somewhat abstract, the issues considered are central to many of

the most serious challenges facing the United Kingdom. One obvious example is the current pressure on government to respond to terrorism and incidents such as the bombings in London in July 2005. How should this be handled? By giving the Home Secretary new powers to detain people for longer periods without being charged for any offence, or new powers to deport those felt to be promoting religious intolerance? By allowing courts to receive evidence obtained as the result of covert surveillance? Or will these developments undermine freedoms essential to British values and the British way of life?

Questions for reflection and discussion

1. Is it necessary for a society to reach a particular level of development before law can play a useful role?

2. What are the consequences for a country or society of not accepting the importance of the rule of law?

3. How can the balance between the preservation of liberty and the maintenance of social order be best preserved?

4. Can law protect the economically weak?

5. What should be the relationship between law and morality? When should things we disapprove of be made unlawful?

6. To what extent can principles of law be employed in the ordering of international affairs?

7. How successful is law in shaping people's behaviour?

8. Are there other functions that you think law plays in the ordering of society? Would you classify these functions as macro or micro?

Further reading

ABEL-SMITH, B., and STEVENS, R., *In Search of Justice: Society and the Legal System* (London, Allen Lane, 1968)

ALLAN, T.R.S., Constitutional Justice—*A Liberal Theory of the Rule of Law* (Oxford, Oxford University Press, 2003)

BRAKE, M., and HALE, C., *Public Order and Private Lives: the Politics of Law and Order* (London, Routledge, 1992)

COTTERRELL, R., *The Sociology of Law: an Introduction* (2nd edn., London, Butterworth, 1992)

DELUPIS, I., *The International Legal Order* (Aldershot, Dartmouth, c.1994)

DICKSON, B., and CONNELLY, A., *Human Rights and the European Convention: the Effects of the Convention on the United Kingdom and Ireland* (London, Sweet & Maxwell, 1997)

DRZEMCZEWSKI, A.Z., *European Human Rights Convention in Domestic Law: a Comparative Study* (Oxford, Clarendon Press, 1997)

DYZENHAUS, D. (ed.), *Recrafting the Rule of Law: the Limits of Legal Order* (Oxford, Hart, 1999)

HUDSON, A., *Towards a Just Society: Law, Labour and Legal Aid* (London, Continuum International Publishing Group, 1999)

JACOBS, F.G., WHITE, R.C.A., and OVEY, C., *The European Convention on Human Rights* (3rd edn., Oxford, Oxford University Press, 2002)

MANSELL, W., *Critical Introduction to Law* (3rd edn., London, Cavendish Publishing, 2003)

ROBERTS, S., *Order and Dispute: an Introduction to Legal Anthropology* (Harmondsworth, Penguin, 1979)

SCHACHTER, O., and JOYNER, C.C. (eds), *United Nations Legal Order* (Cambridge, Grotius, 1995)

SHAPIRO, I. (ed), *The Rule of Law* (New York, New York University Press, 1994)

WARD, I., *Introduction to Critical Legal Theory* (2nd edn., London, Cavendish Publishing, 2004)

Websites

http://www.dca.gov.uk/peoples-rights/human-rights/index.htm *(Ministry of Justice Human Rights Team)*

http://www.echr.coe.int/echr *(European Court of Human Rights)*

http://www.liberty-human-rights.org.uk/ *(Liberty, formerly National Council for Civil Liberties)*

http://www.justice.org.uk/ *(Justice, the British Section of the International Commission of Jurists)*

http://www.un.org/english/ *(United Nations home page)*

http://www.un.org/law/ *(United Nations International Law)*

http://www.icj-cij.org/homepage/index.php?lang=en *(International Court of Justice)*

http://www.un.org/icty/ *(International Criminal Tribunal for the Former Yugoslavia)*

http://www.wto.org/ *(World Trade Organization)*

http://www.uncitral.org/uncitral/en/index.html *(United Nations Commission on International Trade)*

http://www.un.org/Depts/los/index.htm *(United Nations Law of the Sea)*

http://www.icc-cpi.int/home.html&l=en *(International Criminal Court)*

http://www.citizenshipfoundation.org.uk/ *(Citizenship Foundation, promoting citizenship through education about law and democracy)*

http://www.citizen.org.uk/ *(Institute for Citizenship, materials for teachers)*

http://teachingcitizenship.org.uk/ *(Association for Citizenship Teaching)*

3

Law making: authority and process

Introduction

The last chapter considered a number of functions that law plays in the ordering of society. Here we examine the principal law-making institutions and how they work. First, though, we ask: what gives these institutions their authority? What gives law makers their legitimacy?

Power, legitimacy, and authority in the law-making process

One of the macro functions of law identified in Chapter 2 was support for the political order. Law provides much, if not all, of the legal framework within which power is exercised. But simply stating that constitutional principles provide governments or other executive agencies with the power to make law begs a more fundamental question: from where do these constitutional legal principles derive their authority?

The answer is far from easy. Different societies base claims for the legitimacy of their law makers on different theoretical foundations. In broad terms, however, law makers may be said to derive their authority from two principal sources:

(a) the basic constitutional framework or constitutional settlement which operates within that country; and

(b) the underlying political ideology of that country.

The reasons why people are generally more or less willing to accept these as bases for the exercise of power are complex. One is that most people, while accepting that certain services such as education and health need to be provided, do not want to run them themselves. They are happy to let politicians and bureaucrats get on with the job. Furthermore, once a government has established a claim to exercise power, it invariably creates the machinery—police, security services, and the like—whose function is to enforce the law.

But it should always be remembered that even the most fundamental of constitutional arrangements fail if significant groups within a particular society find that constitutional basis unworkable. The fact that in some countries in the world there have been civil wars, that in others there have been *coups d'état,* demonstrates the point. The destruction of the Berlin Wall and the collapse of apartheid in South Africa may be cited as two modern instances. Many countries, even those which now enjoy the most stable and secure of constitutional arrangements, can trace their current situation to resistance to or rebellion against earlier unacceptable constitutional arrangements. The United Kingdom and the United States both stand as examples. It can work the other way as well. The recent attempt to create a new European Constitution foundered, at least for the time being, because of the unwillingness of many citizens of Europe to support it. Constitutional arrangements ultimately depend on the consent of the governed.

In the United Kingdom, and in many other developed countries, that consent is more taken for granted than actively sought (save on particular issues which are the subject of referenda). Here and in other democracies, free and regular elections are seen as the primary mechanism through which continuing consent to govern is implied.

Constitutions and constitutionalism

One basis for the authority given to the law makers can therefore be found in a country's constitution and its related principles of constitutionalism. What are these?

In most countries there exists a *written constitution* or other form of 'basic law' which defines the powers of the law-making institutions of the country. The constitutional arrangements of the United Kingdom are unusual in that there is no formal written constitution. Many of the most important constitutional principles are found not in any written document but in unwritten practice, known as *constitutional conventions.* (*See Box 3.1.*)

These unwritten principles are now accompanied by an increasing number of fundamental statutory provisions.[1] Devolution, reform of the House of Lords, the Human Rights Act 1998, and the Freedom of Information Act 2000 all involve legislation which has transformed the constitutional landscape. The Constitutional Reform Act 2005 went further, significantly changing the role of the Lord Chancellor, making the Lord Chief Justice the Head of the Judiciary, making provision for a new Supreme Court (to replace the judicial branch of the House of Lords), and creating a Judicial Appointments Commission. In addition British membership of the European Union and other international bodies such as the Council of Europe and the United Nations has had significant constitutional implications. These all contribute to the legal framework within which power in the United Kingdom is exercised.

---

[1] See the examples given in Chapter 2 at pp. 13–14.

Box 3.1   Legal system explained

Constitutional conventions

There is a substantial literature on constitutional conventions and the extent to which they have changed over the years. Some examples of constitutional conventions may be noted:

Constitutional monarchy. The theoretical Head of State remains the monarch. The principle of constitutional monarchy means that the Queen takes no active part in the running of the country. Though the parliamentary year starts with the 'Queen's speech' and though bills are given 'royal assent', the Queen does not intervene in the politics of the law-making programme. The Queen is kept informed about what is happening in Parliament and, through audiences with the Prime Minister of the day, is briefed about significant developments. It would be surprising if, on occasion, she did not offer her views on particular issues. But the monarch is not the source of political decision taking or law making.

Prerogative powers. Nevertheless, there are still certain functions of government which are based not in legislative authority, but on the historic exercise of power by the monarch. These are known as 'prerogative powers'. The most dramatic example of this is the power to go to war, which is exercised by ministers not under the authority of any Act of Parliament, but by exercise of prerogative powers. The Home Secretary's 'prerogative of mercy' to reduce a sentence imposed by the courts after a criminal trial may be seen as another example. The government is currently consulting on the question whether these powers should be subject to legislation.

Cabinet government and collective responsibility. The very existence of the Cabinet— the central committee of ministers chaired by the Prime Minister and responsible for determining the government's programme—is another aspect of the British Constitution founded in convention, rather than legislation. The related doctrine of collective responsibility, whereby ministers who do not agree with the policy of the government as determined in Cabinet are supposed to resign from the government, is also based in constitutional convention, rather than constitutional law.

Individual ministerial responsibility. Another constitutional convention is that ministers should take ultimate responsibility for what goes on in their departments. This means that they must answer questions in Parliament or select committees about the work of their departments. On occasion, this may also lead ministers to resign, where something has gone very seriously wrong, though in practice these days this is a rare occurrence.

British *constitutionalism*—the principles which underpin the constitution—rests on three essential features: the *sovereignty of Parliament*, the *rule of law* and the *separation of powers.*[2]

---

[2] Definitions of these concepts have, over the years, been fiercely contested—for examples, see further reading.

- The *sovereignty of Parliament* asserts that the ultimate legal authority for law making in the United Kingdom should be Parliament.

- The *rule of law* insists that power should not be exercised by persons acting by or on behalf of the state, without their being able to point to some form of legal *authority* for their actions. Further, the process by which decisions are reached should be fair. The Constitutional Reform Act 2005, for the first time, gives statutory recognition to the concept of the rule of law.

- The *separation of powers* suggests that, to prevent any particular arm of government from becoming too powerful, there should be separation between the legislative (law making), executive, and judicial functions of government. Thereby each branch of government is subject to *checks and balances*. This in turn leads to the proposition that the judges in particular, and lawyers in general, must act independently of government—now also recognized in the Constitutional Reform Act 2005.

These principles relate to the central issues of power: who may exercise it, how it can be controlled, and how those who exercise power can be called to account.

Political ideology

Stating these principles still leaves unanswered the question: what is the theoretical basis on which power to make law may be asserted by political institutions? To answer this it is necessary to consider the underlying political ideology of the country.

In the United Kingdom, and many other countries, the currently dominant political ideology is *representative democracy,* expressed principally through the holding of regular elections. Democratic theory suggests that society is unable to function as effectively as it might if everyone retained their unique power to control their own life or the lives of others. Instead, by electing Members of Parliament to *represent* the views of electors, individuals pass to those elected some of that control or *sovereignty* which gives them the authority to govern on behalf of the people.

Those in power are also subject to the principle of *accountability.* Thus politicians are regularly called to account for themselves or their political parties when general elections are held. From the electoral process those elected to political office derive their authority to make laws on behalf of the citizens of the country, knowing that if their actions are not approved of by the electorate they will be defeated at the next general election. They are also subject to accountability through a range of *checks and balances* that exist, both within Parliament (such as parliamentary debates or questions to ministers) and outside. These comprise a wide variety of bodies and activities, including the essential part played by the press and other mass media in exposing things that go wrong within government.

Principles in practice

The application of these principles is not as clear in practice as theory might imply.

- First, in the British system, the fact is that the work of Parliament is strictly controlled by the political party which forms the government of the day. There are very few issues on which MPs vote independently of what their party wants. There is the occasional backbench revolt; and the occasional 'free vote' on a matter of conscience where the party 'whip' is not applied. But these are the exception, not the rule.

- Secondly, all legislation in the United Kingdom passes through not only the elected House of Commons, but also the non-elected House of Lords. Although the House of Lords rarely exercises the power it theoretically has to delay bills from becoming law, on many occasions the House of Lords amends, often very substantially, legislation coming to it from the House of Commons. The threat of delay may also result in substantial amendment or even the dropping of legislative proposals. While there is in the Commons a clear link between the democratic process of election and the outcomes of the legislative process, in the Lords this is not so. Even if the constitution of the Lords is reformed, it is unlikely to become a wholly elected body.

- Thirdly, knowing the extent to which the electoral process actually represents the will of the people is very difficult. In the United Kingdom, the 'first past the post' voting system has meant that nearly all recently elected governments have attained power with less than 50 per cent of the popular vote. This leads many, particularly those in the smaller parties who struggle to get elected under the present system, to argue that a fairer voting system would incorporate proportional representation, with seats in Parliament distributed in proportion to votes cast. The primary argument against this apparently attractive proposition is that this tends to lead to coalition governments, in which small minority parties acquire a disproportionately powerful position. Nevertheless, experiments with proportional representation have recently occurred in the United Kingdom in the context of elections of members to the European Parliament and elections to the devolved Parliaments in Wales and Scotland.

- A further issue which is said to weaken the democratic process is the decline in the percentage of the population voting in elections. This has led to suggestions to make it easier for people to vote in elections, for example setting up electronic voting systems in supermarkets or increasing the ease with which people may vote by post. There have even been calls to make voting compulsory, as happens in a number of other countries: Australia is the prime example.

- Fifthly, there are important sources of law other than Parliament. Under the British system of separation of powers, judges in the higher courts have power to make new rules of law. They do this through the development of rules of 'common law'—long-standing principles of law developed over the years, in some cases centuries, by the judges. Many examples of judicial law making can be given:

- the fundamental law of contract. on which much economic activity is based;
- the law of negligence, which relates (among other matters) to dealing with the aftermath of accidents and other forms of injury; and
- the development of the principles *of judicial review,* which is the basis on which judicial control of the administrative arm of government is achieved.

Yet judges are not elected; they do not get their authority from any theory of representative democracy. The legitimacy for their activity has to be found in other constitutional principles, in particular the separation of powers. The judges are recognized to be both a part of the machinery of government and, paradoxically, at the same time independent of it.

Membership of the European Union

One respect in which the law-making process in the United Kingdom has been significantly altered in recent years has arisen from the United Kingdom's membership of the European Union. The fundamental constitutional documents of the Union, starting with the Treaty of Rome and developed by the Treaties of Maastricht, Amsterdam, and Nice,[3] provide not only that member states must abide by those principles of European law that are made by the institutions established by the Treaty of Rome, but also that failure to do this will result in sanctions being imposed by the institutions of the European Union. As a result, the British government is *required* to incorporate certain rules of European law into British law, whether or not it likes them. Furthermore, the House of Lords has decided[4] that if the provisions of a British Act of Parliament are in conflict with European law, then the British Act is to be regarded as of no effect. Until this point was reached, the British courts had never asserted the power to overrule an Act of Parliament, which was always regarded as the sovereign law-making authority. It is these developments that lead many Euro-sceptics to argue, among other things, that joining the European Union has led to an unacceptable loss of parliamentary sovereignty.

One criticism of the institutional arrangements of the European Union is that it runs a 'democratic deficit'. It is argued that too many of the institutions established to run the European Union operate without the authority/legitimacy bestowed by adequate democratic accountability. For example, the exclusive right to initiate legislation is held by the European Commission, whose Commissioners are not directly elected by the people of the European Union. In practice, the powers of Commissioners are constrained by the Council of Ministers, comprising elected ministers from each of

---

[3] Further reforms to the institutional arrangements of the EU are currently under discussion with the intention of introducing a further treaty—the treaty of Lisbon—in 2009.

[4] *Factortame v. Secretary of State for Transport (No. 2)* [1991] 1 AC 603; the jurisprudence of the European Court of Justice had long been clear on the point: Case 6/64 *Costa v. ENEL* [1964] ECR 585.

the member states, and whose approval of legislative proposals was always required.[5] But the European Parliament—the only body with directly elected members—has only a limited part to play in the law-making process, certainly compared with the part played by the British Parliament.

These criticisms have been acknowledged, at least to a degree. Since the Maastricht Treaty was concluded in 1992, and more particularly since the 1997 Treaty of Amsterdam came into effect (on 1 July 1999), the European Parliament has acquired more legislative power. These trends were continued in the Treaty of Nice (2001). While the Parliament still cannot initiate legislative measures, it now has significant power to control the content of measures. Around 75 per cent of all European law making must now be approved by a majority of the European Parliament as well as the Council of Ministers. The poor participation by the British electorate in European elections may be explained, at least in part, by widespread ignorance about the role of the European Parliament and how it has changed.

European Convention on Human Rights and the Human Rights Act 1998

The incorporation of the European Convention on Human Rights[6] into British law, through the Human Rights Act 1998, raises similar issues. All bills presented to the UK Parliament now contain a statement that, in the view of the relevant minister, the bill complies with the Articles of the European Convention. There will be occasions on which particular rules of statute law enacted by the Parliament in London are held by the English courts (as they have from time to time been so held by the European Court of Human Rights in Strasbourg) to be contrary to the Convention. Section 4 of the Human Rights Act specifically prohibits the English courts from declaring legislation invalid. Instead, the Act gives courts the power to issue a 'declaration of incompatibility'. (This formula was adopted to preserve the notion of the sovereignty of Parliament.) This is in effect a direction to the government of the day that a particular statutory provision must be amended in order to comply with the provisions of the European Convention. The reality therefore is that, so long as the UK government is fully signed up to the provisions of the European Convention, its freedom of legislative action is to a degree constrained.

---

[5] Initially, the Council of Ministers had to be unanimous; a single vote against a proposal would result in its not being adopted. In many circumstances the principle of unanimity has been replaced by the principle of qualified majority, which at least enables measures to be introduced despite the opposition of some ministers.

[6] The European Convention on Human Rights is the work of the Council of Europe, *not* the European Union: see below, p. 51.

The law-making institutions

With these points in mind, we take a closer look at the functions of a number of the law-making institutions that exist in the United Kingdom:

- the British Parliament and central government;
- European institutions;
- the courts; and
- other sources of law making.

The British Parliament and central government

The principal law-making body in the United Kingdom is the British Parliament. Its legislative programme is at the heart of the law-making process. By no means all legislative measures are the subject of detailed parliamentary scrutiny (*see Box 3.2*), but the vast bulk of legislative measures derive their authority from the parliamentary process. Even those measures that the British government is required to put into law coming from the European Commission are given the stamp of parliamentary approval.

The nature of the legislative process has undergone significant though inadequately publicized change in recent years—an example of the often understated dynamism that characterizes many developments in the English legal system.[7] The discussion here focuses on the process of enacting an Act of Parliament. Apart from the inherent importance of the subject there is a good practical reason why lawyers need to know about this. There are now circumstances—albeit limited—in which what was said about a bill as it passed though Parliament may be used by a court when dealing with a question of statutory interpretation.[8]

Primary legislation

All Acts of Parliament start as bills. Most bills are accompanied by an Explanatory Note, a detailed note drafted by the bill's sponsoring department, which sets out the

---

[7] One innovation—introduced in November 1999—is that of *backbench debates*. Because of the amount of time the legislative process takes in the House of Commons, backbenchers have only limited opportunity to raise matters of more general concern. Three days each week are now available for backbench debates on matters not related to the legislative programme. These take place not in the chamber of the House of Commons, but in Westminster Hall, which for these purposes is arranged in a horse-shoe formation—thought to be less confrontational than the familiar 'head-on' arrangements in the House of Commons.

[8] *Pepper v. Hart* [1993] AC 593 (HL); on statutory interpretation see below, p. 65.

Box 3.2   Legal system explained

Statute law: the classification of legislative measures

The vast bulk of new law that is brought into effect in England is statute law, that is law which has been passed through Parliament following debate in both the House of Commons and the House of Lords, or law made under the authority of statutes. Statute law comes in a variety of forms:

- primary legislation;
- secondary legislation;
- tertiary legislation; and
- (though not strictly statute law) 'quasi-legislation' or 'soft law'.

Primary legislation is the *Acts of Parliament* that are passed by Parliament. The process of enacting primary legislation consumes a great deal of parliamentary time; indeed lack of time is a significant constraint on the law-making process. Many legislative proposals—particularly those not high on the government's political agenda—are brought forward only when 'time is available'. Lack of time can be used as an excuse for a government delaying measures it does not want to push. But limits on parliamentary time are a real constraint on the opportunities for introducing and amending legislation, even on matters to which government is committed.[9] Most Acts of Parliament are 'Public General Acts', which apply generally in England. They also apply in Wales if they relate to matters not devolved to the Welsh Assembly Government. They often apply in Scotland, though not on matters devolved to the Scottish Parliament. (Each Act contains a section detailing the precise extent of its coverage.) Some are 'Local or Personal Acts' applying only in particular localities or to specific people. (*See further Box 3.3.*)

Primary legislation is supplemented by a vast body of *secondary legislation*—regulations and orders made under the authority of an Act of Parliament. These are known generically as *statutory instruments*. There are typically over 3,000 of these made each year, running to many thousands of pages of text. They are not subject to detailed parliamentary scrutiny, though in many cases statutory instruments cannot be made by the government without consultation with specialist advisory committees. (*See Box 3.5.*)

In addition to primary and secondary legislation, there is a huge amount of *tertiary legislation*—legislative instruments, made under the authority of an Act of Parliament, but which are subject to no parliamentary scrutiny at all. For example, in housing law, numerous powers are given to ministers to issue 'directions' or other instruments, drafted in the form of legislation and which effectively have the force of law, but which are simply issued by the government department in question. Similar examples are found in many other areas of government.

---

[9] However, in emergency, measures can be introduced and passed with extreme rapidity.

Box 3.2 *Continued*

There is, finally, a fourth category of instrument, sometimes referred to as *quasi-legislation* or *soft law,* which comprise statements of good practice or guidance. These may be made under the authority of an Act of Parliament and may in some cases be subject to parliamentary approval. But, as with tertiary legislation, they are subject to no detailed parliamentary discussion. Examples include codes of practice such as the Highway Code or the codes of practice relating to police behaviour made under the Police and Criminal Evidence Act 1984. (See Chapter 5.) Many other examples could be given.

There is a practical problem with tertiary and quasi-legislation. It is not published in the normal way by the Office of Public Sector Information—the official outlet for government publications. For example, ministerial directions are usually made available only to those who need to know about them; ordinary members of the public who wish to know about these documents find them hard to track down. An important issue of principle flows from this. It is frequently asserted that because legislation is published by a single authoritative source, 'everyone is deemed to know the law'. Such a claim is simply not sustainable in the case of such instruments.

background to the bill and explains what it is trying to achieve in policy terms.[10] All bills and notes are published on the internet.

Four distinct types of bill may be identified (for further consideration of these different types of Act of Parliament, *see Box 3.3*):

(1) Government bills, which arise from the political programme of the party in government. This is the largest group, designed to further the political objectives of the government in power. These bills are sponsored by individual ministers.

(2) Law Reform bills, which arise from recommendations made by law reform agencies, such as the Law Commission. These are less politically controversial.[11]

(3) Consolidation bills, which bring together into a single place a wide range of legislative provisions scattered through many Acts of Parliament and thus difficult to find.[12] These measures do not themselves introduce new law but tidy up

---

[10] Since 1999 Explanatory Notes have also been published alongside new Acts of Parliament. These Notes are key to public understanding of legislation, as they are written in plain language and are designed to explain the policy and legal context for to non-lawyers. This is possibly the most important, though again inadequately publicized, procedural innovation of recent years.

[11] For further information on the work of the Law Commission see Chapter 4, p. 85.

[12] Failure to consolidate adds to the complexity of carrying out legal research; printed versions of Acts of Parliament may be quite misleading, having been substantially amended. New computer technology creates the opportunity to keep texts of statutes up to date. In some countries, e.g. Canada, the statute book is automatically consolidated every ten years.

and re-present what is already on the statute book. There is a special procedure to enable such measures to reach the statute book without going through the full parliamentary process discussed below.

(4) Private Members' bills, which are a special type of bill introduced by backbench MPs. (*See Box 3.4.*)

Preparatory stages

Before being presented to Parliament, many bills start the process of becoming law by being included in the political manifesto of the party that won the last general election. Political parties want power in government to turn their ideas into legislative form. Issues that involve a good deal of specialist know-how are frequently the subject of consultation with persons or other agencies outside government. There are various ways in which this is carried out. Commonly, ideas for new policies and related changes in the law are floated in a *Green Paper*,[13] which sets out policy proposals and asks for comments on them. The government usually attempts to steer response by indicating its preliminary view on what should happen.

Box 3.3 Legal system explained

Acts of Parliament: Public General Acts and Local and Personal Acts

Most Acts of Parliament are known as *Public General Acts*. Each Public General Act contains a section which defines to which parts of the United Kingdom the Act applies. Since the devolution of legislative powers to Scotland and Wales, this is not always a straightforward matter. But all such Acts are of *general* application in those parts of the countries to which they are stated to apply. There are special rules relating to legislation which is effective in Northern Ireland.

By contrast, *Local and Personal Acts* (together 'Private Acts') are of limited scope only. They may apply only to a local area (say a town) or to a specific institution (say a body such as a university), or a particular individual. The procedure by which Local and Personal Acts become law is quite different from the procedure by which Public General Acts become law. The detail is not considered here, but in essence such Acts are passed through a procedure involving committees of the House, not the full House of Commons.

Private Acts must be sharply distinguished from *Private Members' Acts* (see Box 3.4).

---

[13] So called because years ago they were published with green covers. For some years, however, image-conscious governments have used designers and printers to produce Green Papers with covers containing all the colours of the rainbow!

Box 3.4   Legal system explained

Private Members' Acts

Private Members' bills are introduced by MPs who are not members of the government. They are subject to special rules relating to their content. The most important is that they cannot contain any provision that would result in the expenditure of public money. These bills are also subject to special procedural rules, which mean that only a very few such measures reach the statute book in any given year.

The backbenchers who bring these bills forward are selected following a ballot—a process which takes place early in each parliamentary session. Private Members' bills are debated only on Fridays—a day when the pressure of government business is usually less. Twenty Private Members are able to introduce their measures following the ballot, but those near the top of the list have a greater chance of seeing their bills introduced into law. For a bill to have any chance of success it must either be supported by the government, or at least not actively resisted by the government.

The Housing (Homeless Persons) Bill 1976 is a good example: as originally drafted it would have given a range of legal rights to the homeless which the government regarded as wholly unacceptable. In that case, the government offered the bill's sponsor, the late Stephen Ross, an alternative bill, which he took forward. With this government support the bill passed into law.

Private Members' bills can be used to introduce measures on which there are fierce divisions of opinion, but where those divisions are not the subject of party political debate. An excellent example of this is the Abortion Act 1967, which was a very important, obviously controversial, measure introduced by Mr David Steel, in relation to which none of the main political parties wished to tie their political reputations. The willingness of a Private Member to take such an issue forward means that the political parties, in particular the government party, can to an extent distance themselves from the issue.

Over the last fifteen years or so, about eight out of twenty Private Members' bills have reached the statute book each year. There are three other means by which backbenchers may attempt to introduce legislation: 'presentation bills', Ten Minute Rule bills, and bills from individual members of the House of Lords. The numbers of such bills passing into law are tiny and are not considered further here.

Following initial consultation, a further and firmer statement of the government's policy objectives may be published in a *White Paper*[14] that summarizes responses to the consultation and sets out what the government plans to do.

---

[14] They too are no longer distinguished by the colour of their covers.

The Queen's speech

Each session of Parliament[15] opens with the Queen's speech. Written by the government, it sets out the legislative priorities for the coming parliamentary session. Getting a slot in the Queen's speech is a key objective for ministers seeking to introduce a bill into Parliament. Without it, their legislative ambitions cannot be advanced.[16] The details of the Queen's speech are determined each year by a Cabinet committee.

Procedural changes

Until recently, parliamentary practice required all bills to be presented first to Parliament. Failure to do this was regarded as an insult to Parliament. The process of enacting bills has recently undergone three important changes.

Consultation. The wisdom of the principle that bills must not see the light of day until they are brought to Parliament became subject to increasing challenge. As the result of important procedural changes,[17] an increasing number of bills are now published in draft and circulated for comment and criticism by those most likely to be affected, prior to their formal introduction into Parliament.[18] The Select Committee on Modernization has recommended that this procedure be followed as much as possible.[19]

Hearings. In addition there are now cases where a draft bill is subject to special hearings by a committee of MPs—a practice common in the United States and other countries but not until recently used here.[20] Thus, in the case of the Financial Services and Markets Bill 1999 a consultation paper was issued in July 1998, with a draft bill attached to it. This was the subject of consultation with those likely to be affected by it. In addition it was the subject of hearings before two parliamentary committees: one, the Treasury Committee of the House of Commons;[21] the other, a joint committee of the House of Commons and House of Lords, both of which issued reports on the draft bill. All these consultations led to further changes to the bill being made before it was formally introduced into the House of Commons in June 1999.

Carry forward. A further significant procedural experiment has been introduced whereby a bill can be considered over two parliamentary sessions. If the passage of

[15] The date is usually in November. Following a general election, the opening of the session will start shortly after the results are declared and the new government formed. The November date applies in those years when there is no general election.

[16] The only exception to this is emergency legislation needed to deal with an urgent and unexpected issue.

[17] See Select Committee on the Modernization of the House of Commons, *The Legislative Process* (July 1997) (HC 190,1997–1998).

[18] The Employment Rights (Dispute Resolution) Act 1998 is an example.

[19] Modernization of the House of Commons Select Committee, 2nd Report, *A Reform Programme, HC* 1168 September 2002; www.publications.parliament.uk/pa/cm/cmmodern.htm.

[20] An early example was the pre-legislative scrutiny by the Social Security Select Committee of the government's draft bill on pension sharing on divorce, published in June 1998.

[21] Their report, *Financial Services Regulation,* was published in February 1999, with a response from government in March 1999.

a bill through Parliament is not completed before Parliament is prorogued in late October/early November, it can be taken forward into the following parliamentary session. One example was the Financial Services and Markets Bill 1999 mentioned above. The Select Committee on Modernization has recommended wider use of this practice, which is common in most other political systems with Westminster-style parliamentary procedures.[22]

The advantage of these developments is clear. Those affected are given the opportunity to comment on the adequacy of the legislation from a practical point of view before it reaches its final form. The ability to carry bills from one parliamentary session to another means that there can be greater flexibility over the dates on which bills can be introduced into Parliament. The practice of 'front-loading'—the presentation of new bills in the first half of each parliamentary session—is, to some extent, mitigated. It also represents a sensible attempt to prevent the detail of complex legislation being rushed through Parliament, at the end of a parliamentary session, often with undesirable drafting consequences.

Parliamentary stages

The formal procedure for passing an Act starts with the presentation of a bill in one of the Houses of Parliament. Most measures designed to advance the political objectives of the government are presented first in the House of Commons; less controversial measures (including consolidation bills) may start in the House of Lords. The analysis here assumes the bill starts in the House of Commons.

The bill's policy objectives will have been determined by the political imperatives of the government or other person presenting the bill. Those policies are transformed into legislative form by specially trained lawyers known as Parliamentary Counsel.

The parliamentary process starts with a *first reading*, a formal stage when the House orders the bill to be printed.[23] No further progress can be made until it has been printed.

The first opportunity for debate arises at the *second reading*. Here the minister responsible sets out the main policy objectives; the opposition parties set out their objections. This is followed by comments from other Members of Parliament. At the end of the debate, there is a summing up by a government minister. It is rare for a government bill to be defeated at this stage.[24] If a bill requires either the raising of taxation or the expenditure of public money, Parliament also has to pass (respectively) a Ways and Means Resolution or a Money Resolution.

---

[22] Carry forward is only possible within a parliamentary session; bills that fail to be enacted because a general election is called cannot be carried forward, even if the new government is formed by the same political party as the outgoing government. In such cases, the bill must be reintroduced and start the parliamentary process anew.

[23] All bills are printed on a light-blue-coloured paper, to distinguish them from the subsequent Act, which is printed on white paper.

[24] This was the fate suffered by the Shops Bill 1986, designed to deregulate Sunday trading.

The bill then moves to the *committee stage*.[25] Detailed scrutiny of the text is carried out by a group of MPs, which may range in size from sixteen to fifty, known as a standing committee. They consider the clauses[26] of the bill, as drafted, consider amendments proposed to those clauses, and determine whether or not such amendments should or should not be accepted. This is a highly 'political' stage in the legislative process. Not only do the opposition members put down such amendments that they have thought of, but members of the standing committee are also subject to intense lobbying from groups outside Parliament, with a view to their putting down amendments which reflect the interests of those lobbying groups. (These groups will also exert pressure in other ways—press releases, airing their views on TV and radio, and so on.)

Given that the government party always has a majority on the committee, and those MPs from the government side are instructed to vote as the Whip tells them, the government usually either gets its way, or makes only those concessions which it is prepared to accept. Despite this degree of control, bills are frequently amended and often emerge from the overall process significantly changed from the form in which they were first advanced. Very occasionally, where a bill is being rushed though Parliament, or involves significant constitutional change, the committee stage may take place in the whole House.

Next comes the *report stage*. Here what has happened to the bill in committee is reported to the main House. This may provide the government with the chance to undo things that the committee may have done to the bill which the government does not like. It is often the point at which amendments which the government wishes to introduce into the bill (perhaps following debate in committee) are introduced.

Finally comes the *third reading,* a more formal stage in which the bill in its amended form is brought together but no more amendments are made. The bill then goes to the House of Lords, where it begins a similar process.

The progress of a bill through Parliament is now regulated by a *programme order,* formally approved by Parliament following the second reading. This sets out the dates by which each stage of the bill is to be completed. Since programme orders were introduced in 1998, guillotine motions have become extremely rare. One effect of programme orders should be noted: not infrequently substantial parts of a bill may pass into law without debate.

[25] The committees of the House of Commons which look at bills are known collectively as standing committees. Rarely, on a very controversial measure or on an urgent measure that is being rushed through the parliamentary process, the committee stage may be taken 'on the floor of the House', in other words before the whole House of Commons. Standing committees should be carefully distinguished from 'select committees' which have the task of examining the activities of government carried out in the various government departments.

[26] Each separate provision in a bill is called a clause; after the bill has passed through Parliament and become an Act, clauses become sections. A new procedural innovation, being piloted with the current Legal Services Bill as it goes through the House of Commons, is the provision of Explanatory Notes for members of the standing committee.

The House of Lords

Procedure in the House of Lords is broadly similar to that in the Commons. The major differences are:

(i)   the committee stage is taken on the floor of the House. There are no standing committees of peers whose task it is to report back to the House as a whole;

(ii) there is no guillotine, and thus debate on amendments is not restricted; and

(iii) amendments can be made at the third reading stage.

These potentially can be, and on occasion are, a source of delay. In theory the House of Lords is able to wreck or seriously delay legislation. But peers are aware that, given their status as a non-elected legislative body, the ultimate decision on legislation must lie with the elected House of Commons. While they do not in practice wholly destroy bills, there have been a number of occasions in recent years where they have secured significant amendments or even caused a bill to be withdrawn.[27]

Once the Lords' stages are complete, there has to be a process for the Commons and the Lords to agree a single version of the text. Particularly at the end of the parliamentary year (late October/early November) this can lead to dramatic horse-trading between Lords and Commons, especially where measures are very controversial. In the last resort, the House of Lords does have power under the Parliament Act 1911 to delay a Commons bill for up to one year (though not a money bill). If there is an ultimate impasse, then the view of the elected legislature, the House of Commons, prevails. The most recent occasion on which the Parliament Act was invoked was in relation to the passing of the Hunting Act 2004.

Royal assent and commencement

Finally comes the *royal assent*. This has not been withheld since 1707, but, reflecting the fact that the United Kingdom is a constitutional monarchy, remains a formal step that has to be completed.

The mere fact that an Act has completed the legislative process does not mean it at once becomes effective. Commonly, new administrative arrangements have to be put in place before an Act can become operational. In such cases, the legislation will be effective only when a *Commencement Order*—a special type of statutory instrument (see below)—is made. (The Easter Act 1928 has still not been brought into force.) It is clearly essential that those who may seek to take advantage of new rules of law discover whether or not statutory provisions are in force. This could involve difficult detailed research. The availability of statutes on-line, through legislation database services

---

[27] The Criminal Justice (Mode of Trial) Bill 1999, which sought to limit rights to jury trial, was introduced in the House of Lords, but was withdrawn following an adverse vote there. The government decided to introduce a new bill, revised in content but with the same title, in the House of Commons; this was the subject of a wrecking amendment in the House of Lords. See further Chapter 5.

Box 3.5   Time for change

Case Study: House of Lords consideration of the
Constitutional Reform Bill 2004

As part of its programme of constitutional reform, in June 2003, the government announced that it had decided to abolish the post of Lord Chancellor and create a new Supreme Court (to replace the House of Lords' judicial function). This generated considerable controversy, not least among the senior judiciary who feared that such a step could undermine the conventional constitutional balance of power between the judicial and executive branches of government. It was also discovered that, in any event, simple abolition of the post without legislation was not technically possible.

There followed a period of public consultation on the three principal elements of reform (Lord Chancellor, Supreme Court, and judicial appointments), and the government published summaries of the responses on 26 January 2004. The Supreme Court and judicial appointments issues were also considered by the Constitutional Affairs Committee of the House of Commons, which reported on 3 February 2004. One of its recommendations was that the Constitutional Reform Bill would be 'a clear candidate for examination in draft'. A number of speakers in a keenly argued debate in the House of Lords on 12 February 2004 made the same point.

Nevertheless, the government decided to introduce the Constitutional Reform Bill into the House of Lords without prior discussion. It became clear that, such was the degree of opposition to the Bill, it stood little chance of being passed by the House of Lords. However the Lords were also conscious that to deny progress to what the government regarded as an important measure would be a risky step to take.

The compromise was to 'rediscover' a procedure—not used in relation to a government bill for about ninety years—of referring the Bill to a specially constituted Select Committee of the House of Lords. The Committee held nine days of hearing evidence and spent a further eleven days deliberating. They made numerous drafting changes to the Bill, though on the two key issues—abolition of the post of Lord Chancellor and creation of the Supreme Court—the Committee remained divided.

The effect of the process was to give people outside Parliament a chance to comment on the Bill, as now happens with consideration of draft bills, but also to make detailed changes to the Bill, as standing committees of the House of Commons do at the committee stage of a bill.

Although the Select Committee did not agree on everything, the Bill, as amended, was recommitted to the House of Lords, from which it finally emerged as the Constitutional Reform Act 2005.

One of the most important features of the Select Committee's Report is that it published the hitherto unpublished agreement reached by the Lord Chancellor and the Lord Chief Justice on the guarantees needed to ensure the continuing independence of the judiciary. For further information about the concordat, as the agreement is known, see p. 80.

such as *Lexis-Nexis* and the new Statute Law database, has made it easier to find out whether new legislation is in force.

Reports of debates

The debates on all the parliamentary stages are the subject of verbatim reporting in the Official Reports of the Houses of Parliament (known collectively as *Hansard*). Thus it is possible to research what was said and by whom at each stage of the parliamentary process. These reports also detail how MPs voted. These reports are available on the internet.

Secondary legislation

Because of the time needed to ensure the passage of legislation through Parliament, modern practice is for Acts of Parliament to contain the essential principles of legislation only. The detail is filled in by *secondary legislation* made under the authority of the Act, but which is not subject to the full parliamentary scrutiny that a bill undergoes. Secondary legislation is technically known as *statutory instruments,* which come in two forms, *regulations* (the most common) and *orders.*

Underpinning the creation of secondary legislation are a number of controls designed to ensure that governments only introduce measures which they have authority to introduce:

(1) regulations are subject to formal vetting by the Joint Committee on Statutory Instruments;

(2) many categories of statutory instruments also have to be shown in draft to particular bodies or organizations detailed in the 'parent' Act. Many governmental advisory committees are given the specific task of commenting on and vetting proposed regulations. (*See Box 3.6.*) Some parent Acts require the government not just to consult with a specific nominated body, but with 'such bodies as appear to have an interest in the legislation'. This is code for requiring the government to discuss the content of proposed delegated legislation with a range of interested groups;

(3) there is the potential for some parliamentary input, though this rarely happens. All regulations are subject either to a *negative resolution procedure* or to an *affirmative resolution procedure.* (Two particular types of SI, Commencement Orders (which bring Acts of Parliament, or parts of Acts of Parliament into effect) and Orders in Council, are not subject to any parliamentary procedure.) The *negative resolution procedure* is the more common. It means that, once laid before Parliament, a new regulation becomes effective on the date stated in the regulation, *unless* Parliament passes a resolution stating that the regulations should be annulled. Given that regulations are introduced by government and that (usually) the government has a majority in the House of Commons, annulment happens very infrequently. By contrast, the *affirmative resolution procedure* means that a regulation laid before Parliament cannot become effective unless Parliament adopts a resolution which states *positively* that

the regulation should become effective. It cannot be said that this process gives the House of Commons much control over the detail, since debate is permitted only on the underlying issues, not the specific details. But affirmative resolution debates do give some opportunity for opposition parties to make broad political points about the regulation in question;[28]

(4) in an extreme case, the validity of a statutory instrument may be challenged in the courts and, if found to be *ultra vires* (outside the legal framework provided by the parent Act), will be declared by the courts to be a nullity.[29]

Box 3.6   Time for change

Case Study: consultation on regulations: social security and administrative justice

An interesting example of the use of a specialist committee to review delegated legislation is the work of the Social Security Advisory Committee which looks at draft regulations relating to social security. It not only considers the proposals itself, but also consults on those proposals with a wide range of bodies and pressure groups outside government. It reflects on these comments before making its own report to the government. The government then decides whether or not to accept the advice of its Committee.

When it brings forward the final version of the regulations, the government is required to publish a special report which not only reproduces the report from the Advisory Committee, but also details why the government has (or more often has not) followed the advice of the Committee.

This represents a particular form of accountability which to some extent replaces normal parliamentary debate; arguably it is more relevant since most of those consulted have a specialist interest in and knowledge of the area. This is a model which, it has been forcefully argued, should apply in other regulation-making contexts.[30]

Another example is the work of the Administrative Justice and Tribunals Council which scrutinizes draft statutory instruments relating to the practice and procedures of tribunals and inquiries.

---

[28] An example is found in the annual up-rating of social security benefits. The relevant regulations are subject to the affirmative resolution procedure. Debate on whether the new amounts should be 50p more or less is not permitted; but general debate about social security provision and social welfare policy is allowed.

[29] Although a relatively rare occurrence, there are examples. See, *R v. Secretary of State for Trade and Industry, ex p Thomson Holidays, The Times,* 12 January 2000, CA and *R v. Secretary of State for the Environment, Transport and the Regions and Another, ex p Spath Holme Ltd* [2000] 1 All ER 884, HL.

[30] Harden, I., and Lewis, N., *The Noble Lie: The British Constitution and the Rule of Law* (London, Hutchinson, 1986).

Amending legislation

The process of amending legislation is usually done by passing a new Act which alters an Act already on the statute book. Thus amending legislation has to take its turn in finding a slot in the legislative programme. On occasion, ministers have sought to make their lives easier by providing that provisions in an Act of Parliament can be amended by statutory instrument, thereby avoiding Parliament. These provisions, called 'Henry VIII clauses',[30] are not regarded with favour.

One consequence of the passing of amending legislation is that it can make it hard to find out what the current law is on a particular subject. A very important recent development has been the launch of the Statute Law Database, which provides details of how and when legislation has been amended. It is not yet complete, in the sense that not all legislation on the statute book is currently in the database; but its scope is expanding. It is a very important new legal resource.

Regulatory reform

In recent years, it has come to be accepted that where changes in legislation which impose unnecessary burdens can be removed they should be without waiting for a full parliamentary legislative slot. The first Act to move in this direction, the Deregulation and Contracting-Out Act 1994, provided that, subject to detailed safeguards, ministers could lay orders before Parliament which had the effect of amending legislation. The power was used forty-eight times to remove burdens from business and individuals which might not otherwise have received parliamentary time. This trend continued with the Regulatory Reform Act 2001, which gave ministers wider powers to lay orders before Parliament to amend legislation, so long as any such amendment removed burdens. This Act has, in turn, been replaced by the Legislative and Regulatory Reform Act 2006, which came into force at the start of 2007.

The passage of all these bills has been very controversial, as backbench MPs and indeed those outside government fear the powers could allow ministers to make significant legislative change without exposing their arguments to parliamentary scrutiny. Many of these fears were, arguably, overstated; certainly ministers' powers to amend legislation are significantly circumscribed. (For further information on the Legislative and Regulatory Reform Act, *see Box 3.7.*)

Comment

Given the domination of the parliamentary timetable by the government machine, it is sometimes asked whether the amount of time spent debating proposals in relation to which the outcome is totally or largely predictable is worthwhile. Elected Members

---

[30] Reflecting the propensity of that monarch to ride roughshod over Parliament.

Box 3.7   Legal system explained

The Legislative and Regulatory Reform Act 2006

Scope of the Act

In relation to powers to amend legislation, ministers are given power to make any provision by order, called a legislative reform order, which would remove or reduce any burden, or remove or reduce the overall burdens, to which any person is subject as a direct or indirect result of any legislation. Burdens are defined as: a financial cost; an administrative inconvenience; an obstacle to efficiency, productivity, or profitability; or a sanction, criminal or otherwise, which affects the carrying on of any lawful activity. Each of these concepts is defined further in the legislation. One clear limit is that ministers can only use their power to reform an area where there is already a legislative framework. It could be used to replace one statutory regime with another where this removes or reduces burdens. But it cannot be used to introduce an entirely new regulatory regime. So, for example, it would not be possible to create an entirely new legislative framework relating to a new area of consumer protection, employment rights, or environmental protection simply because there are considered to be good policy reasons for doing so.

Ministers are also given power to amend the powers of regulators so that their functions comply more closely with defined Principles of Good Regulation. These are that regulatory activities should be carried out in a way that is transparent, accountable, proportionate, consistent, and should be targeted only at cases in which action is needed.

Save where a minister wants simply to restate existing law, he or she must meet six conditions.

1. There are no non-legislative solutions which will satisfactorily remedy the difficulty which the order is intended to address.
2. The effect of the provision made by the order is proportionate to its policy objective.
3. The provision made by the order, taken as a whole, strikes a fair balance between the public interest and the interests of the persons adversely affected by the order.
4. The provision made by the order does not remove any necessary protection.
5. The provision made by the order will not prevent any person from continuing to exercise any right or freedom which he might reasonably expect to continue to exercise.
6. The provision made by the order is not constitutionally significant.

The Act sets out the procedures ministers must follow. First, the minister must consult on his proposals for an order. He must then lay a draft order and an explanatory document before Parliament. The order must be made by statutory instrument in accordance with the negative resolution procedure, or the affirmative resolution procedure

Box 3.7   *Continued*

(see above, p. 46) or the super-affirmative resolution procedure (see below). The minister's recommended procedure applies unless either House of Parliament requires a higher level of procedure.

Super-affirmative procedure

The super-affirmative procedure affords greater parliamentary scrutiny than the ordinary affirmative resolution orders procedure. First, the minister must lay a proposed legislative reform order before Parliament in draft, together with a full explanatory document. Following a sixty-day period of parliamentary consideration, during which time the proposal is referred automatically and simultaneously to two parliamentary committees, the committees make their first reports to their respective Houses. If the reports are favourable, the next stage is for the minister formally to lay a draft order in each House, along with an explanation of any changes made to the original draft proposal. If the minister accepts any changes proposed to the draft order by the committees or others between this stage and the final vote on the order, he must formally withdraw the draft order he has laid and replace it with another which incorporates the changes. The ability to make changes (minor or otherwise) to the draft order is a key feature of the order-making power, which is not available to statutory instruments dealt with in the usual way.

The final procedural stages for parliamentary scrutiny of draft regulatory reform orders are set out in standing orders. The Commons committee produces a report on the draft order within fifteen days. The Lords committee has no set time period but usually reports within the same time period. Each House then considers the relevant committee report on the draft order (this is the main feature that makes this form of parliamentary consideration 'super-affirmative').

of Parliament do not, in general, have any detailed control over the content of Acts of Parliament; indeed, there is no guarantee that all provisions of bills are subject to considered debate. The vast bulk of legislation—secondary legislation—reaches the statute book with no consideration by Members of Parliament at all.

Nevertheless it should be remembered that much of the detail of the parliamentary process was developed in an age where the party machine and the discipline over the parliamentary party provided by the Whips was not as it is today. But the enormous power of the modern party machine in government to dominate the legislative process is perhaps the best reason for retaining the detailed process that currently exists. This arises from the very political theories, noted above, which underpin the British Constitution and its system of government. Although ministers may be able to achieve their desired goals in the end, the process ensures that they will have been subject to challenge by elected Members of Parliament. Without these procedures it would be far harder for ministers seeking to defend a particular measure to claim legitimacy for their legislative acts.

European law-making institutions

There has been much debate about the impact that the involvement of the United Kingdom 'in Europe' has had on British law and the English legal system. Two quite separate institutional frameworks are often confused. They are:

- the Council of Europe; and
- the European Union.

The Council of Europe

The Council of Europe was established after the end of the Second World War. Its task was to prevent a repeat of the human rights outrages of the Second World War period. More recently it has engaged in a process of assisting those countries of the former Eastern Bloc to create the institutional arrangements that will assist them to develop democratic principles. Its most significant act in terms of its impact on English law was the creation in 1950 of the European Convention on Human Rights. This is a charter of fundamental rights and freedoms agreed by all the member states of the Council of Europe. As is common with all treaties, the Convention did not come into effect until it had been ratified by a number of governments. This happened in 1953. The Convention has been amended a number of times. The current version, amended by Protocol 11, came into effect in November 1998.

Normally treaties seek to regulate relationships between nation states. They may provide that one country may take action against another where there is an alleged breach of an international treaty obligation. The European Convention on Human Rights is different. In it, provision is made for *individuals* to take proceedings where it is alleged that a government is in breach of its obligations under the treaty. Individuals cannot start proceedings unless the government in question has permitted this to take place. In the case of the United Kingdom, the right of an individual to take proceedings against the British government for alleged breaches of the Convention was agreed in 1966.

The impact of the Council of Europe on the law making process in the United Kingdom has been indirect. Where cases are taken before the European Court of Human Rights in Strasbourg which result in a decision that a rule of British law or some practice of the British government is contrary to the provisions of the Convention, this leads to the British government changing the law to bring it into line with the Convention, as interpreted by the Court.[31] The Interception of Communications Act 1985, which regulates phone-tapping, was the result of an adverse decision by the Court of Human Rights.

Now that the terms of the European Convention have been directly introduced into British law following enactment of the Human Rights Act 1998, most of the Articles of the European Convention have become directly enforceable in the English courts. It is specifically stated in the Human Rights Act that, in interpreting its provisions, English judges must take account of the jurisprudence developed by the European Court of Human Rights in Strasbourg.

The Act has two principal effects on the law-making process in the United Kingdom. First, in presenting bills to Parliament, ministers must declare that in their opinion proposed legislation complies with Convention provisions. Secondly, as noted,[32] British courts now have power to declare a legislative provision incompatible with the provisions of the Convention. Although not declaring an Act of Parliament, or a provision in an Act, unlawful, this puts overwhelming pressure on ministers to introduce changes so that the incompatibility is removed. In this important sense, the legislative freedom of ministers is reduced.

There is much debate about the impact of the Human Rights Act. The British government introduced a number of measures to deal with law it thought was not Convention-compliant; the Regulation of Investigatory Powers Act 2000 is an example. Policy-makers within government are very conscious of the need to ensure that new policies will be Convention-compliant. To that extent the Act has had significant impact. New legislation is also scrutinized for compliance by a newly created Parliamentary Joint Committee on Human Rights.

Legal arguments based on the Human Rights Act have been advanced in a significant number of cases in the upper courts (High Court, Court of Appeal, and House of Lords). However the extent to which these arguments have been upheld in the courts has so far been relatively limited.

In 2006 the Lord Chancellor published a review on the implementation of the Human Rights Act which came to much the same conclusion. Apart from counter-terrorism measures (for a case study, see Box 3.8) the review concluded that the impact of the Human Rights Act had been beneficial. One possibly unexpected consequence of its enactment is that judges in the court in Strasbourg take more notice of what British judges say on human rights issues.

What the long-term impact of the Act will be is harder to gauge. It should be remembered that, despite the ability of the judges in the United Kingdom to apply the provisions of the Convention, they do not have the last word; applications to the European Court of Human Rights in Strasbourg can still be made. One idea, raised in the recent

---

[31] There have been over thirty adverse decisions of the Court affecting the United Kingdom.
[32] Above, p. 35.

Box 3.8   System in action

Case study: impact of Human Rights Act on prevention of terrorism law.

The power of the Human Rights Act was revealed dramatically in the House of Lords case, *A and Others* v *Secretary of State for the Home Department* [2004] UKHL 56.

In outline the facts were that, following attacks in the United States on 11 September 2001 by the terrorist group Al-Qaida, the UK government considered that it was necessary to derogate from the right to liberty provided by Article 5(1)(f) of the European Convention for the Protection of Human Rights and Fundamental Freedoms. Article 5(1)(f) guaranteed that no-one was to be deprived of his liberty save in 'the lawful arrest or detention of a person ... against whom action is being taken with a view to deportation or extradition'. Derogation is permitted by Article 15 of the Convention where there is a 'public emergency threatening the life of the nation'. Accordingly, the Human Rights Act 1998 (Designated Derogation) Order 2001 was made and the Anti-terrorism, Crime and Security Act 2001 enacted. Section 23 of the 2001 Act provided that a suspected international terrorist could be detained (without charge) under specified provisions of the Immigration Act 1971 despite the fact that his removal or departure from the United Kingdom was prevented, whether temporarily or indefinitely, by a point of law which wholly or partly related to an international agreement, or a practical consideration. The appellants were all non-UK nationals who faced the prospect of torture or inhuman treatment if returned to their own countries, who could not be deported to any third countries, and were not charged with any crime. Thus, without the derogation from Article 5(1)(f) of the Convention, they could not have been detained. All had been certified by the Secretary of State as suspected international terrorists and detained under section 23 of the 2001 Act. They contended that section 23 of the 2001 Act and the 2001 Order violated the prohibition on discrimination under Article 14 of the Convention as they allowed only suspected terrorists who were non-UK nationals to be detained when there were British nationals, equally dangerous, who could not be so detained.

Initially, the Special Immigration Appeal Committee upheld their argument. The Court of Appeal reversed that decision. The case went to an exceptionally large, nine-person, House of Lords. They reversed the Court of Appeal.

The Lords took the view that the Convention regime for the international protection of human rights required national authorities, including national courts, to exercise their authority to afford effective protection. The courts were not precluded from scrutinizing the issues raised. Matters of the kind in issue did not fall solely within the discretionary area of judgment belonging to the democratic organs of the state. Any restriction of the right to personal liberty had to be closely scrutinized by the national court. The public emergency on which the United Kingdom had relied to derogate from Article 5 of the Convention was the threat to security presented by Al-Qaida terrorists and their supporters. While the threat to the security of the United Kingdom derived from foreign nationals, some of whom could not be deported, the threat did not derive solely from such foreign nationals. Section 23 of the 2001 Act did not rationally address the threat presented by Al-Qaida terrorists and their supporters because it did not

Box 3.8 *Continued*

address the threat presented by United Kingdom nationals; it permitted suspected foreign nationals to pursue their activities abroad; and permitted the detention of persons who were not suspected of presenting any threat to the security of the United Kingdom as Al-Qaida terrorists or supporters. The choice of an immigration measure to address a security problem had the inevitable result of failing adequately to address that problem (by allowing non-UK suspected terrorists to leave the country with impunity and leaving British suspected terrorists at large) while imposing the severe penalty of indefinite detention on persons who, even if reasonably suspected of having links with Al-Qaida, might harbour no hostile intentions towards the United Kingdom. Section 23, being discriminatory, could not be strictly required within Article 15 and so was disproportionate. In providing for the detention of suspected international terrorists who were not United Kingdom nationals but not for the detention of suspected international terrorists who were United Kingdom nationals, section 23 unlawfully discriminated in breach of Article 14 of the Convention against the enjoyment of liberty under Article 5. The foreign nationality of the appellants did not preclude them from claiming the protection of their Convention rights. Suspected international terrorists who were United Kingdom nationals (unremovable from the United Kingdom) were the relevantly analogous comparators. The aim of section 23 was to protect the United Kingdom against the risk of Al-Qaida terrorism. The risk was thought to be presented by both non-UK and UK nationals. The effect of section 23 was to permit the former to be deprived of their liberty, but not the latter. The appellants had been treated differently because of their nationality or immigration status. The decision to detain one group of suspected international terrorists defined by nationality or immigration status and not another could not be justified and was a violation of Article 15 and inconsistent with the United Kingdom's other obligations under international law.

The response of government was to enact, with great speed, the Prevention of Terrorism Act 2005, which had the effect of permitting the continued detention of the detainees. But the passage of this bill was highly controversial. It did not become law without the government having to make significant concessions on its terms. In addition, the government committed itself to bringing a further measure before Parliament early in 2006. The resulting Terrorism Act 2006 was enacted in March 2006. This expands the scope of offences that can be committed in relation to terrorist activity. It also extended to 28 days the period during which police have power to detain suspects without charge. (There is ongoing debate whether this period is sufficient or should be even longer.)

Thus, as well as being a case study in the power of the Human Rights Act, it also illustrates that Parliament can still play a significant role in settling the details of extremely controversial legislative proposals. It also demonstrates clearly the significance of the independence of the judiciary in these key debates on balancing civil liberty and state security.

Source: Summary of the facts and of the House of Lords judgment adapted from the headnote in the All England Law Reports.

paper on the Governance of Britain, is whether there should be a new British Bill of Rights and Duties.

The European Union

Although being a signatory to the European Convention on Human Rights has had an indirect impact on United Kingdom law making, the accession of the United Kingdom to the European Economic Community in 1973 has had a direct impact on the English legal system. Ever since it became a member of the European Union, there has been an obligation on the United Kingdom to incorporate rules of law prescribed by the institutions of the European Union: the European Commission, the European Council of Ministers,[33] and the European Parliament.

The fundamental purpose of the European Union is to create a huge free market for the provision of goods and services throughout the area of the EU. In order to achieve this, European law seeks to provide a framework within which trade between the countries of the EU can fairly take place. Thus, for example, the EU law provides for the promotion of competition and the regulation of anti-competitive practices.[34] It aims to liberalize industries, such as telecommunications or the airlines, to allow greater freedom of consumer choice. It seeks to prescribe EU-wide standards for the manufacture of goods, in order to protect consumers and to try to ensure that industry overheads are broadly in line. Examples include European standards on the manufacturing of cars or the quality of food labelling. The European Commission also engages, on behalf of the member states, in negotiations with international bodies such as the World Trade Organization.

In more recent years, the EU has sought to develop other wider areas of activity. For example, the EU now seeks to promote human rights and tries to support measures for social cohesion. Thus certain common standards of social security provision for workers are set down, as well as entitlements for citizens of one country in the EU to work in other countries of the Union. There are specific rules relating to measures of employment protection, including safety at work and the prohibition of discriminatory employment practices, particularly those based on gender and race or ethnic origin. In response to criticism about the inability of the EU to intervene in situations of conflict that might seem to warrant a European-wide approach, moves have been made towards the creation of a common foreign and security policy and a common defence policy. There have also been important initiatives in the area of justice and home affairs.

---

[33] Although in the formal descriptions of the EU there is only one Council of Ministers, there is in fact a substantial number of Councils of Ministers reflecting the different portfolios of those ministers, for example, agriculture, foreign policy, economic matters, trade matters, and the like. The supreme Council of Ministers is that which comprises the leaders of the governments of the Union, brought together to determine the most fundamental issues affecting the EU.

[34] For example, the content of the Competition Act 1998 was greatly influenced by the demands of EU law and policy.

The aim of the much discussed, but poorly understood, proposals for the adoption of a European Constitution was both to draw these developments together and to build on them. Had the European Constitution been adopted, it would have replaced a number of existing treaties with a single document setting out the powers and responsibilities of the EU and its constituent institutions, and incorporated a proposed European Charter for Fundamental Rights. The European Constitution was intended to complete a process of institutional reform initiated by the Nice Treaty (2001) designed to make the working of the EU more efficient, particularly with the increase in the size of the EU to twenty-five member states, following accession of countries from Eastern Europe. More generally, it was hoped that the adoption of a single constitution would make the work of the EU and its institutions more comprehensible to those who live within the EU.

Following adverse results in referenda held in France and the Netherlands in the summer of 2005, the plan for a new European Constitution was put on hold. However, pressure for further institutional reform has not gone away. As this edition is being prepared, the EU has published the draft of a new treaty on institutional reform which was agreed in Lisbon at the end of 2007, with a view to implementation in 2009. There is much conflict between those who argue that the proposed new treaty is an attempt to reintroduce the proposed Constitution by the back door, and those who argue that it has a much more limited, technical objective, namely enabling the expanded EU to function more efficiently.

The existence of law-making powers in the institutions of the EU means that, in relation to matters covered by the EU, British law-making institutions no longer have exclusive power. In the language of common political debate, the 'sovereignty of Parliament' has been diminished.

In recent years a different principle developed within the EU—'subsidiarity'— designed to ensure that the European institutions exercise their law-making powers only in relation to those matters which are truly essential to the working of the aims and objectives of the Common Market and which can only be achieved by inter-governmental co-operation. Other, subsidiary, matters are to be left to the law-making bodies in member states. It is beyond the scope of this work to assess the extent to which adoption of the principle of subsidiarity has in fact reduced the amount of law making activity undertaken in the institutions of the EU. But the tensions between law-making bodies within the United Kingdom and those outside cannot be ignored.

The law-making processes of the EU are extremely complex. They are not at all like the parliamentary processes familiar in the United Kingdom. Under the European Treaties, the European Commission has the exclusive right to initiate proposals for legislation. Whether or not proposals become law, and if so in what terms, depends on the outcome of complex negotiations and consensus-building between the Commission, the Council of Ministers, and the European Parliament. The details of these procedures changed following the Treaty of Nice (2001). They would have changed further had the European Constitution come into effect and will change further if the Treaty of Lisbon is successfully implemented. The nature of the legislative process is more like that in the United States, where the President proposes legislation and the Congress decides whether or not it passes into law—the whole process relying on negotiation between the White House and Capitol Hill.

A number of technical points need to be made about the different types of law that emerge from the EU institutions.

First, all the institutions of the EU draw their ultimate authority from the treaties that underpin the establishment of the EU.[35] These may be regarded as the *primary legislation* of the EU. While many of these fundamental provisions of Community law are designed to deal with obligations between states, some have been held by the European Court of Justice to have 'direct effect' in the determination of individual rights and duties. For treaty provisions to have this effect, the content of the provision must be clear; the provision must be self-executing, in the sense that it imposes a specific duty; and the provision must not contain any conditions or qualifications. There are many European Court of Justice decisions which have held particular treaty Articles to be of direct effect; for example Article 81,[36] which outlaws anti-competitive agreements, or Article 141, establishing the principle of equal pay between men and women.

Secondly, where a treaty provision is found to be of direct effect it may be both vertically and horizontally effective. 'Vertical' effectiveness arises when an individual uses a treaty provision to challenge an act of the government or some other public body; 'horizontal' effectiveness arises where one individual or other body wishes to use EU law to challenge the behaviour of another individual body of similar status.

Thirdly, more detailed legislative measures which seek to implement the detailed policies of the EU can collectively be described as the *secondary legislation* of the EU. This emerges in three different guises: regulations, directives, and decisions.

Under Article 249 of the Treaty establishing the European Community, *regulations* are—like the treaty provisions considered above—of 'direct effect', that is to say they automatically become part of the internal law of each of the member states of the EU. An example is Regulation 1408/71, which deals with aspects of social security law and the need to insure workers under a scheme of national insurance. As with treaty provisions, regulations may have both vertical and horizontal effectiveness.

Directives are more general in tone. They set down standards towards which member states are required to aim, but some discretion as to the detail of how that is to be done is left to the member states. The recent debate in the United Kingdom about the implementation of the Working-Time Directive, which seeks to regulate the number of hours worked each week, provides a good example. The principle of direct effect may arise if there is a complaint that a government has failed so to incorporate

---

[35] In particular, the Treaty of Rome, the Single European Act, the Treaty of Maastricht (the Treaty on European Union), the Treaty of Amsterdam, and the Treaty of Nice. Although called a Constitution, the European Constitution would technically have been just another Treaty, bringing together (with important changes) all the existing Treaties.

[36] Following the adoption of the Treaty of Amsterdam in 1997, the Treaties were officially consolidated and the Articles renumbered.

the provision into national law. In the United Kingdom, directives are usually brought into effect in statutory instruments.

Decisions are rulings on particular matters addressed to either governments of member states, corporations, or individuals. For example, an argument about whether a particular take-over bid was or was not anti-competitive could be the subject of a decision. Decisions are binding on those to whom they are addressed (Article 249).

In addition to these forms of secondary legislation, the EU may also make *recommendations* and *opinions,* but these do not have any direct effect.

The courts

There are three principal ways in which English courts contribute to the development of English law:[37]

- *The development of common law.* England is a 'common law' country. This means that many of the principal doctrines of law have been established, not by Parliament, but through cases determined in the higher courts.

- *Statutory interpretation.* Courts play a crucial role in the interpretation of the statutes that Parliament has enacted.

- *Procedural law.* Courts also make important contributions to the development of procedures which the courts follow.

The contribution of European Courts is considered below (p. 68).

The development of common law

It may seem odd today, but the power of the judiciary to make law was, for many years, said not to exist. Judges said their power was merely to 'discover' basic principles of the common law. No-one seriously believes this now. It is recognized that judges do make law. There is however often unease about the theoretical basis for this power. Certainly it cannot derive from any theory of representative democracy; judges are not elected. Rather, the power of the judiciary depends on the doctrine of the *separation of powers,* that to prevent dictatorial powers from being asserted by any one branch of government there must be checks and balances in the constitution. The independence of the judiciary is at the heart of this separation. (*See further Box 3.9.*)

The judges have the primary task of ensuring adherence by ministers and other agents of the state to the principles of the *rule of law.* Until very recently, no specific legislative provision gave the judiciary that power. Rather it has been the assertion

---

[37] It should be stressed only the higher courts—the House of Lords, the Court of Appeal, and the High Court—have authority to make law. For further discussion of the courts see Chapter 9.

of this power by leading judges over the years, and the place that they occupy in the structure of the government, that has resulted in the development of this fundamental judicial function. One consequence of the passing of the Constitutional Reform Act 2005 is that, for the first time, statutory recognition is given to the importance of judicial independence and the need for the Lord Chancellor and other ministers not to seek to influence (other than by argument in court) the judiciary.

The law-making powers of the judiciary are themselves supported by two other fundamental principles: the hierarchical structure of the courts and the doctrine of precedent.

Box 3.9   Legal system explained

Independence of the judiciary

The key claim made for the judges, indeed for adjudicators of all kinds (see Chapter 9), is that they must not only be, but be seen to be, independent. Judicial independence relates centrally to the constitutional function of judges in interpreting and applying law outside the constraints of internal government departmental policies. Judges and adjudicators not perceived as independent are fatally compromised in the eyes of the public, particularly by those whose disputes are being resolved by them. One of the strong claims for adjudicators in the English legal system is that, with rare exceptions, they both appear to be independent and do act independently. This is not to say that they may not bring their own views of the world into play when reaching decisions or determining facts. But claims of corruption of those who hold judicial office—the worst case that could be imagined for compromising judicial independence—are not heard.

As a result of the passing of the Constitutional Reform Act 2005, judicial independence is, for the first time, subject to statutory protection. Section 3 of the Constitutional Reform Act states, in part:

The Lord Chancellor, other ministers of the Crown, and all with responsibility for matters relating to the judiciary or otherwise to the administration of justice must uphold the continued independence of the judiciary.

The following particular duties are imposed for the purpose of upholding that independence: The Lord Chancellor and other ministers of the Crown must not seek to influence particular judicial decisions through any special access to the judiciary. The Lord Chancellor must have regard to—

(a) the need to defend that independence;
(b) the need for the judiciary to have the support necessary to enable them to exercise their functions;
(c) the need for the public interest in regard to matters relating to the judiciary or otherwise to the administration of justice to be properly represented in decisions affecting those matters.

The hierarchical structure

The idea of courts being arranged within a hierarchical framework is quite straightforward. The courts are organized on the basis of seniority (*see Diagram 3.1*); the higher the level of seniority, the greater the authority of the court. Thus the decisions of the

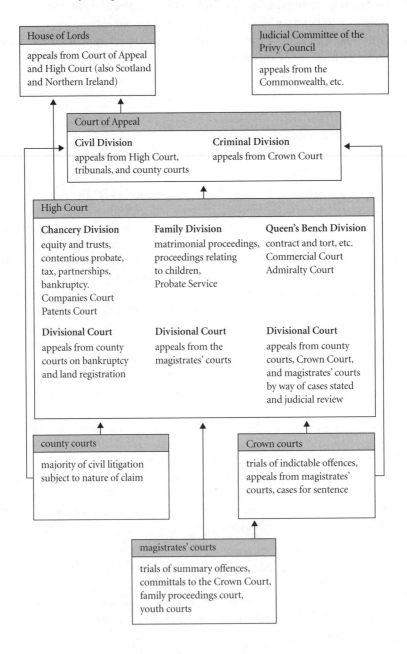

Diagram 3.1 An outline of the court structure in England and Wales

Source: Judicial Statistics, 2005 (Cm 6903) (London, The Stationery Office, 2005).

House of Lords[38] are the most authoritative; those of the Court of Appeal are next; those of the High Court third. Decisions of courts at lower levels are not regarded as precedents, though very occasionally the judgment of a county court judge on a novel point of law may get reported. (On the importance of law reporting *see Box 3.10.*)

There have been occasions on which this hierarchical structure has been challenged, most notably by the late Lord Denning when, as Master of the Rolls, he was the senior judge in the Court of Appeal. He argued that, since most appeals ended in his court and did not proceed to the House of Lords, his court should have similar law-making power to that of the House of Lords. His arguments did not prevail, though they provoke a broader question: do we need all the levels of court, in particular all the levels of appeal, that currently exist?

Box 3.10   Legal system explained

Law reporting

An essential part of the ability of the courts to develop principles of common law or to give authoritative interpretations of statutory principles rests on the publication of law reports—which contain the reasoned judgments prepared by judges in particular cases, from which general principles are then drawn.

Decisions as to which cases get reported are not, in general, taken by members of the judiciary themselves, but by editorial teams responsible for the publication of law reports. Many sets of law reports are now published. Maintaining a complete library of all sets of reports is a very expensive business, only possible for the best-endowed university libraries, the libraries of the Law Society and the Inns of Court, and the most prosperous law firms.

It should be stressed that the production of law reports is not seen as a function of government (though some government departments do in fact publish the text of decisions in specialist areas, such as taxation cases and immigration appeal reports).

The most authoritative of the generalist sets of law reports are those published by the Incorporated Council of Law Reporting, which publishes a range of reports, including: Appeal Cases (decisions of the House of Lords), the Queen's Bench Reports, and the Chancery Division Reports. The Council also publishes the Weekly Law Reports. There is a requirement that if a case is reported in these reports, that is the version that must be used, at least in the High Court and Court of Appeal.

Other sets of law reports are published by commercial publishers. The most widely available generalist set is the *All England Law Reports,* published by Butterworths. In

---

[38] Although the name is the same, the House of Lords sitting as a court is quite distinct from the House of Lords acting in its legislative capacity. The judges in the House of Lords can take part in debates in the House of Lords, but they sit on the cross benches—outside the control of any political party—and by convention usually only intervene in debates on law reform or the administration of justice. The judicial functions of the House of Lords will, under the terms of the Constitutional Reform Act 2005, be transferred to the new Supreme Court, discussed in Chapter 9.

Box 3.10 *Continued*

addition there is now a wide range of specialist reports available in areas ranging from local government, to housing, from education to family law, from criminal appeals to judicial review. Many sub-specialisms in legal practice now have their own sets of law reports. Law reports are also reported in the broadsheet newspapers; the most used are those reported in *The Times.*

Legal electronic databases

In addition to reports in paper format, there is an increasing tendency for law reports to be published in electronic format. For many years a vast electronic database, *Lexis-Nexis,* has been available, providing full-text versions of decisions from a range of the most senior courts. The use of these reported cases as precedents has, however, been limited by the refusal of the judiciary to take into account judgments that appear only in the Lexis format. If they have not been reported elsewhere, in printed form, they have not been usable.

The internet

A more recent development has been the appearance of a range of decisions on the internet. The House of Lords has all judgments since 14 November 1996 on line; Her Majesty's Court Service website carries reports selected by the judges from the Court of Appeal and Administrative Court. There are other on-line sources available too (see the list of websites on the Online Resource Centre for this book). For those who have access to the internet, the costs of obtaining the report of a particular case are limited to the costs of going on line and printing the text. The provision of the reports themselves is at present free. In order to facilitate the use of these sources, a system of 'neutral citation' of judgments has been introduced. (*See Box 3.11.*) It seems inevitable that, as more information technology becomes available in court-rooms, the judges will become more accepting of the citation of cases on screen rather than in hard copy from books.

Box 3.11 Legal system explained

Neutral citation of judgments

Since 11 January 2001 every judgment of the Court of Appeal and of the Administrative Court, and since 14 January 2002 every judgment of the High Court, has been prepared and issued as approved with single spacing, paragraph numbering (in the margins), and no page numbers. In courts with more than one judge the paragraph numbering continues sequentially through each judgment and does not start again at the beginning of each judgment. A unique reference number is given to each judgment.

Box 3.11   *Continued*

Each Court of Appeal judgment starts with the year, followed by EW (for England and Wales), then CA (for Court of Appeal), followed by Civ (for Civil) or Crim (for Criminal) and finally the sequential number. For example *Smith v. Jones* [2001] EWCA Civ 10.

In the High Court, abbreviated as HC, the number comes before the divisional abbreviation and, unlike Court of Appeal judgments, the latter is bracketed: (Ch(ancery)), (Pat(ent)), (Q(ueen's) B(ench)), (Admin(istrative)), (Comm(ercial)), (Admlty(Admiralty)), (TCC (Technology and Construction Court)), or (Fam(ily)) as appropriate. For example, [2002] EWHC 123 (Fam) or [2002] EWHC 124 (QB) or [2002] EWHC 125 (Ch).

Paragraph numbers are referred to in square brackets. Thus paragraph 59 in *Green v. White* [2002] EWHC 124 (QB) would be cited: *Green v. White* [2002] EWHC 124 at [59]; paragraphs 30–35 in *Smith v. Jones* would be *Smith v. Jones* [2001] EWCA Civ 10 at [30]–[35]. Page numbers are not given.

This 'neutral citation' is the official number attributed to the judgment and must always be used at least once when the judgment is cited in a later judgment. It is designed to facilitate the use of websites so that the confusion that is caused by differences in pagination that occur when information is downloaded to different computers with different printers is avoided.

The doctrine of precedent

This is also a simple idea, though not always easy to apply in practice. The essence of precedent is that a principle of law, established in one case, must be applied in a similar situation in a later case. Such a rule of law continues to be applied until either another court decides that, for some reason, the case was incorrectly decided, or for some other reason cannot be allowed to stand; or until a court higher in the hierarchy overturns the decision; or until Parliament decides to change the law by passing a new Act of Parliament which has the effect of overruling or altering the rule that has been laid down by the court.

There have long been arguments for and against the use of precedent. Against, it is argued that precedent introduces unnecessary rigidity into the law, thereby preventing legal doctrine from developing as society develops. In its favour, the use of precedent is said to bring certainty to the law by enabling people to know how issues in the future will be resolved. The principle of law in one case which forms the precedent is known by the Latin phrase, the *ratio decidendi*. Any part of a judgment that does not form part of the *ratio* is not part of the precedent, and thus not relevant in later cases. These are referred to as *obiter dicta*.

There are many reasons this apparently straightforward principle can be exceptionally hard to apply in practice.

(1) The facts on which the ratio of one case is based never replicate themselves precisely in a later case. Thus lawyers wishing to argue that a particular precedent

does not apply to the later case will seek to *distinguish* the two fact situations, thereby, they hope, rendering the earlier decision irrelevant.

(2) Given the large number of reported decisions, there may be situations where a decision reached in one case was reached in ignorance of other relevant decisions. The argument is then made that the precedent in question was made incorrectly or, again to use the Latin, *per incuriam*.

(3) Again because of the very large number of cases that are now reported, there may be two decisions in the law reports that are simply inconsistent, so that a straightforward application of a particular decision to a new situation is not possible.

(4) Since 1966, the House of Lords has taken to itself the authority, in very exceptional circumstances, to change its mind and alter a precedent. It may therefore, on occasion and notwithstanding the existence of clear precedents, decide that earlier cases were wrongly decided and that the law should now be changed.

There are also more technical reasons why the doctrine of precedent is not always simple to apply in practice. It can be very hard to decide what the precedent is. When the House of Lords found[39] that a manufacturer of ginger-beer was negligent after it allowed a decomposed snail to enter a ginger-beer bottle, was this a case about not allowing snails into ginger-beer bottles? Or about not allowing foreign bodies in general into manufacturing processes? Or was it about the duty of care which any person—including a professional person giving advice to a client—should demonstrate towards others? In short, what was the 'level of generality' at which the particular instance of snails in ginger-beer bottles was to be treated in future cases?

Even if the principle of law which can be derived from the cases is clear—such as the principle of negligence, that one person owes a 'duty of care' to his 'neighbour'—who will be categorized for these purposes as a neighbour? And what will be the standard of behaviour that will result in a conclusion that the 'duty of care' has been broken? If teachers take a party of teenage pupils to the seaside, and one of the pupils is washed out to sea by a freak wave, were the teachers in breach of a duty of care in those circumstances to the pupil who drowned? Or did the fault lie with the pupil who ignored advice and went clambering onto the rocks from which he was swept?

Much of the litigation that arises out of the principles of the law of negligence is not seeking to redefine the principles of the law, but rather exploring the extent to which those principles should apply in new situations of risk. This is not the place for a detailed analysis of the law of negligence. The point to be stressed here is that, even though at one level the law may be quite clear, the situations to which the law may be applied in future can be far from clear.

---

[39] In *Donoghue v. Stevenson* [1942] AC 562.

Statutory interpretation

Statutory interpretation is another way in which the courts with authority within the hierarchical structure are able to develop the law. The work of the courts interpreting statutes may not be as dramatic as developing principles of common law, as judges clearly have to work within the texts that have been prescribed by Parliament through the legislative process. Nevertheless the interpretative process can lead to the clarification of words in statutes, and thus in the implementation of those statutory rules. (For a particular example *see Box 3.12*.)

The power of the court to interpret statutes has increased now the Human Rights Act 1998 has been brought into force. British courts not only interpret legislative provisions, but also test the substance of legislative provisions against the standards laid down in the Human Rights Act, which derive from the Articles of the European Convention on Human Rights. In cases where the courts find that they must declare a statute or provision within a statute to be incompatible with the Convention—thus in effect requiring ministers to change the law—the courts acquired a significant new power to develop English law.

One question that may be asked is: why—if Parliament has passed legislation—should there be any need for the courts to intervene at all? There are two basic reasons why this needs to happen: the unpredictability of fact situations and the ambiguity of language.

Box 3.12   System in action

Case study: statutory interpretation: the case of Mr Fitzpatrick[41]

In current housing law, a tenant can pass his right to occupy premises on death to a 'member of his family'. The question has arisen in a number of cases over the last fifty years: who is a member of the family? Initially, in the 1940s, it was held that the phrase was limited to blood relatives; thus the former mistress of a deceased tenant could not take over the tenancy, despite having lived together with her partner for many years. Later, in the 1960s, it was held that, with changes in the nature of relationships and society's attitudes, the mistress of a deceased male tenant could in such a circumstance be regarded as a member of the family and thus take over the tenancy.

More recently still, in 1999, the House of Lords decided that the long-standing homosexual partner of a deceased tenant could similarly take over the tenancy. The judges found that, in terms of love and affection and thus the attributes of family, a distinction could no longer sensibly be drawn between a couple of the same sex living together and a couple of different sexes. Reference was made to the provisions of the European Convention on Human Rights protecting family and family life.

This case illustrates that, even within a single statutory framework, there is scope for developing the law by interpretation which reflects changes in social practices and attitudes.

---

40 *Fitzpatrick v. Sterling Housing Association* [1999] 3 WLR 1113, HL.

The unpredictability of fact situations

However detailed the provisions of statutes or statutory instruments may be, they can only set down rules at a certain level of generality. There will always be those whose particular situation is not captured *precisely* by the legislative provisions. In such cases the facts will need to be determined by the courts—in itself not always a straightforward task—and once this has been done, a judgment reached as to whether or not the relevant legislative provision covers that situation. Particularly where legislative provisions seek to impose some burden or penalty on the citizen, there is a general judicial policy that this should not happen unless those provisions quite clearly 'bite' on the individual circumstances concerned. To give an example: the 'tax avoidance industry' engages in the detailed analysis of tax legislation to see whether arrangements can be made to enable those who might otherwise have to pay tax quite legitimately to avoid paying it.[41]

Many apparently pedantic points taken in some criminal trials are, similarly, the result of the principle that a person should not be able to be convicted of a crime unless the factual situation that has been established in the court is quite clearly caught by the relevant statutory provisions.

The ambiguity of language

The other justification for the role of the courts is that the meaning of language is not itself precise. There may be ambiguities arising from the way particular rules have been drafted. There may be differences in the meaning of words chosen. Some statutory provisions are deliberately drafted using words such as 'reasonable' or 'fair' which do not have a precise meaning and which therefore give scope to officials and others for the exercise of discretion or judgement. There may be changes in the meaning of a word—(*see Box 3.12*)—resulting from broader developments in society.

There is, in the literature on statutory interpretation, a set of principles—rather inaccurately described as 'rules'—designed to be of assistance. These include:

- the literal rule;
- the golden rule;
- the mischief rule; and
- the 'unified common approach'.

The *literal rule* is what it implies. The words of a statute should be given their literal meaning. This does not solve the problem of linguistic ambiguity—words may have more than one literal meaning.

---

[41] The distinction between tax avoidance, which if successful is lawful, and tax evasion, which is clearly unlawful, should be noted. In recent years, governments have become increasingly adept in their attempts to thwart the tax avoiders. Tax incentives—schemes which attract tax advantages and are part of the government's fiscal policy, e.g. tax relief on pension premiums—are quite different.

The *golden rule* suggests that the courts should use the literal rule unless this would lead to manifest absurdity.

The *mischief rule* asks the judge to consider what was the legislative purpose of the Act—what was the 'mischief' the Act was trying to deal with. Any question of interpretation should be resolved in such a way as not to thwart that purpose. The problem with this view is: how does it relate to the concept of the independence of the judiciary? If the mischief rule is rigidly adhered to, does this not result in the judges losing their independence and doing the government's job for it? On the other hand, if legislative intention is wilfully ignored by the judge, how does that square with the constitutional principle that the primary law-making authority should rest with the democratically elected Parliament, not the unelected judiciary?

It will be quickly appreciated that these principles are not consistent with each other; they offer great scope for reaching different conclusions. The reality is that different judges favour different approaches; indeed individual judges are themselves not consistent.

The *unified common approach* is the label now used to suggest that judges should adopt a broader, less specific approach. It implies that judges should start by considering the literal meaning of the words; but if they are really not clear or would lead to absurd results then the judge should consider what the purpose of the Act was and interpret the Act so as to advance that purpose.

The inference should not be drawn from this discussion that the bases on which the judiciary interprets legislation are so varied that there is no principle at all. Reading the reported judgments in decided cases reveals that those judges in the higher courts whose decisions get reported go to great lengths to try to ensure that their decisions are founded in rationality and principle. But that there are different approaches cannot be denied, and the inevitable consequence is that there is some inconsistency of outcome. The ability of different judges to arrive at different decisions in individual cases is seen most clearly in cases that go to appeal, when courts are quite frequently divided in their views.

Procedural law

A third way in which judges make law is by the development of new procedures. A number of examples may be briefly mentioned:

- the day-to-day practice of litigation is regulated by rules of procedure which are drafted by the judiciary—Rules Committees—acting under legislative authority. Many rules of court are supplemented by Practice Directions, also made by the judiciary (see Chapter 8);

- the rules of evidence—what evidence is or is not admissible in a court of law—has to an important degree been developed by the judiciary, though supplemented by very important statutory provisions, for example, the Police and Criminal Evidence Act 1984, the Civil Evidence Act 1991, or the Criminal Justice Act 2003 (see further Chapter 5);

- a number of powers of the court are asserted on the basis of what it claims as its 'inherent jurisdiction'—the High Court's powers of wardship over children may be given as an example (see Chapter 7); and

- perhaps the most important judicial development of the last generation has been the shaping of the rules and practice relating to judicial review, which goes to the heart of the powers of the judiciary to render government departments and other public bodies legally accountable for their actions (see Chapter 6).

The European Courts

The European Union has, as one of its constituent bodies, the European Court of Justice, which sits in Luxembourg. The Council of Europe has the European Court of Human Rights, which sits in Strasbourg. Both courts have played a significant role in the development of the jurisprudence of, respectively, the European Union and the European Convention on Human Rights.

It is hard to summarize the 'European' approach of the judges in these courts. The legal instruments of both the European Union and the Council of Europe, with which the European Courts have to deal, are drafted in the relatively more broad-brush European continental tradition than in the more linguistically precise tradition familiar in the United Kingdom. As a consequence the approach of judges in the European Courts has been to decide cases very much bearing the purposes of the relevant treaty provisions in mind. British legal minds often regard this as a rather distinct approach. Perhaps more accurately it may be said to represent something of a hybrid between the British approaches to common law and statutory interpretation. Decisions of the European Courts lead to the development of legal principle on a case-by-case basis, not dissimilar to the common law tradition. At the same time, these developments are set within the framework of treaties and other instruments which have emanated from the institutions of the European Union and the Council of Europe and which require interpretation by the courts.

Other sources of law making

At the end of this lengthy account, the existence of other sources of law making will be mentioned only briefly.

Local and regional government

Local government has long had power to make by-laws—a form of tertiary legislation (*see above, Box 3.2*)—since by-laws are made under the authority of Acts of Parliament but apply only in the area of the local authority in question.

Under the terms of the Scotland Act 1998 the Scottish Parliament was granted authority to pass legislation in areas within its competence. Under the Government of Wales Act 1998, the National Assembly for Wales was given power to pass secondary legislation, again within the scope of its areas of competence. Limited powers to make primary legislation have been granted to the Welsh Assembly Government by the Government of Wales Act 2006. The Northern Ireland Act 1998 similarly grants legislative power to the Northern Ireland Assembly.

Other rule-making agencies

A great deal of rule making is also undertaken by industry regulators: for example the Civil Aviation Authority or the regulators of the privatized utilities.[42] Major rule-making powers have been conferred on the Financial Services Authority.[43] The rules made by these bodies fall outside the parliamentary framework though in most cases they are based on legislative authority conferred by Act of Parliament.

Other international institutions and bodies of international law

We have considered the Council of Europe and the EU in context above. Many other international institutions also have an impact on detailed rules of English law. There are many industries, for example aviation and telecommunications, where at least some of the legislative framework results from the provisions of international treaties. Increasing globalization of economic activity combined with increasing pressure to deal with some of the major issues of the day—the environment, genetic engineering, global warming, international trade—ensures that this trend will develop.

It is also relevant to note the existence of a separate body of private international law—in essence rules of English law, designed to assist in the determination of private law rights and entitlements which have an international dimension.

Conclusion

Law making is a central feature of modern government. It is theoretically based in democratic principle, though by no means all sources of law derive their authority from those principles. Law making and other normative statements also occur in a variety of formats. This all makes for considerable complexity that has increased enormously in recent years. It is unlikely that the ordinary person in the street is aware of more than a fraction of the law which in theory affects her. It is fanciful to claim that ordinary people can be assumed to know the law. One of the challenges facing modern

---

[42] Baldwin, R., *Rules and Government* (Oxford, Oxford University Press, 1995).
[43] Financial Services and Markets Act 2000.

society is how new technologies can be used to transform this vast mass of legal information into knowledge that can actually be used by the ordinary citizen.

Questions to test knowledge

1. What is the difference between a select committee and a standing committee?
2. What is the difference between a Private bill and a Private Members' bill?
3. What is the difference between primary legislation and secondary legislation?
4. What is a programme order? Why is it important?
5. What is a regulatory reform order?
6. Which body is responsible for the Treaty of Nice?
7. Which body is responsible for the European Convention on Human Rights?
8. Where is the Council of Europe based?
9. Where is the European Court of Justice located?
10. What is the difference between common law and civil law countries?

Questions for reflection and discussion

1. Do you agree with the view that there is a lack of engagement between ordinary people and the work of government? What are the arguments for and against making voting compulsory?

2. Would proportional representation result in fairer electoral outcomes? Would it lead to less efficient government?

3. Should the (legislative) House of Lords be reformed? Should it become a fully elected body?

4. Should the (judicial) House of Lords be reformed? Should it become a Supreme Court?

5. Should more or less time be spent debating legislative proposals in Parliament?

6. How significant a restraint on law-making powers is the European Convention on Human Rights and Fundamental Freedoms?

7. Should there be a British Bill of Rights?

8. Is there a 'democratic deficit' in the institutions of the EU? If so, how should it be overcome?

9. Should judges make law?

10. Does the independence of the judiciary impose unacceptable limits on the power of the executive?

11. How can citizens become better informed about the law and legal system?

Further reading

BENOIT-ROHMER, F., and KLEBES, H., *Towards a Pan-European Legal Area* (Strasbourg, Council of Europe, 2005)

BIRCH, A.H., *Representative and Responsible Government: an Essay on the British Constitution* (Ann Arbor, Mich., UMI, 1989)

BIRKINSHAW, P., *Government and Information: The Law Relating to Access, Disclosure and Their Regulation* (3rd edn., Manchester, Tottel Publishing, 2005)

—— *Freedom of Information: The Law, the Practice and the Ideal* (3rd edn., Cambridge, Cambridge University Press, 2001)

BOGDANOR, V. (ed), *The British Constitution in the Twentieth Century* (Oxford, Oxford University Press, 2004)

BRAZIER, A. (ed), *Parliament, Politics and Law Making: Issues and Developments in the Legislative Process* (London, Hansard Society, 2004)

BRAZIER, R., *Constitutional Practice: the Foundations of British Government* (3rd edn., Oxford, Oxford University Press, 1999)

—— *Ministers of the Crown* (Oxford, Clarendon, 1997)

BUTLER, D., BOGDANOR, V., and SUMMERS, R. (eds), *Law, Politics and the Constitution* (Oxford, Oxford University Press, 1999)

COSGROVE, R.A., *The Rule of Law: Albert Venn Dicey, Victorian Jurist* (London, Palgrave Macmillan, 1980)

FINE, B., *Democracy and the Rule of Law: Liberal Ideals and Marxist Critiques* (London, Pluto Press, 1984)

HARDEN, I., and LEWIS, N., *The Noble Lie: the British Constitution and the Rule of Law* (London, Hutchinson, 1986)

HARTLEY, T.C., *Constitutional Problems of the European Union* (Oxford, Hart, 1999)

—— *The Foundations of European Community Law: an Introduction to the Constitutional and Administrative Law of the European Community* (4th edn., Oxford, Oxford University Press, 1998)

HOLLAND, J.A., *Learning Legal Rules* (6th edn., Oxford, Oxford University Press, 2006)

MARSHALL, G. (ed), *Ministerial Responsibility* (Oxford, Oxford University Press, 1989)

McLEOD, I., *Legal Method* (6th edn., London, Palgrave Macmillan, 2007)

PAGE, E.C., *Governing by Numbers: Delegated Legislation and Everyday Policymaking* (Oxford, Hart, 2001)

TWINING, W., and MIERS, D., *How to do Things with Rules: a Primer of Interpretation* (4th edn., London, Butterworths, 1999)

VILE, M.J.C., *Constitutionalism and the Separation of Powers* (2nd edn., Indianapolis, Ind., Liberty Fund, c1998)

ZANDER, M., *The Law-making Process* (6th edn., London, Butterworths, 2004)

Websites

http://www.justice.gov.uk/guidance/elections.htm *(MoJ website of guidance on elections)*

http://www.electoralcommission.gov.uk/ *(Website of the agency that oversees election policy and practice)* http://www.electoral-reform.org.uk/ *(Electoral Reform Society)*

http://www.electoral-reform.org.uk/article.php?id=5 *(Site providing links to accounts of different voting systems)*

http://www.hansardsociety.org.uk/ *(Hansard Society—promoting effective democracy)*

http://www.charter88.org.uk/ *(Charter 88, campaigning organization for increased democracy)*

http://www.justice.gov.uk/publications/governanceofbritain.htm *(Link to text of the Green Paper on Constitutional Reform, 2007)*

http://www.parliament.uk/ *(Home page of the UK Parliament)*

http://www.parliament.uk/business/bills_and_legislation.cfm *(Site for bills presented to Parliament)*

http://www.opsi.gov.uk/acts.htm *(Office of Public Information—text of Acts of Parliament)*

http://www.parliamentary-counsel.gov.uk/ *(Parliamentary counsel—statute draftsmen)*

http://www.statutelaw.gov.uk/ *(statute law database)*

http://www.royal.gov.uk/output/Page6.asp *(The monarchy today)*

http://www.number-10.gov.uk/output/Page1.asp *(Office of the Prime Minister)*

http://www.ssac.org.uk/ *(Social security advisory committee)*

http://www.atjc.gov.uk/ *(Administrative Justice and Tribunals Council)*

http://www.publications.parliament.uk/pa/ld/ldjudgmt.htm *(House of Lords judgments)*

http://www.hmcourts-service.gov.uk/cms/judgments.htm *(Links to selection of judgments of the Court of Appeal and other judgments)*

http://www.wordwave.co.uk/ *(Law reporting site)*

http://www.bailii.org/ *(British and Irish legal information)*

http://www.kent.ac.uk/lawlinks/ *(Lawlinks—portal to huge range of legal sites)*

http://www.coe.int/ *(Council of Europe portal)*

http://ec.europa.eu/index_en.htm *(European Commission)*

http://curia.europa.eu/en/index.htm *(European Court of Justice)*

http://www.echr.coe.int/echr/ *(European Court of Human Rights)*

http://www.bihr.org/ *(British Institute of Human Rights)*

http://www.justice.org.uk/ourwork/index.html *(JUSTICE—home page of Human Rights organization)*

http://www.justice.org.uk/jshrn/home.htm *(JUSTICE Students Human Rights Network)*

http://www.liberty-human-rights.org.uk/ *(Homepage of Liberty—campaigning human rights organization)*

http://www.dca.gov.uk/peoples-rights/human-rights/index.htm *(Ministry of Justice site)*

http://www.justice.gov.uk/docs/full_review.pdf *(Lord Chancellor's review of the Implementation of the Human Rights Act)*

http://www.scottish.parliament.uk/home.htm *(Scottish Parliament)*

http://www.wales.gov.uk/index.htm *(Portal to the National Assembly for Wales and the Welsh Assembly Government)*

http://www.niassembly.gov.uk/ *(Northern Ireland Assembly)*

http://www.pleas.org.uk/ *(Public Legal Education taskforce site)*

PART II

THE INSTITUTIONAL FRAMEWORK

This Part consists of five chapters. The first (Chapter 4) looks at the contributions made by government departments to the shaping of the English legal system. Primary attention is paid to the Ministry of Justice, but the role of other departments is also considered. The remaining chapters discuss each of the branches of the justice system. The distinction made in most English legal system books between criminal and civil justice is replaced by a more functional classification: criminal justice, administrative justice, family justice, and civil and commercial justice. In each of these chapters a 'holistic' approach is adopted. The focus is not just on what goes on in courts (or other formal adjudicatory bodies), but embraces those aspects of the justice process which occur outside these formal settings as well as within them.

4

Shaping the institutional framework: the role of government

Introduction

One way in which the English legal system has changed over the years has been the increasing involvement of government in shaping and reforming the legal system. Central government has provided substantially increased funds not only for running court services and publicly funded legal services, including paying the salaries and fees of the judiciary, but also for the huge array of other services which are part of or impact upon the legal system. The police, prison, and probation services and administrative tribunals are obvious examples. As government must be concerned with keeping levels of public expenditure under control and securing value for money, it is always looking for ways of delivering services in a more cost effective way. Any understanding of the forces of change within the legal system must include analysis of the part played by government. The principal actors considered here are:

- the Ministry of Justice;
- the Home Office; and
- other central government departments.

Lurking behind all of them is the Treasury.

The Ministry of Justice

The Ministry of Justice (MoJ)was established in 2007. It was the culmination of a dramatic process of constitutional change that had seen the former Lord Chancellor's Department become the Department for Constitutional Affairs (in 2003). The new MoJ plays the central role in the development of policy relating to the legal system.

There had long been calls for the creation of a Ministry of Justice. Many argued that the former split between the Lord Chancellor's Department/Department of Constitutional Affairs and the Home Office (with the latter largely responsible for criminal justice) prevented the development of a coherent overall justice policy.

There was also concern about the post of the Lord Chancellor. Historically, the Lord Chancellor had always been a member of the non-elected House of Lords, not the House of Commons. He (there have been no female Lord Chancellors) was always a qualified lawyer. And he embodied a peculiar position in the government, apparently breaching the principle of the separation of powers, since he was simultaneously a member of the executive (the Lord Chancellor is a member of the Cabinet); the head of the judiciary; and, as Speaker of the House of Lords, a member of the legislature.

When the 2003 changes were made, it was originally intended that the historic post of Lord Chancellor should simply disappear, and that the chief minister should become a Secretary of State, just like any other head of a government department. Closer analysis revealed that legislative change was needed to achieve this outcome. The Constitutional Reform Bill in fact contained a clause which would have abolished the post of Lord Chancellor. This became one of a number of issues which were fiercely contested during the passage of the bill through Parliament. In the end a political compromise was achieved. It was agreed that the post of Lord Chancellor would be retained. But he would no longer be the Speaker of the House of Lords; nor would he remain the Head of the Judiciary—this responsibility would pass to the Lord Chief Justice. Nor would the posts of Secretary of State and Lord Chancellor necessarily be held by the same person. In future the Secretary of State would be exclusively a member of the executive branch of government.

The government also secured the principle that the office would in future no longer have to be held by a member of the House of Lords. But the Constitutional Reform Act 2005 uniquely limits the power of the Prime Minister in relation to the person who may be appointed Lord Chancellor. The convention that the Lord Chancellor should always be a senior barrister is dropped. Instead, the Act states that the Prime Minister must appoint someone 'qualified by experience'. This is defined in section 2 of the Act as experience as a Minister of the Crown; as a member of either House of Parliament; as a qualifying legal practitioner; as a teacher of law in a university; or with 'such other experience that the Prime Minister considers relevant'. The present Secretary of State/Lord Chancellor, Jack Straw MP, is the first to be appointed after the new law came into effect.

The MoJ (and its predecessors) is a department that has grown markedly in both size and importance within government. There was an occasion in the 1920s when its Permanent Secretary—the head civil servant—was able to record that not one item of post had been received! For many years the former Lord Chancellor's Department (LCD) was seen as a bit 'odd' in the overall government structure. In most government departments, lawyers are used as specialists advising on questions of law, drafting bills and regulations and the like, rather than being closely involved in the development of policy. In the LCD, the Permanent Secretary—the head civil servant—was required by law to be qualified as a practising lawyer. As a consequence he was perceived as slightly different from his counterparts in other departments, who were not required to have specific professional qualifications. This rule was abolished in 1997. Since then the Permanent Secretary has not been a lawyer.

Over the last decade, the MoJ (and its predecessors) have come to operate much more like other large service-delivery departments. As will be discussed in the pages that follow, the department has radically altered the management of the courts, through the creation of Her Majesty's Court Service. It has created a new Tribunals Service. It is making major changes to the ways in which the legal profession is regulated. No longer can the MoJ be regarded as at the periphery of government.[1]

Principal responsibilities

The MoJ's website summarizes its primary activities under the following headings:

- the National Offender Management Service: administration of correctional services in England and Wales through Her Majesty's Prison Service and the Probation Service, under the umbrella of the National Offender Management Service;
- youth justice and sponsorship of the Youth Justice Board;
- sponsorship of the Parole Board, Her Majesty's Inspectorates of Prison and Probation, Independent Monitoring Boards, and the Prison and Probation Ombudsmen;
- criminal, civil, family, and administrative law: criminal law and sentencing policy, including sponsorship of the Sentencing Guidelines Council, the Sentencing Advisory Panel, and the Law Commission;
- the Office for Criminal Justice Reform: hosted by the MoJ but working trilaterally with the three CJS departments, the MoJ, Home Office, Attorney-General's Office;
- Her Majesty's Courts Service: administration of the civil, family, and criminal courts in England and Wales;
- the Tribunals Service: administration of tribunals across the UK;
- legal aid and the wider Community Legal Service through the Legal Services Commission;
- support for the judiciary: judicial appointments via the newly created Judicial Appointments Commission, the Judicial Office, and Judicial Communications Office;
- the Privy Council Secretariat and Office of the Judicial Committee of the Privy Council;
- constitutional affairs: electoral reform and democratic engagement, civil and human rights, freedom of information, management of the UK's constitutional arrangements, and relationships including with the devolved administrations and the Crown Dependencies; and

---

[1] For an official statement of the aims and ambitions of the new Ministry, see *Justice: A new approach* (2007) at http://www.justice.gov.uk/publications/justicenewapproach.htm.

- MoJ corporate centre: focused corporate centre to shape overall strategy and drive performance and delivery.

This is a substantial, indeed daunting, list of responsibilities. It is not actually complete, as it does not mention its very significant work in relation to the regulation of the legal and law-related professions. Nor does it mention its very important role in commissioning and undertaking the empirical research needed to inform its policy making.

The point to stress here is that no aspect of the justice system has remained unchanged in recent years. But it is the MoJ that shapes the policy. In short, government injects into the English legal system a dynamism that is often not fully appreciated—both in the sense of its not being understood by those outside the system, and its not being welcomed by those inside. The fact is that many of the images of and pre-conceptions about law and the legal system mentioned in Chapter 1 have been swept away or radically altered by new policy initiatives from the MoJ.

Most of the headings listed above are considered in their appropriate context. Here we consider those activities that do not fit easily into other chapters.

Her Majesty's Court Service

Her Majesty's Court Service (HMCS) is an executive agency of the MoJ. It started operation on 1 April 2005. It was formed by merging the Court Service (set up in 1995) and the Magistrates' Courts Service (which had been run separately). The creation of HMCS was one of the main recommendations of a review of the Criminal Justice system carried out by Sir Robin Auld in 2001. He argued that a unified court service should be able to offer a more coherent and flexible court system.

In common with other areas of government, HMCS is required to deliver defined standards of service to all those who come through the doors of the courts—whether as claimants, those defending claims, those appearing as witnesses, jurors, other friends and relatives, or general members of the public—standards unheard of only a few years ago. Many of the key tasks required of HMCS are those of administrative efficiency: dealing with people courteously; dealing with issues expeditiously but fairly; handling matters as economically as possible and seeking to reduce costs; and—in the civil courts—recovering from parties to proceedings the costs associated with the provision of court services.

The HMCS is engaged in a major programme of investment in computerization and new information technologies. While this will not be complete for a number of years, the implications, not only for the more efficient running of the existing system, but also for introducing fundamental change into the operation of the system, are enormous. Computerization should help with practical issues such as the listing of cases for hearing, and, more broadly, tracking the progress of cases through the system to ensure that they are not subject to unnecessary delay.

Increasingly sophisticated telecommunications and information technologies allow for routine proceedings to take place without the need for personal attendance at court. Professional lawyers can be relieved from wasting time attending court on purely procedural matters. Parties to proceedings could similarly be allowed to 'attend' court from a distance. HMCS completed the roll out of its XHIBIT service in March 2006. This is a website providing up-to-date information about the progress of criminal cases listed in courts. It runs Money Claim Online that enables persons to bring an action for debt using the internet. It also runs Possession Claim Online which similarly enables certain possession proceedings to be started online.[2]

Clearly parties are still required to attend trials. But a great deal of routine procedural work does not require attendance; it just wastes resources. Similarly facilities are being developed to enable more evidence to be presented through video links, thus making it easier for witnesses, who may be unable or reluctant to attend a particular court, to appear.

New forms of electronic data collection also have the potential for reducing the amounts of paper that have to be brought to court for major trials. Use of legal databases will also considerably improve the library facilities available in courts to the judiciary—outside the principal courts these are woefully inadequate.

As a result of these and other developments, the HMCS is also taking a strategic look at the location of its court buildings and their configuration. There is scope for rationalization of the land and buildings currently occupied by the courts. Among the initiatives currently being taken forward is the creation of more unified court centres where both criminal and civil cases are dealt with. In many cases, court closures become very contentious, particularly where a courthouse is an historic building that has existed for many years. There are also arguments about the need for access to justice—in the literal sense that if a citizen is summoned to court, or seeks to take proceedings in court, he or she should not be too distant from a court centre. It is likely that, despite objections, the number of court buildings around the country will reduce over the next decade. New building also permits courts to adopt new forms of working. These require new forms of court design, in particular to take advantage of the opportunities created by the increased use of technology.

The efficiency of the courts in delivering the services they are required to provide, and ensuring they are delivered to the required standard, will be monitored by Her Majesty's Inspectorate of Court Administration. (This is another new body, replacing an Inspectorate that had in the past only looked at the operation of magistrates' courts.)

Support for the judiciary

Although reforming the post of Lord Chancellor to make it more democratically accountable may have initially seemed straightforward, it generated enormous controversy (*see above, Box 3.5*). The senior judiciary were extremely worried that an office,

---

[2] The on-line services of HMCS are listed at: http://www.hmcourts-service.gov.uk/onlineservices/index.htm.

which had historically been a strong defender of the independence of the judiciary, might lose its effectiveness. The outcome of the protracted and often heated discussions between the then Lord Chancellor, and the then Lord Chief Justice, Lord Woolf, resulted in publication of a concordat. This sets out how the judiciary-related functions of the Lord Chancellor would in future be carried out. There are three specific issues to be drawn from the concordat.

First, the concordat establishes the basis of the division between the functions of the Secretary of State and the Lord Chief Justice. Broadly, the Secretary of State has responsibility for determining fundamental issues, such as the level of resource available to enable the courts and tribunals to operate. These include obvious matters such as pay and pensions and the provision of accommodation. The Lord Chief Justice has responsibility for ensuring the effective deployment of the resources that are available.

Secondly, the importance of the Secretary of State continuing to guarantee the independence of the judiciary was recognized. A section in the Constitutional Reform Act 2005 enshrines the principle in law.

Thirdly, there was to be greater transparency in a number of areas in which, hitherto, it had been argued this was lacking. The making of judicial appointments (see below) is the obvious example. (It was also important to ensure that judicial appointments would not be subject to political intervention.) There were also other issues where, in future, there would be greater procedural transparency. These included matters such as the disciplining of judges and dealing with complaints against them.

The principles set out in the concordat were subject to severe test when the announcement of the creation of the Ministry of Justice was made in 2007. Judges feared that the inclusion particularly of the National Offender Management Service in the overall activity of the new Ministry would result in resources being taken away from courts and tribunals to fund shortfalls in prisons and probation budgets. Eventually agreement was reached that appropriate levels of funding would be guaranteed.

Directorate of Judicial Offices for England and Wales

To reinforce the institutional separation of the judiciary from the executive, a new Directorate of Judicial Offices for England and Wales was established in 2005. It comprises: the Judicial Office; the Judicial Communications Office; and the Judicial Studies Board.

Judicial Office

The Judicial Office comprises a team of officials brought together to support the new role of the Lord Chief Justice. Among its most important tasks is the upholding of the concordat considered in the previous paragraphs. The new Office has taken over personnel functions associated with any large organization. It is responsible for the disposition of the judiciary around the court system. It also enables the development of new management processes such as appraisal of judicial performance. For the first time, senior members of the judiciary are involved in the management of judges—a role which for many is novel, requiring the acquisition of new skills. It is also responsible for dealing with complaints about the judiciary. This function in particular involves a complex interaction between the Lord Chancellor and the Lord Chief Justice, especially where a serious complaint about a judge is upheld and the question arises whether that individual should remain a judge.

Judicial Communication Office

The Judicial Office is also supported by a new press office, the Judicial Communication Office. This is intended not only to provide a link between the Judicial Office and the media, but also to assist with internal communication amongst the judiciary.

Judicial Studies Board

The Directorate of Judicial Offices has also taken over formal responsibility for the work of the Judicial Studies Board (JSB). The JSB is another part of the English legal system that has developed significantly in recent years. For a long time, many judges assumed that they knew all that there was to know about law and legal process, and that therefore judicial training was unnecessary; some regarded it as an impertinence to suggest otherwise. Notwithstanding this complacent view, there has been an increasing acceptance that judicial training is needed. As early as the 1960s, judicial conferences were convened to address the particular issue of inconsistency in sentencing practices by the judiciary.

The scope of judicial training was put on a more normal footing in 1979 with the creation of the Judicial Studies Board. Over the last (nearly) thirty years the Board has grown in size and stature and now delivers a very considerable programme of judicial training, not only to judges sitting in criminal trials, but also those handling civil trials, and to the chairs of a wide range of tribunals. It also sets the framework for the training of magistrates.

In delivering its programmes, the JSB provides both *induction* courses, which must be taken before a judge begins to sit, and *continuation* courses, which are offered on a three-yearly cycle. In addition to these regular programmes, the JSB also arranges special programmes. For example there were special programmes to introduce the judiciary to the Human Rights Act 1998 prior to its coming into force in October 2000; and when Lord Woolf's reforms to the civil justice system were introduced in 1999, on how the new system would work. Most controversial was a programme, in 1995–6, to provide ethnic awareness training to the judiciary—an issue which arose from perceived differences in the ways in which people from different ethnic groups might be treated in the courts.[3] This remains an issue of great importance for the work of the courts, as well as other actors in the legal system.[4]

---

[3] Hood, R., in collaboration with Cordovil, G., *Race and Sentencing: a Study in the Crown Court: a Report for the Commission for Racial Equality* (Oxford, Clarendon Press, 1992).

[4] Macpherson of Cluny, Sir William, *The Stephen Lawrence Inquiry Report* (Cm 4262) (London, Stationery Office, 1999).

Besides course provision, the JSB also provides written guidance on the running of trials in *Bench Books*—loose-leaf volumes of information that judges keep beside them for easy reference while performing their judicial functions. It has produced a CD-Rom for training purposes. Through its Equal Treatment Advisory Committee (formerly the Ethnic Minorities Advisory Committee) it has developed advice and training for judges to ensure that parties to proceedings in courts or tribunals feel they have been treated equally and not been subject to any form of discrimination. The JSB has sponsored one or two more practical books, notably the *Guidelines for the Assessment of Damages in Personal Injury Cases,* designed to ensure greater consistency in reaching awards for damages in personal injury cases. It also produces a journal.

The development of the role of the JSB is a fascinating example of the evolution of policy and practice. It did not stem from high-profile parliamentary debate or the enactment of special legislation. Rather, senior officials in the former LCD, working with influential members of the judiciary, saw this as an important part of the management of a modern judicial system. Pockets of resistance among the judiciary—which undoubtedly existed years ago—have been replaced by an acceptance, reflected in professional life more generally, that continuing education is a proper, indeed essential, part of professional development. Newly appointed judges now expect training; and those in post acknowledge the need for opportunities to reflect on their work.

This is not to say that the model so far developed is perfect. The amount of training which English judges receive is still modest. Unlike the situation in some other jurisdictions, there is no university law school which offers a specialist post-graduate diploma or degree in judicial science. There is always more that can and should be done. Nevertheless, the development of professional judicial studies has been one of the most significant developments in the English legal system in the past two decades. It has not attracted the public attention that it deserves.

Judicial appointments

The process of making judicial appointments is another feature of the English legal system that has undergone rapid change. For many years, it was shrouded in secrecy. Appointments were offered to a relatively small circle of barristers, mostly practising in London. The expansion of the legal profession and the opening of judicial appointments to solicitors were among the factors that meant such procedures were no longer viable. Written criteria for judicial appointment have been in the public domain for well over fifteen years. But this was not enough for critics of the system. Over the last eight years, there has been substantial further reform.

It started in 1999 when the Lord Chancellor invited Sir Leonard Peach to review the process of judicial appointments. (He was also asked to look at the process of selection of QCs.) Sir Leonard noted that many judicial recruitment practices had, in recent years, developed in accordance with the best personnel management practice. Most appointments were advertised; proper job descriptions and person specifications had been developed; and there was a comprehensive system of feedback, on request, to unsuccessful candidates. In his view the most controversial aspect of the process was the consultation process. He thought this required a visibility it did not then have, to ensure that candidates could have confidence that information about them was well founded, and not based on hearsay.

To improve the situation Sir Leonard recommended: that consultee forms should be redesigned; that candidates should provide more information by way of self-appraisal; and that there should be greater opportunity for those not well known in the main judicial centres to nominate consultees, whose views should automatically be sought. Sir Leonard did not recommend, as some had argued, that the process should be taken outside the government machine. Instead he suggested the creation of a post of *Commissioner for Judicial Appointments,* who would both provide an ombudsman facility for disappointed individuals and organizations, and undertake a regular audit of applications on a sample basis of current procedures. These would be used to inform recommendations for improvements in process.

The Commission for Judicial Appointments was created in 2001. The Commissioner's functions included: reviewing procedures to ensure that selection was on merit, and investigating any complaints arising out of the application of appointment procedures. In its first report, published in 2002, the Commissioner noted that much had been done to make the appointment process more transparent. But he also stated that applicants for judicial appointment needed to understand: the criteria against which their applications were assessed; the processes by which their applications are assessed; the weight placed on different aspects of their applications; the role played by consultees, in particular automatic consultees, in the assessment process; the identity of those who are consulted; and the process by which consultees' comments are taken into account. Consultees needed to understand: their role in the appointment process; the criteria against which applications will be judged; the importance of relating their comments to the criteria; and the process by which their comments will be taken into account. Failure to do this might lead to a perception of unfairness.

Despite all these changes, the critics were still not satisfied. Indeed the Commissioner recommended that further reforms be made. It was argued that so long as judicial appointments were the responsibility of the senior judicial minister, this undermined the independence of the judiciary. When the Department for Constitutional Affairs was created in 2003, it became clear that further steps would have to be taken about the question of judicial appointments.

The government decided that a key feature of the Constitutional Reform Act 2005 would be the creation of a new Judicial Appointments Commission, supported by a Judicial Appointments and Conduct Ombudsman. The Commission began work in April 2006. It has recently published its first annual report.

The first year of its existence has not been trouble free. Various criticisms were made, particularly of its slowness in reaching decisions and of the complexity of the whole process. To an extent, operational criticism was unfair; the Commission had to establish quite new methods of working, and it had some difficult transitional procedures to cope with. Its second year will be a better test of its capabilities.

One of its particular aims is to increase judicial diversity. Some interpret the focus on judicial diversity as meaning that those targeted—women, members of ethnic minorities, and people with disabilities—will receive preferential treatment. This is not what the Commission wants or is allowed to do. What it is, quite properly, doing is encouraging all those qualified to apply for judicial appointment to do so. Thus it has run road shows and taken other steps to draw to members of the legal profession that the process to appointment has changed and is more open.

A number of important changes have also been made to the threshold qualification for being able to apply for judicial appointment. The Tribunals Courts and Enforcement Act 2007 provides that, rather than eligibility for office being based on possession of rights of audience for a specified period, those who wish to apply for judicial office will have to show that they possessed a relevant legal qualification for the requisite period and that while holding that qualification they have been gaining legal experience. In respect of many of the offices, the number of years for which a person must have held such qualification before becoming eligible for judicial office is also reduced. It is hoped that with greater flexibility, a wider variety of people will put themselves forward.

Table 4.1 sets out the latest published figures relating to diversity in the judiciary. These indicate that there has been some improvement in the gender balance of appointments in the lower tiers of the judiciary; but the numbers of women in the top judicial jobs remains very small. The numbers from ethnic minority origin also remain extremely small.

Table 4.1 Annual Diversity Statistics—as at 1st April 2007

Post	Total	Female No.	Female %	Of Ethnic Minority Origin No.	Of Ethnic Minority Origin %
Lords of Appeal in Ordinary	12	1	8.3	0	0.0
Heads of Division (excl LC)	4	0	0.0	0	0.0
Lord Justices of Appeal	37	3	8.1	0	0.0
High Court Judges	108	10	9.3	1	0.9
Circuit Judges (inc TCC)	639	73	11.4	9	1.4
Recorders	1206	182	15.1	53	4.4
District Judges (inc Family Division)	450	101	22.4	14	3.1
Deputy District Judges (inc Family Division)	780	219	28.1	30	3.85
District Judges (MC)	139	33	23.7	7	5.1
Deputy District Judges (MC)	169	42	24.85	9	5.3
Total	3544	664	18.7	123	3.5

Source: Judicial Communications Office

The Law Commission

The Law Commission was established by Act of Parliament in 1965 to keep the law of England and Wales under review.[5] It is the most important standing body devoted to questions of law reform. Though independent in character, it falls within the overall responsibility of the MoJ. The Commission is chaired by a High Court judge, currently Mr Justice Etherton. He is supported by four other commissioners, who in turn are assisted by teams of lawyers, research assistants, and a small secretariat.

In carrying out its functions it does not attempt to review all the law all the time. Rather it determines, on a regular basis, programmes of work it intends to carry out. (At any one time, the Commission will be engaged on between twenty and thirty projects, at different stages of development.) In addition, the Commission seeks to *codify* areas of law that have become extremely complex, and to *repeal* legislation that is no longer of practical use.[6] The current ninth programme contains projects on criminal law (including a review of the law of homicide); commercial law (including work on illegal transactions); property and trusts law (including cohabitation); and public law (including a project on the reform of housing law). The tenth programme will be announced in 2008.

Its work starts with analysis of the existing law, including, where relevant, consideration of how other countries have dealt with the issue in question. It then drafts a preliminary consultation paper setting out a statement of the existing law, explaining why that area of law needs reform, and indicating its preliminary views on how the law might be reformed, on which it seeks comments from members of the public. Having analysed those comments, the Commission develops its ideas into recommendations for the reform of the law. It usually commissions the drafting of a bill designed to capture the outcome of these policy formulations.[7]

However, the mere fact that this stage in the law-making process has been reached by no means guarantees that the bill so drafted becomes law. It still has to go through the parliamentary process discussed in Chapter 3. And no further progress can be made if parliamentary time cannot be found. About two-thirds of the Commission's proposals for reform have reached the statute book.

Research

Unlike many other large-spending government departments, the former DCA had a very poor level of investment in empirical research. Specific policy-related research projects were commissioned from time to time. But policy initiatives too often derived from anecdotal evidence, pressure from individual influential judges or groups of judges, powerful professional bodies such as the Law Society and the Bar Council, or

---

[5] There is a separate Law Commission for Scotland.

[6] Since 1965, over 5,000 measures have been removed from the statute book as a result of this work.

[7] One of the particular features of the Law Commission is that Parliamentary Counsel are seconded to it for the purpose of drafting commission bills.

the ideas or even prejudices of government ministers or Members of Parliament. Over the last 10 years, the DCA established its own research unit with control over a (modest) budget dedicated to the development of specially commissioned policy-related research. Initially all the research was carried out by academics or other research agencies on a research contract basis. The unit now supplements this effort with an in-house research team.

One of the consequences of the creation of the MoJ is that the very much larger ,research activity formerly within the Home Office will be brought into the new Ministry. The details of exactly how the new department will organize its research activity are not yet clear. But one of the opportunities that is created is for researchers to be encouraged to see the links between criminal and civil justice issues that was previously harder to achieve.

The research work of the MoJ is further complemented by that of the Legal Services Research Centre, which works within the Legal Services Commission. It has done pioneering work on the need for legal and advice services, how people use those services, and the gaps in service provisions.

It must be right in principle to attempt to develop policy that is going to affect large numbers of people's lives on the basis of hard information rather than soft anecdote. The present government is properly committed to the principle of 'evidence-based' policy development. This is very important and should develop further in the coming years.

The Home Office

The Home Office was the other government department with a central role in shaping the institutional framework of the English legal system, particularly in relation to the development of the criminal justice system considered further in Chapter 5. Much of the drive for increased efficiency within the criminal justice system, leading to significant changes to the ways in which criminal processes operate, derived from Home Office initiatives. For example, the Home Office has promoted a number of measures designed to make the police force more efficient.

Most recent was the creation of the Serious Organised Crime Agency (SOCA). This is a new agency sponsored by, though working independently of the Home Office. It brought together the National Criminal Intelligence Service, the National Crime Squad, that part of HM Revenue and Customs that dealt with drug trafficking, and part of the UK Immigration Service dealing with organized immigration crime.[8] One of the key features of policing in England and Wales is that there is no national police force, but rather a different police force operating in each county. Arguments in favour of the creation of a national police force are met by the counter-argument that that would lead to too great a centralization of police power and a lack of local

---

[8] See the Serious Organised Crime and Police Act 2005.

accountability. It is recognized, however, that serious organized crime cannot be dealt with effectively by fragmented local forces. SOCA is a national agency, designed, as its name suggests, to tackle serious organized crime.

Although most of its functions relating to the criminal justice system have been transferred to the MoJ, the Home Office still takes the lead in relation to a number of issues which have an important impact on law making and the role of law in England and Wales. These include: crime reduction; immigration and nationality; drugs prevention; and race equality and diversity, including anti-discrimination legislation. Particularly controversial areas for which it is responsible include: dealing with internal terrorist threats—which includes the issue of the extent to which people should be able to be detained without charge while inquiries are made; handling claims of asylum-seekers; anti-social behaviour and the introduction of identity cards.

Other government departments

One other department, which is closely associated with the development of the justice system, is the Attorney-General's Department. The Attorney-General occupies an interesting though complex position in government. Partly the A-G acts as a kind of in-house lawyer, giving independent advice to government; the A-G is also ultimately responsible for the work of the Director of Public Prosecutions and the Crown Prosecution Service (Chapter 5). But the department is also engaged in activity designed to improve the working of the justice system.

The impact of other government departments on the English legal system is less focused than the examples given above but is nonetheless considerable. For example, the Department for Children, Schools and Families works closely with the Ministry of Justice on issues relating to family justice (see Chapter 7) and also on dealing with young offenders (see Chapter 5).

The new Department for Business Enterprise and Regulatory Reform does much work on regulation (taking in the activities of the Better Regulation Executive). Much of this work involves detailed consideration of existing rules and regulations, how they might be simplified, and how they can be made more effective without over-burdening industry and commerce. It also has responsibility for consumer protection. Both of these streams of work underpin issues relating to civil and commercial justice (see Chapter 8). This department is also responsible for employment matters, including policy that may end up with people taking cases to employment tribunals (see Chapter 6). It is this department that also provides much of the funding for advice, especially through the Citizens' Advice Bureaux (see Chapter 10).

The Department for Communities and Local Government has a wide range of policy under its control. These include both planning and housing—both of which are issues which may lead to use of the administrative justice and civil justice systems (Chapters 6 and 8).

One of the great challenges for government as a whole is to ensure that, as far as possible, policy initiatives arising in one department reflect and work with (rather than against) policies arising in other departments. While the principle of a joined-up approach to the delivery of policy is broadly accepted, it is far from easy to deliver this in practice.

Questions for reflection and discussion

1. If the Chancellor of the Exchequer is not necessarily an economist, how experienced in the law should the Secretary of State for Justice be?

2. How can the independence of the judiciary be best protected?

3. Is the appraisal of judicial performance desirable? Can it be achieved without adversely affecting judicial independence?

4. Should judges be elected (as they are in some parts of the USA)?

5. Is judicial training desirable? How might it be developed?

6. Should there be a national police force?

7. How can government policy making on justice issues be made more coherent?

8. Should the Attorney-General remain as a government minister or have a role more independent of government?

Further reading

ABEL-SMITH, B., and STEVENS, R., *In Search of Justice: Society and the Legal System* (London, Allen Lane, 1968)

MALLESON, K., and BANDA, F., *Factors Affecting the Decision to Apply for Silk and Judicial Office* (London, LCD, 2000)

OLIVER, D., *Constitutional Reform in the United Kingdom* (Oxford, Oxford University Press, 2003)

POLDEN, P., *Guide to the Records of the Lord Chancellor's Department* (London, HMSO, 1988)

STEVENS, R., *The Independence of the Judiciary: The View from the Lord Chancellor's Office* (rev. edn., Oxford, Clarendon Press, 1997)

WOODHOUSE, D., *The Office of the Lord Chancellor* (Oxford, Hart, 2001)

Websites

http://www.justice.gov.uk/ *(Ministry of Justice home page)*

http://www.justice.gov.uk/whatwedo/whatwedo.htm *(MoJ site giving more detail about their work)* http://www.hmcourts-service.gov.uk/ *(Homepage of Her Majesty's Court Service)*

http://www.publications.parliament.uk/pa/ld200304/ldselect/ldcref/125/12514.htm *(Text of the concordat on the transfer of the Lord Chancellor's Judicial-related functions)*

http://www.cjsonline.gov.uk/ *(Homepage for Criminal Justice System online)*

http://www.tribunals.gov.uk/ *(Homepage for the Tribunal Service)*

http://www.lawcom.gov.uk/ *(Law Commission)*

http://www.jsboard.co.uk/ *(Judicial Studies Board)*

http://www.justice.gov.uk/publications/research.htm *(MoJ research unit publications site)*

http://www.homeoffice.gov.uk/rds/ *(Home Office research)*

http://www.lsrc.org.uk/ *(Legal Services Research Centre)*

http://www.judicialappointments.gov.uk/ *(Judicial Appointments Commission)*

http://www.parliament.uk/parliamentary_committees/conaffcom.cfm *(Homepage of the Constitutional Affairs Committee of the House of Commons, looking at the work of the MoJ)*

http://www.attorneygeneral.gov.uk/ *(Attorney-General's homepage)*

http://www.ucl.ac.uk/laws/socio-legal/empirical/ *(Report of inquiry into the importance of empirical research in law.)*

5

The criminal justice system

Introduction

Criminal law is central to the relationship between law and society. It seeks to regulate behaviour; it provides sanctions against those who break those rules. It is intimately linked with key social policy objectives, such as the maintenance of law and order and preservation of the peace, security of the individual, and the protection of property. It is also linked to other objectives, especially the protection of human rights and individual freedoms. Indeed, one of the great difficulties law makers face when thinking about the development of rules of criminal law and criminal procedure is how to achieve a proper balance between the provisions of the criminal law and the preservation of liberty and the freedom of the individual. These issues are currently seen in sharp relief in discussions about how we should respond to threats of terrorist activity. Furthermore, the boundaries of the criminal law change over time. They are not always set by the outcome of purely rational debate and argument; they also reflect the preferences and prejudices of politicians. The criminal justice system is that branch of the English legal system in which the criminal law is administered.

Any idea that the criminal justice system can be understood simply by looking at the work of the criminal courts can be quickly disabused by considering the wide range of agencies involved. They include:

- the police service;
- the Crown Prosecution Service;
- the Serious Fraud Office;
- other investigating/prosecuting authorities;[1]
- magistrates' courts;
- the Crown Court;
- the appeal courts;
- the Criminal Cases Review Commission;
- the prison service;

[1] For example, the Revenue and Customs, or the Health and Safety Executive; *see Box 5.7.*

- the national probation service for England and Wales;
- the Criminal Defence Service;
- the Criminal Injuries Compensation Scheme for victims; and
- other victim and witness care services.

Altogether, the criminal justice system affects large numbers of people.[2] It is a huge employer. It consumes a great deal of public money: currently in excess of £13bn a year (over £200 for each man, woman, and child). Over half goes on policing. The prison service receives around £2bn; criminal legal aid, £1.3bn; the probation service, £0.6bn. These sums are not trivial; yet there is always pressure to spend more. Calls for increased expenditure have to be set in the context of these figures. Opportunities for doing things more cheaply need to be identified as well. The efficiency of the criminal justice system—to ensure that its social objectives are met, while at the same time keeping control of expenditure levels—is, as in other areas of social policy, a constant challenge for government. One of the most controversial measures, contained in the Offender Management Act 2007, is the extent to which provision of offender management services, in particular probation services, might be contracted out to private or voluntary sector suppliers.

The criminal justice system has been the subject of much political controversy, many official inquiries, and considerable change. To give just a few examples: a Royal Commission on Criminal Procedure reported in 1981; a further Royal Commission on Criminal Justice reported in 1993; and a review of the criminal courts was published in 2001, together with a major review of sentencing policy. Nearly every year there is new legislation on some aspect of the criminal justice system. Reform of the criminal justice system is a key element in the present government's legislative programme. This is reflected in the establishment, in 2004, of the Office for Criminal Justice Reform (*see Box 5.1*).

Some argue that the system is loaded in favour of those accused of criminal activity and against those who are the victims of crime or, more generally, 'the interest of society at large'. This leads to calls for a re-balancing of the system in favour of victims and witnesses. Others strongly disagree, pointing to the serious miscarriages of justice that have occurred over the years and the need to protect individuals from wrongful involvement in the criminal justice system. The pace and scope of these changes pose serious and difficult questions about how government should respond. In the pages that follow, each part of the system is considered. First, though, we consider the social theories that underpin the criminal justice system.

---

[2] A longitudinal study carried out by the Home Office showed that 34 per cent of *all* males born in this country in 1953 had, by 1993, received at least one conviction for a criminal offence of a more serious nature; the figure for females was 8 per cent. Reported in Taylor, R., *Forty Years of Crime and Criminal Justice Statistics, 1958–1997* (London, Home Office, Research and Development Section, 1999).

> **Box 5.1** Legal system explained
>
>
>
> ### The Office for Criminal Justice Reform (OCJR)
>
> OCJR is a cross-departmental team working together to provide an improved service to the public. It reports on an equal basis to the Ministry of Justice, the Home Office, and the Law Officers' Departments. Its goal is to deliver the National Criminal Justice Board's vision of what the criminal justice system will look like in 2008. The key components of the vision are that:
>
> - victims and witnesses will receive a consistent, high standard of service from all criminal justice agencies;
> - more offences will be brought to justice through a more modern and efficient justice process;
> - rigorous enforcement will revolutionize compliance with sentences and orders of the court;
> - the public will have confidence that the criminal justice system is effective and it serves all communities fairly; and
> - the criminal justice system will be a joined up, modern, and well run service, and an excellent place to work for people from all backgrounds.

Theories of criminal justice

Just as the social functions of the criminal law may be seen to be quite diverse, so too are the different social theories or models that underpin the criminal justice system.[3] From the criminological literature, a number of 'models' of the criminal justice system may be identified. These include:

(1) the *due process* model, in which the primary social goal may be said to be 'justice', and where there is an emphasis on fairness, and the rules needed to protect the accused against error and to restrain the exercise of arbitrary power;

(2) the *crime control* model, in which the primary social goal is punishment, and where the focus is on ensuring that the police are able to obtain convictions in the courts;

(3) a *medical model* in which the emphasis is on the rehabilitation of the offender, giving decision takers discretion to achieve this;

(4) the *restorative justice* model, in which the emphasis is on getting the offender to recognize his or her responsibility in committing the offence and to make amends to the victim;

---

[3] The following is derived from the excellent book by King, M., *The Framework of Criminal Justice* (London, Croom Helm, 1981).

(5) the *bureaucratic model* in which the emphasis is on the management of crime and the criminal, and the efficient processing of offenders through the system;

(6) a *status passage* model, in which the emphasis is on the denunciation and degradation of the offender, involving a shaming of the offender, reflecting society's views of the offender; and

(7) a *power model* in which the emphasis is on the maintenance of a particular social/class order, which reinforces the values of certain classes over others.

None of these models offers a uniquely correct interpretation of the criminal justice system. The explanatory power of each model varies, depending on the person looking at the system. The defence lawyer or the defendant will take a different view from the policeman or the prosecutor, the victim, or the Home Secretary. Thinking about these models, however, both highlights the tensions and conflicts that—perhaps inevitably—exist in this complex sector of the justice system. It also helps to identify the assumptions that are all too often left unstated in considering developments in the criminal justice system. The reader should reflect on how recent developments in criminal justice fit into the models thus identified.

Understanding the criminal justice system

To gain some understanding of the criminal justice system, it is necessary to break the overall structure into more manageable parts. The approach adopted here is to look at the system in three segments:

- pre-trial stages;
- trial stage; and
- post-trial stages.

Each of these is further subdivided.

Pre-trial stages

Before any alleged criminal gets anywhere near a court-room, a number of crucial preliminary steps are taken, each of which may affect the outcome of the case, and indeed whether a case ever reaches court at all. The following analysis of the stages that an allegation of criminal activity may go through before trial provides a structure that does not occur as neatly as this in practice; but it should help the reader see the overall shape of the criminal justice system more clearly.

The committing, reporting, and recording of crime

It may be obvious that the first step in any criminal process is that some criminal act should have been *committed*. By itself that will (save in the most exceptional circumstances) not be sufficient to launch any kind of criminal process. Unless the offence is *reported* to the authorities, either by the victim or by some other person who has seen the incident or has come to realize that some criminal activity has taken place, no further action will follow. (On criminal statistics, *see Box 5.2*.)

The agency to which most crime is reported is the police. But many other agencies also have criminal law enforcement responsibilities. For example:

- local authorities have responsibilities for areas like environmental pollution and public health;
- central government departments have responsibilities for investigating a wide variety of potential criminal activity—for example social security benefit fraud, tax evasion, and other types of fraudulent commercial activity;
- health and safety agencies have duties to prosecute breaches of health and safety legislation (for example unlawful emissions of radioactive material); and
- in very rare circumstances, an individual him- or herself may commence a criminal prosecution.

Although the police are the largest single agency to which crimes are reported, the total number of criminal offences committed each year which are dealt with by bodies other than the police exceeds the total offences reported to the police. Nonetheless, for present purposes we concentrate on the role of the police.

Research shows clearly that, if a victim of crime is unwilling to report a crime and get the police to investigate it, then in all save the gravest situations no effective further action will be taken in relation to that alleged offence.[4] The initial act of reporting is crucial.

Furthermore, if the police are perceived as being unsympathetic in any particular context, then this reduces the likelihood of alleged offences being reported. For example, some years ago the police were perceived—whether rightly or not—as being unsympathetic to female victims of alleged rape. The police took this criticism seriously and made strenuous efforts to demonstrate that this was not the case. In so far as the criticism had validity, the police determined to change their practices. At the time it could be predicted that the number of reported rape cases would increase. This has indeed happened. It may well be that an increase in numbers of reported rapes is the result of more rapes occurring. But at least some of the increase is attributable to a more reliable pattern of reporting and recording. (There is still evidence that the number of rapes is under-reported, but this may be more due to fears victims may have about how they are going to be dealt with by the courts.)

---

[4] Cretney, A., and Davis, G., *Punishing Violence* (London, Routledge, 1995).

Box 5.2   Legal system explained

Criminal statistics[5]

One technical point needs to be made in this context. Most press reports about levels of crime are based on official criminal statistics. These are data brought together from figures prepared by each police force of incidents of crime reported to and recorded by them. There are at least two problems with these data as a measure of levels of criminality in the community.

First, as is the case with all data, their value is dependent on the quality of the input. There is always the possibility of error in data collection and entry. Some reporting practices may distort patterns of criminality. The thief who steals a crate of milk bottles from outside a front door may be recorded as having stolen one item (the crate); or twelve items (each individual bottle). In statistical terms this is a very considerable difference. There is also a tendency to relate crime figures to arguments for resources. If Chief Constables think more resources will be available to fight crime if trends are upwards, this may—even if only subconsciously—lead to an increasing trend in the figures; if success in reducing crime is to be rewarded this might encourage a downward pressure on figures.

Secondly, the figures relate to reported and recorded crime. Many factors influence reporting and recording. For example, if insurance companies insist on theft from cars or property being reported this may lead to an increase in the rate of recorded crime; conversely a relaxation in their practices may lead to a reduction in recorded crime.

It is not argued here that the figures for recorded crime do not reflect trends in criminality in the community. But one should be cautious about drawing the simple conclusion, as is usually done in the media, that published statistics of recorded crime represents 'the crime figures'. It is more complex than that.

Corroboration of these points is found in the *British Crime Survey*,[6] in which a sample of the population is interviewed about its experience of crime as well as the criminal justice system. Although this survey by no means covers the totality of the population, the sample of over 40,000 people is drawn on the basis of accepted practices for creating social survey databases. The conclusion to be drawn from the *British Crime Survey* is that a very different picture of criminality and the individual experience of crime is presented there, compared with the picture presented by the *Criminal Statistics*. This is illustrated clearly in Diagram 5.1 on p. 110.

Another example is domestic violence. There is a widespread assumption that the police are reluctant to get involved in domestic disputes. Whether or not this perception is correct does not much matter. The number of cases of domestic violence

---

[5] These are prepared by the Home Office and published annually by the Stationery Office.

[6] This is also undertaken by the Home Office. The survey, established in 1982, reported irregularly until 2000. Since 2001 it has reported on an annual basis.

Box 5.3   System in action

The Domestic Violence, Crimes and Victims Act 2004

In response to the criticism that domestic violence is not taken seriously enough, Parliament has passed this new Act. It makes the following provisions:

- creates significant new police powers to deal with domestic violence including making it an arrestable, criminal offence to breach a non-molestation order, with a penalty of up to five years in prison;
- makes common assault an arrestable offence;
- gives stronger legal protection for victims by extending the use of restraining orders—giving courts the power to impose a restraining order where the defendant has been acquitted but the court believes an order is necessary to protect the victim from harassment;
- provides for a code of practice, binding on all criminal justice agencies, so that all victims receive the support, protection, information, and advice they need;
- allows victims to take their case to the Parliamentary Ombudsman if they feel the code had not been adhered to by the criminal justice agencies;
- sets up an independent commissioner for victims to give victims a voice at the heart of government and to safeguard and promote the interests of victims and witnesses, encouraging the spread of good practice and reviewing the statutory code;
- amends the Protection from Harassment Act 1997 to ensure that victims have their say if an application is made to vary or terminate a restraining order that is protecting them from abuse or harassment;
- strengthens the civil law on domestic violence so that cohabiting same-sex couples have the same protection as heterosexual couples, and extending the availability of non-molestation orders to couples who have never lived together or have never been married; and
- creates a new offence of familial homicide for causing or allowing the death of a child or vulnerable adult.

reported to the police is considerably lower than the total number of incidents that actually take place. The Home Office estimates that, on average, a victim experiences thirty-five incidents of domestic violence before going to the police. (*See Box 5.3*.)

Even if an alleged offence is reported, the police may not think that there is sufficient information to justify the *recording* of the alleged incident. If the matter is not recorded, no further action will be taken.

Finally, even if a crime is both reported and recorded, no effective further action necessarily results. Many reports of petty theft, for example, are not taken further by the police—they do not have the resources to carry out the required investigations.

The investigation stage—police powers

Once a crime has been reported to the relevant agency (still using the police as the main example) the next stage is the investigation. In the case of major incidents this involves the consumption of considerable resources with large numbers of police spending a lot of time on an investigation. In less important cases, the investigation stage may be extremely cursory. (There are cases where the conceptually distinct processes of reporting and investigating are in practice blurred. The police may gain intelligence that a criminal act is being planned. This leads to investigation in advance of the commission of the offence. If the offence is actually committed, the preliminary intelligence-gathering may also result in the gathering of sufficient evidence to justify the arrest of the person or persons concerned and their being charged with the commission of an offence.) The Police and Justice Act 2006 has created a new National Policing Improvement Agency, designed to promote good policy practice for the country's different police forces.

For the criminal investigation bodies to be able to do their work, they need special powers. In the case of the police, their powers were the subject of major reform in 1984, with the enactment of the *Police and Criminal Evidence Act 1984* (PACE). The statutory powers of the police are accompanied by important *codes of practice,* which should also be observed by the police.[7] A joint Home Office/Cabinet Office review of the codes was undertaken in the summer of 2002, with the results published in November 2002.[8] This concluded that the codes played an important part in the criminal justice process, but that, nearly twenty years after the coming into force of PACE, they could be updated. Some amendments were made in 2003. As a result of the passing of the Serious Organised Crime and Police Act 2005, and the Drugs Act 2005, all the PACE codes were revised. The newly revised codes came into effect on 31 December 2005, save Code C which was revised in July 2006 along with the introduction of Code H.

The government is currently engaged in a review of the Police and Criminal Evidence Act. It was launched in March 2007. Responses to the consultation paper were published in July 2007. Further policy developments may be anticipated in 2008.

The principal powers enabling the police to carry out their functions are:

- the power to stop and search;
- the power to arrest and detain;
- the power to question; and
- the power to enter and search premises.

---

[7] There are now eight codes of practice. Originally there were five: Code A on Powers of Stop and Search; Code B on Search and Seizure; Code C on Detention, Treatment, and Questioning of Persons; Code D on the Identification of Persons; Code E on Tape Recording. A sixth code, F, on Visual Recording of Interviews was issued in May 2002. A seventh code, G, on the Statutory Power of Arrest by Police Officers was introduced in the 2006 revision. An eighth code, H, on the detention and questioning of those suspected of terrorism was issued in July 2006.The codes have also been adapted to apply to immigration officers in their work.

[8] *Pace Review: Report of the Joint Home Office/Cabinet Office Review of the Police and Criminal Evidence Act 1984* (London, Home Office, 2002).

The precise order in which these powers are used in any particular case naturally depends on the circumstances. The extent of police powers, how they are interpreted and applied by the police, and the balance between those powers and the liberty of the individual are constant sources of controversy.

Stop and search

The powers of the police to stop and search people or vehicles are contained in section 1 of the Police and Criminal Evidence Act 1984. The law provides that a constable must have reasonable grounds for believing that, by exercising his/her powers, stolen goods, or an offensive weapon, or a knife or other bladed or sharply pointed article, or articles adapted for use in burglary, theft or obtaining by deception, or a vehicle that has been taken without authority will be found.

These general powers are supplemented by other powers to stop and search to be found in other specific Acts of Parliament—e.g. relating to terrorism, drugs, firearms, or alcohol at sporting events. For example, under section 43(1) of the Terrorism Act 2000 a constable may stop and search a person whom the officer reasonably suspects to be a terrorist to discover whether the person is in possession of anything which may constitute evidence that the person is a terrorist. These searches may only be carried out by an officer of the same sex as the person searched. The Criminal Justice and Public Order Act 1994, section 60, also created an extensive power to stop and search 'in anticipation of violence'. However this power may not be exercised unless a police superintendent has authorized its use in a particular locality.

In exercising these powers, the police are required to follow procedures set down in section 2 of PACE, which, among other things, requires the officer to give his/her name, state why the search is taking place, and record that the stop and search has occurred (unless this is not practicable).

The language of the legislation gives considerable room to the individual police officer to decide whether or not the conditions for carrying out a stop and search are met. The exercise of the power has been controversial, in particular because of evidence that people from the ethnic minorities are more likely to be stopped and searched than those from the majority white communities. (*See further Box 5.4.*) These issues have become particularly acute following the bombings in London in July 2005.

To try and ensure that use of stop and search powers are used as fairly as possible, the Home Office established a Stop and Search Action Team. The Home Office also publishes annual statistics on race and the criminal justice system, which includes an analysis of information about the use of stop and search powers.[9] Although somewhat inconclusive, there seems to be some evidence that if the police take a 'softly, softly' approach to stop and search, levels of crime rise. What is clear is that, while the power is an important one, it is one that must be used sensibly and with care if it is not to exacerbate local community feelings and make the task of policing harder. It is an issue which the Home Office keeps under regular review.

[9] Details of the 2005 statistics can be found at http://www.homeoffice.gov.uk/rds/pdfs06/s95overview0405.pdf

Box 5.4   System in action

The impact of stops and searches on crime and the community

Impact on crime

- *Detection*—Evidence suggests that searches probably detect offenders for only a small proportion of all the crimes they address. However, they can make a more notable contribution to arrests.
- *Disruption*—Searches can directly disrupt criminal activities, although evidence suggests this effect is likely to be small in relation to overall crime. Search arrests can also disrupt crime through the incapacitation or desistance of offenders. However, it is difficult to assess the extent to which this occurs on existing evidence.
- *Deterrence*—There is little solid evidence that this occurs. However, police stops, more generally, may have a role in preventing crime.
- *Order maintenance*—It is possible that a focus on low-level crime problems helps prevent the development of more serious crime problems. However, the role or effectiveness of searches in this regard is unknown.
- *Intelligence*—Information gained from a search encounter can be fed back into police work. This is potentially true of stops in general, as well as just searches. The research suggests that the effectiveness of searches is greatest when they are based on strong grounds for suspicion and make the best use of intelligence.

Impact on the community

The research shows that the experience of being searched is associated with reduced confidence in the police. It is likely, therefore, that this will contribute directly to lower levels of confidence in the police among those from minority ethnic groups. It also notes that people were less satisfied with stop or search encounters when they were searched, not given convincing explanations, or not treated politely or fairly.

Lower levels of satisfaction with encounters among ethnic minority people appears to occur because they disproportionately experience these problems. Problems with community relations could be reduced by making efficient use of searches, responding constructively to disproportionality, and improving the management of encounters.

Conclusions

Were it not for the controversy surrounding searches, no doubt they would be seen as one useful 'tool in the toolbox' for the police. By using stops and searches in an appropriate way, it is likely that effectiveness can be maximized and community costs can be reduced.

Source: Police Stops and Searches: Lessons from a programme of research (Home Office, 2000).

Arrest

Broadly there are two types of arrest—with warrant, and without warrant.

- An arrest *with warrant* takes place under the authority of a warrant issued by a magistrate. A warrant may be issued after information has been given to the magistrate, on oath, that the person named has or is suspected of having committed an offence.

- There are a number of powers to arrest *without a warrant*. PACE, section 24 has been amended by the Serious Organised Crime and Police Act 2005 to provide that the police should have a general power to arrest without warrant persons who have committed or are suspected of committing an offence and that it is necessary that the person should be arrested without a warrant. To show that an arrest without warrant is necessary, one of the following reasons must be present: (a) to enable the name of the person in question to be ascertained (in the case where the constable does not know, and cannot readily ascertain, the person's name, or has reasonable grounds for doubting whether a name given by the person as his name is his real name); (b) correspondingly as regards the person's address; (c) to prevent the person in question—(i) causing physical injury to himself or any other person; (ii) suffering physical injury; (iii) causing loss of or damage to property; (iv) committing an offence against public decency; or (v) causing an unlawful obstruction of the highway; (d) to protect a child or other vulnerable person from the person in question; (e) to allow the prompt and effective investigation of the offence or of the conduct of the person in question; (f) or to prevent any prosecution for the offence from being hindered by the disappearance of the person in question.

  ((c)(iv) applies only where members of the public going about their normal business cannot reasonably be expected to avoid the person in question.)

- The amended law also clarifies the circumstances in which a citizen may make an arrest. The exercise of the citizen's power of arrest is limited to arresting those committing or suspected of committing an indictable offence.

In addition, there are a number of specific powers to arrest without warrant under particular Acts of Parliament, e.g. the Mental Health Act 1983. Finally there is a common law power to arrest where a breach of the peace is taking place or is reasonably anticipated.

For an arrest to take place without a warrant, the person making the arrest must make it clear, by words or action, that the person arrested is under compulsion. The person arrested must be informed of the ground for the arrest, either at the time of arrest or as soon as possible thereafter, for example where it is not practicable to provide the information before the person to be arrested tries to run away. There is no legal power simply to detain persons for questioning without first making an arrest.[10]

---

[10] In practice, this does happen. When persons are said in a news bulletin to be 'helping the police with their inquiries', this is an indication that they have not been arrested, but nonetheless 'persuaded' to attend the police station 'voluntarily'.

An arrest is the first stage in a process that may eventually lead to a criminal trial. Research suggests that, despite the legal framework created by PACE, a very large number of arrests lead to no further action being taken. This raises the question of the extent to which police practice on arrest conforms to the legal rules relating to arrest.

Detention

Once a person has been arrested, that person may be detained in a police station to enable further investigation (including questioning of the person) to be carried out. One of the principal changes brought about by PACE was that a detailed set of statutory provisions was put in place to regulate the time a person could be detained in custody. Under Part IV of the Act (as amended), arrangements must be made for a staff custody officer, usually but not necessarily a police officer, to keep the detention under review. The police have, in general, twenty-four hours in which they must either charge the arrested person with an offence, or release the person, either with or without bail. Exceptionally, authorization for detention without charge for up to thirty-six hours may be given.

In the context of responses to terrorist events, there are now special but significant powers to detain those suspected of these classes of offence for considerably longer periods. These are said by the police and other investigating agencies to be needed in order that they can complete essential inquiries. Opponents of these measures argue that they are unnecessarily draconian, and likely to create more problems than they resolve. These arguments were exposed in the sharp differences of view in Parliament during debate on the Terrorism Bill, which became the Terrorism Act 2006. There a government attempt to extend the period of detention without charge to ninety days was defeated, and replaced by twenty-eight days. The issue of the period of detention continues to resurface and is likely to be revisited in the near future. Because powers to detain without either charge or trial are so exceptional, a new PACE code, H, was introduced in July 2006 to regulate police practice in this area.

Once charged the person may be further detained but must be brought before a magistrates' court as soon as practicable. The magistrates decide whether the person can then be released on bail or remanded in custody.

Part V of PACE[11] sets out detailed provisions for the treatment of those who have been detained. Usually, a person detained is entitled to have someone informed of that fact, and to have access to legal advice, which gives the right to consult privately a solicitor at any time. There are powers to delay these rights where this is thought necessary, e.g. to prevent evidence being destroyed. The statutory rules and code also set out in detail the physical conditions in which people should be detained; these include details about the provision of drinks and refreshment.

The Criminal Justice Act 2003 extended the powers of the police to enable them to take fingerprints and a DNA sample from a person whilst in police detention

---

[11] Supplemented by *The Code of Practice for the Detention, Treatment and Questioning of Persons by Police Officers* (Code C) (London, TSO, revised edn. 2006).

following arrest. Fingerprints can now be taken electronically. Thus the police can confirm in a few minutes the identity of a suspect where that person's fingerprints are already held on the national fingerprint database. This prevents persons who may be wanted for other matters avoiding detection by giving the police a false name and address. Fingerprints taken under this provision can also be subject to a speculative search across the crime scene database to see if they are linked to any unsolved crime. The DNA profile of an arrested person is loaded onto the national DNA database. It can also be subject to a speculative search to see whether it matches a crime scene stain already held on the database. Both these new powers can assist the police in the detection and prevention of crime. Currently the database holds information on just over five per cent of the population. A senior judge recently suggested that all citizens should be required to provide a DNA sample for the national database, arguing that this would help the innocent as much as the wrongdoer; this was fiercely criticized by civil liberty groups.

Questioning

The power to question suspects detained by the police is the subject of detailed guidance in Code C. The police regard the power to question as crucial. Questioning often leads to the suspect providing a confession. This leads to considerable savings later in the criminal process, as most of those confessing plead guilty.

Confessions raise two particular problems: 'induced' confessions; and false confessions.

Induced confessions are, as the name implies, confessions that have arisen from the police offering inducements to the suspect to confess—for example, early release on bail, the suggestion that a confession may lead to less serious charges being made against the alleged criminal, or that in some other way the outcome will be less serious than it would otherwise be. Such inducements can colour the reliability of the confession.

Rules of evidence which apply in court are designed to ensure that induced confessions are not made, by preventing the evidence obtained from them from being presented in court. Many police practices, for example the tape recording of interviews or the requirement to issue a formal caution to those who may be charged with an offence, are designed to eliminate improper police behaviour. However, it seems unlikely that the police will never seek to induce a confession, for example in a location where there are no tape recorders. Furthermore the present form of the 'caution'[12] provides some incentive to people to make statements at an early stage.

False confessions are more problematic. Contrary to common sense and expectation there have been cases where a person being questioned by the police has confessed to a

---

[12] 'You do not have to say anything. But it may harm your defence if you do not mention when questioned something which you later rely on in court. Anything you do say may be given in evidence'. This form of words provoked much criticism when introduced, as it was argued that it undermined the right of silence, one of the principal sources of protection for the accused.

crime that he has not in fact committed. This can arise from the very considerable psychological pressure which people are under when detained in a police station. This was one of the issues which led to the establishment of the Royal Commission on Criminal Evidence and Procedure in 1979.[13]

Entering and searching premises

The last general power available to the police (and other crime investigation agencies) is the power to enter and search premises for evidence, and where relevant to seize that evidence. Many specific Acts of Parliament give power to grant warrants to the police for particular purposes, for example, investigating drugs offences or theft. Section 8 of PACE (as amended by the Serious Organised Crime and Police Act 2005) creates a general power enabling magistrates to grant warrants to search for evidence relating to a serious arrestable offence. A warrant may relate to specific premises, or more generally to all premises controlled by an individual. As with other police powers, these statutory provisions are supplemented by statutory safeguards and a code of practice.[14] Certain types of material are excluded from this provision, for example, items subject to legal privilege;[15] and certain other categories of excluded material.[16]

There are also circumstances where the police are empowered to enter and search premises without a warrant: for example to arrest someone suspected of committing an arrestable offence or to save life and limb or prevent serious damage to property.[17]

Comment

There can be no doubting the powers that the police have over the ordinary citizen. The range of powers, considered in outline above, may be seen as a sensible code, enabling the police to go about their business of investigating crime and catching suspects. Nevertheless, there are always concerns, backed by specific examples of police malpractice, which demonstrate that the police act beyond the powers given to them. This in turn means that further controls on police behaviour to prevent the exercise of powers beyond the legally prescribed limits are essential.

Where examples of the planting of evidence or the use of oppressive questioning techniques are demonstrated, some critics argue that use of illegally obtained evidence is endemic to police practice. Others, including the police themselves, argue that such abuses are simply the result of individual 'rotten apples', and that, so long as

---

[13] See Irving, B., *Police Interrogation: A Study of Current Practice* (Research Study No. 2 for the Royal Commission on Criminal Procedure) (London, HMSO, 1980).

[14] *Code of Practice for the Searching of Premises by Police Officers and the Seizure of Property found by Police Officers on Persons or Premises* (Code B) (London, TSO, 2005).

[15] Principally communications containing legal advice from a professional legal adviser to his/her client.

[16] For example, personal records and journalistic records. There is a procedure whereby a circuit judge may be asked to make an order granting access to such material or, in an extreme case, to grant a warrant to search for this sort of material: PACE, s. 9 and Sch. 1.

[17] PACE, s. 17.

steps are taken to remove them, the basic activities of the police are undertaken within both the letter and the spirit of the law.

The police who fail to act within the scope of their legal powers may be the subject of internal disciplinary proceedings, or worse. Potentially the most effective deterrent against breaking the rules arises from the fact that any evidence obtained improperly may not be able to be given in court. As the police know that during the investigative/ information-gathering stage these rules of evidence will be applied should a case reach court and be contested, the rules should shape the ways in which evidence is obtained by the police. However, as is noted later, the law of evidence gives judges considerable discretion whether or not evidence should be excluded. The practical consequences of bending or ignoring the questioning rules are not always predictable.

As in other aspects of professional and public life, there is now much more for- mal accountability than was the case some years ago. The overall efficiency of police forces is the responsibility of Her Majesty's Inspectorate of Constabulary. The cre- ation of the Independent Police Complaints Commission[18] (replacing the Police Complaints Authority) has resulted in new mechanisms for individuals to pursue grievances against the police. In addition, each year a number of cases against the police are brought before the courts by individuals, for example seeking damages for false imprisonment or compensation for damage to property.

Suggestions, made by some, that police activity is characterized by wholesale mal- practice and corruption are not justified. Many who have incidental brushes with the police find they operate strictly according to the book and in a perfectly proper fash- ion. However, it is also true that there are more circumstances than those which hit the headlines in which the police do not behave strictly according to the rule book.

Next steps

On completing the first two stages, the police have a number of choices. They may:

- take no further action, e.g. where insufficient evidence has been obtained;
- give an informal warning;
- issue a formal caution (for adults) or reprimand or warning (for youths) from a senior police officer—this should only follow an admission of guilt and informed consent by the offender (or his/her parents or guardian in the case of a juvenile);[19]
- exercising powers under the Criminal Justice Act 2003, issue a conditional cau- tion. This may be given where there is sufficient evidence to charge a suspect with an offence which he or she admits, and the suspect agrees to the caution. It is for the CPS to decide whether a conditional caution is appropriate, and for the police to administer it. If the suspect fails to comply with the conditions, he or she is

[18] Police Reform Act 2002, Part 2.
[19] 60 per cent of offenders under the age of eighteen were cautioned for indictable offences in 1997.

Box 5.5   System in action

Use of cautions

The 2005 Criminal Statistics show that 299,000 offenders were cautioned for all offences in 2005—17 per cent more than in 2004. Cautions include 119,000 juveniles who were given reprimands or final warnings under the Crime and Disorder Act 1998, a rise of 13 per cent compared with 2004. The cautioning rate for indictable offences (i.e. the number of offenders cautioned as a percentage of those found guilty or cautioned) rose by four percentage points to 38 per cent. As well as cautioning offenders the police also issued 146,500 penalty notices for disorder (PNDs) and 57,700 warnings for cannabis possession in 2005.

liable to be prosecuted for the offence. A code of practice relating to conditional cautions was published in October 2004 (*see further, Box 5.5*).

- refer the papers to the prosecuting authorities for a decision on whether to charge the person with having committed a particular offence. (For all but minor and routine cases, the decision to charge is no longer made by the police, but by the prosecuting authorities. This change, made by the Criminal Justice Act 2003, resulted from pilot projects which showed that involving the prosecutor at an earlier stage led to more accurate charges and earlier guilty pleas.)

In practice very many reported and recorded crimes are dealt with in the first four of the ways listed above. It is statistically much more likely that a case will end at this point and not proceed to formal prosecution. Those who argue that the criminal justice system should be based on the 'due process' model will realize that, in this majority of cases, the formal protections of that model are effectively not available to the accused. The 'attrition' of reported incidents down to indictments actually dealt with in the Crown Court is demonstrated in *Diagram 5.1* on p. 110.

If a person is charged with an offence, a further decision needs to be taken whether the person charged is to be detained in custody or released on bail. *(See Box 5.6.)*

The decision to prosecute

This decision to charge an alleged offender is, except in minor cases, taken by prosecutors in the Crown Prosecution Service (CPS). (For other prosecuting authorities *see Box 5.7*.) The CPS is a public service, headed by the Director of Public Prosecutions (DPP), and answerable to Parliament through the Attorney-General. It was established in 1986 following enactment of the Prosecution of Offences Act 1985. Before then, the decision to prosecute was usually taken by the police themselves. This led to the criticism that, in some cases which had involved miscarriages of justice, the interrelation

Box 5.6 Legal system explained

Bail or custody

A fundamental principle of the criminal justice system is that a person is deemed to be innocent until proved guilty. It is wrong to deny an innocent person his liberty. Yet consideration of the real world suggests that some accused of crime are simply too dangerous to be allowed to remain at liberty until any case against them has been determined. They have to be remanded in custody, either for their own good or for the good of society at large.

Decisions about whether to release persons on bail (i.e. subject to a requirement that they surrender to custody at a specified time and place) can be taken at any stage in the criminal trial process until the final determination of the last appeal. Thus bail may be granted by the police, magistrates' courts, Crown Courts, the High Court, and the Court of Appeal (Criminal Division). The granting of bail, by whichever agency is involved, is subject to the principles laid down in the Bail Act 1976. The Act creates a statutory presumption that bail should be granted unless specified circumstances exist which mean that bail should not be granted. These make it easier to justify remanding in custody persons charged with an offence that may result in a sentence of imprisonment, than those charged with one which would not.

In some cases, the presumption is reversed. For example, following the passing of the Criminal Justice Act 2003, there is a presumption that bail will not be granted for a person aged eighteen or over who is charged with an imprisonable offence, and tests positive for a specified Class A drug, if he refuses to undergo an assessment as to his dependency or propensity to misuse such drugs, or following an assessment, refuses any relevant follow-up action recommended, unless the court is satisfied that there is no significant risk of his re-offending on bail. Also, when deciding whether to grant bail in respect of an offence which appears to have been committed while the defendant was on bail for another offence, courts are required to give particular weight to that fact when assessing the risk that (if granted bail) the defendant may commit further offences.

In practice the vast majority of those against whom criminal proceedings are taken are granted bail. Nevertheless there are those who argue that bail is granted too readily. In particular, there is disquiet about the numbers of crimes committed by people while they are out on bail. Notwithstanding these fears and the apparent policy of the Bail Act, numbers of those remanded in custody awaiting trial or sentencing or an appeal have increased sharply over the years and have exacerbated the problem of prison overcrowding. This has led policy-makers to consider other options, such as the electronic tagging of defendants so that the authorities can keep track of those persons even though they have not been detained in custody.

There are two types of bail: conditional bail and unconditional bail.

Box 5.6   *Continued*

Conditional bail

The police and courts can impose any requirements needed to make sure that defendants attend court and do not commit offences or interfere with witnesses whilst on bail. Conditions can also be imposed for the defendant's own protection or welfare (where he is a child or young person). Common conditions include not going within a certain distance of a witness's house, or being subject to a curfew. If a defendant is reported or believed to have broken a bail condition, they can be arrested and brought before a magistrates' court which may then place the person in custody.

Unconditional bail

If the police or court think that the defendant is unlikely to commit further offences, will attend court when required, and will not interfere with the justice process, they are usually released on unconditional bail.

Breach of bail

Defendants who do not stick to their bail conditions, or fail to attend court on the set date, are in breach of bail. They are liable to be arrested and may have their bail withdrawn. They may be remanded in custody and might not get bail in the future. Failing to appear at court as required is a criminal offence and they can also be prosecuted for this offence.

of investigation and prosecution had resulted in the police inappropriately exercising their powers to prosecute. The Royal Commission on Criminal Procedure 1981 recommended a separation of the investigation and prosecution functions, to introduce an element of independence into the latter.

This was extremely controversial. In the early years, the police in particular were very unhappy. The CPS was also confronted with many public challenges. It was said that they employed poor quality staff; their work was hampered by poor quality administration; and their decisions were often criticized. Notwithstanding these early criticisms, the role of the CPS has been retained, and it has grown in confidence and maturity. There are now fewer complaints, at least in the mass media, about its role in the criminal justice system.

The basic procedure is that, after the police have investigated a crime, the case papers are passed to the CPS. One of the CPS lawyers—a Crown Prosecutor—reviews the papers to decide whether or not to go ahead with the case. The prosecutor's decision

Box 5.7   Legal system explained

Case study: other prosecuting agencies: the Serious Fraud Office

As noted in passing above, there are many other prosecuting agencies apart from the police. Local authorities, the taxation authorities, and the social security authorities are just some of the other public bodies that have the legal powers both to investigate criminal activities and to bring prosecutions before the courts. Limits on space prevent any detailed discussion here. The prosecution policy of the Director of Revenue and Customs Prosecutions is set out at www.hmrc.gov.uk/prosecutions/prosecution-policy.htm.

One particular agency, in relation to which this short note is provided, is the *Serious Fraud Office* (SFO). This was established by the Criminal Justice Act 1987.[20] It was designed to increase the capability of the authorities to investigate serious and complex fraud cases. The Director of the SFO, appointed by the Attorney-General, works with specially appointed staff. In this area, the investigation and prosecution functions have been kept together. The Director and, by extension, staff have wide powers to require those under investigation (and others believed to have relevant information) to answer questions, and to furnish information. The SFO focuses on the most serious fraud cases; other cases are pursued in the normal way through the Fraud Investigation Group within the CPS.

The work-load of the SFO is not extensive but is very intense. For example, during the reporting year ending in April 1999, it worked on the investigation or prosecution of ninety-four cases; but the total value of the sums involved was well in excess of £1 bn. During the same year, eighteen trials involving thirty-eight defendants were concluded. The principal defendants were convicted in all but one of those trials.

is based on two tests set out in the *Code for Crown Prosecutors*. (There is much public ignorance about these tests. *See Box 5.8 for* some of the details.)

Notwithstanding the general approach of the CPS there are still cases where the CPS comes under heavy criticism, either from the police or from a victim (or her family). Particular problems arise in very emotive cases, which may have attracted considerable media publicity, where therefore there is a great pressure to prosecute, but where the evidence to satisfy the tests sketched out above may just not be there. In making its decisions, the CPS cannot always reach conclusions that attract universal approval.

The CPS employs a considerable number of staff. They work in different parts of the country on a regional basis. There is also a Central Casework group which deals with especially important cases, such as deaths in police custody, cases involving the Official Secrets Act, or cases involving terrorism.

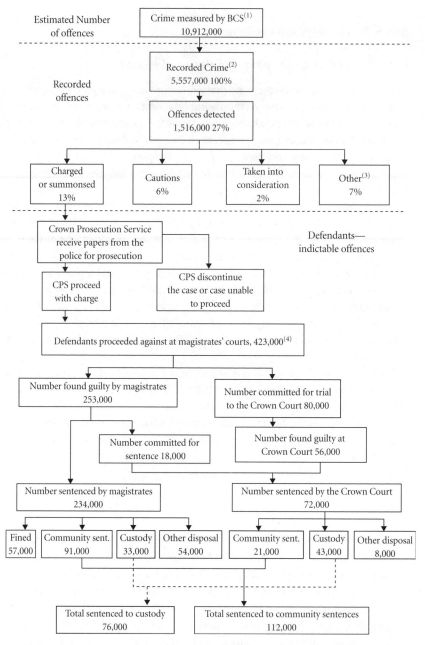

1. Covers crimes against households and individuals, reported in the 2005/06 British Crime Survey interviews, that were not necessarily reported to the police. This set of offences is not strictly comparable to recorded crime.
2. Covers all indictable, including triable either way, offences plus a few closely associated summary offences.
3. Includes formal warnings for cannabis possession, penalty notices for disorder, and non-sanction detections.

Diagram 5.1 Flows through the criminal justice system, 2005

Source: Criminal Statistics, 2005 (Home Office Statistical Bulletin 19/06).

Box 5.8 Legal system explained

Code for Crown Prosecutors: the decision to prosecute

Crown Prosecutors make charging decisions in accordance with the Full Code Test, other than in those limited circumstances where the Threshold Test applies. The Threshold Test applies where the case is one in which it is proposed to keep the suspect in custody after charge, but the evidence required to apply the Full Code Test is not yet available. Where a Crown Prosecutor makes a charging decision in accordance with the Threshold Test, the case must be reviewed in accordance with the Full Code Test as soon as reasonably practicable, taking into account the progress of the investigation.

The Full Code Test has two stages. The first stage is consideration of the evidence. If the case does not pass the evidential stage it must not go ahead no matter how important or serious it may be. If the case does pass the evidential stage, Crown Prosecutors must proceed to the second stage and decide if a prosecution is needed in the public interest.

The evidential stage

Crown Prosecutors must be satisfied that there is enough evidence to provide a 'realistic prospect of conviction' against each defendant on each charge. They must consider what the defence case may be, and how that is likely to affect the prosecution case.

A realistic prospect of conviction is an objective test. It means that a jury or bench of magistrates or judge hearing a case alone, properly directed in accordance with the law, is more likely than not to convict the defendant of the charge alleged. This is a separate test from the one that the criminal courts themselves must apply. A court should only convict if satisfied that it is sure of a defendant's guilt.

When deciding whether there is enough evidence to prosecute, Crown Prosecutors must consider whether the evidence can be used and is reliable. There will be many cases in which the evidence does not give any cause for concern. But there will also be cases in which the evidence may not be as strong as it first appears. Crown Prosecutors must ask themselves the following questions:

- Can the evidence be used in court?
- Is the evidence reliable?
- Is it likely that the evidence will be excluded by the court?
  (There are certain legal rules which might mean that evidence which seems relevant cannot be given at a trial. For example, is it likely that the evidence will be excluded because of the way in which it was gathered? If so, is there enough other evidence for a realistic prospect of conviction?)
- Is there evidence which might support or detract from the reliability of a confession? Is the reliability affected by factors such as the defendant's age, intelligence, or level of understanding?

Box 5.8 *Continued*

- What explanation has the defendant given? Is a court likely to find it credible in the light of the evidence as a whole? Does it support an innocent explanation?
- If the identity of the defendant is likely to be questioned, is the evidence about this strong enough?
- Is the witness's background likely to weaken the prosecution case? For example, does the witness have any motive that may affect his or her attitude to the case, or a relevant previous conviction?
- Are there concerns over the accuracy or credibility of a witness?

Crown Prosecutors should not ignore evidence because they are not sure that it can be used or is reliable. But they should look closely at it when deciding if there is a realistic prospect of conviction.

The public interest stage

In 1951, Lord Shawcross, who was Attorney-General, made the classic statement on public interest, which has been supported by Attorneys-General ever since: 'It has never been the rule in this country—I hope it never will be—that suspected criminal offences must automatically be the subject of prosecution'. (House of Commons Debates, volume 483, column 681, 29 January 1951.)

The public interest must be considered in each case where there is enough evidence to provide a realistic prospect of conviction. Although there may be public interest factors against prosecution in a particular case, often the prosecution should go ahead and those factors should be put to the court for consideration when sentence is being passed. A prosecution will usually take place unless there are public interest factors tending against prosecution which clearly outweigh those tending in favour, or it appears more appropriate in all the circumstances of the case to divert the person from prosecution. Crown Prosecutors must balance factors for and against prosecution carefully and fairly.

Some common public interest factors in favour of prosecution

The more serious the offence, the more likely it is that a prosecution will be needed in the public interest. A prosecution is likely to be needed if:

- a conviction is likely to result in a significant sentence;
- a conviction is likely to result in a confiscation or any other order;
- a weapon was used or violence was threatened during the commission of the offence;
- the offence was committed against a person serving the public (for example, a police or prison officer, or a nurse);
- the defendant was in a position of authority or trust;

Box 5.8   *Continued*

- the evidence shows that the defendant was a ringleader or an organizer of the offence;
- there is evidence that the offence was premeditated;
- there is evidence that the offence was carried out by a group;
- the victim of the offence was vulnerable, has been put in considerable fear, or suffered personal attack, damage, or disturbance;
- the offence was committed in the presence of, or in close proximity to, a child;
- the offence was motivated by any form of discrimination against the victim's ethnic or national origin, disability, sex, religious beliefs, political views, or sexual orientation, or the suspect demonstrated hostility towards the victim based on any of those characteristics;
- there is a marked difference between the actual or mental ages of the defendant and the victim, or if there is any element of corruption;
- the defendant's previous convictions or cautions are relevant to the present offence;
- the defendant is alleged to have committed the offence while under an order of the court;
- there are grounds for believing that the offence is likely to be continued or repeated, for example, by a history of recurring conduct;
- the offence, although not serious in itself, is widespread in the area where it was committed; or
- a prosecution would have a significant positive impact on maintaining community confidence.

A prosecution is less likely to be needed if:

- the court is likely to impose a nominal penalty;
- the defendant has already been made the subject of a sentence and any further conviction would be unlikely to result in the imposition of an additional sentence or order, unless the nature of the particular offence requires a prosecution or the defendant withdraws consent to have an offence taken into consideration during sentencing;
- the offence was committed as a result of a genuine mistake or misunderstanding (these factors must be balanced against the seriousness of the offence);
- the loss or harm can be described as minor and was the result of a single incident, particularly if it was caused by a misjudgment;
- there has been a long delay between the offence taking place and the date of the trial, unless the offence is serious; or the delay has been caused in part by the defendant;
- the offence has only recently come to light; or the complexity of the offence has meant that there has been a long investigation;

Box 5.8   *Continued*

- a prosecution is likely to have a bad effect on the victim's physical or mental health, always bearing in mind the seriousness of the offence;
- the defendant is elderly or is, or was at the time of the offence, suffering from significant mental or physical ill health, unless the offence is serious or there is a real possibility that it may be repeated;
- the defendant has put right the loss or harm that was caused (but defendants must not avoid prosecution or diversion solely because they pay compensation); or
- details may be made public that could harm sources of information, international relations or national security.

The Crown Prosecution Service does not act for victims or the families of victims in the same way as solicitors act for their clients. Crown Prosecutors act on behalf of the public and not just in the interests of any particular individual. However, when considering the public interest, Crown Prosecutors should always take into account the consequences for the victim of whether or not to prosecute, and any views expressed by the victim or the victim's family. It is important that a victim is told about a decision which makes a significant difference to the case in which they are involved.

Source: Extracts from the *Code for Crown Prosecutors* (CPS, 2004).

Monitoring

Because of concerns about the quality of the work of the CPS, an inspectorate was established in 1996 to monitor the quality and consistency of decision taking across the country, and to try to ensure the spread of good practice. Initially, the creation of the Inspectorate was the result of executive action; recent legislation has, however, put the existence and powers of the authority onto a statutory footing.[20] Particular incidents may, additionally, be the subject of special inquiry.[21]

The trial stage

As we have seen, there are many reasons criminal offences do not all result in an offender being brought before the courts. Even when a case is so brought, the public image of what then happens is far removed from the typical case. The impression given

[20] Crown Prosecution Service Inspectorate Act 2000. This followed a recommendation in the Glidewell Report, *Review of the Crown Prosecution Service* (Cm 3960) (London, The Stationery Office, 1998). The Inspectorate publishes an annual report on its work.

[21] See, e.g., His Honour Gerald Butler QC's report, *Inquiry into CPS Decision-Making in Relation to Deaths in Custody and Related Matters* (London, The Stationery Office, 1999).

in the news media or in TV drama series is that prosecutions result in full-scale trials in the Crown Court. The reality is quite different. The vast bulk of criminal trials are disposed of in the magistrates' court, and the vast bulk of them—both in the Crown Court and in the magistrates' court—are determined on the basis of a plea of guilty. The trial is a statistical rarity.

All prosecutions start in the magistrates' court. Whether they finish there depends on how the case is classified. (For classification of criminal cases *see Box 5.9*.) The most serious cases—indictable offences—are forwarded ('committed') to the Crown Court for disposal. The vast majority of criminal cases—summary cases—are disposed of in the magistrates' court. Cases which are triable either way, i.e. either summarily or on indictment, are determined in the appropriate court, once a decision on the classification of the case has been made.

Box 5.9 Legal system explained

Classification of criminal cases

There are four potential classes of criminal case.

1. *Offences triable only on indictment.* These are the most serious cases, such as murder, manslaughter, and rape. If the defendant pleads not guilty, these cases must be tried in the Crown Court, before a jury.
2. *Offences triable summarily.* These are all offences created by statute, where the statute provides that they are summary offences. These cases are determined by magistrates. There is no right to trial by jury. There have been some attempts at reclassifying certain offences as summary only, in particular, small thefts; but political arguments about 'taking away rights to a jury trial' have made change difficult.
3. *Offences triable either way.* These are offences, also created by statute, where the Act provides that they may be dealt with either summarily or on indictment. In such cases, the accused currently chooses how he wishes to be tried, before magistrates or before a jury. Opting for trial in the Crown Court exposes the accused to the prospect of more serious sentences, as the Crown Court has wider powers of sentence than the magistrates' courts, though the latter can commit a case to the Crown Court where they think their powers of sentence are inadequate. (See further below.)
4. *Summary cases triable on indictment.* In specific cases an accused may have a charge that he has committed a summary offence added to a charge that he has committed an indictable offence. These can now both be dealt with in the same trial in the Crown Court.[22]

---

[22] Criminal Justice Act 1988, s. 40; see also s. 41.

The functions of the courts

Criminal trial courts have two principal functions:

- dealing with the case, which includes determining guilt where the defendant has pleaded not guilty, as well as deciding on the correct sentence; and

- ensuring that, so far as possible, the trial is fair.

They may also have to deal with other procedural questions, such as whether or not to grant bail or remand a person in custody. (See above, *Box 5.6.*)

Dealing with the case

In cases where the accused pleads not guilty, the court has to hear the evidence, in the light of that evidence reach findings of fact, in the light of those findings determine whether the accused person is or is not guilty of the alleged crime, and, if guilty, pass an appropriate sentence. In the magistrates' courts all these functions are performed by the magistrates. In the Crown Court, the findings of fact and the question of guilt are determined by the jury. Before the jury start their work, they are provided with a summing-up of the case by the trial judge, an exercise designed to help them focus on the issues they have to decide. If a conviction results, then, subject to further pleas in mitigation and reports on the accused from other agencies such as the probation service, sentence is passed by the trial judge.

Many think that the function of the court is to determine the truth about the events that have led to a person appearing in court. In practice the function of the trial is rather different. The prosecution must prove 'beyond reasonable doubt' that the accused committed the offence alleged. The function of the defence, therefore, is to throw sufficient doubt on what the prosecution is alleging so that the burden of proof is not established. If the burden of proof is not established, the defendant must be acquitted.

In cases where the defendant pleads guilty, the only issue for the court, again subject to pleas in mitigation made on behalf of the accused and other reports, e.g. from social workers or probation officers, is to determine sentence.

Ensuring the fairness of the trial

Fairness is at the heart of the due process model of criminal justice. A great deal of the law of criminal procedure and evidence is designed to ensure that the accused gets a fair trial. It is in this context that many of the tensions between the 'due process' model and the 'crime control' model may be seen. A number of initiatives have been taken in recent years which have shifted the balance from the former to the latter. The question is whether the balance has now gone too far. The full detail of the relevant law is beyond the scope of this book. However two examples will be briefly considered: evidence and disclosure.

Evidence. The law on criminal evidence is designed to ensure that only relevant material is put before the court and to prevent material being put before the court which would be unfairly prejudicial to the defendant. Among the rules which exclude evidence in a criminal trial are:

- *the rule against hearsay evidence.* In general, only evidence given by witnesses in court is admitted. What others said to a witness cannot be admitted, as the person who made the statement cannot be challenged (cross-examined) about its veracity. The Criminal Justice Act 2003 relaxes these principles. It is now provided that witness statements can be used as evidence, subject to a number of safeguards, where the witness is identified but unavailable to testify or the statement is contained in a business document. The court is also given a discretion to admit hearsay evidence where it would not be contrary to the interests of justice for it to be used. In addition, witnesses' previous statements have been made more widely admissible at trial. This enables witnesses to refer to their statement whilst giving evidence in court and permits greater use of video recorded statements for crucial evidence in serious cases;

- *the rule preventing the giving of information about a person's past record.* In general, the prosecution was not able to disclose to the court evidence about the person's history, particularly criminal record, unless the accused wished to challenge the veracity of a prosecution witness, say a policeman. Under the Criminal Justice Act 2003, this principle is also relaxed. Judges are given power to let juries hear about a defendant's previous convictions and other misconduct where relevant to the case. The court can exclude evidence of previous misconduct if it thinks that the jury will give it disproportionate weight (in other words, if the relevance of the evidence to the case is outweighed by any prejudicial effect). The starting point, however, is that relevant evidence is admissible. This proposal, which derived in part from a detailed study of the issue by the Law Commission, was extremely controversial. Lawyers' organizations and civil liberty groups argued that a person should be tried only for the crime for which he has been prosecuted; to introduce evidence of previous misconduct would undermine the presumption that a person should be regarded as innocent until proved guilty. Those in favour of the proposal argued that such evidence will not be admitted generally, but only where it is relevant to the case in question.[23]

In some circumstances, there are precise rules of law which relate to the admissibility of evidence. For example, where it is proposed to rely on a confession, section 76 of PACE requires the prosecution to demonstrate beyond reasonable doubt that the confession was not made by oppression of the person who made it, or as a result of inducements made to the person giving it which might render the confession unreliable.

Section 78 of PACE also gives the judge/magistrate a general discretion to exclude evidence that would otherwise be admissible and relevant 'where the admission of

---

[23] E.g., the fact that X had convictions for robbery would not be admitted if X was being prosecuted for rape; however evidence that X had been found guilty of other charges of serious assault against women would be.

the evidence would have such an adverse effect on the fairness of the proceedings that the court ought not to admit it'. Evidence obtained by the police in breach of the rules relating to questioning and interrogation can fall into this category.

Disclosure. A separate issue relates to the question of what evidence should be disclosed by the prosecution to the defendant and vice versa. One of the most significant causes of serious miscarriages of justice arises when the prosecution withholds evidence which it has acquired during the process of its investigation but which weakens the case which the prosecution is seeking to build against the accused.

This was a central issue considered by the Royal Commission on Criminal Justice which reported in 1993. As a result of, though not fully accepting, its recommendations, the former Conservative government introduced a new legal regime relating to disclosure, contained in Parts I and II of the Criminal Procedure and Investigations Act 1996. (*See Box 5.10.*) Disputes about whether or not documents should be disclosed are also resolved by the court at a pre-trial hearing.

An important innovation in the way the courts work has been the creation, in 2004, of a new Criminal Procedure Rules Committee whose task it is to create a code of

---

Box 5.10   System in action

Disclosure of evidence

The Royal Commission on Criminal Justice was appointed in 1991 against a background of cases where there had been clear miscarriages of justice: the 'Guildford four', the 'Maguire seven', the 'Birmingham six', and the Judith Ward cases are amongst the best known. In addition, the courts in a number of cases had been developing the (then) common law relating to disclosure. The result had been to place increased responsibility to disclose on the police. This provided an opportunity to the defence to mount fishing expeditions to find out what information the police had. The Royal Commission sought to strike a balance between the duties of the prosecution and the rights of the defence.

The Royal Commission proposed that a new scheme for disclosure should be enshrined in statute, accompanied by a code of practice or a more detailed statutory instrument.

In May 1995, the then government published a consultation paper, which led to the Criminal Investigations and Procedure Act 1996. This has been amended by the Criminal Justice Act 2003. In outline, this provides:

(1) the investigator (usually the police) must preserve material gathered during the investigation and make available to the prosecutor material falling into defined key categories, plus a list of other material which has been acquired;

(2) the prosecutor must serve on the defence material on which the prosecutor intends to rely to found her case;

Box 5.10 *Continued*

(3) the prosecutor must also disclose prosecution material that has not previously been disclosed and which might reasonably be considered capable of undermining the case for the prosecution against the accused, or of assisting the case for the accused. There is a continuing duty on the prosecutor to disclose material that meets the new test. The prosecutor is specifically required to review the prosecution material on receipt of the defence statement and to make further disclosure if required under the continuing duty; and

(4) the defence statement must set out the nature of his defence including any particular defences on which he intends to rely. It must also indicate any points of law he wishes to take, including any points as to the admissibility of evidence or abuse of process. The judge is required to warn the accused about any failure to comply with the defence statement requirements. There is also a requirement for service of an updated defence statement to assist the management of the trial, requiring the accused to serve, before the trial, details of any witnesses he intends to call to give evidence (other than himself) and also details of all experts instructed including those not called to give evidence. The new obligation on the defence to provide details of the witnesses it intends to call will be accompanied by a code of practice governing the conduct of any interviews by the police or non-police investigators with defence witnesses disclosed in accordance with the requirement.

Any disputes about disclosure are to be resolved by the court in a pre-trial hearing.

The main features of the process are: (a) that it is statute-based; (b) that it puts the responsibility on the prosecution to decide what should be disclosed; and (c) that it requires that the defence should make disclosure of its case before the start of the trial.

The accompanying *code of practice* (made under the authority of Part 2 of the 1996 Act) requires the appointment, in any criminal investigation, of an 'officer in charge', plus a separate 'disclosure officer' who will be responsible for the administration of the investigation, including the operation of the disclosure scheme. The 'investigator'—the police or other officer carrying out the investigation—is made responsible for retaining material gathered or generated by the inquiry. The disclosure officer prepares the schedule of unused material, together with a list of any sensitive material (e.g. relating to national security or information given in confidence). The disclosure officer must send these schedules to the prosecutor, accompanied by copies of any material relating to the unreliability of witnesses or confessions or containing any explanation by the accused for the offence. Once the defence statement is filed, the disclosure officer is to look at all the files again and draw attention to any which may assist the defence. He must then certify to the prosecutor that, to the best of his knowledge and belief, the duties imposed by the code have been complied with.

In a decision by the European Court of Human Rights, it was held that where the prosecution withheld evidence because it was claimed to be immune from disclosure

> **Box 5.10**   *Continued*
>
> on the grounds of public interest, the failure to put it before a trial judge so as to per-
> mit him to rule on the question of disclosure deprived an accused person of the right
> to a fair trial.[24]
>
>   The effectiveness of these arrangements depends to a large extent on the willing-
> ness of particular individuals, on both the investigation and prosecution sides, to oper-
> ate the scheme in accordance with the statutory provisions and code of guidance. A
> report, published in 2000 by the Crown Prosecution Service Inspectorate,[25] gave a
> disturbing account of routine failures to follow the rules.

criminal procedure that applies throughout the criminal courts. This is modelled on
the Civil Procedure Rules Committee, and is designed to give judges greater authority to manage the progress of criminal trials. The Rules were published and came into
force in 2005. They consolidate rules governing the practice and procedure of the
criminal courts—the criminal division of the Court of Appeal, the Crown Court, and
magistrates' courts, which were scattered among almost fifty separate sets of rules,
containing a total of nearly 500 individual rules. The rules are intended to be evolu-
tionary, rather than revolutionary, but are designed to change some of the culture of
the criminal trial process, in particular through judicial case management. It is too
early to assess whether these objectives are being met.

Magistrates' courts[26]

Magistrates' courts have a long history. They have a distinct character in that they
depend very heavily on volunteer/lay persons to determine decisions. Much of the
claim to legitimacy for the magistrates is that benches are composed of persons who
come from the community affected by the alleged criminal activity.[27] (For types of
magistrates' courts *see Box 5.11*.)

Functions

All criminal trials start in the magistrates' courts. In carrying out their judicial
function, there are two distinct types of procedure which they control: *committal*

---

[24] *Rowe and Davis v. United Kingdom, The Times,* 1 March 2000.

[25] Crown Prosecution Service Inspectorate, *Report on the Thematic Review of the Disclosure of Unused Material* (London, CPS, 2000).

[26] The magistrates' court also has responsibilities in certain family matters. These are considered below in Chapter 7.

[27] An independent research report on magistrates was published by the Home Office in December 2000. See Morgan, R., and Russell, N., *The Judiciary in the Magistrates' Courts* (London, Home Office, 2000).

Box 5.11   Legal system explained

Types of magistrates' courts

There are two distinct types of magistrates' courts which operate in England and Wales: the *lay justices'* courts, and the *district judge* (formerly *stipendiary*) *magistrates'*[28] courts. Lay justices' courts are made up of (usually) three lay persons (i.e. persons with no specific legal qualifications), known as Justices of the Peace (JPs), who sit and determine criminal cases. They receive legal advice on their powers from the *Justices' Clerk*, a specially appointed official who is legally qualified. JPs provide their services on a voluntary basis; they receive expenses, for example for travel and subsistence, and, where appropriate, can claim a loss of earnings allowance. Apart from that, however, they are unpaid. By far the majority of magistrates' courts are lay justices' courts.

District judge magistrates' courts are run by district judges, who are qualified lawyers and sit on their own, rather than in panels of three. They used to sit only in those areas of the country designated by the government as appropriate for such courts. As the result of a change in the law, they are now able to sit in any magistrates' court in the country, thus giving court managers greater flexibility in the use of this source of judicial manpower.[29]

---

proceedings and *summary trials*. In addition they have responsibility for enforcing non-custodial penalties, especially fines.

Committal proceedings and sending for trial

The function of committal proceedings is to ensure that, even though the case will be tried in the Crown Court, magistrates are satisfied that there is a case for the defendant to answer. It used to be the case that committal proceedings were fully reported in the press and other mass media; but this led to the criticism that such publicity made it difficult to find members of a jury who had not heard about the case. The law was therefore changed; publicity to committal proceedings can be given only where the defendant permits this.

It is only very rarely that magistrates find there is no case to answer. From January 2001, all indictable only cases are automatically sent for trial in the Crown Court following the appearance of the defendant before magistrates. Traditional committal proceedings therefore now occur only in the case of an offence triable either way, where it is decided that the trial should be on indictment.

In 2005, just over 80,000 cases were committed to the Crown Court for trial (down from over 91,000 in 1997). Much of this decrease is attributable to a change in procedure

---

[28] Stipendiary magistrates were renamed District Judges (Magistrates' Courts) by the Access to Justice Act 1999, s. 78.

[29] Access to Justice Act 1999, s. 78 and Sch. 11.

whereby accused persons are required to enter a plea—guilty or not guilty—in the magistrates' court.[30] Thus those who would have been sent to the Crown Court for trial and who would then have pleaded guilty are no longer committed for trial to the Crown Court, though they are committed for sentence. (On sentencing generally, see further below.)

Summary trials

All other prosecutions are dealt with summarily, that is to say by the magistrates themselves. In 2005 some 1.90 million defendants were proceeded against in the magistrates' courts: ninety-five per cent of prosecutions are dealt with in this way. And the vast majority of these cases (sixty-two per cent) were determined by a plea of guilty, rather than following a trial.[31]

Committals for sentence

In all cases where guilt is established, whether or not there is a trial, the magistrates have to impose a penalty. The powers of magistrates to impose sentences are limited. However they can commit a case to the Crown Court where they decide that their powers of sentence are inadequate. The number of cases referred to the Crown Court has increased from around 14,800 cases in 1997, to about 20,000 in 2005. The reason for this increase is the procedural change noted above which requires the accused person to indicate how he will plead (guilty or not guilty) before any decision as to which court should hear the case is made.

Fine enforcement

In many cases where the penalty imposed is a fine, the magistrates have to follow this up with enforcement proceedings.

Youth courts

A vast amount of criminal activity is carried out by people, mainly male, at a relatively early age. Juvenile delinquency and measures to try to deal with it—not always with conspicuous success—have been on the policy agendas of governments for many years. Current debates about anti-social behaviour, drug and alcohol abuse, and general fear of violent crime are fuelled at least in part by a general perception that we live in a 'yob culture'. There are major tensions between the desire to prevent juvenile crime and deal firmly with those young persons found guilty of criminal activity, and the desire not to blight young lives unnecessarily by giving them criminal records which may prevent them entering the job market or otherwise making a positive contribution to society.

---

[30] Criminal Procedures and Investigations Act 1996, s. 49, introducing the Magistrates' Court Act 1980, s. 17A.

[31] *Criminal Statistics, 2005* (Home Office Statistical Bulletin 19/06, 2006).

There have also been fierce debates about where the responsibility for youth crime should lie—with individual offenders, with their parent(s), with schools and teachers, or with the wider society which is said to fail to provide the educational and employment opportunities that might make them more productive members of society.

The issue was reviewed by the government in 1997, in the White Paper *No More Excuses*.[32] This led to two Acts, the Crime and Disorder Act 1998 and the Youth Justice and Criminal Evidence Act 1999. These contained provisions, not only to process young offenders (those under the age of eighteen) through the criminal justice system more quickly, but also to try to demonstrate to them the effect their actions have had on the lives of others.

The Crime and Disorder Act 1998 led to the creation of *youth offending teams*— multi-disciplinary agencies brought together at the local level to devise effective programmes to prevent offending and re-offending by young people. Their work is kept under review by the *Youth Justice Board*. The Board is also responsible for funding crime prevention schemes.

The 1998 Act also replaced a non-statutory policy whereby police could merely decide to caution a young offender, with a new statutory 'final warning'. Once an offender has received one, any further offence leads to criminal proceedings in court.

When dealing with young offenders, magistrates' courts are technically known as *youth courts*. When sitting as a youth court, magistrates are subject to special procedural rules designed to ensure that cases are dealt with as speedily as possible. Magistrates also have a special range of sentencing options. In most cases, some form of community order will be appropriate. These include: community punishment and rehabilitation order; supervision order; action plan order;[33] attendance centre order; curfew order;[34] parenting order;[35] drug treatment and testing order; reparation order[36] as well as fine, conditional discharge, and absolute discharge. Where it is essential to keep a young person in custody, a detention and training order is available.[37]

As a result of the Youth Justice and Criminal Evidence Act 1999, magistrates may make a referral order to refer first-time offenders to a *youth offender panel*.[38] This is intended to work with the young offender to establish a programme of

[32] (Cm 3809) (London, The Stationery Office, 1997).

[33] A three-month programme of community-based intervention combining punishment, rehabilitation, and reparation, designed to address specific causes of offending.

[34] This is designed to protect young children from the risk of involvement in crime. This may involve requiring the child to be at home at particular times or to stay away from certain people or places.

[35] Which could require parents to attend counselling and guidance sessions, and to ensure their children attend school.

[36] E.g., requiring the offender to write a letter of apology to a victim; or to clean up graffiti or repair criminal damage.

[37] It replaces the sentences of a *secure training order* and *detention in a young offenders' institution*.

[38] The power to refer is available only in the youth court. A young offender tried in the Crown Court may, however, on conviction be referred to the youth court for sentence in a case where the trial judge regards that as appropriate.

behaviour for the young offender to follow. The programme is explicitly based on the theory of 'restorative justice', to ensure that the offender takes responsibility for the consequences of his offending behaviour; makes restoration to the victim; and achieves re-integration into the law-abiding community. Whether these objectives will be achieved is, as yet, too early to determine. It must also be questioned whether the theory of restorative justice is the only theory behind the new programme; other 'justice models'—including the 'crime control' and the 'bureaucratic'—appear to be in play as well.

In 2001, the Home Office published a *Good Practice Guide for Youth Courts*.[39] This evolved from an experiment in two courts which sought to achieve four key objectives:

- effective engagement with defendants and their parents to probe the reasons for offending and to encourage plans to change behaviour;
- changing courtroom layouts to facilitate better communication;
- making the court process more open by lifting reporting restrictions where appropriate, and exercising discretion to allow others such as victims to attend court; and
- giving feedback to sentencers on the outcome of sentences.

The guide is designed to encourage youth courts to respond positively to such initiatives to counter public perceptions that they were not delivering effective justice.

In addition to the work of the youth courts, other measures designed to curb anti-social behaviour have also been introduced. These include: local child curfews; anti-social behaviour orders; and acceptable behaviour contracts. As in other areas of the justice system the pace of change has been extremely fast. There now seems to be a strong case for a period of consolidation and evaluation of what has been done rather than more change.

Many of the initiatives designed to prevent anti-social behaviour have been brought together under the label of the Respect Agenda. The Respect Taskforce, which led work in this area, has been brought into a new Youth Taskforce established in October 2007. It will work to deliver the goals set out in *Aiming high for young people: a ten year strategy for positive activities* published by the Government in 2007. The government is seeking to promote a more positive tone in relation to young people, replacing some of the negative rhetoric that has been so prominent over the last decade. The government has also announced, in October 2007, a review of the best ways to engage communities in the fight against crime.

---

[39] *The Youth Court: Changing the Culture of the Youth Court* (London, Home Office, 2001).

The Crown Court

Jurisdiction and organization

The Crown Court is where the most serious criminal cases–cases tried on indictment—are disposed of. The Crown Court is divided into three tiers located in 92 court centre locations around the country. These centres are further grouped into six circuits.[40]

- First-tier courts are those in which High Court judges, circuit judges and recorders sit. They have higher levels of security to deal with the most difficult prisoners. The full range of criminal work, together with High Court civil work (see Chapter 8), is dealt with in these courts.
- Second-tier courts are the same, though no civil work is conducted in them.
- Third-tier courts are presided over only by circuit judges or recorders.

The offences dealt with in the Crown Court are themselves divided into three classes, under directions given by the Lord Chief Justice.[41] The aim is that the most serious offences are dealt with by the most senior judges. Distribution of business is the responsibility of the presiding judges—judges specially nominated in each circuit to have responsibility for the efficient running of trial lists.

The Crown Court also has powers to sentence persons convicted in the magistrates' court where the magistrates have decided that their own powers of sentencing are inadequate. In addition, the Crown Court hears appeals from decisions of the magistrates' court.

Work-load

Committals and cases sent for trial. According to the 2005 *Judicial Statistics,* in that year the Crown Court had just over 80,000 cases committed to it. Only 77,000 cases were actually dealt with in 2005. Just under 28,000 followed a plea of not guilty—i.e. just under 40 per cent. Thus less than half went to trial. A considerable number of trials were 'cracked trials', i.e. cases originally listed for trial, but where the accused changed his plea from not guilty to guilty, most commonly on the day of the trial. There were over 14,500 cracked trials in 2005.

Of those pleading not guilty to all charges, 66 per cent were acquitted. This represents over 17 per cent of the total number of defendants dealt with by the Crown Court during the year. Of these, 31 per cent were acquitted as the result of a verdict of not guilty by the jury; the remainder were either discharged by the judge (57 per cent) or acquitted on the direction of the judge.

Of those convicted after pleading not guilty 21 per cent were convicted on the basis of a majority verdict; the rest were convicted by the unanimous decision of the jury.

---

[40] Midland and Oxford; North Eastern; Northern; South Eastern; Wales and Chester; and Western. The 'Old Bailey' is the name given to the Central Criminal Court in London, a Crown Court in the South Eastern Circuit.

[41] These are set out in *Judicial Statistics, 2005* (Cm 6799) (London, The Stationery Office, 2006).

Committals for sentence. Around 33,000 committals for sentence were made; just about the same number of cases were dealt with.

Appeals. Just over 12,800 appeals from magistrates' courts were made, and a similar number were dealt with. Of these, over 40 per cent were allowed or resulted in a variation of the sentence.

Waiting times. The average waiting time for those pleading guilty was 12 weeks; for those pleading not guilty, 21 weeks. Those held in custody waited, on average, 14 weeks for their trial; those on bail waited, on average, 16.2 weeks.

Hearing times. The average hearing times were:

- For not guilty pleas, 9.8 hours;
- For guilty pleas, 1.3 hours;
- For sentence, 0.6 hours;
- For appeals, 1.1 hours.

Comment

The most obvious point is that, as in the magistrates' courts, full-scale trials following a plea of not guilty are a statistical rarity.

- A significant percentage of those who plead not guilty are ultimately acquitted, though far more are on the direction of the judge rather than as the result of a jury verdict.

- The newspapers may give the impression that cases in the Crown Court take significant amounts of time, particularly where there is a full trial. Although trials take longer than other forms of disposal, on average they last just under 10 hours (less than two days of court time).

- The 'success rate' in appeals could be seen as raising some questions about the quality of magistrates' decisions, though the total number of appeals is a tiny proportion of the total number of cases dealt with by the magistrates.

Issues in the criminal justice trial system

Charge and plea bargaining

The high level of guilty pleas in both the magistrates' and Crown Courts may suggest that the police and prosecution allow only the strongest cases to come before a court. But it may nonetheless seem surprising that in a system where the theory is that all are innocent until proved guilty so few accused actually take advantage of the due process model of criminal justice and submit the evidence presented by the prosecution for testing before either the magistrates or a jury.

Of course there are cases where the evidence is so overwhelming that a guilty plea is the only sensible option for the accused. But in less clear-cut cases, at least part of the answer to this puzzle arises from the fact that those within the criminal justice system work quite hard, through various forms of bargaining, to ensure that accused persons plead guilty. This saves considerable amounts of court time (as the statistics for average hearing times set out above clearly show) and thus expense and other resources. There are various practices which may occur to assist the accused in deciding what plea to enter.

First, there may be a negotiation between the prosecutor and the defence about the charge to be proceeded with before the courts. If the accused is willing or can be persuaded to plead guilty to a charge which carries a less severe penalty, the prosecution may then decide not to pursue an alternative charge which could arise from the same factual situation, which might attract a more severe penalty.

Secondly, there may be an indication that if a plea of guilty is entered, then, in passing sentence, the judge may reduce the sentence he might otherwise have imposed. Direct negotiations between defence lawyers and judges on sentence, commonplace in the United States, do not take place here. Further, the decision in *R v. Turner*[42] makes it clear that judges may not indicate the sentence they are planning to impose, nor indicate how that sentence might change were the defendant to plead guilty.

However, at the end of a hearing, the Criminal Justice and Public Order Act 1994, section 48(2), requires a judge to give reasons for any reduction in the sentence from what would normally be expected for the offence in question taking normal sentencing guidelines into account. The Criminal Justice Act 2003 also requires courts to take into account the stage in the proceedings at which the guilty plea was offered, and the circumstances in which it was made. It is known that in practice judges allow a discount of between 25 and 33 per cent in cases where the defendant pleads guilty. The earlier the plea, the higher the discount.

The formal legal position on these practices is that undue pressure must not be put on defendants to enter any particular plea, as this may lead the innocent to plead guilty to a crime they did not commit. In other words, such practices do not fit with the due process model of the criminal justice system. The reality is, however, that justice is frequently negotiated, a practice justified by the added efficiency that it brings to the system, thus fitting the crime control model. The extent to which such practices should be condoned is the subject of considerable debate in the criminal justice literature.

Jury trial

A second issue of considerable current importance relates to the use of juries to determine the facts in Crown Court trials. Three issues can be considered separately: are juries competent to decide cases? to what extent should the accused be entitled to choose trial by jury in those cases where a choice is open to them? should the classification of indictable offences (for which the right to trial by jury arises automatically) be altered?

The competence of juries. Jury trial is perceived by many as one of the great strengths of the English criminal justice system. There is an enormous literature on

---

[42] [1970] 2 QB 321, CA.

Box 5.12   System in action

Case study: the case of Mr Ponting

There have certainly been historically significant, if rare, cases where juries appear, despite the weight of evidence, to have acted on their conscience to protect civil liberty by finding persons not guilty of crimes which may be said to have significant political overtones. The example of the acquittal of Clive Ponting is often cited. Ponting was a former civil servant, accused of offences under the Official Secrets Act 1911 after he had passed to a Member of Parliament confidential documents relating to the sinking of an Argentinian battleship during the Falklands War in 1982. Despite a ruling from the judge that Ponting had no authorization to pass the documents on, and that there was no other lawful justification for his action, the jury acquitted him. It was assumed that the jury had decided that the moral arguments in favour of his doing what he did outweighed the legal arguments that what he did was unlawful.

juries, asserting their importance as a defender of civil liberty and a bulwark against oppression by the state. Indeed, the use of juries may be said to legitimate decision-taking in the criminal justice system by enabling decisions to be taken by ordinary lay people. This reinforces the independence of the judicial system in this context and thus fits with the constitutional separation of the courts from other decision-making bodies. (*See Box 5.12.*)

Important changes to the constitution and functions of juries have been made over the years. Before 1972, occupation of a house with a prescribed rateable value was one of the criteria for selection.[43] Since then most of the restrictions on jury qualification have gone (with the exception of mentally disordered persons and certain groups of convicted persons). This has led to profound changes in jury composition, certainly in terms of their class composition. Since 1981, selection for jury service has been by random selection using a computer. Perhaps the most significant change occurred in 1967 when the ability of juries to determine cases on the basis of majority verdicts was introduced.[44]

Despite the arguments in favour of jury trial, which have considerable force, little is actually known about how juries function. Direct research into the work of the jury has never been permitted. The only research currently available is through the use of 'surrogate' juries dealing with hypothetical situations.

There have been many suggestions that particular types of case—lengthy and complex fraud trials are given as the prime candidates—are not suitable for jury trial. This

---

[43] Changes were made in the Criminal Justice Act 1972.

[44] See now the Juries Act 1974, s. 17. Majority verdicts are subject to an important *Practice Direction* [1967] 1 WLR 1198, and [1970] 1 WLR 916 which regulates their use. Current data on the use of majority verdicts are given in the text above.

has led to alternative proposals being adopted, for example judges sitting with a panel of lay assessors, or such cases being heard by a panel of judges rather than just a single judge. (There are significant dangers in allowing facts to be found from disputed evidence by a single adjudicator.)

Part 7 of the Criminal Justice Act 2003 makes provision for the possibility of trials without a jury. First, it enables the prosecution to apply for a trial of a serious or complex fraud case to proceed in the absence of a jury. The judge may order the case to be conducted without a jury if he is satisfied that the length or complexity of the case (having regard to steps which might reasonably be taken to reduce it) is likely to make the trial so burdensome upon the jury that the interests of justice require serious consideration to be given to conducting the trial without a jury.

Secondly, the Act provides for a trial to be conducted without a jury where there is a real and present danger of jury tampering, or continued without a jury where the jury has been discharged because of jury tampering. The court must be satisfied that the risk of jury tampering would be so substantial (notwithstanding any steps, including police protection, that could reasonably be taken to prevent it) as to make it necessary in the interests of justice for the trial to be conducted without a jury. In trials already under way where the jury has been discharged because of jury tampering, the trial will continue without a jury unless the judge considers it necessary in the interests of justice to terminate the trial. In that event, he may order a retrial, and if he does he will have the option of ordering that the retrial should take place without a jury.

There is a right of appeal to the Court of Appeal for both prosecution and defence against a determination made by a court on an application for a trial without a jury, and against a court order to continue a trial in the absence of a jury, or to order a retrial without a jury, because of jury tampering. Where a trial is conducted or continued without a jury and a defendant is convicted, the court will be required to give its reasons for the conviction. At the time of writing, four years after enactment, these provisions have not been brought into effect, though they may be if the Fraud (Trials without a Jury) Bill 2007, currently before Parliament, is enacted into law.

Some believe that juries are too ready to acquit defendants. But there are no serious proposals that jury trial should be abolished. Such a step would be seen as politically unacceptable, and as too great a move from the due process model to the crime control model of criminal justice.

Choice of mode of trial. A quite distinct issue, though also a matter of considerable controversy, is the question of who should have the right to choose jury trial in those cases which are triable either way. The present government originally proposed, following the Royal Commission on Criminal Procedure's report in 1993, that the decision should be made by the magistrates before whom all such cases initially come, and not left to the discretion of the accused. Powerful voices dissented, arguing that such a change would involve a fundamental issue of principle which, once conceded, would further undermine the due process model of criminal justice. It looks as though the government has decided not to pursue this issue having unsuccessfully tried twice in recent years to get such a proposal through Parliament.

Should the classification of indictable offences be altered? There is a quite distinct argument that the present classification of offences allows some cases to be tried by juries where this does not seem warranted by the seriousness of the offence. There have been examples of this happening in recent years.[45] There have been other attempts to reclassify certain types of minor theft as summary offences, thereby denying those accused of them the right to trial by jury. Proposals for change are always countered by the 'thin end of the wedge' argument, that any step in this direction will encourage governments to take further steps in the same direction, thereby reducing the scope of jury trial still further. The Criminal Justice Act 2003 took a step in this direction by increasing the sentencing powers of the magistrates' courts from six to twelve months. Thus they are now able to deal with a number of more serious offences which before had to go to the Crown Court for sentencing.

Representation

The criminal defence system is discussed below, Chapter 10, p. 272.

Sentencing

In the same way that the criminal justice system as a whole may be seen to depend on a variety of conflicting social theories, so too is sentencing policy and practice based on a variety of conflicting theories. The literature on theories of sentencing is extensive. Ashworth has classified the approaches under five main headings:

- desert (retributive) theories;
- deterrence theories;
- rehabilitative theories;
- incapacitative theories; and
- restorative (reparative) theories.

Desert or retributive theories take as their focus the idea that punishment is a natural or appropriate response to crime, at least as long as it is proportionate to the crime committed. It is assumed that a person who commits a crime deserves to be punished; and that society is entitled to see that retribution is exacted from the offender. The problem of determining whether sentences are in fact proportional to the offence is, of course, a matter on which there can be great room for debate—and often is when the press criticize judges for apparently light (occasionally over-harsh) sentencing.

Deterrence theories offer a slightly different view. Here the perspective is on deterring future offending behaviour by punishing the offender currently before the authorities. Such a theory would then justify harsher penalties being imposed on an offender who has committed the same offence on more than one occasion than would be the case for a first offender. The research literature does not offer great confidence that, in practice, policies

---

[45] The Criminal Justice Act 1988 reclassified a number of motoring offences as summary only.

of deterrence work. Nonetheless they are very important politically, and indeed have led to the adoption of mandatory sentences for certain categories of repeat offenders.

Rehabilitative sentencing focuses on the offender and efforts to change his behaviour so that he can become a full and productive member of society. It may be assumed that offenders are in some way unable to cope with life and thus need professional support to change. It involves elements of diagnosis and treatment; it also implies that particular decisions need to be tailored to the individual offender.

Incapacitative sentencing focuses on the need to identify particular individuals or groups who are likely to do serious harm in the future, and who therefore need to be removed from society ('incapacitated') to prevent such harm occurring. The difficulties of imposing what may be severe penalties on the basis of what may happen in the future are obvious, but arise, for example, in the context of convicted paedophiles.

Restorative approaches concentrate more on the victim and the need for the offender to make amends to the victim. Restorative justice shares with rehabilitative models the belief that such outcomes will encourage the offender to change his way of life, but the focus on the victim is distinctive. The use of these approaches in youth justice has been noted above.

The Criminal Justice Act 2003 for the first time set out a statutory list of the principles and purposes of sentencing, reflecting the approaches outlined above. Given the conflicting nature of these theories, it is not entirely obvious what the purpose of doing this was. As with general theories of criminal justice, different rationales for sentencing practice need to be understood so that not only the present law but also possible alternatives to it can be assessed.[46]

Determining sentencing policy is extremely hard. Politicians seek to reassure the public that they are taking crime seriously and therefore place emphasis on the deterrent effect of penalties, particularly custodial sentences. They are supported in this by sections of the mass media which make rational discussion of sentencing policy and practice extremely difficult. Concern about the complexity of the law on sentencing led the government, in 2006, to launch a consultation *Making Sentencing Clearer* on whether a simpler approach would be possible, The consultation responses were published in 2007. What policy initiatives will result are not at present known.

Research tends to show that, in many cases, so-called deterrent sentences do not in general deter. This leads to arguments that there should be more emphasis on rehabilitation and reparation. Certainly, the range of penalties available to the courts has grown in recent years. In particular new forms of 'community sentence', in which the offender is obliged to undertake some form of reparative work in the community and for the victim, have been introduced. The problem with community sentences is convincing the public that they are not a 'soft-option'. (For some basic facts on current sentencing outcomes *see Box 5.13*.)

---

[46] The powers of the courts to sentence offenders were consolidated in the Powers of Criminal Courts (Sentencing) Act 2000; they have already undergone major revision, particularly resulting from the enactment of the Criminal Justice Act 2003.

Box 5.13   System in action

Sentencing: some basic facts

In 2005, some 1.49 million offenders were sentenced, having been found guilty of indictable or summary offences.

In the Crown Court, 58 per cent of those sentenced for indictable offences (44,000 offenders) were sentenced to immediate custody, 26 per cent to a community sentence, 2 per cent were fined, and 3 per cent received an absolute or conditional discharge.

The fine was by far the most frequent outcome in the magistrates' courts, used in well over 1 million determinations (73 per cent of the total). Use of community sentences by the magistrates' court increased to 182,000 (13 per cent). In the Crown Court, fines were imposed in just 4 per cent of cases, and community sentences were used in about 30 per cent of cases.

The magistrates' courts and Crown Court together sentenced 108,000 persons to immediate custody in 2005.

Source: Criminal Statistics, 2005 (The Home Office, Statistical Bulletin, 19/06, 2006).

A major review of sentencing policy was published in 2001. Many of the recommendations made in it are now incorporated in the Criminal Justice Act 2003. The principal features of the radically reformed sentencing regime are set out in *Box 5.14*.

Sentencing practice is frequently the subject of (usually adverse) press comment, often ill-informed. Judges and magistrates are often criticized for sentencing too lightly. Yet there are proportionately more people in prison in England and Wales than in almost any other European country. Although more community sentences are now handed down than custodial ones (particularly by magistrates) prison overcrowding remains a source of considerable tension in the criminal justice system. Judges are told both to impose severe sentences where necessary and not to send people to prison unless absolutely essential. Both the design and implementation of sentencing policy is extremely controversial. At least in part this is because there are strongly held assumptions about the effectiveness of particular forms of case disposal which are not borne out either in practice or in the results of research. It is a topic on which rationality is often found to be in short supply.

Assets recovery

An additional form of penalty arises from the principle of assets recovery. Although this has been possible in specific contexts (e.g. seizing the proceeds of drug trafficking) for some time, the principle was put on a more general basis in the Proceeds of Crime Act 2002. This created the Assets Recovery Agency. Its principal objectives are: to disrupt organized criminal enterprises through the recovery of criminal assets, thereby alleviating the effects of crime on communities; and to promote the use of

Box 5.14   System in action

Criminal Justice Act 2003: the principal features

Magistrates' sentencing powers. The Act extends magistrates' sentencing power from six to twelve months. This should reduce the number of cases sent to the Crown Court, particularly those committed there for sentence.

Sentencing Guidelines Council. The Act has established a Sentencing Guidelines Council. Its task is to draft and promulgate sentencing guidelines which are to be taken into account by all criminal courts. The Council acts on recommendations made to it by the Sentencing Advisory Panel. Its guidance relates both to the Crown Court and the magistrates' court. It also offers 'allocation guidelines' when decisions on mode of trial need to be made. As guidelines they are not determinative of individual cases. Courts are required to have regard to them. Significant deviation from them would be the basis for appeals.

Generic community sentences. The Act creates a single community sentence under which the range of measures currently attached to the different types of community orders remain available. It also sets out the tests that must be met before a community order is made. The statutory tests are also supplemented by guidance from the Sentencing Guidelines Council.

Short custodial sentences. These were identified as particularly problematic. They were too short to offer the offender any rehabilitation but when the offender came out from prison, there was no further supervision for him. Recidivism was common. The 2003 Act offers three alternatives. First is 'custody minus'. A short prison sentence can be suspended for up to two years while requirements to do some work in the community which are set by the court are undertaken. If the offender breaches any of the requirements, the custodial term is activated, and the sentence becomes one of custody plus. Committing a further offence during the period of suspension also counts as breach.

Second is 'intermittent custody'. The Act creates a new sentence of intermittent custody in which the custodial element can be served intermittently (for example at weekends). The licence period, complete with requirements set by the court, is served in between the custodial periods and beyond (if applicable).

Third is 'custody plus'. This sentence consists of a custodial period of between two and thirteen weeks, followed by a period of at least six months served in the community on licence within an overall sentence envelope of less than twelve months. Some of the options under the generic community sentence are available as licence conditions.

Sentences of over twelve months. For offenders serving a sentence of over twelve months (apart from the sentences for dangerous offenders outlined below) release is made automatic at the halfway point. They remain on licence until the end of the sentence.

Sentences for dangerous offenders. The Act introduces a new scheme for the sentencing of dangerous adults. Offenders who have committed a specified sexual or violent

Box 5.14 *Continued*

offence and have been assessed as dangerous are to be subject to a life sentence, if the maximum penalty is life. If the maximum penalty is less than this (but is for ten years' imprisonment or more), the offender is subject to a sentence of 'imprisonment for public protection'. The court may impose an 'extended sentence' where the maximum term is between two and ten years' imprisonment. Release from all of these sentences is at the discretion of the Parole Board. These provisions, referred to as indeterminate sentences, are designed to ensure that the most dangerous offenders who continue to pose a risk to the public are kept in prison for an indeterminate period. Recent data shows that judges are using indeterminate sentences far more widely than had been anticipated. A key issue is that one of the ways that those serving indeterminate sentences may seek an application for parole is to show they have taken courses on issues that might help their rehabilitation. However, relevant courses are not always available in the prisons where they are held. This situation is currently the subject of court challenge.

financial investigation as an integral part of criminal investigation, within and outside the Agency, domestically and internationally, through training and continuing professional development. It has been subject to the criticism that its impact to date has been somewhat limited with only rather modest amounts of assets being recovered. In view of these criticisms, the government has decided to abolish the Agency in 2008 and move its work into the Serious Organised Crime Agency (SOCA).[47]

The post-trial stages

Criminal appeals[48]

Those convicted in magistrates' courts can appeal to the Crown Court, either against conviction or against sentence. In 2005, there were over 12,800 appeals from the magistrates' courts to the Crown Court. Of these, about 25 per cent were allowed.

Appeals from the Crown Court can be made to the Court of Appeal (Criminal Division), but only with the leave of the court. In 2005, the Court of Appeal dealt with 7,023 applications for leave to appeal, of which 5,178 were against the sentence imposed, and 1,661 were against conviction. About 1,900 of these applications were granted. Of the appeals actually determined by the full Court of Appeal, over 37 per

---

[47] Provision for this is made in the Serious Crimes Bill 2007 currently before Parliament.

[48] For consideration of appeals in civil cases, see below, Chapter 8, p. 222.

cent of appeals against conviction were allowed, and over 71 per cent of appeals against sentence were allowed.[49]

There is the possibility of a further appeal to the House of Lords, but this can only be exercised with the permission of the court. In 2005, the House of Lords gave leave in only a handful of cases.

Criminal Cases Review Commission

One of the most serious challenges facing the criminal justice system is ensuring that miscarriages of justice do not occur. Notwithstanding the opportunities for appeal and the outcomes of appeals, there will always be cases where the full facts have not emerged at trial or on subsequent appeal, possibly because there have been failures by the police or prosecution to put evidence before the court.

The Criminal Cases Review Commission was established in 1997.[50] It usually considers only those cases that have been through the normal judicial appeal process. It started undertaking casework at the end of March 1997; by the end of August 2007 it had received over 10,000 applications. Of the cases accepted for review, which is only a small percentage of the total, 375 had been referred back to the Court of Appeal. Of the cases dealt with by the Court of Appeal, the conviction was quashed in 235 cases.

Reviews are conducted by case review managers. Decisions on the outcome of the work of the case review managers are taken by the Commission. The Commission has eleven members, appointed from a variety of backgrounds. Any decision to refer a case back to the Court of Appeal is taken by a committee of at least three members.

The function of the Commission is to consider whether there would be a real possibility that a conviction, finding of fact, verdict, or sentence would not be upheld by the court, were a reference back to be made. In relation to reviews of convictions, there has to be either a legal argument or evidence which had not been raised at the trial or on appeal, or other exceptional circumstances; in relation to sentencing, again there has to be legal argument or information about the individual or the offence which was not raised during the trial or on appeal.[51]

Parole and the work of the Parole Board

Even though the court may have imposed a custodial sentence in a particular case, this does not mean that the convicted person will serve the whole period of the sentence.

---

[49] Data from *Judicial Statistics, 2005* (Cm 6799) (London, The Stationery Office, 2005).

[50] Criminal Appeal Act 1995, Part II. This followed recommendations from the Royal Commission on Criminal Justice, 1993. It has had its powers extended to enable it to consider cases where the verdict of 'guilty but insane' was reached: Criminal Cases Review (Insanity) Act 1999. Although this verdict was abolished in the mid-1960s, there is a small number of people whose cases were so determined, who might wish to take advantage of these new provisions. Since 1964 the verdict in such cases is 'not guilty by reason of insanity': Criminal Procedure (Insanity) Act 1964.

[51] A detailed account of the work of the Commission can be found in its *Annual Reports* (London, Criminal Cases Review Commission, annual).

Sentences are subject to review by the Parole Board. This body has been in operation since 1968.[52] Its primary function is to make risk assessments which inform decisions whether prisoners can be released back into the community early. While protection of the public is crucial, the Board seeks to enhance the rehabilitative effect of prison in cases where that seems possible. The responsibilities of the Board vary, depending on different types of case. Important changes to the work of the Board were made by the Criminal Justice Act 2003 (see below).

Determinate sentence cases

Cases determined under the Criminal Justice Act 1991 Where a convicted person was sentenced to a fixed term of imprisonment on or after 1 October 1992, he becomes eligible for parole half-way through his sentence (backdated to include any time spent in custody on remand before the trial).[53] Thus a prisoner sentenced to four years on 2 January 1994, who had also spent six months in custody on remand, became eligible for parole on 2 July 1996—the Parole Eligibility Date (PED).

Six months before the PED, officers of the Parole Board begin gathering the information together to enable a panel from the Parole Board to take an initial decision on whether the prisoner may or may not be suitable for parole. The prisoner may also be interviewed by a Parole Board member. In addition to written reports, the panel is required to take into account *directions* made by the Home Secretary. These give guidance on particular issues on which the panel must be satisfied before finding in favour of the prisoner. While the decision to grant parole is formally one for the Secretary of State, he has delegated his decision-taking powers to the Board in all cases where the prisoner was sentenced to a period of less than fifteen years.[54] At this stage the decision of the Board is a discretionary one; cases are referred to as *discretionary conditional release* (DCR) cases. The latest Annual Report from the Board records that in 2005–6 parole was granted in 49.4 per cent of the 7,300 applications it considered (a lower percentage than previous years).

Whether or not prisoners are released following a Parole Board review, determinate prisoners are automatically released two-thirds of the way through their sentence. However, all those released either after a parole decision or under the automatic process remain subject to supervision by the Probation Service and are subject to recall either for re-offending or for other breaches of the probation supervision until 75 per cent of the period of the sentence has expired. Although the supervision of the Probation Service ends at that point, the remaining 25 per cent of the sentence can be reactivated if the person is subsequently committed for another criminal offence.

The Criminal Justice Act 2003 made recall to custody an executive decision—by the prison and probation services—rather than by the Parole Board, itself. The

---

[52] It was established under the provisions of the Criminal Justice Act 1967.

[53] For those sentenced before 1 October 1992, the date of eligibility for parole arose one-third of the way through the sentence.

[54] Until 1998 the upper limit for Parole Board decisions was sentences for less than seven years.

offender has the right of appeal to the Parole Board, and even if the offender chooses not to exercise this right the Parole Board nonetheless scrutinizes all recall decisions to ensure they are fairly taken. By allowing the Parole Board to focus on assessing decisions of recall, the Act removed an anomaly whereby the Parole Board both advised on recalls and acted as an appeal body against those same recalls.

Cases determined under the Criminal Justice Act 2003 For these cases, prisoners are automatically released on licence once they have served half their sentence. They remain on licence until the end of their nominal sentence. Thus the Board is no longer involved in the initial decision to release. However, they retain a key role in deciding what should happen should a decision be taken to recall a prisoner for breach of the licence. The Parole Board reviews such cases, if necessary holding an oral hearing to hear representations from the prisoner. The House of Lords held in the case of *Smith and West* [55] that those recalled had the right to make oral representations. This has resulted in a very significant increase in oral hearings: 1,900 in 2005–2006, up 42 per cent on the previous year. The role of the Board has, therefore, become more like an administrative tribunal, less like a decision-taking agency.

Life sentences

The Parole Board also has important responsibilities in relation to life sentences. There are two sorts of life sentence: *mandatory* life sentences, where the judge must impose a life sentence (as in the case of a conviction for murder); and *discretionary* life sentences, where this was the sentence that the judge decided was appropriate because of the risk that the offender would commit another offence. (The Board also has responsibilities relating to those subject to the new indeterminate sentence of Imprisonment for Public Protection: *see above Box 5.14.*)

The starting point is a decision on *the tariff*. This is the minimum period which the prisoner is to serve. Under the provisions of the Crime (Sentences) Act 1997, the tariff for mandatory lifers was fixed by the Home Secretary taking into account a recommendation of the trial judge. Following a decision of the European Court of Human Rights,[56] the House of Lords declared that the imposition of the tariff was indistinguishable from sentencing, and thus in effect part of the trial process.[57] As Article 6 of the European Convention on Human Rights requires that tribunals deciding criminal trials must be independent, the role of the Home Secretary was incompatible with Article 6.[58] The tariff in all cases is now set by the trial judge.

---

[55] [2005] UKHL 1.

[56] *Stafford v. United Kingdom* (Application No. 46295/99, 28 May 2002).

[57] R *v. Secretary of State for the Home Department, ex p Anderson* [2002] UKHL 46. In the same judgment, the Lords also held that a mandatory life sentence for murder was not incompatible with the provisions of the European Convention on Human Rights.

[58] In R *v. Secretary of State for the Home Department, ex p V and T* [1998] AC 407, the House of Lords held that it was unlawful for the Home Secretary to set a tariff relating to a young person which did not take into account the provisions of the UN Convention on the Rights of the Child. The European Court of Human Rights has now held in *T v. United Kingdom, V v. United Kingdom* (1999) 30 EHRR 121 that setting a tariff is

Three years before the expiry of the tariff, the case is reviewed by the Parole Board which considers whether or not a prisoner is suitable to be moved to the more relaxed regime of an open prison. On the expiry of the tariff, the Parole Board considers whether the prisoner is suitable for release on licence. If it decides to release on licence, the prisoner will still be subject to supervision by the Probation Service, for at least four years. At that point (or later) the Home Secretary may decide that the supervision requirements can be lifted. The prisoner remains liable to recall and for the balance of his sentence to be reactivated for the rest of his life, should there be reason for so doing, such as subsequent offending.

If the Parole Board concludes that, on the expiry of the tariff, release would not be appropriate, the case is reviewed normally every two years.

Procedure

The process of reaching these decisions does, however, vary. In the case of *mandatory* lifers, the decision-taking process is similar to that for determinate sentences. Reports are prepared; an interview is held by a member of the Parole Board with the prisoner; and a decision is reached on the papers. Mandatory lifer panels are specially constituted to include a judge and a psychiatrist. Again the panel is required to take into account *directions* prescribed by the Home Secretary. Originally, the actual decision was taken by the Home Secretary; the Parole Board panel could only make a recommendation. The Criminal Justice Act 2003 provides that the Board should take the decision.

For *discretionary* lifers, the process of review involves the compilation of a dossier of reports. But there is then a fundamentally important difference. An oral hearing (rather like a tribunal hearing) is listed before a discretionary lifer panel of the Parole Board (which includes a judge and a psychiatrist). The prisoner is entitled to legal representation at this hearing. At the conclusion of the hearing, the panel may recommend transfer to open prison conditions, or may in appropriate cases direct release. In 2005–6, the Board arranged over 1,900 hearings relating to discretionary lifers or those subject to indeterminate sentences who were seeking release on parole. (This was over 40 per cent higher than the previous year.)

The place of the victim

One of the ways in which the criminal justice system has been transformed in recent years is through increased recognition of the victim of crime. As has already been noted, the position of the victim is fundamental to the whole criminal justice system since the victim's report that a crime has been committed is, save for the most serious

---

a sentencing function which should not be carried out by a member of the executive arm of government but by an independent tribunal.

offences, the key to further steps being taken in the criminal process. Further, as also noted, the viewpoint of the victim is one of the factors taken into account by the CPS in reaching a decision whether or not to prosecute a case. There are respects in which sentencing policy reflects the impact the criminal activity may have had on the victim. Much of the activity in the youth justice system is designed to make the offender aware of the victim's perceptions of what he has done. The Home Office sought to bring support for victims (and witnesses) together in its *Victims' Charter* (originally published in 1997).

In recent years the place of the victim has started to have greater statutory recognition. Many of the provisions in the Criminal Justice Act 2003, for example those relating to bail or the use of video links, are designed to assist victims and other witnesses to give evidence.

More specifically the Domestic Violence, Crime and Victims Act 2004 contains a number of provisions designed to ensure that the victim is kept informed about the progress of a case, and about the release of a prisoner. Among the measures included are, first, the Victim's Charter is transformed into a statutory code of guidance, which must be endorsed by Parliament.

Second it provides that, where a court convicts a person (the 'offender') for a sexual or violent offence and imposes a prison sentence of a minimum of twelve months, the local probation board must take reasonable steps to establish whether the victim of the offence wishes to make representations about whether the offender should be subject to conditions on release (and if so, what conditions), or wishes to receive information about those conditions. If the victim does express such a wish, the relevant local probation board becomes responsible for forwarding any representations the victim makes to the authority responsible for making the decisions about release. The board is also responsible for informing the victim whether the offender will be subject to any conditions in the event of release; for providing details of any conditions about contact with the victim or his family; and for providing any other information it considers appropriate. Similar provisions apply where an offender has been detained under the provisions of the Mental Health Act.

Third, the jurisdiction of the Parliamentary Commissioner for Administration is expanded so that she can investigate and report on complaints that a duty under the code of practice for victims has been breached. These relate to complaints that any person has failed to comply with a duty to victims relating to the need to keep victims informed. The Parliamentary Commissioner has the same powers to obtain evidence and examine witnesses as she has in relation to complaints of maladministration.

Fourth, the Act provides for the creation of the post of Commissioner for Victims and Witnesses. The Commissioner's primary functions are: to promote the interests of victims and witnesses of crime and anti-social behaviour; and to take steps to encourage good practice in their treatment and to keep the code of guidance under review. The Commissioner is given various ways in which he can carry out these functions, including making a report to the Secretary of State, commissioning research, and making recommendations to an authority within his remit (a broadly defined group of those working in and around the criminal justice system). Further, the Commissioner must provide advice on issues relating to victims and witnesses of crime and anti-social behaviour when requested to do so by any government minister. The authorities within the Commissioner's remit may also ask the Commissioner to give specific advice in connection with the information they provide, through whatever medium, to victims and witnesses.

Fifth, the Act provides for the appointment of a Victims' Advisory Panel which the Home Secretary can consult on matters relating to victims and witnesses of crime and of anti-social behaviour. The Panel is required to publish an annual report if the Secretary of State has consulted it during a particular year. This replaces the non-statutory Victims' Advisory Panel which met for the first time on 3 March 2003. The membership of the current Panel comprises ten voluntary lay members, who have direct experience of victimization, three co-opted members representing wider victims' interests, representatives of voluntary organizations to which the government provides core funding to provide direct services to victims and witnesses, and senior officials from criminal justice agencies. The most recent development has been the possibility of the victim's relatives being able to make a statement to the court in murder and manslaughter cases.

Three further developments may be briefly noted: victim support schemes, the criminal injuries compensation scheme, and compensation orders.

Victim support schemes

There are now about 365 local victim support schemes with some 15,000 volunteers offering help to over 1.5 million victims. In the Crown Court, there are another 1,500+ volunteers helping over 120,000 victims and witnesses who have to attend court. These do a great deal of work trying to reassure the victims of crime that they have not been targeted, but are simply the victims of opportunistic criminal activity. They also help victims and other witnesses cope with the stress and strain of appearing in court.

The Criminal Injuries Compensation Scheme

This has been in operation for many years. This state-funded scheme was revised in 2001. It is administered by the Criminal Injuries Compensation Authority. Currently, the scheme pays about £200 million compensation to some 39,000 successful claimants. (Around 50 per cent of applications are unsuccessful.) The scheme is limited to those victims who have been injured as the result of violent criminal activity directed towards them. Critics point out that other negative consequences of being the victim of crime are not thus compensated.

Two specific points may be noted. First, the amounts of compensation paid are defined in a statutory tariff; they are not assessed in the same way as damages for personal injury in civil litigation. This leads to complaints that the scheme under-compensates the victims of crime, particularly where they have suffered other than by way of physical injury. Second, as a result of amendments in the Domestic Violence, Crime and Victims Act 2004, it is now provided that the courts, when making a compensation order (see below), can require sums obtained from the offender to be used to compensate the Compensation Injuries Fund (in cases where an award from the fund has been made).

Compensation orders

In addition to this statutory scheme, it may also be noted that since 1972 the criminal courts have had power to order those convicted of crimes to pay compensation to their victims. These powers have been developed so that there are circumstances in which a compensation order may be imposed as the sole penalty. Since 1988, the courts have been required to consider making compensation orders in defined groups of cases involving death, injury, loss or damage, and to give reasons where an order is not made. And since 1991 the limits on the sums which magistrates may order as compensation have been increased. These developments may be seen as more reparative forms of outcome for the criminal justice system.

A strategic approach to criminal justice?

Underpinning all the reforms of the criminal justice system that have been considered above has been the recognition by successive governments of the need for a more integrated approach to dealing with crime. Numerous initiatives have been taken in recent years to try to deliver this. Indeed the pace of change has been breath-taking. Things have moved so quickly that it is often hard to assess the impact of all this change on the ground. The objective of a more integrated approach is clearly sensible. But these often involve getting those working in the criminal justice system to work in new ways. Unless there is a clearly defined and well-run programme of change management, the outcomes may not be as fully integrated on the ground as system planners may hope. At present, the effects of all these changes are not clear; too much has happened too recently.

There are complaints from many quarters about the pace of change. But clearly the government wants results, not least to satisfy political demands to be seen to be getting on top of crime. The latest strategic statement is to be found in the *Strategic Plan for Criminal Justice 2004–2008*. Two newly emerging themes may be noted in this final section. First, a new approach to the delivery of criminal justice is the subject of a very important trial in Liverpool—the Community Justice Centre (*see Box 5.15*).

Secondly, a new approach to the role and work of the various criminal justice inspectorates was proposed in a consultation in 2005. If it had gone ahead it would have led to the creation of a new Justice and Community Safety Inspectorate. While the paper made a powerful case for reform, there were concerns that an amalgamated inspectorate would become less focused on specific problems in the criminal justice system (e.g. prison conditions) that need addressing. Despite the government's initial commitment to the idea, the proposal for a single inspectorate is not currently being advanced. (See Box, 5.16).

Box 5.15   Time for change

Case study: the North Liverpool Community Justice Centre

This new initiative is designed, in the government's words, 'to improve quality of life in the area by reducing criminal activity and the fear of crime, while providing advice and support to the community'. It is based on a successful project in New York City. The centre, which opened fully in 2005, is the first of its kind in England and Wales. It is designed to work in partnership with local people to provide help with a wide range of problems and deal with offences committed against the community that affect quality of life, for example vandalism, fly-tipping, and graffiti. The centre also provides access to support, social, and education services for both offenders and local residents. It contains a court-room, run by a single judge, who works closely with the community, to provide consistency for offenders and check that they carry out the sentences they have been given. Over 200 North Liverpool residents including parents, teenagers, senior citizens, the long-term unemployed, and local business people joined with probation officers and ex-offenders to help develop plans for the Community Justice Centre and discuss how a more holistic approach to low-level offending can have a positive impact on their local neighbourhoods.

Findings from independent research among a number of residents, which covered the wards of Anfield, Everton, Kirkdale, and Walton within the Atlantic Partnership area, give a clear indication of how the Community Justice Centre can provide a new approach to dealing with criminals damaging the quality of life for residents. Research showed that the overall perception is that crime in the area is a problem, with major areas of concern being drugs and youth gangs. Against this background, over three-quarters of those participating believed that the Community Justice Centre is, or could be, a good idea. Nearly three-quarters of the residents interviewed were concerned that offenders should be sent to court, be sentenced and rehabilitated quickly. They also believed that sentences should be set that involve completing work to benefit the local neighbourhood. Over half thought that the community should have a say in the type and location of unpaid work done as part of a sentence. Two-thirds of those interviewed supported the idea of a single judge who will make sure that offenders carry out their sentences and three-quarters thought the community should be able to report what is going on in their area, safely. There is clear agreement that the centre should place an emphasis on dealing with anti-social behaviour-type offences, like car crime, criminal damage, and fly-tipping. (There are now a dozen community justice courts in operation around the country.)

Box 5.15   *Continued*

Judge David Fletcher, who leads the centre, has said:

There is a lot of support out there for the idea of community justice. Residents are telling us they want improvements to their quality of life, including the need for people to
feel safer, have better support and a better environment to live in. The centre represents
the most radical change to occur in the justice system for decades. While focusing on
reducing crime through tackling its root causes and offering long-term support to the
community, we can help all law-abiding citizens to be heard, without fear of reprisal or
intimidation.

Merseyside Police, the Crown Prosecution Service, probation and youth offending
teams all have offices on-site to provide a joined-up, problem-solving approach to
offending. The centre also aims to bring a number of other community advice and
support services under one roof.

Box 5.16   Time for change

Inspectorates in the Criminal Justice system

The current inspection regime comprises: Her Majesty's Inspectorate of Constabulary
(HMIC); Her Majesty's Crown Prosecution Service Inspectorate (HMCPSI); Her Majesty's
Inspectorate of Court Administration (HMICA); Her Majesty's Inspectorate of Prisons
(HMI Prisons); and Her Majesty's Inspectorate of Probation (HMI Probation). Although
constituted differently, they all predominantly ensure the safe and proper delivery of
the services inspected and promulgate good practice.

- HMIC has a stated purpose to promote the efficiency and effectiveness of policing
  through inspection of police organizations and functions to ensure agreed standards
  are achieved and maintained, good practice is spread, and performance is improved.
  It has a developing remit, with its inspection responsibilities growing to include
  Her Majesty's Revenue and Customs (HMRC) enforcement work and the Serious
  Organised Crime Agency (SOCA)—two large non-police agencies. It also provides
  advice and support to the Home Secretary, police authorities and forces and plays a
  role in the development of future leaders.
- HMCPSI has a stated purpose to promote continuous improvement in the efficiency,
  effectiveness, and fairness of the prosecution services within a joined-up criminal
  justice system, through the process of inspection, evaluation, and identification of
  good practice. It inspects the Customs and Excise Prosecutions Office on a non-
  statutory basis.

Box 5.16 *Continued*

- HMICA has responsibility for inspecting and reporting on the performance of court administration. It will also have a duty to inspect and report on the performance of the Children and Family Court Advisory Support Service (CAFCASS).
- HMI Prisons has a remit to inspect prison establishments and to report on the conditions of those establishments, the treatment of prisoners and other inmates, and the facilities available to them. The Inspectorate also undertakes inspection of immigration removal centres and, by invitation, the military corrective centre.
- HMI Probation reports on the work and performance of the National Probation Service and of Youth Offending Teams (YOTs), particularly on the effectiveness of work aimed at reducing re-offending and protecting the public. It contributes to policy and service delivery by providing advice and disseminating good practice.

HMI Prisons and HMI Probation are jointly developing a shared approach to inspection of offender management as it is developed by the National Offender Management Service (NOMS).

The five inspectorates undertake both single agency inspection and joint inspection:

Single agency inspection: The statutory remit of each inspectorate requires them to inspect and report on the performance of their relevant organization (or for prisons the treatment and conditions of those in custody). This can be done via cyclical inspection of an area, risk-based inspection of an area, or thematic inspections on a particular topic. Given the current remit of the five inspectorates, their primary attention is on the safe and proper delivery of services within their separate organizations.

Joint inspection: This can take the form of either routine or thematic inspections conducted by more than one inspectorate, on a particular topic involving more than one inspected organization. These can be done both within the CJS and outside in areas such as education, health, or local services, for example HMI Prisons routinely inspects with OfSTED, the Royal Pharmaceutical Society and the British Dental Board. Currently joint inspections are resourced from existing budgets and must take into account the resource demands of single agency inspection. To facilitate cross-CJS inspection, in 1998, the Chief Inspectors established a Criminal Justice Chief Inspectors Group (CJCIG) to undertake inspections within the CJS on a joint basis. Since then the number of joint inspections has increased; initially they were thematic in nature, but since 2003 the five inspectorates have combined together to start inspecting Criminal Justice Areas (or Local Criminal Justice Boards).

The Consultation Paper argued that there was a need for institutional reform :

- the police reform programme had introduced fundamental changes to the police service that call for the examination of the remit of HMIC, to consider how police inspection can support a modernized police service and fit with new bodies such as the National Policing Improvement Agency;

Box 5.16   *Continued*

- the changes to the charging process, which involves CPS lawyers in police stations deciding on charges in all but minor cases, and providing the police with early legal advice before and during the charging process, have introduced a new partnership approach between the police and the CPS (the prosecution team). This involves the CPS working with the police locally to implement performance measures and procedures. These new arrangements require a joined up inspection regime to support effective implementation and delivery; and
- the creation of a National Offender Management Service (NOMS) has initiated major change in the delivery of correctional services, introducing end-to-end management of offenders, whether they serve their sentence in prison, the community, or both. The creation of a purchaser–provider split in the provision of services means that NOMS will focus on specifying service standards and procuring services rather than running them directly, a shift a new inspection regime needs to address.

Notwithstanding the arguments for bringing together the large number of existing inspection functions, the proposed new inspectorate is not to be being taken forward for the time being.

Source: Adapted from *Inspection Reform: A Consultation Document* (CJS, March 2005).

Comment

There can be little doubt about the importance the present government attaches to reform of the criminal justice system. Not content with all the changes that have already been made, there are clear political suggestions that yet more change is in the air. Another strategy document, *Cutting Crime: a new Partnership 2008–2011* was published in 2007. An important question must be: should there be a period of reflection before the introduction of any further institutional or legislative change? Or do political pressures on Home Secretaries prevent this?

Questions for reflection and discussion

1. What do you think are the primary objectives of the criminal justice system? How far are they consistent?
2. How can the tension between the 'due process' and 'crime control' models be managed?
3. Do the police have too many/too few powers?
4. Should everyone be required to provide a DNA sample for the national DNA database?
5. Are the rules of evidence too heavily weighted in favour of the alleged offender?

6. Should the criminal justice system become more 'victim-focused'?

7. What are the primary objectives of sentencing policy?

8. Are too many people sentenced to prison? What are the alternatives to prison?

9. Can mandatory sentences be justified? Or should sentencers always retain sentencing discretion?

10. Should the rules relating to jury trial be changed?

11. Should it be possible to undertake research into the jury?

12. Do you think the community justice centre model offers a sensible way forward for the criminal justice system?

13. Should the pace of reform be reduced?

Further reading

ASHWORTH, A., *Sentencing and Criminal Justice* (4th edn., Cambridge, Cambridge University Press, 2005)

—— and REDMAYNE, M., *The Criminal Process* (3rd edn., Oxford, Oxford University Press, 2005)

AULD, LORD JUSTICE, *A Review of the Criminal Courts of England and Wales* (London, The Stationery Office, 2001)

BALDWIN, J., and McCONVILLE, M., *Jury Trials* (Oxford, Clarendon Press, 1979)

BARCLAY, G., and TAVARES, C. (eds), *DIGEST 4—Information on the Criminal Justice System* (London, Home Office, 1999)

BELLONI, F., and HODGSON, J., *Criminal Injustice: An Evaluation of the Criminal Justice Process in Britain* (London, Palgrave Macmillan, 1999)

CAVADINO, P., and GIBSON, B., *Introduction to the Criminal Justice Process* (2nd edn., Winchester, Waterside Press, 2002)

CLEMENTS, P., *Policing a Diverse Society* (Oxford, Oxford University Press, 2006)

CORNISH, W.R., *The Jury* (Harmondsworth, Penguin, 1971)

CRAWFORD, A., and NEWBURN, T., *Youth Offending and Restorative Justice:* *Implementing Reform in Youth Justice* (Cullompton, Willan Publishing, 2003)

DAVIES, M., *Criminal Justice: An Introduction to the Criminal Justice System in England and Wales* (3rd edn., Harlow, Longman, 2005)

ELLISON, L., *The Adversarial Process and the Vulnerable Witness* (Oxford, Oxford University Press, 2002)

HALLIDAY, J., *Making Punishments Work: Report of a Review of the Sentencing Framework for England and Wales* (London, Home Office, 2001)

HAWKINS, K., *Law as Last Resort: Prosecution Decision-making in a Regulatory Agency* (Oxford, Oxford University Press, 2003)

HENHAM, R., *Sentence Discounts and the Criminal Process* (Aldershot, Dartmouth, 2001)

HOOD, R., in collaboration with CORDOVIL, G., *Race and Sentencing: a Study in the Crown Court: a Report for the Commission for Racial Equality* (Oxford, Clarendon Press, 1992)

McCABE, S., and PURVES, R., *The Jury at Work: a Study of a Series of Jury Trials in which the Defendant was Acquitted* (Oxford, Blackwell for the Oxford University Penal Research Unit, 1972)

McCabe, S., and Purves, R., *The Shadow Jury at Work: an Account of a Series of Deliberations and Verdicts where 'Shadow' Juries were Present During Actual Trials* (Oxford, Blackwell for the Oxford University Penal Research Unit, 1974)

McConville, M., and Mirsky, C.L., *Jury Trials and Plea Bargaining: A True History* (Oxford, Hart, 2005)

—— and Wilson, G. (eds), *The Handbook of the Criminal Justice Process* (Oxford, Oxford University Press, 2002)

Macpherson of Cluny, Sir William, *The Stephen Lawrence Inquiry Report* (Cm 4262) (London, The Stationery Office, 1999)

Maguire, M., Morgan, R., and Reiner, R. (eds), *The Oxford Handbook of Criminology* (3rd edn., Oxford, Clarendon Press, 2002)

Padfield, N., *Text and Materials on the Criminal Justice Process* (4th edn., Oxford University Press, forthcoming, 2008)

Robertshaw, P., *Jury and Judge: the Crown Court in Action* (Aldershot, Dartmouth, 1995)

Sanders, A., and Young, R., *Criminal Justice* (3rd edn., Oxford University Press 2006)

Walker, N., *Policing in a Changing Constitutional Order* (London, Sweet & Maxwell, 2000)

Websites

http://www.cjsonline.org/index.html *(Portal to criminal justice system)*

http://www.cjsonline.gov.uk/the_cjs/departments_of_the_cjs/ocjr/index.html *(Home page of the Office for Criminal Justice Reform)*

http://www.justice.gov.uk/about/criminal-proc-rule-committee.htm *(Criminal procedure rules committee)*

http://police.homeoffice.gov.uk/operational-policing/powers-pace-codes/pace-code-intro/ *(Introduction to police powers)*

http://www.met.police.uk/stopandsearch/ *(Report on use of stop and search powers)*

http://police.homeoffice.gov.uk/operational-policing/powers-pace-codes/ *(Text of PACE codes)*

http://police.homeoffice.gov.uk/operational-policing/powers-pace-codes/stop-search1.html/?view=Standard *(Stop and Search Action Team)*

http://www.sentencing-guidelines.gov.uk/ *(Homepage of the Sentencing Guidelines Council and link to the Sentencing Advisory Panel)*

http://www.hmcourts-service.gov.uk/onlineservices/xhibit/index.htm *(Information about the HMCS Xhibit scheme tracking cases through the criminal courts)*

http://www.apa.police.uk/apa/ *(Association of Police Authorities)*

http://inspectorates.homeoffice.gov.uk/hmic/ *(HM Inspectorate of Constabulary, with links to other inspectorates)*

http://www.cps.gov.uk/ *(Crown Prosecution Service)*

http://www.cps.gov.uk/victims_witnesses/code.html *(Sets out the Code of Practice for Crown Prosecutors)*

http://www.hmcpsi.gov.uk/ *(Crown Prosecution Inspectorate)*

http://www.sfo.gov.uk/ *(Serious Fraud Office)*

http://www.legalservices.gov.uk/criminal.asp *(Criminal Defence Service)*

http://www.ipcc.gov.uk/ *(Independent Police Complaints Commission)*

http://www.cjsonline.gov.uk/witness/help_and_support/index.html *(Witness care service)*

https://www.cica.gov.uk/portal/page?_pageid=115,1&_dad=portal&_schema=PORTAL/ *(Criminal Injuries Compensation Authority)*

http://www.noms.homeoffice.gov.uk/ *(National offender management service)*

http://www.probation.homeoffice.gov.uk/output/Page1.asp *(National Probation Service)*

http://inspectorates.homeoffice.gov.uk/hmiprobation/ *(HM Inspectorate of Probation)*

http://www.hmprisonservice.gov.uk/

http://inspectorates.homeoffice.gov.uk/hmiprisons/ *(HM Inspectorate of Prisons)*

http://www.ppo.gov.uk/ *(Prisons and probation ombudsman)*

http://www.yjb.gov.uk/en-gb/ *(Youth justice board)*

http://www.respect.gov.uk/ *(Homepage for the respect agenda)*

http://www.hm-treasury.gov.uk/media/2/6/cyp_tenyearstrategy_260707.pdf *(Aiming high for young people: a ten year strategy for positive activities)*

http://www.magistrates-association.org.uk/

http://www.jc-society.com/ *(Justices' Clerks' Society)*

http://www.statistics.gov.uk/CCI/nscl.asp?ID=5004&x=126&y=15 *(National Statistics crime and justice statistics)*

http://www.homeoffice.gov.uk/rds/bcs1.html *(British Crime Survey)*

http://www.homeoffice.gov.uk/rds/pdfs06/hosb1906.pdf *(2005 Criminal statistics)*

http://www.ccrc.gov.uk/ *(Criminal Cases Review Commission)*

http://www.paroleboard.gov.uk/

http://www.victimsupport.org.uk/ *(Victim Support)*

http://www.homeoffice.gov.uk/documents/victims-charter?version=1 *(Victims' Charter)*

http://www.homeoffice.gov.uk/science-research/using-science/dna-database/

http://www.homeoffice.gov.uk/documents/crime-strategy-07/

6

The administrative justice system

Introduction

Although the criminal justice system, discussed in the previous chapter, is institutionally extremely complex, the primary focus of the system—on the regulation of forms of social behaviour, and dealing with those who transgress the rules—is relatively clear. By contrast, the very concept of 'administrative justice' is controversial, meaning different things to different people. Traditional analyses of the legal system, focusing exclusively on criminal and civil law, have failed to acknowledge a separate system of 'administrative justice'. Instead, it gets wrapped up in general discussion of the civil justice system.

In part, this reflects the continuing influence of the nineteenth century writer A. V. Dicey, who argued that there should not be a separately identifiable body of *droit administratif* (administrative law). He thought that this would result in public officials being given legally preferential treatment and thus offend against the fundamental principle of the rule of law, that all should be equal under the law.

Over 100 years on, the reality is that the state plays a large part in the regulation of society; and there is a vast array of institutions employing individuals who provide public services. Although there may still not be a conceptually distinct branch of the law which may be described as administrative law, as there is for example in many of the countries in Continental Europe, any understanding of the modern English legal system must involve recognizing the distinct concept of administrative justice.

The primary focus of this chapter is on the institutions in which administrative law is practised. First, however, we reflect on the nature of administrative law and the role it plays in modern society.

The role of administrative law: authority and values

As already noted, one of the features of the twentieth century—which has continued into the twenty-first—has been the significant role of government in developing and implementing a vast range of social policies. Implementation of social policy depends on law. Administrative law:

- provides authority for public servants to deliver government policy, whose legitimacy is enshrined in the laws (primary, secondary, and tertiary—*see above, Box 3.2*) passed through the parliamentary system;
- authorizes the raising and expenditure of public funds;
- sets limits to the powers of public officials;
- creates the institutional mechanisms for calling public officials to account; and
- provides means for the redress of individual grievances or resolution of complaints by the citizen.

In addition to the functional attributes of administrative law, administrative justice embraces certain *values* or *principles,* which should underpin good administration by state officials, and others who deliver services on behalf of the state. These include: openness (or transparency); fairness; rationality (including the giving of reasons for decisions); impartiality (independence) of decision-takers; accountability; the prevention of the exercise of arbitrary power and the control of discretion; consistency; participation; efficiency; equity; and equal treatment.

These underlying values of administrative justice are not wholly consistent one with the other. There may be circumstances in which openness may properly yield to confidentiality; where fairness of process may conflict with efficiency. Each of these values is contingent upon the context in which it is asserted. One of the challenges for those who govern, and for those who criticize government, is to achieve an appropriate balance between conflicting values.

The details of particular areas of substantive public law (for example rules relating to social security) are not for discussion here. Rather the focus is on the mechanisms of accountability which exist to keep officials in check and which provide means of resolving disputes when things go wrong. But readers should reflect on the tensions between the different values in administrative justice in the context of particular administrative activities—for example, the determination of asylum applications; or the collection of taxes; or the granting of planning permissions; or the payment of social security benefits.

Administrative justice: the institutional framework

A great variety of bodies and processes make up the institutional framework of administrative justice. They include:

- courts;
- tribunals;
- inquiries;

- ombudsmen;

- complaints procedures.

Each of these is considered below. This is another area where there has been rapid development over the last fifty years. It is one of the most dynamic areas of the English legal system.

This way of conceptualizing the framework of administrative justice is not wholly orthodox. Practising lawyers tend to think of administrative law as, in essence, the special process available in the High Court known as *judicial review*. Academic lawyers go beyond this court-focused approach to include in their analyses comments on other mechanisms for the resolution of disputes. But the treatment tends to be somewhat superficial, and even here the balance is normally tilted in favour of the court's role.[1] There are perfectly good reasons for this:

(1) The *qualitative* importance of the law of judicial review is clear. It is the reported decisions of judges in the Administrative Court and above that have developed the jurisprudence of judicial review. The fundamental principles—procedural fairness, and limiting the exercise of discretionary power by officials—are the creation of the courts. The range of persons permitted to bring proceedings by way of judicial review has been expanded. The numbers of bodies and institutions subjected to the principles of judicial review have been significantly widened. The grounds on which judicial review may be sought have also been developed. Judicial review provides the legal background against which the administrative justice system operates. This is largely the work of the courts—judges asserting their independence over the executive. The importance of this work has been expanded by the Human Rights Act 1998, which enshrines further principles against which official actions can be tested in the courts.

(2) It is in the courts that practising lawyers earn good money and develop formidable reputations. With rare exceptions, legal aid is not available to pay for legal representation before tribunals or other dispute resolution/grievance handling fora. This reduces the incentive for legal practitioners to get to know about the wider world of administrative justice.

(3) The work of this wider range of bodies is often not the subject of formal published documentation. Legal scholars find it hard to access the material needed for a full review of the administrative justice system as a whole.

Nevertheless, concentration on judicial review—a procedure that results in about 4,000 applications being brought before the courts each year (with only a much smaller number going to a full hearing)—means that other procedures for the delivery of administrative justice are not paid the attention they are due. For example, the Appeals Service, which adjudicates on social security disputes, decided nearly 165,000 appeals in 2006–7; the Asylum and Immigration Tribunal disposed of over

---

[1] There are honourable exceptions: Harlow, C. and Rawlings, R., *Law and Administration* (2nd edn., London, Butterworths, 1997).

156,000 immigration appeals in the same period; Employment Tribunals dealt with nearly 80,000 cases; Mental Health Review Tribunals determined over 11,500.[2] Many other examples could be given. The large number of ombudsmen that now exist handle thousands more cases in a year. A variety of complaints procedures deal with countless other grievances. *Quantitatively* these other mechanisms are far more significant than the courts. This account seeks to redress the balance.

There are two important reasons for making this argument which arise not just from a desire to be different. First, what the administrative justice system—taken as a whole—provides is a vast test bed for the development and evaluation of new procedures:

- decisions being taken on the papers;
- decisions by a single judge;
- decisions by three- (or more-) person tribunals; and
- procedures involving the unrepresented and inarticulate.

It is one of the great wasted opportunities that those who have sought in recent years to introduce change into the civil justice system should have paid such scant attention to what goes on in practice in the administrative justice system. It provides a rich source of ideas regarding how things might be done differently. Those who in the past may have looked down their noses at the administrative justice system as 'not being proper courts' should think again. It is here that alternative procedures are to be found, often working extremely well.

Secondly, the failure to see the administrative justice system in a more holistic fashion prevents people from seeing the enormous variety of ways that exist for seeking the redress of citizens' grievances. This broader approach is currently at the heart of the government's programme of reform of the administrative justice system (see below). It is a theme that was taken up by the National Audit Office (NAO) in its important report on citizen redress (*see Box 6.1*).

Box 6.1   Time for change

Citizen redress

An important and distinctive feature of public services are the arrangements in place for getting things put right, remedying grievances or securing a second view of a disputed decision. We use the 'citizen redress' label to denote all the administrative mechanisms that allow citizens to seek remedies for what they perceive to be poor treatment, mistakes, faults, or injustices in their dealings with central government departments or agencies. Of course,

---

[2] Council on Tribunals, *Annual Report, 2006/2007* (HC 733) (London, TSO, 2007), Appendix G.

Box 6.1   *Continued*

redress mechanisms may not find in favour of the citizens making complaints or bringing appeals. Indeed, in a well-run administrative system the large majority of cases investigated should prove to be unfounded. Yet even in such cases the redress processes used should provide people with assurance that they have been fairly and properly treated or that a disputed decision has been correctly made under the relevant rules.

The systems currently in place for the citizen to seek remedy when things go wrong have developed over time and for a variety of different purposes. Inevitably, this has resulted in complexity and variations in attitude and approach. Against this backdrop, this report is not a single definitive analysis of redress; instead it is a first attempt to map the overall picture. It draws out key themes which can be explored further by the NAO working in conjunction with ombudsmen and other key participants, to help identify ways in which the effective handling of redress can, in turn, lead to major improvements in the quality of services the citizen receives.

The main mechanisms for achieving redress currently are: customer complaints procedures; appeals and tribunals systems; references to independent complaints handlers or ombudsmen; and resort to judicial review (and other forms of legal action).

In cases where something is found to have gone wrong, one important outcome of such mechanisms may be the payment of compensation. The different redress mechanisms interconnect strongly. From the citizens' point of view they offer a range of different options and opportunities for trying to achieve very similar or connected outcomes. And from government organizations' points of view, the efficacy of some redress procedures may imply fewer cases running through other routes. For instance, good basic complaints-handling systems should minimize the number of cases referred on to ombudsmen or leading to legal actions.

Yet public sector redress systems have developed piecemeal over many years and in the past they have rarely been systematically thought about as a whole. Central government organizations make a strong distinction between complaints and appeals. Complaints concern processes and how issues have been handled. They have traditionally been considered as part of the internal business arrangements of departments and agencies. They are often thought about primarily in terms of customer responsiveness and business effectiveness. Appeals systems and tribunals concern the accuracy or correctness of substantive departmental or agency decisions. They conventionally form part of the administrative justice sphere. They are often considered primarily in terms of citizens' legal rights, natural justice, and a range of related quasi-judicial criteria. This bifurcated approach may have some advantages, but it is very distinctive to the public sector and has no counterpart in private sector firms. Rigidly separating complaints from appeals also means that many public service organizations are essentially providing two different basic systems of redress, which are set up and organized on different lines. And citizens also have to grapple with two very different concepts of redress, instead of a more integrated concept of 'getting things put right' . . .

Citizen redress procedures have an importance for the overall quality of public services that goes far beyond their direct costs. Complaints are an important source of feedback to central departments and agencies about where things are perceived by citizens as going wrong, a view also stressed by the Parliamentary Ombudsman. Hence they are a significant source of information on possible improvements in organizational arrangements. Similarly the availability of

Box 6.1   *Continued*

appeals and tribunals options is intended to provide an effective incentive for officials to make considered decisions which are right first time. Providing a range of administrative procedures for citizens to seek remedies or redress is also a key area of civil rights, providing vital safeguards against arbitrary or ill-founded decision making by government organizations. So it is clearly essential that any changes made to citizen redress arrangements do not restrict established rights to independent review and an opportunity to state one's case.

However, it is also possible that the current workings of citizen redress institutions may not be optimally configured to deliver what the public most want. Current arrangements have built up over long periods, largely in separated ways, often specific to one policy sector or one government organization. So the existing ladder of redress options may not be as accessible or as useful to citizens as it could be. It also may well not deliver what citizens most want. Redress systems should be purposefully targeted to deliver valued benefits to citizens in a timely way, rather than just following through on established procedures whose added value for citizens remains unclear.

In the past there were separate channels in government for dealing with complaints, appeals, and ombudsmen processes. The complaints route has mostly been seen as a matter for departments or agencies to run in a decentralized way as they see fit, within only the general discipline provided by ombudsmen comments. Appeals and tribunals confer important citizens' rights and are legally mandated and so in business terms are an inescapable cost. They were previously regulated in a separate, more legal manner by the then Lord Chancellor's Department with input from the Council of Tribunals. As a result, citizen redress arrangements have apparently not been monitored or costed in any systematic way by central departments (such as the Cabinet Office or the Treasury). The onus has been on departments and agencies to consider the effectiveness and efficiency of their own redress schemes as part of their wider drive to improve efficiency.

Source: Extracted from Citizen Redress: *What citizens can do if things go wrong with public services,* National Audit Office, 2005.

Costs

Although most of the procedures (save the courts) are provided free to the individual, they clearly cost money to run. The relationship between that cost and the output of the bodies and procedures funded cannot be ignored. In the same report, the NAO provided some first estimates of the costs of the administrative justice system, as broadly conceived here. (*See Box 6.2.*) It may be argued that, though significant, these costs are small compared with expenditure on public services taken as a whole. But this is not sufficient reason for not thinking critically about the present system and whether it could be made more efficient. A consequence of the failure to see administrative justice in the round is that it makes it hard to appreciate the amount of money spent on the provision of administrative justice systems.

Box 6.2 Legal system explained

The costs of the administrative justice system

The National Audit Office estimated that nearly 1.4 million cases are received through redress systems in central government annually and are processed by over 9,300 staff at an annual cost of at least £510 million. Appeals and tribunal cases account for just under three-fifths of the redress load, seven-tenths of the annual costs, and two-thirds of the staff numbers. Complaints are much cheaper to handle, accounting for two in five redress cases but an eighth of the annual costs. Cases handled by independent complaints handlers or ombudsmen are a small part of the total. But because they often concern more complex or hard-to-resolve issues they are perhaps inevitably more resource-intensive than basic complaints handling.

There are currently very wide differences amongst departments and agencies in the ways that they define and record complaints. The NAO survey shows that around half of central government organizations, including departments operating in areas of major interest to many citizens, cannot effectively answer how many complaints they have received in either of the last two years. In some cases complaints are not distinguished from 'enquiries'. Even when complaints are systematically monitored in some way, departments and agencies vary greatly in how they define an interaction with citizens as 'a complaint'. Most government organizations operate with an inclusive view of complaints as 'any expression of dissatisfaction', including major departments handling tax and welfare issues—and they also record high numbers of complaints. But others include major restrictions on recording interactions with dissatisfied customers as complaints. Some of these organizations use additional 'no blame' concepts such as 'corrections' and others do not count complaints made and resolved at local or regional level.

Even the apparently clearer concept of 'an appeal' has important variations in meaning in different administrative settings. In some organizations a large number of customer interactions are processed into the appeals system with minimal effort on citizens' part, whereas in other cases citizens must make more of an effort to initiate an appeal. So our findings here are necessarily qualified by difficulties in measurement and inadequacies in many government organizations' recording systems, especially for the costs of redress.

The overall public expenditure costs of handling complaints and appeals can be assessed very roughly as the cost per new case and research suggests the following data:

- complaints cost an average of £155 per new case;
- appeals cases cost an average of £455 per new case;
- the costs for independent complaints handlers and for ombudsmen vary a lot, ranging between £550 and £4,500 per case, but mostly around £1,500 to £2,000.

Box 6.2 *Continued*

There are very wide variations around these average numbers. For instance the cost per complaint claimed by organizations can be as low as £10 per case in a few cases for those that are reviewed and settled by grass roots or 'street level' staff.

In addition to the direct administrative costs of complaints, appeals, and other redress systems, processing these cases can indirectly create substantial additional expenditures for some particular areas of the central government, via legal aid costs paid to those people eligible for this assistance. From information supplied by the Legal Services Commission the NAO can say that these additional costs are a minimum of £198 million in central government (primarily in the area of immigration and asylum appeals), plus a small amount in welfare benefit appeals. A minimum additional £24 million is incurred in the National Health Service. The actual full costs involved here are likely to be much greater than this.

The numbers suggest that there is considerable potential for departments, agencies, and appeals bodies to review their practices and to bear down upon any procedures or approaches which unnecessarily encourage the occurrence of complaints or appeals, or their progression up the ladder of redress options. Cutting down the initial numbers of complaints or appeals, resolving more complaints and appeals more speedily and pro-actively, and improving the cost efficiency of current redress arrangements, could all make appreciable savings in public money, savings which could then cumulate with every passing year. If reductions of 5 per cent could be made in the current costs of redress systems, the NAO estimate[s] that the Exchequer would save at least £25 million per year less the cost of implementation.

Source: Adapted from Citizen Redress: *What citizens can do if things go wrong with public services,* National Audit Office, 2005.

The courts

The heart of the administrative justice system is the Administrative Court, part of the High Court, where the fundamental principles of *judicial review* have been developed. The essence of judicial review is straightforward. Public officials must act within the constraints of the law. If they do not, the courts will declare a decision to be unlawful. In general judges limit themselves to this; they do not usually substitute their own decisions for that of the original decision-taker.

The primary tasks of judges in judicial review cases are:

- *to interpret statutory provisions.* There are many situations, particularly when a new piece of legislation has been passed, when the law may need clarification. Deciding the limits of the law, and whether or not a person acted within the law or outside it, is a clear judicial task;

- *to control discretion.* In some situations the legislation has been drafted to give officials flexibility in the application of the law to the particular case. Where a statute states that the minister 'may' act in a certain way or reach a 'reasonable' decision, these are examples of discretionary power. The judges have developed the principle that the exercise of discretion must not be 'unreasonable';[3]

- *to determine the validity of secondary legislation.* English courts have resisted the temptation to decide, as does the Supreme Court in the United States, that particular items of legislation are unlawful, though it has recently been decided that they should do so if an item of British legislation is contrary to the law of the EU.[4] Under the Human Rights Act, the courts have power to declare a provision in an Act of Parliament incompatible with the rights set out in the Human Rights Act. However, the courts have long asserted the power to declare secondary legislation unlawful, on the basis that the statutory instrument was beyond the powers of the minister as established by the primary Act of Parliament;[5]

- *to determine the fairness of procedures.* The courts have also determined fundamental principles of fairness in the lower courts, in other tribunals, and in a range of other contexts in which decisions affecting the citizen are made. Where these principles apply, the person must know the basis of the case against her, and be given an opportunity to be heard; and

- *to prevent bias.* In addition, the judges have insisted that adjudicators in the courts and other fora must not be 'biased', in the sense that they must not have a personal interest in the outcome of any particular case.

Judicial review has not just developed in a vacuum. It is a response to the fact that people no longer accept official decisions as easily as they once did. The reasons for this are complex: better public education; a more consumerist society; the development of this type of legal practice by legal practitioners. But government has also expanded its activities. It seeks to regulate large tranches of human activity. It is not surprising that use of judicial review, or the threat of such use, should now be part of the politics of modern public administration.

One consequence of the development of judicial review has been an increased use by pressure groups of the courts for testing the validity of legislation or its interpretation. The taking of test cases, called 'cause lawyering' in the USA, has become a part of contemporary legal practice.[6] The Human Rights Act 1998 has provided a new focus for such work as challenges about the compliance of legislation and policy with the European Convention on Human Rights are made.

---

[3] *Associated Provincial Picture Houses Ltd v. Wednesbury Corporation* [1948] 1 KB 223, CA.

[4] *Factortame v. Secretary of State for Transport (No. 2)* [1991] 1 AC 603.

[5] *R v. Secretary of State for Trade and Industry, ex p Thomson Holidays, The Times,* 12 January 2000, CA; and *R v. Secretary of State for the Environment, Transport and the Regions, ex p Spath Holme Ltd* [2000] 1 All ER 884, HL.

[6] See, for example, the work of the Public Law Project: www.publiclawproject.org.uk/.

Tribunals

The places where the vast majority of disputes between the citizen and the state get resolved are known collectively as tribunals. Some, such as the General Commissioners of Income Tax, trace their history back to the late eighteenth century. Most are the creation of the twentieth century, reflecting increased involvement of the state in the lives of its citizens.

For the first twenty to thirty years of that century, there was considerable concern about the use of tribunals as a mechanism for the resolution of disputes. It was argued that only courts had the constitutional authority to perform this function. (It was, perhaps, one of the advantages of the lack of a written constitution that, despite this claim, there was no written constitutional principle that *required* all dispute resolution bodies to have the status of 'court'.) The development of tribunals was a pragmatic response to the problems caused for the court system when, at the end of the nineteenth century, jurisdiction to deal with disputes arising under the Workmen's Compensation Acts was given to the county court. This resulted in those courts drowning in that work, preventing them from dealing effectively with other business. When the National Insurance Act 1911 was passed, creating the first social security benefits, appeals against decisions were not to the courts, but to a tribunal, the sportingly named *Committee of Referees* with a further right of appeal to the equally sporting *Umpire*.

Criticism of the use of bodies other than the courts for resolving disputes led to fierce criticism, not least from the then Lord Chief Justice, Lord Hewart, who in 1929 published his famous polemic *The New Despotism*. This resulted in the establishment of the Committee on Ministers' Powers, under the chairmanship of Lord Donoughmore, which in 1932 reported that, in its view and subject to safeguards, tribunals were a necessary if not desirable part of the fabric of the English justice system.

The issue was revisited after the Second World War when, in 1955, a further committee under Sir Oliver Franks was established, in the wake of a scandal known as the Crichel Down affair, to review tribunals and inquiries. The report of his committee was published in 1957. By this time many more tribunal systems were in existence. Franks accepted that, subject to basic principles of openness, fairness, and impartiality, tribunals should be accepted as a part of the adjudicative structure. Since that time, there has been no serious discussion about the need for tribunals. Indeed, their number has continued to grow (alongside other institutional developments, to which we shall come below). The position of tribunals is even more secure following the enactment of the Human Rights Act 1998, since Article 6 of the European Convention on Human Rights requires the existence of courts or tribunals to determine a person's civil rights.

Reforming the tribunals system

This is the background against which the new Tribunals Service has been created. In May 2000, the Lord Chancellor appointed Sir Andrew Leggatt (a retired judge of the

Court of Appeal) to undertake a major review of tribunals. His report, *Tribunals for Users: One System, One Service,* was published in August 2001. It set out a long list of recommendations, the central one being a call for a unified Tribunal Service.

Publication of the report caused considerable consternation in the corridors of Whitehall. Government departments came to see that implementation of the review's proposals would involve some ceding of their current portfolio of functions to another department, never an attractive prospect. However, after a protracted period of discussion within government, the Lord Chancellor announced early in 2003 that the central recommendation was accepted. The White Paper setting out the government's intentions was published in the summer of 2004. This not only set out the framework for the new service, but also argued that it was important to look at dispute-resolution in the round. There should be clear and flexible pathways for the citizen to obtain redress when things went wrong.[7]

The new Tribunals Service came into being in April 2006. At first it operated under powers transferred to it by statutory order. The passing of the Tribunals, Courts and Enforcement Act 2007 gives a further impetus to the reform programme.

The Act creates two new, generic tribunals: the First-Tier Tribunal that will deal with the bulk of cases arising from official decision-taking; and the Upper Tribunal, which, in the main, will hear appeals from decisions taken by the First-Tier Tribunal. Existing tribunals will be brought into this new framework. The Act allows tribunals in either tier to be grouped into 'chambers' so that the many pre-existing tribunals can be brought together in a practically functional way. When necessary, new tribunal jurisdiction may be brought into this generic framework. The Act also formally creates the post of Senior President, currently the Court of Appeal judge, Sir Robert Carnwath. The Act provides that legal members of tribunals will, in future, be given the title of judge.

While its first target is to bring into the service those tribunals previously sponsored by the former Department of Constitutional Affairs, together with the Appeals Service (social security tribunals), a further Consultation Paper was published in November 2007 setting out ideas for the expansion of the Service to other tribunals.

The aim of the Service is to reduce the current bewildering variety of practices and procedures of existing tribunals; to enable judicial manpower to be used more effectively, by enabling tribunals chairs and members to sit in more than one tribunal; and to rationalize routes of appeal to an upper tier tribunal. An early target is the creation of a single body of procedural rules to guide the work of tribunals.

In creating the new service, care must be taken to preserve the distinctive characteristics of tribunals. Most important is that the qualifications of tribunal judges should match the tasks they are required to perform. At present most tribunals have legally qualified chairmen. But this is not universal. General Commissioners for Income Tax who determine tax cases, and Valuation Tribunals, which determine property values, operate with only non-legally qualified persons on the tribunal. Some tribunals take

---

[7] See *Transforming Public Services: Complaints, Redress and Tribunals,* July 2004.

advantage of other professional expertise as well, for example, valuers or accountants or doctors. This brings an expertise to the tribunal that is not usually available in court (unless experts are specially appointed).

Secondly, many tribunal systems make extensive efforts to deal with appellants who—as the result of a lack of availability of legal aid—either have to represent themselves or have to rely on lay advocates. The social security appeal system, for example, prides itself on its 'enabling role'. Unlike the adversarial approach of the courts, where the judges tend to take a back seat while the argument, for and against, is presented by advocates for both sides, members of tribunals take a more interventionist role, seeking to draw relevant information from the parties by appropriate questioning. It is in this variety of forensic methods that much of the potential innovation of the tribunal system is to be found, and from which the courts—if they knew what went on in the best-run tribunals—might have much to learn.

The new service will however be able to address some of the unnecessary variations found in the former system, particularly relating to the management of tribunals, the training of tribunal judiciary, and the reporting of the most important appeal decisions.

Inquiries

Historically there was an important conceptual distinction between a tribunal and an inquiry. Whereas a tribunal usually had statutory authority to adjudicate a dispute and reach a final decision which, subject to any right of appeal, determined the matter, an inquiry gathered information, in the light of which a government minister would decide the issue.

In practice, this distinction has become increasingly blurred. Mental Health Review Tribunals, for example, when dealing with mental patients who have been detained in a mental hospital as a result of a court order, can only make a recommendation to the Home Secretary that a patient should be released from hospital; it is the Secretary of State (or his officials) who takes the final decision. So too, many inquiries lead directly to a decision being taken, rather than a report to a minister which would form the basis for a decision.

Planning inquiries and related procedures

The principal use of the inquiry as an institution in the administrative justice system is found in the context of the planning process. In a geographically small country with a substantial population, it has long been accepted that the state has an interest in determining how land should be used. The planning process seeks to balance the competing interests relating to land use of urban dwellers, rural dwellers, industrialists, scientists, the pursuers of leisure interests, the providers of transport systems, and other utility providers (gas, electricity, water), to give just some examples. The bulk of planning decisions are taken by local authorities, acting as local planning authorities. Strategically important decisions—for example over the siting of a new airport—may be 'called in' for determination by the Secretary of State within central government.

Once a planning decision has been reached, rights of appeal are provided. Whereas in other contexts a tribunal has been established to deal with appeals, in the planning context appeals are dealt with by planning inspectors. Originally, planning inspectors held inquiries and in the light of their findings made recommendations to the Secretary of State in the central government. These procedures were 'inquiries' in their original sense. As a result of changes in the law, planning inspectors now make the final determination in all but the most complex or important cases, where they still make recommendations to the Secretary of State. In most cases, the functions of the planning inspectorate are indistinguishable from the functions of a tribunal. Planning inspectors have three ways of proceeding:

- written representations;
- hearings; and
- inquiries.

Statistically, the inquiry is the least frequently used mode for determining planning appeals.

- *Written representations* are, as the name implies, a means of dealing with an appeal purely through written representations. This is the speediest and cheapest of the procedures and is particularly suitable for the determination of relatively small matters, e.g. an extension to a dwelling.

- *Hearings* involve the appellants and the local planning authority in a hearing before a planning inspector, but the process is consciously 'low-key'. Planning inspectors are trained to run hearings proactively to try to avoid the need for the use of expensive legal representation. The inspector shapes the hearing by assisting the parties to identify the issues that need to be addressed. Typically, the hearing is used in cases slightly more significant than those dealt with by written representation, but not as large scale as those going to inquiry.

- *Inquiries* are used primarily for major planning issues. (Inquiries are also used to determine the shape of local planning authorities' local plans, which provide the background against which individual planning applications are decided.) Inquiries involve hearing a wider range of persons with an interest in the decision—for example, environmental groups or trade associations—than written representations or hearings. Procedurally they are more formal, with the parties usually using barristers or solicitors to represent their interests. Inquiries can take a very long time; the public inquiry into the Fifth Terminal at London Heathrow Airport took over five years to complete.

Particular and ad hoc inquiries

In addition to planning inquiries, which are held on a regular basis, many other particular forms of inquiry are put in place as the need arises, for example, inquiries into serious rail accidents or other disasters.

The government may also use an ad hoc inquiry to deal with the aftermath of a particular incident. Recent examples include the inquiry into events at the Bristol Children's Hospital, or the Scott inquiry into the Arms for Iraq affair. The Council on Tribunals has issued advice on matters that government should take into account when establishing such ad hoc inquiries.[8] Local authorities and other public bodies may also establish inquiries into a range of issues, as they arise.[9]

Review

Another form of redress of grievance is review. This involves officials who took the initial decision reviewing that decision to see whether or not it is correct or should be revised. In some cases, the reviewer is the initial decision-taker; in others the reviewer is another official, usually more senior. Reviews may lack the independence that characterizes an appeal to a tribunal or an inquiry. But they provide an easy and quick means of rectifying a decision where something has clearly gone wrong. Reviews are found in two basic forms: formal and informal.

- *Formal* reviews are those which are required by law to be carried out. In some cases, such as review of decisions relating to the Social Fund, there is no tribunal process available at all—all appeals go through the review process.
- *Informal* reviews are not required by law but officials nonetheless carry them out as part of their routine administrative procedures. In the case of social security appeals, for example, any appeal by a social security claimant against a decision of the Benefits Agency triggers an internal official review to check whether the decision appealed against is or is not correct. There is evidence that more cases are revised in favour of claimants at this stage than at the appeal stage.[10]

Reviews as a feature of the administrative justice system have been the subject of considerable criticism. In the same way that, in the context of criminal justice, decisions by the police to deal with suspects administratively—e.g. by issuing a caution—are criticized for undermining the due process model of criminal justice, so too is review seen by some as undermining the due process model of administrative justice. For example, Sainsbury argues strongly that the review process is objectionable in principle, in that there cannot be independence where reviews are conducted essentially within the organization that made the initial decision. He also objects to review on the practical ground that, by introducing another layer of decision-taking, this may have the effect

---

[8] *Advice to the Lord Chancellor on the Procedural Issues arising in the context of Public Inquiries set up by Ministers,* July 1996 (HC 114) (London, HMSO, 1996).

[9] Some of the issues are discussed in Law Commission, *In the public interest: Publication of Local Authority Inquiry Reports* (Law Com 289) (Cm 6272) (London, TSO, 2004).

[10] See Baldwin, J., *et al., Judging Social Security* (Oxford, Clarendon Press, 1992).

of denying claimants the right to appear before a tribunal to hear their case—at least in situations where review is a preliminary to appeal before a tribunal.[11]

Against this, others suggest that models of administrative justice should be based not just on due process but also on other values, such as cost-effectiveness and efficiency. This might lead to the conclusion that review is not so objectionable, but is a pragmatic and sensible way of ensuring that mistakes are corrected without the expense and delay of a tribunal hearing. They can be organized so as to meet the objection that they lack independence. Indeed, when well organized, review has all the hallmarks of independence and due process.[12]

While the theoretical objections can perhaps be overstated, the review mechanism—in its various guises—will remain in the repertoire of the dispute resolution procedures of the administrative justice system, and should thus be seen as a part of that system. The question is not so much whether review should be part of the system at all; rather, consideration should be given to those cases where review is appropriate and those where it is not.

Practical experience suggests that the primary reason decisions taken by officials are often found to be wrong is not that the official has misunderstood the law to be applied to the case in question, but that the factual information on which the decision is based is in some respect wanting. It should therefore make sense to find ways of getting at the relevant facts other than by the relatively expensive and long-drawn-out process of a tribunal hearing. In this context, review may be particularly valuable. However, if the way in which the review works is that no effort is made to see whether new evidence is forthcoming, or that those who may have a case to take to a tribunal become so disheartened that they fail to pursue their claims in full, then review may be criticized as not adding value to the repertoire of administrative justice procedures.

Ombudsmen

The Parliamentary and Health Service Ombudsman

The Ombudsman concept was introduced into the United Kingdom from Scandinavia in 1967. The first Ombudsman was formally known as the 'Parliamentary Commissioner for Administration' (PCA), though she is now described as the *Parliamentary Ombudsman*. The Ombudsman's original function was to investigate complaints and allegations of *maladministration* in UK government departments and related agencies which may have resulted in injustice.

---

[11] Sainsbury, R., 'Internal Reviews and the Weakening of Social Security Claimants' Rights of Appeal' in Richardson, G., and Genn, H. (eds), *Administrative Law and Government Action* (Oxford, Clarendon Press, 1994).

[12] Harris, M., 'The Place of Formal and Informal Review in Administrative Justice' and Scampion, J., 'New Procedures' in Harris, M., and Partington, M. (eds), *Administrative Justice in the 21st Century* (Oxford, Hart, 1999).

Two particular features of the Parliamentary Ombudsman's jurisdiction should be noted. First, members of the public are not entitled to complain directly to the PCA; they must get their complaint referred to the Ombudsman by a Member of Parliament. MPs are not actually obliged to refer cases to her, if they think they can deal with the matter themselves. The reason for this is that, when the Ombudsman concept was introduced, there were those who argued that it might undermine the primary responsibility of Parliament and its members to call ministers (and their officials) to account. The MP filter, as it is known, was not part of the original Scandinavian Ombudsman concept, where direct access by the public was permitted.

Secondly, the Parliamentary Ombudsman cannot order that any particular consequence should follow a finding of maladministration. She can only persuade a government department, for example, to pay compensation to an aggrieved citizen. Again, in other countries, the Ombudsman has power to enforce his decisions. The Ombudsman is currently drawing up guidance on the principles to be adopted when considering what remedies should be offered to those who are found to have suffered maladministration. The range of remedies is much wider than those offered by the courts.

Since first established, the scope of the Ombudsman's work has been broadened considerably, first to deal with complaints about the Health Service, more recently to deal with complaints about the Victims' Charter.

As Health Service Ombudsman she investigates complaints about failures in National Health Service (NHS) hospitals or community health services, about care and treatment, and about local NHS family doctor, dental, pharmacy, or optical services. Any member of the public may refer a complaint direct to her, i.e. it does not have to come through a Member of Parliament, though normally she pursues a complaint only if a full investigation within the NHS complaints system has been carried out first. She can only consider issues arising in the NHS in England. (See below for the position in Wales and Scotland.)

Since April 2006, when the Victims' Code took effect (see above, p. 139), the Ombudsman has provided a complaints-handling service for victims of crime who have a complaint about the way in which any of the criminal justice agencies has carried out its obligations under the code. Such cases are subject to the MP filter.

Besides investigating and, where appropriate, redressing grievances, the Ombudsman sees her function as improving the quality of administration. She endeavours to ensure that her reports contain general guidance on good practice from which government or health departments may learn. In April, she published general principles of good administration. There are six: getting it right; being customer focused; being open and accountable; acting fairly and proportionately; putting things right; and seeking continuous improvement. Though these may seem obvious, it is surprising how often these basic principles get ignored in practice. Summaries of her investigations are published regularly and are available on her website. She also produces an *Annual Report*.

For the first time, in 2005, she published a joint report covering both her parliamentary and health service work. Issues particularly considered were: problems with the new tax credits system; the operations of the Child Support Agency; NHS funding of continuing care for people with long-term healthcare needs; and the need for a truly patient-focused NHS complaints procedure. The Annual Report is considered by a specialist Select Committee of the House of Commons, who interview her as well as senior civil servants from departments that have been criticized by her. Thus Parliament is kept informed about the Ombudsman's work and the impact it has had on government departments.

Public service ombudsmen in Wales and Scotland

As a result of devolution, the detailed arrangements for Wales and Scotland have been changed. In Wales, until fairly recently, complaints could be taken to four separate ombudsmen: the Commission for Local Administration in Wales, Health Service Commissioner for Wales, the Welsh Administration Ombudsman, and also the Social Housing Ombudsman for Wales. These have been brought together into a single scheme, called the Public Service Ombudsman for Wales, which started work on 1 April 2006.

In Scotland there is a Scottish Public Service Ombudsman who deals with complaints about Scottish public bodies previously dealt with by the Scottish Parliamentary Ombudsman, the Health Service Ombudsman for Scotland, the Local Government Ombudsman for Scotland, and the Housing Association Ombudsman for Scotland. The Ombudsman has also taken over the Mental Welfare Commission for Scotland's function of investigating complaints relating to mental health and complaints against Scottish Enterprise and Highlands and Islands Enterprise.

Local government ombudsmen

The Ombudsman concept has been extended to local government. There are three local government ombudsmen covering all local authorities in England. They investigate complaints against principal councils (not town, parish, or community councils) and certain other bodies in England, Scotland and Wales. By law, some kinds of complaint cannot be considered. Examples are personnel complaints and complaints about the internal running of schools.

As with other ombudsmen, the objective of the local government ombudsmen is to secure, where appropriate, satisfactory redress for complainants and better administration by local authorities. Since 1989, they have had power to issue advice on good administrative practice, drawing lessons from the cases they have handled. To date, six guidance notes have been published: on setting up complaints procedures; good administrative practice; council housing repairs; local authority members' interests; the disposal of land; and remedies when things have gone wrong.

Following a review of the Parliamentary and Health Services Ombudsman and the English local government ombudsmen, the government recently agreed that, where a complaint raises matters relating both to central and to local government, the two organizations could investigate it jointly.[13]

---

[13] The Regulatory Reform (Collaboration between Ombudsmen) Order 2007. See also *Reform of Public Sector Ombudsmen Services in England: A consultation paper,* published by the Cabinet Office in August 2005.

Others

Increasingly, Ombudsman or Ombudsman-type offices are being created which are more specialist in nature. For example, a new *Office for Legal Complaints* is being created, to handle consumer complaints in respect of all bodies providing legal services, subject to oversight by the Legal Services Board;[14] a new *Judicial Appointments and Conduct Ombudsman* has been created by the Constitutional Reform Act 2005, to deal with complaints about judicial appointments and judicial conduct; the *Independent Police Complaints Commission* which—as the name implies—deals with complaints against the police; a *Prisons and Probation Ombudsman,* who deals with complaints about the prison and probation service; and the *Independent Housing Ombudsman,* who deals with complaints against (primarily) registered social landlords (housing associations).

The rise of private sector ombudsmen

Over the last fifteen years or so, a peculiarly British phenomenon has emerged. A considerable number of private sector industries have set up their own sector-wide ombudsman schemes to deal with those customer complaints that cannot be resolved within a particular company. These include the Estates Agents Ombudsman, the Banking Ombudsman, the Insurance Ombudsman, and the Building Societies Ombudsman. By contrast with the PCA and the other public sector ombudsmen, where the levels of complaints have been relatively low, many of these private sector ombudsmen have had large case-loads to deal with. They offer a 'mass-market' dispute resolution procedure, as opposed to the more 'Rolls-Royce' work of the PCA.[15]

Following the Financial Services and Markets Act 2000 a Financial Services Ombudsman scheme brought together many of these private schemes. It operates under statutory rather than industry-determined powers. It has a substantial case-load and is able to award compensation up to £100k. It has effectively replaced the courts as the forum for the resolution of consumer disputes with financial services providers.

Process

A common feature of all ombudsmen's procedures is that they operate on an 'inquisitorial' or 'investigative' basis. The complaint is made; the relevant ombudsman's staff investigates the complaint, taking further evidence both from the government department or other agency concerned and the complainant. In the light of the investigation a conclusion is reached on whether or not there was in fact maladministration. Many investigations result in a finding that the department or agency in question behaved perfectly responsibly, and the complainant was being unreasonable. Where there was

---

[14] This replaces the existing Legal Services Ombudsman and Legal Services Complaints Commissioner, once the Legal Services Act 2007 is brought into force.

[15] Williams, T., and Goriely, T., 'A Question of Numbers: Managing Complaints Against Rising Expectations' in Harris, M., and Partington, M. (eds), *Administrative Justice in the 21st Century* (Oxford, Hart, 1999).

a finding of maladministration, there is comment on whether the response of the department was appropriate. Many findings of maladministration lead to no more than the writing of a letter of apology, which is often all that the complainant wanted in the first place. Usually there is no possibility of an oral hearing (though the Pensions Ombudsman is required to offer this).

The European Ombudsman

In addition to developments in England and Wales, the Ombudsman concept also extends to the work of the European Union. The creation of a European Ombudsman was approved in the Maastricht Treaty; the statute giving him his authority was agreed in 1994. He took up office in 1995 and has been issuing annual reports on his work since 1996.

He operates on the basis of *The European Ombudsman Implementing Provisions*. These not only set out in general terms the principles on which the Ombudsman carries out his work, but also list the powers he has when determining cases: these include the possibility of making 'critical remarks' where no more general conclusions can be drawn from the case under investigation; and the making of a 'report with draft recommendations', where it appears that some more general lessons may be learned.

In addition, and unlike the national ombudsmen in England and Wales, the European Ombudsman has a very broad power to instigate his 'own-initiative' inquiries. One fruit of this, to date, has been the preparation of a set of draft recommendations, which have been put both to the European Commission and to the European Parliament and Council of Ministers, relating to the adoption of a *Code of Good Administrative Behaviour*. His reason for doing this was the result of reflecting on many of the individual complaints he had received, which indicated that maladministration might have been avoided had clearer information been available about the administrative duties of Community staff towards its citizens. The code was approved by the European Parliament and published in March 2002.

Other complaints-handling bodies

It might be thought that, with the creation of ombudsmen to deal with issues at a high level and with the more recent development of a wide variety of complaints-resolution procedures in individual government departments, there were now adequate means for the redress of citizens' complaints. In fact, other bodies and procedures have been created with more specific remits than the ombudsmen's but more general authority than an internal complaints procedure. Only a few examples are given here.

- The *Adjudicator* investigates complaints from people and businesses about the work of HM Revenue and Customs, the Insolvency Service, the Public Guardianship Office, and the Valuation Office Agency. The Adjudicator does not look at issues of law or of tax liability, because tribunals resolve these problems. But she does look into excessive delay, mistakes, discourtesy of staff and the use of discretion.

- The *Independent Case Examiner* investigates complaints about maladministration by the Child Support Agency, when clients are dissatisfied with the outcome of the Agency's internal complaints service. She also deals with complaints about the Northern Ireland Social Security Agency.

- The *Independent Adjudicator for Higher Education* operates an independent student complaints scheme under the Higher Education Act 2004. All higher education institutions in England and Wales are required to comply with the rules of the scheme. The service is free to students. The adjudicator handles individual complaints against higher education institutions, and may publish recommendations about how they deal with complaints and what constitutes good practice.

- The *Immigration Services Commissioner,* an independent public body set up under the Immigration and Asylum Act 1999, is responsible for ensuring that all immigration advisers fulfil the requirements of good practice. His office is responsible for regulating immigration advisers in accordance with the Commissioner's Code of Standards and Rules, including taking criminal proceedings against advisers who are acting illegally.

The number and variety of these bodies has grown significantly over the last ten years.

'Collective' administrative justice—regulators of privatized utility providers

Another context for the resolution of disputes arises from the privatization of the main utility providers—water, gas, telecommunications, for example. Following privatization, the provision of services by state monopolies was, in the main, replaced by private monopolies. New regulatory offices—including OFWAT, OFGEM and OFTEL—were established to regulate these new industries to prevent abuse of market power in the setting of prices, and to create the conditions in which other suppliers could come into the market to provide the competition essential for consumer protection. These regulatory offices have also had some responsibility for the development of procedures for dealing with individual customer complaints and complaints from others wishing to enter particular market sectors.[16]

This is not the place to consider the work of these industry regulators in detail. But their existence does need to be noted and the fact that they too now play a part in the overall framework of administrative justice.

---

[16] See McHarg, A., 'Separation of Functions and Regulatory Agencies: Dispute Resolution in the Privatised Utilities' in Harris, M., and Partington, M. (eds), *Administrative Justice in the 21st Century* (Oxford, Hart, 1999).

Putting people first

Notwithstanding all these dispute resolution institutions and procedures, there is a powerful argument that they would not be necessary if those who delivered public services were fully focused on delivering a high-quality service themselves. 'Getting it right first time' should be preferable to making the citizen complain, or appeal, or go to an ombudsman. This general issue has been a particular concern of government for nearly twenty years. First came the concept of the Citizens' Charter, later rebadged by the Blair government as *Service First*. By contrast with the Ombudsman, where the concept moved from the public sector to the private, the Citizens' Charter involved private sector ideas about standards of customer care and service delivery being brought into the public sector. Though the initial introduction of the charter, in 1991 by the government of Mr Major, was seen as rather gimmicky, it provided further impetus to promoting service standards in the public sector.

Since then much attention has been given to improving the quality of public service delivery. Under the Blair government, the Office of Public Sector Reform defined four principles for public service delivery: national standards to ensure that people have the right to high-quality services wherever they live; devolution to give local leaders the means to deliver these standards to local people; more flexibility in service provision in light of people's rising expectations; and greater customer choice. Much of this is driven by the desire to enhance the use of information technology in the delivery of public services.

A review of progress was commissioned in 2006. The resulting report, *Service Transformation: A better service for citizens and businesses, a better deal for the taxpayer* by Sir David Varney was published in 2006. Responsibility for taking these issues forward lies with a Delivery Council, established within the Cabinet Office.

Many issues of considerable political importance derive from these initiatives. For example, the emphasis of the government on setting standards and targets (and dealing with the consequences of failing to meet them) derives from these principles. So too does the extremely controversial issue of the extent to which private sector companies should be involved in the delivery of public services. Particularly contentious examples arise in relation to the provision of health care, education, and prison services.

It is difficult to gauge the extent to which these principles are being delivered in practice. The nature of political debate and reports in the media is to focus on things that are not happening rather than on the positive developments that are occurring. There are often good reasons to think that progress is slower than ministers would like. In many parts of the country, public service pay levels make it hard to recruit staff of adequate quality. Some forms of public service are very stressful to deliver, which increases the problems of staff recruitment and retention. And, some areas of social administration are very complex; however well staff do their jobs, there will be grounds for appeal or seeking reviews of decisions. Examples of services being delivered to much higher standards do not attract the same attention, though reports of the many official Inspectorates suggest that good services are offered in many areas of government.

There seems little doubt that there will continue to be a focus on the need for public services to deliver a better service to the public. Administrative justice should be based on a desire to ensure that official decisions are right first time. To the extent that the institutional procedures considered in this chapter are needed, this may reflect the facts that standards of administrative justice are not as high as they should be.

Overview of the administrative justice system

The Administrative Justice and Tribunals Council

Since 1959, tribunals and inquiries were kept under review by the Council on Tribunals. It had a statutory responsibility to advise and report to government on the work of the tribunals and inquiry systems under its jurisdiction; to comment on drafts of procedural regulations, on which the Council must be consulted; and to deal with such other matters as might be referred to it. For example, the Council was regularly consulted on proposals to establish new tribunals or to introduce changes to existing tribunals, for example by changing their procedural rules or by expanding the range of cases which may go before the tribunal. In addition the Council prepared a number of reports relating to general issues about the operation of tribunals and inquiries. For example, in 1997 it produced a report on the independence of tribunals, reasserting the importance of this fundamental principle in the operation of tribunals.[17] In 2002 it produced the first *Framework of Standards for Tribunals*. In 2003 it produced the second edition of a guide to drafting procedure rules that might be adopted by tribunals.

A particular feature of the Council was that its members had, in the vast majority of the tribunal systems under its authority, a statutory right to attend hearings. As a result of these visits many items of concern to the Council emerged, which have been translated into proposals for change. They include:

- the need for training of tribunal chairmen and members;
- the importance of the role of the clerk and administrative support generally in ensuring the smooth running of tribunals; and
- the need for adequate levels of resource to enable the work of the tribunals to be done effectively.

The *Annual Reports* of the Council provide a rich repository not just of information about developments in the administrative justice system, but also of the principles and practices which should be adopted in that system. The obvious limitation of the work of the Council was implicit in its name; its focus is limited to the tribunals and inquiry system over which it has been given a supervisory function.

---

[17] *Tribunals: Their Organisation and Independence* (Cm 3744) (London, TSO, 1997).

The Leggatt review of tribunals saw the Council as a key part of the administrative justice system and recommended that its role should be enhanced. From
November 2007, the Council has been transformed into an Administrative Justice and
Tribunals Council. A Welsh Committee is formally established, with effect from June
2008. Details of the new Council's powers are set out in the Tribunals Courts and
Enforcement Act 2007. These are broadly drawn. While the new Council will continue with the work of its predecessor, how it responds to its wider remit will only
emerge after it has had the chance to settle into its new role. One innovation that
should have been introduced by the Act, but was not, is that the Annual Reports of the
new Council should be presented not just to the Secretary of State, but also to a special
Select Committee of the House of Commons (as the Parliamentary Ombudsman does
to the Public Administration Select Committee). This would have helped ensure that
at least some members of the House of Commons took a specific interest in the structure and workings of the administrative justice system as a whole.

The British and Irish Ombudsmen's Association (BIOA)

BIOA is a private organization founded by the ombudsmen in 1995 to ensure that only
those bodies that subscribe to certain procedural standards use the label 'ombudsman'.
In particular, they wanted to make clear that ombudsmen in the private sector of the
economy, who were privately financed, are truly *independent* of their paymasters. It
has also undertaken other activity, such as developing principles for the training and
procedures to be adopted by individual ombudsman systems. One feature particularly
worthy of note—and which it is surprising does not exist in other parts of the English
legal system—is the link with the neighbouring common law jurisdiction, Ireland.
(There would be advantage in thinking of other areas of the justice system where there
might be opportunities for the British and the Irish to learn from each other.)

Audit and quality control

The discussion of administrative justice so far has focused on the wide variety of fora,
ranging from the courts to informal complaints-handling procedures, available to the
individual citizen, dissatisfied with some aspect of public administration. There are
now many avenues for challenging the legality of a decision, or the use of a discretionary power, or the process by which a decision was made.

Other mechanisms have also been introduced to try to ensure quality of performance and the provision of good public services which provide value for money. As
Ison has argued, if officials get the initial decision right, then the consumers of public
services should be better satisfied and have less need to use the myriad appeal and
complaints mechanisms outlined above.[18] (Indeed, one of the criticisms that can be

---

[18] Ison, T., 'Administrative Justice: Is it such a good idea?' in Harris, M., and Partington, M. (eds),
Administrative Justice in the 21st Century (Oxford, Hart, 1999).

made of many of these processes—the ombudsmen are perhaps an exception—is that there is rather little institutional commitment to the idea of considering what *general* lessons might be drawn from the resolution of the *individual* appeal or complaint. The very process of encouraging disputes to be resolved on an individual basis may disguise structural questions which, if addressed by the government department or other agency, might have prevented the problem arising in the first place.)

Among the alternative techniques now used to try to achieve these more general objectives are:

- the use of audit to ensure that value for money in the provision of public services is achieved;
- the use of inspectorates to ensure the quality of service provision;
- the provision of benchmarking statistics to provide baseline data against which performance by public sector agencies may be measured; and
- the conclusion of public service agreements, designed to encourage the modernization of service delivery, support proposals for reform, and increase accountability by the setting of clear aims and objectives.

The time has come to appreciate the importance of the application of these techniques to the administrative justice system.

Questions for reflection and discussion

1. Are tribunals properly seen as part of the English legal system?

2. Can tribunals ever be truly 'user-friendly'? How can those who cannot afford representation before a tribunal be best assisted to make their case?

3. What are the arguments for and against keeping tribunals as three-person bodies?

4. Should there be a direct right of access by members of the public to the Parliamentary Ombudsman? Does the 'MP filter' serve any useful purpose?

5. Should all ombudsmen be able legally to enforce any award compensation or other remedy they recommend for proven maladministration?

6. Are there too many avenues for complaint when things go wrong?

7. What mechanisms, apart from courts and tribunals, seem most suited to reviewing the quality and administrative action and controlling the power of state officials?

Further reading

BRIDGES, L., MESZAROS, G., and SUNKIN, M., *Judicial Review in Perspective* (London, Cavendish, 1995)

ELLIOTT, M., *The Constitutional Foundations of Judicial Review* (Oxford, Hart, 2001)

GENN, H., *Tribunals for Diverse Users* (DCA Research Series) (London, DCA, 2006)

—— and GENN, Y., *The Effectiveness of Representation at Tribunals: Report to the Lord Chancellor* (London, Queen Mary College, Faculty of Laws, 1989)

HARLOW, C., and RAWLINGS, R., *Law and Administration* (2nd edn., London, Butterworths, 1997)

HARRIS, M., and PARTINGTON, M. (eds), *Administrative Justice in the 21st Century* (Oxford, Hart, 1999)

LEWIS, N., and BIRKINSHAW, P., *When Citizens Complain: Reforming Justice and Administration* (Buckingham, Open University Press, 1993)

NATIONAL AUDIT OFFICE, *Citizen Redress: What Citizens Can Do if Things Go Wrong with Public Services* (HC21, 2004–5) (London, The Stationery Office, 2005)

RICHARDSON, G., and GENN, H. (eds), *Administrative Law and Government Action* (Oxford, Clarendon Press, 1994)

SENEVIRATNE, M., *Ombudsmen—Public Services and Administrative Justice* (Cambridge, Cambridge University Press, 2002)

SMITH, R.G., *Medical Discipline, The Professional Conduct Jurisdiction of the General Medical Council, 1858–1990* (Oxford, Oxford University Press, 1994)

WOOLF, LORD, JOWELL, J., and LE SUEUR, A.P., *De Smith's Judicial Review of Administrative Action* (6th edn., London, Sweet & Maxwell, 2002)

Websites

http://www.tribunals.gov.uk/ *(Homepage for information about the new Tribunals Service)*

http://www.appeals-service.gov.uk/

http://www.employmenttribunals.gov.uk/default.asp

http://www.employmentappeals.gov.uk/ *(Employment Appeals Tribunal)*

http://www.tribunals.gov.uk/tribunals/asylum.htm *(Links to four separate tribunals dealing with asylum and immigrationl)*

http://www.irs-review.org.uk/ *(Independent review service of the social fund inspectorate)*

http://www.rpts.gov.uk/ *(Residential property tribunal service)*

http://www.planning-inspectorate.gov.uk/ *(Planning inquiries)*

http://www.ombudsman.org.uk/ *(Parliamentary and Health Service Ombudsman)* http://www.ombudsman.org.uk/improving_services/good_administration/index.html *(The principles of good administration)*

http://www.bioa.org.uk/ *(British and Irish Ombudsmen's Association—portal for links to most ombudsman sites)*

http://www.dh.gov.uk/en/Policyandguidance/Organisationpolicy/Complaintspolicy/ NHScomplaintsprocedure/index.htm *(NHS complaints procedure)*

www.dca.gov.uk/foi/index.htm *(Still current MoJ page on Freedom of Information and Data Protection)*

http://www.parliament.uk/parliamentary_committees/public_administration_select_ committee.cfm *(Select Committee of the House of Commons with responsibility for reviewing the reports of the PCA)*

http://www.lgo.org.uk/ *(Local Government Ombudsman)*

http://www.ipcc.gov.uk/ *(Independent Police Complaints Commission)*

http://www.ppo.gov.uk/ *(Prisons and probation ombudsman)*

http://www.ihos.org.uk/ *(Independent Housing Ombudsman)*

http://www.financial-ombudsman.org.uk/ *(Financial Services Ombudsman)*

http://www.adjudicatorsoffice.gov.uk/ *(Adjudicator's Office—deals with range of complaints relating to taxation, national insurance contributions)*

http://www.ind-case-exam.org.uk/ *(Independent Case Examiners—deals with complaints of maladministration against the Child Support Agency and other agencies)*

http://www.euro-ombudsman.eu.int/code/en/default.htm *(European Ombudsman Code of Good Administrative Behaviour)*

http://www.euro-ombudsman.eu.int/lbasis/en/statute.htm *(European Ombudsman Statute)*

http://www.euro-ombudsman.eu.int/lbasis/en/provis.htm *(European Ombudsman imple-menting provisions)*

http://www.ofgem.gov.uk/Pages/OfgemHome.aspx *(Homepage of the Office of Gas and Electricity Markets)*

http://www.ofcom.org.uk/ *(Office of Communications)*

http://www.ofwat.gov.uk/aptrix/ofwat/publish.nsf/Content/navigation-homepage(ofwat) *(Office of Water Services)*

www.ajtc.gov.uk/

http://www.publiclawproject.org.uk/ *(Private charity offering access to public law remedies)*

http://www.cpl.law.cam.ac.uk/ *(Cambridge University Centre for Public Law)*

7

The family justice system

Introduction

The role law should play in the regulation of family relationships is controversial. Some argue that law should have only a residual function leaving people to structure their lives as a matter of private choice and personal morality. Others argue that society has a legitimate interest in family policy, particularly where children are involved. Furthermore, if support is not given to families, this leads to other undesirable social consequences, for example anti-social behaviour, youth criminality, and under-age pregnancy.

Institutional change

The institutional framework within which family policy is developed has undergone considerable change in recent years. Ministerial boundaries have been redrawn and new agencies created. This short chapter can do little more than highlight some of these changes, which set the context within which the family justice system operates.

Shortly after the Blair Labour government was elected in 1997, the government published an important policy paper, *Supporting Families*. While acknowledging the limits of the law, the government nevertheless stated that it wished to focus on five key issues, where it claimed government can make a difference: ensuring all families have access to advice and support; improving family prosperity and reducing child poverty through the tax and benefit system; making it easier for families to balance work and home; strengthening marriage and reducing the risks of family breakdown; tackling the more serious problems of family life, such.as domestic violence, truancy, and school-age pregnancy. One of the outcomes of the paper was the creation of the National Institute (now just Institute) for Parenting and the Family. (*See further Box 7.1.*)

Many of the issues raised in the *Supporting Families* paper have been taken forward. There have been reductions in child poverty. The framework for dealing with youth criminality has been subject to great change, particularly with an increased focus on keeping children and young people out of court, and, if court cannot be avoided, focusing on principles of restorative justice to encourage offenders to understand the impact of their behaviour on others (see Chapter 5). At the same time, it has been increasingly recognized that those responsible for raising families may also need support.

Box 7.1   Time for change

Institute for Parenting and the Family

This private charity was set up in 1999 following publication of *Supporting Families*. Its role is to bring together organizations, knowledge, and know-how. The Institute has adopted a manifesto setting out its principal objectives:

1. a national overarching family policy to ensure that families are at the centre of policy development on health, education, childcare, work, the law, tax and benefits, housing, transport, community safety, neighbourhood renewal, culture, and media;
2. a universal, co-ordinated network of family support services, including support for parents of teenagers, so parents have a place to go for help when they need it, and high quality services for parents who are struggling and for vulnerable children;
3. a family justice system that offers support for parents and children during family relationship difficulties and separation whilst continuing to put children at the centre of every decision;
4. a continuing commitment to support parents' work–life balance;
5. a childcare strategy that provides parents with real choices and high quality affordable childcare;
6. an ongoing commitment to the fight against child and family poverty;
7. a legislative framework which encourages businesses, the public, and the voluntary sector to make their services family-friendly, and protects the interests of parents and children;
8. a community regeneration strategy built on the recognition that local neighbourhoods are fundamental to the health and well-being of families; and
9. a commitment to consulting parents about issues which affect their children and families.

Source: Adapted from the website of the *Institute for Parenting and the Family* (2007).

The political importance of family policy has been recognized in significant changes to the machinery of government, In summer 2003 a Children's Minister was appointed within the (then) Department for Education and Science. Following further changes in July 2007, there is now a Department for Children, Schools and Families. The Minister, Beverley Hughes, MP, now attends cabinet meetings when social policy issues are under discussion.

In relation to children and family policy, the Department is working under two general policy headings. *Every Child Matters* is the policy designed to ensure that all children, whatever their background or their circumstances, have the support they need to: be healthy; stay safe; enjoy and achieve; make a positive contribution; and achieve economic well-being. These rather general aims cover a wide range of more detailed policies including: more assistance with the provision of childcare (the Childcare Act was passed in 2006 to help parents who want to go out to work); better integration of social services for children through Children's Trusts; and assistance with parenting skills (with grants being made to voluntary and community sector agencies to support this).

Many other initiatives have been taken forward under the government's *Sure Start* programme. This aims to: increase the availability of childcare for all children; improve health and emotional development for young children; and support parents as parents and in their aspirations towards employment. Sure Start covers children from conception through to age fourteen, and up to age sixteen for those with special educational needs and disabilities. One of the principal ways of delivering these objectives is through the creation of Children's Centres. These bring together childcare, early education, health, and family support services for families with children under five years old. The government aims to have created 2,500 centres by 2008.

In addition, under the Children Act 2004, the post of Children's Commissioner was created. His function is to ensure that ministers are continually reminded of and advised about the child's perspective in policy-making.

Law and the family

For present purposes, the principal functions of the law relating to the family may be defined as:

(1) to define the rules for the validity of marriage;

(2) to prescribe the bases on which marital relationships may be brought to an end through divorce or nullity;

(3) to deal with the consequences of divorce and other relationship breakdown, in particular questions of responsibility for children, financial support, and the division of property rights;

(4) to provide a framework for the protection of children, including care and adoption;

(5) to provide a framework for dealing with issues of domestic violence.

The last two are not dependent on the existence of a marriage; the first two are. The third is largely dependent on the existence of a marriage, though there is a limited though complex involvement of the law on the breakdown of *de facto* relationships.

The extent to which the law should be involved in the regulation of *de facto* relationships is currently the subject of considerable debate. For example, there has been fierce argument about the extent to which, if at all, the provisions for distributing property on the breakdown of a marriage should or should not apply to (heterosexual) *de facto* relationships where parties have lived together as a family, but without formally getting married. The Law Commission has recently reported on this subject. A Government response is awaited.

Equally controversial have been questions of the extent to which, if at all, those involved in homosexual relationships might be subject to analogous principles. The Civil Partnerships Act 2004 provides a legal framework within which same-sex couples can obtain legal recognition of their relationship by forming a civil partnership. They may do so by registering as civil partners of each other provided: they are of the same sex; they are not already in a civil partnership or lawfully married; they are not within the prohibited degrees of relationship; they are both aged 16 or over (and, if either of them is under 18 and the registration is to take place in England and Wales or Northern Ireland, the consent of appropriate people or bodies has been obtained). The Act also sets out the legal consequences of forming a civil partnership, including the rights and responsibilities of civil partners.

It is also important to note that, underpinning much development of the domestic law of England and Wales, there is an important international law dimension, particularly relating to the law which affects children. Although the International Convention on the Rights of the Child 1989 does not have direct impact on English law (unlike the law of the EU or the European Convention on Human Rights) it has considerable political significance. The effect of the Convention is kept under review by the Committee on the Rights of the Child, part of the United Nations Human Rights Commission.

Four particular issues have emerged in the last twenty years as factors which should influence not only the structure of the family justice system, but also the roles that people who work within that system should perform.

- First, there has been the important realization that if a marriage (or indeed other long-term relationship) does break down, the process of bringing that relationship to a formal end should—wherever possible—reduce the inevitable feelings of stress, rejection, and failure that accompany such a process, rather than add to them.

- Secondly, there is now a clearer acceptance, recognized in law, that the welfare of the child must be protected wherever possible.

- Thirdly, there is much concern about the extent to which parents who have separated should be able to maintain contact with their children.

- Fourthly, there is much greater awareness of the problem of domestic violence and other forms of abuse which occur in the family home. There have been a number of important legal developments designed both to assist victims of abuse, and also to send the broader educational message that such behaviour is not acceptable.

These issues have informed much of the institutional development of the family justice system and the attitudes of those who practise within it.

Family justice: the institutional framework

England and Wales has no specialist family court. Rather there is a complex set of arrangements with different courts having a range of powers to determine the different issues that may arise in family law. While the idea of a separate family court has not been accepted by government, it is accepted that, in most areas of family work, the relevant judiciary should be specially suited to the particular tasks it has to perform.

In many instances judges must undertake specialist training before they can determine family cases, particularly those relating to children. The training embraces not only instruction on the law and legal procedures, but also issues relating to theories of child development and principles of social work. The difficulty of resolving cases relating to children can hardly be overstated, since the outcome of such cases may be that children are removed from one parent and transferred to another, or are removed from the parent(s) altogether and placed under the care and supervision of others. Judicial training is designed to ensure that as appropriate decisions as possible are taken.

While turning its face against a specialist family court, the government has decided that there should be a single code of procedure for the different courts. Under the Courts Act 2003, a Family Procedure Rules Committee was established with the ultimate objective of writing a new uniform set of Family Procedure Rules. At the end of 2005, the Committee completed the first stage of the process with uniform rules arising from the Adoption and Children Act 2002. It is currently dealing with a number of other issues, for example relating to different routes of appeal. The government also created the Family Justice Council to keep the family justice system as a whole under review. (*See Box 7.2.*)

There is one important, and controversial, respect in which the family courts operate differently from most other courts and tribunals. Much of their work is closed to the public. This has long been justified on the ground that publicity, especially between warring parents, could be extremely damaging to children. On the other hand, there have been counter-arguments that private hearings enable judges to reach decisions that do not always appear to be fair. The present government has wavered on the issue. In 2006 it issued a consultation paper suggesting that, among other things, the media should have access to proceedings as of right, though with a power given to the court to exclude and to set reporting restrictions. There were sharp responses to these proposals. In particular, organizations representing children argued strongly that such an approach would not work in the interests of the children. The government has decided not to go ahead with its original proposals. Instead, in July 2007, it issued a further consultation paper. It now argues that the better way forward is to exclude the media, though give courts the power to admit the media in particular cases. Final decisions on these issues are pending.

Box 7.2 Time for change

The Family Justice Council

The Council was established in July 2004. Its terms of reference require it to facilitate the delivery of better and quicker outcomes for families and children who use the family justice system by:

- promoting improved interdisciplinary working across the family justice system through inclusive discussion, communication, and co-ordination between all agencies;
- identifying and disseminating best practice throughout the family justice system by facilitating a mutual exchange of information between local committees and the Council, including information on local initiatives;
- consulting with government departments on current policy and priorities and securing best value from available resources;
- providing guidance and direction to achieve consistency of practice throughout the family justice system and submitting proposals for new practice directions where appropriate;
- promoting commitment to legislative principles and the objectives of the family justice system by disseminating advice and promoting inter-agency discussion, including by way of seminars and conferences as appropriate;
- promoting the effectiveness of the family justice system by identifying priorities for, and encouraging the conduct of, research;
- providing advice and making recommendation to government on changes to legislation, practice, and procedure, which will improve the workings of the family justice system.

Source: Adapted from *Family Justice Council website, 2007.*

Children

From October 1991 (when the Children Act 1989 came into force) there has been a common jurisdiction across all the tiers of the court structure for dealing with issues relating to children. The structure is designed to enable cases to be disposed of at the most appropriate court level. Three levels of courts need to be considered:

- family proceedings courts;
- the county court; and
- the High Court.

Family proceedings courts

Family Proceedings Courts are magistrates' courts which deal with family matters. The lay magistrates who sit in them are drawn from specially selected family panels, the members of which have all been trained and receive on-going training. The district judges who sit in family proceedings are also specially trained. In this jurisdiction they sit with lay justices. Family proceedings courts have jurisdiction to deal with both public and private law cases relating to children. (For the distinction between public law and private law cases, *see Box 7.3*.) All public law cases start in the family proceedings court. (Despite their name, family proceedings courts do not deal with divorce.)

This is a busy jurisdiction. Nearly 13,500 public law applications were made in the family proceedings court in 2005; nearly 15,000 private law applications were made during the same period.

The county court

County courts are divided into five distinct categories:

- non-divorce county courts, with no power to deal with any family law matters;
- divorce county courts, which can issue all private law family proceedings but from which, if a matter is contested, it is referred to a family hearing centre for trial;

Box 7.3 Legal system explained

Public law and private law children cases

In relation to children, an important distinction must be drawn between public law cases and private law cases. *Public law* cases are brought by public authorities—in particular the social services departments of local authorities—or other agencies such as the NSPCC. They may be seeking orders from the court relating to the care, supervision, or emergency protection of children. *Private law* cases are those brought by private individuals, usually the parents of the child, seeking orders relating to the child in the context of a divorce or the separation of the parents.

One of the principal objectives of the Children Act 1989 was to ensure that the voice of the child was heard. To assist in this, in most public law applications, the court appoints a children's guardian to assist the child, unless the court is satisfied that this is not needed to protect the interests of the child. The role of the guardian is to ensure that the court is fully informed of facts relevant to determining the best interests of the child. She also seeks to ensure that the court is made fully aware of the child's feelings and wishes. Guardians are provided by the Children and Family Courts Advisory and Support Service (CAFCASS), established in 2001 by the Criminal Justice and Court Services Act 2000. In defined cases, the guardian is also required to appoint a solicitor to act for the child, to ensure proper legal representation.

In private law cases, an analogous role is played by the Childrens and Family Reporter, also appointed by CAFCASS.

- family hearing centres which can issue and hear all private law family cases whether or not they are contested;

- care centres, with full powers to deal with all private law and public law matters;

- specialized adoption centres, which have power to issue, hear and process adoption applications under guidance issued by the President of the Family Division.[1]

The circuit judges and district judges who deal with matters relating to children under the Children Act 1989 have to be specially nominated[2] for family work by the Lord Chancellor. They are not so nominated without receiving special training and guidance. They are formally known as 'nominated care judges'.[3] The circuit judges who are nominated have full powers to deal with all public and private law matters. District judges who have been nominated as care judges can hear uncontested public law cases, and contested private law cases. In addition to the nominated care judges there is also a group of circuit family judges who can deal with private law matters, but not public law matters.

County courts have a very large case-load. In 2005 they received nearly 86,000 private law applications, plus around 8,500 public law cases.

The High Court

Although there are no formal training requirements for High Court judges who do family work, nonetheless they sit in a separate division of the High Court—the Family Division. There are seventeen such judges, plus a President, specially appointed to give leadership to this specialist group of judiciary. The smallness of their number enables them to operate in a collegiate style with a fair degree of common purpose and approach.

The High Court has power to hear all cases relating to children. It has exclusive power to decide matters relating to wardship, whereby the court assumes responsibility for the child, taking over from the parents. It also hears appeals from family proceedings courts. The work-load of the High Court is numerically trivial by comparison with those of the other two courts—just 253 public law and 292 private law applications in 2005. But its more important decisions are reported and thus develop the jurisprudence of the family justice system.

---

[1] *Adoption Proceedings—A New Approach* (London, Lord Chancellor's Department, 2001).

[2] One exception is that circuit judges who are not nominated can still hear cases involving requests for injunctions arising from allegations of domestic violence and some other matrimonial work.

[3] There are also designated family judges who, besides undertaking normal judicial duties as nominated care judges, also chair local Family Court Business Committees and Family Court Forums—both mechanisms for improving working relationships between the courts and their users.

Orders

The Children Act 1989 provides for a wide range of orders which can be made by the courts. They include:

- care/supervision orders;
- emergency protection orders;
- exclusion requirements; and
- 'section 8' orders.

Care/supervision orders

These are made on application by either a local authority or the NSPCC.[4] Before an order may be made, the court must be satisfied either that a child is suffering or is likely to suffer significant harm, and that the harm or likelihood of harm is attributable to:

(1) the care given to the child; or

(2) the likelihood of the care not being what it would be reasonable to expect a parent to give a child;

or that the child is beyond parental control.

If the court is so satisfied, it may make an order:

(1) placing the child in the care of a designated local authority; or

(2) putting the child under the supervision of a designated local authority or probation officer.

Such orders cannot be made in relation to a child who has reached the age of seventeen (sixteen if the child is married).

The effect of a *care order* is to impose a duty on the local authority to keep the child in care, to exercise parental responsibility over the child, and determine the extent to which a parent or guardian may meet his or her parental responsibility towards the child.[5] The effect of a *supervision order* is to impose a duty on the supervisor to advise, assist, and befriend the child, and to take the necessary action to give effect to the order, including whether or not to apply to vary or discharge it.

Emergency protection orders

These may be made where the court is satisfied that there is reasonable cause to believe that a child is suffering, or is likely to suffer, significant harm if not removed to accommodation provided by the applicant, or that the child should not remain in the place

---

[4] The National Society for the Prevention of Cruelty to Children. It is the only 'authorized person' under the terms of the Children Act able to bring such proceedings.

[5] The impact of placing children in care, particularly in care homes run by the authority, can be extremely severe; see Tribunal of Inquiry into Child Abuse, *Lost in Care* (HC 201, 1999–2000) (London, The Stationery Office, 2000).

where she is currently living. Emergency protection orders may be sought where anyone, including a local authority, believes that access to a child is being unreasonably refused.

Exclusion requirements

From October 1997, the courts have had power to order the exclusion of a suspected abuser from a child's home, where ill-treatment of the child is alleged, and either an interim care order or an emergency protection order has been made. A power of arrest can be added to the exclusion requirement, so that anyone in breach may be instantly arrested. Before an exclusion requirement can be ordered, the court must be satisfied that there will still be a person remaining in the premises with the child, and that that person has agreed to care for the child and has consented to the exclusion requirement.

'Section 8' orders

Orders made under section 8 of the Children Act include:

- *residence* orders, determining where the child should live;
- *contact* orders, deciding whom the child may see;
- *prohibited steps* orders, to prevent a defined action(s) taking place; and
- *specific issue* orders, dealing with particular aspects of a child's upbringing.

During 2005, a total of 97,418 section 8 orders were made, the vast bulk of them relating to residence and contact.

Problems with the enforcement of these orders, highlighted by the recent activities of direct campaign organizations such as Fathers 4 Justice, have resulted in the government introducing new rules for dealing with parental separation. Following publication of a Green Paper, *Parental Separation: Children's Needs and Parents' Responsibilities* in July 2004, and the White Paper *Parental Separation: Children's Needs and Parents' Responsibilities, Next Steps* in January 2005, a draft Children (Contact) and Adoption Bill was published and subjected to pre-legislative scrutiny in the first half of 2005. The resulting Children and Adoption Bill was introduced into Parliament in summer 2005 and became an Act in 2006.

The Act has two objectives. First it wants to promote the quality of contact between parent and child. The Act gives the court power to direct a party to take part in an activity that would promote contact with a child. Contact activities include attendance at programmes, classes or counselling sessions designed to improve the quality of contact time, or to address a person's violent behaviour. This may occur during the proceedings, even if the court does not make a contact order, or by making such activity a condition in a contact order. Second, it gives the court wider powers in cases involving breach of a contact order by adding: a power to make enforcement orders imposing an unpaid work requirement; and a power to order one person to pay compensation to another for a financial loss caused by a breach. These powers are in addition to their powers as to contempt and their ability to alter the residence and contact arrangements relating to a child.

Adoption

The other main activity of the courts in relation to children concerns adoption, whereby the rights, duties, and obligations of a child's natural parents are legally extinguished and are vested, by order of the court, in the adoptive parents. It is essential that the court is satisfied that the adoptive parents are suitable and have consented to the adoption. Where possible it is also necessary to obtain the consent of the parents (including any guardian with parental responsibility), though this may be dispensed with if there is evidence that the natural parent has persistently ill-treated the child or that consent is being unreasonably withheld. Once again, the primary objective of the courts is to safeguard and promote the welfare of the child. This includes taking the views of the child into account.

After a long period of gestation, major changes to the law of adoption were made in 2002.[6] The intention is, while continuing to protect children, to make it easier for those wishing to adopt children to do so, thereby increasing the number of adoptions currently sanctioned by the legal process. The government is particularly anxious that more children, currently in the care of local authorities, should be adopted. Judicial statistics reveal, however, that the number of adoptions has been falling. In 2005 some 4,000 orders were actually made (a decrease of 12 per cent on the previous year), around 22 per cent being in favour of the child's step-parents.

Matrimonial matters

The other principal work of the courts in the context of the family relates to the dissolution of marriages. For these purposes the courts are the county courts, except those designated as *non-divorce county courts*.

A marriage may be dissolved in two ways: divorce and nullity. *Divorce* is much more frequently used. To obtain a divorce, the petitioner must prove that the marriage has broken down irretrievably. This can be demonstrated by proof of: adultery; behaviour

---

[6] The Adoption and Children Act 2002. The history of this measure can be traced back at least ten years. See Department of Health and Welsh Office, *Review of Adoption Law* (London, HMSO, 1992); *Adoption: The Future* (Cm 2288) (London, Department of Health, Welsh Office, Home Office and Lord Chancellor's Department, 1993); *Adoption—A Service for Children: Adoption Bill—A Consultative Document* (London, Department of Health and Welsh Office, 1996); Prime Minister's Review, *Adoption* (London, Performance and Innovation Unit, July 2000); White Paper, *Adoption—a New Approach* (Cm 5017) (London, The Stationery Office, 2000).

which the petitioner cannot reasonably be expected to live with; desertion for at least two years; two years' separation where the respondent consents; five years' separation where there is no such consent. Evidence of irretrievable breakdown is usually considered by a district judge. If proved, a provisional measure, the *decree nisi,* is made. The divorce becomes final only after a final decision, the *decree absolute.* The existence of this two-stage process is to provide an opportunity, albeit rarely used, for second thoughts. Most cases are disposed of on the basis of paper evidence without the need for a hearing.

Where children are involved, the court must be satisfied with the arrangements for their welfare. These must be written down and, if possible, agreed between the parents. If agreement is not possible, the judge may order the parents to come to court so that the issues may be resolved. If the issues are uncontested at this point, the judge may issue a *section 8 order* (see above).

The divorce case-load is enormous.[7] In 2005, over 151,000 petitions for divorce were filed; just over 150,000 decrees nisi were made, and over 142,000 decrees absolute were made.

Nullity is the other mode of dissolving a marriage. However this can be used only where there is proof that the marriage either was void in the first place (e.g. because one of the parties was under the age of 16 or was already married), or was voidable (e.g. because one of the parties was pregnant by someone else at the time of the marriage or the marriage was not consummated due to incapacity or wilful refusal). To obtain a decree of nullity, a two-stage process, similar to the divorce process, must be gone through. By contrast with divorce, this mode of dissolution is rare: 436 petitions were filed in 2005.

Judicial separation is an alternative procedure for those who do not wish to or who for some reason cannot get divorced. It does not terminate the marriage, but legally absolves the parties to a marriage from the obligation to live together. Just 387 separation decrees were granted in 2005.

Ancillary relief

Ancillary relief refers to the powers of the court to make orders linked to divorce or other matrimonial proceedings. These relate to maintenance (periodical payments to an ex-spouse) and to lump sum payments or property orders (usually dealing with the matrimonial home). As with divorce, the courts for these purposes are the county courts.

---

[7] Numbers of divorces have grown enormously over the last fifty years, reflecting both changes in social attitudes and changes in the law. Even in 1968 only 54,000 petitions were filed. The peak was in 1990, when 191,615 petitions were filed.

The powers of the courts to deal with maintenance orders relating to the children of the marriage have largely been taken over by the child support system (see below). Since April 1993, most new applications for maintenance have been dealt with by the Child Support Agency. Initially there was a plan to transfer then existing court orders to the Agency. However the controversies and operational chaos that surrounded the Agency led to an indefinite deferment of this plan. Thus the county courts still have to make a large number of orders relating to the maintenance of children. In 2005, over 15,000 such orders were made.

In 2005, the courts also made over 15,000 orders relating to the payment of a lump sum or the transfer of property and approved another 50,000 ancillary relief orders which were made with the consent of the parties.

Enforcement

One of the problems with the maintenance system was that people just did not pay. Enforcement procedures are available. For example, where the relevant ex-spouse is in work, the other former spouse may ask the county court for an *attachment of earnings order* which requires the employer to pay a proportion of salary or wages to that former spouse. In 2005, 640 applications for such an order were made, and 623 were granted. In addition it is possible to register the maintenance order in the magistrates' courts which are made responsible for collecting the maintenance. 1,033 registration orders were made in 2005.

Failure to pay is a contempt of court, the ultimate sanction for which may be an order committing the person in contempt to prison. This is a threat that on occasion can be used to stimulate the payments due. However the reality is that enforcement of periodical maintenance payments against an ex-spouse who is not willing to make such payments is not easily achieved.

Procedural reform

Detailed reform of procedures relating to ancillary relief was introduced in June 2000. These were designed to promote early settlement between the parties, to eliminate unnecessary delay, and to keep costs down.[8] As with the broader reforms to the civil justice system (see Chapter 8), the key is active judicial case management, combined with the need for proportionality—ensuring that the costs of the proceedings are proportionate to the assets in dispute. Both sides are required to make the other party aware of how costs are mounting up, particularly if there is unnecessary delay in reaching a conclusion. A further innovation is that the parties are required to undergo a financial dispute resolution appointment in which, with the assistance of a judge,

---

[8] An extreme example of costs not being proportionate to the resources available is found in *Piglowska v. Piglowska* [1999] 2 FLR 763 (HL).

an attempt is made to help the parties agree an outcome, rather than have a solution imposed on them by the judge.

Child support

One of the most controversial structural changes made to the family justice system has been the creation of the child support system.

The principle behind its establishment in 1993[9] was straightforward. Far too many single parents, mostly women, found it impossible either to obtain an order for the maintenance of their children or, if they did obtain one, were unable to enforce it. A consequence of this was that lone parents were heavily dependent on the provision of social security benefits for the financial resources needed to bring up their children, rather than being supported by the child's natural but absent parent. Indeed during the preceding decade, while the number of children living in lone-parent families increased substantially, the proportion of children receiving maintenance fell. In 1989, 23 per cent of lone parents claiming income support were receiving maintenance, compared to around 50 per cent in 1979. The child support system was intended to reverse this decline, by providing consistent rules for assessing maintenance liability and a readily accessible means for collecting and enforcing payment that was due. A system for getting absent parents to pay for their children had been introduced in Australia in the 1980s, apparently with great success. Thus, it was argued, a similar scheme could be introduced in the United Kingdom.

From the outset the British scheme was dogged by controversy. One crucial difference between the British and Australian models was that, in the former, for every pound paid by the absent parent a pound of social security benefit was lost; in Australia, for every dollar of maintenance paid by the absent parent, the parent with care lost only 85 cents of her social security payments. Although the Australian model was less advantageous from a purely public expenditure point of view, it had the supreme psychological advantage that the absent parent felt that (usually) he was, by making the payments, actually improving the quality of life for his child(ren). In the United Kingdom, there was no such positive incentive.

The force of these criticisms was to a limited degree acknowledged by the previous government in the Child Support Act 1995. This introduced the *Child Maintenance Bonus,* intended as an incentive to encourage parents with care into work, and the *departures* scheme which allowed for the normal rules for the assessment of child support liability to be departed from in order to take account of exceptional circumstances not recognized in the formula-based assessment.

---

[9] Child Support Act 1991.

However, these changes did not go far enough. In 2000, the Labour government passed further legislation to enable reform of the child support system to be put in place.[10] The government defined the principal problems to be dealt with thus:

- while the Child Support Agency (CSA) has almost 1.5 million children on its books, only around 300,000 gain financially from child support payments. Of these 300,000, only around 100,000 see the benefit of all the maintenance that is due;
- the complexity of the current formula led to long delays in assessing liability. This in turn made it difficult to ensure that child support was paid regularly. Because the assessment process is complex, the CSA had less time to help parents understand what they should pay or chase up non-payment; and
- families living on income support do not gain from the payment of maintenance as their benefit is reduced by an amount equal to the maintenance paid.

The key changes provided for in the Child Support, Pensions and Social Security Act 2000 included:

- the formula for assessing child support was replaced with a simpler system of rates;
- the processes for applying for child support and the way in which child support liability is decided were simplified;
- there are clear penalties for parents who deliberately misrepresent their circumstances to the CSA—and for those who refuse to provide the information needed to calculate liability and collect maintenance;
- there is the possibility of varying the normal rate of maintenance liability to recognize certain exceptional costs and sources of income;
- there are rights to appeal against decisions on child support liability and the processes by which liability will be kept up to date;
- the formation of a complete and comprehensive collection scheme with financial and other penalties for late and non-payment; and
- improvements to the provisions for establishing paternity.

Given the history of the scheme, there was much scepticism as to whether the problems that attracted so much criticism would in fact be addressed, particularly given the reluctance of absent parents in particular to co-operate with the working of the scheme. Indeed, implementation of the new scheme was delayed because of problems with the supporting information technology. The reformed scheme started, for new cases only, in March 2003.

---

[10] The Child Support, Pensions and Social Security Act 2000. Proposals were first published in July 1998 in the consultation document *Children First: a New Approach to Child Support* (Cm 3992) (London, The Stationery Office, 1998). This led to the White Paper, *A New Contract for Welfare: Children's Rights and Parents' Responsibilities* (Cm 4349) (London, The Stationery Office, 1999).

Since then, the Agency continued to be subject to serious criticism, with constant and critical comments from the Independent Case Examiner, and adverse reports from the Parliamentary Ombudsman. It was the subject of an investigation by the Work and Pensions Select Committee of the House of Commons.

All these pressures led to the Government, in 2006, commissioning a special review of the child support scheme by Sir David Henshaw. He argued for a fresh start with a redesigned scheme. The government accepted many of his recommendations and published a further White Paper—*A New System of Child Maintenance*—in 2006. In June 2007, a Child Maintenance and Other Payments Bill was introduced into the House of Commons. If enacted, the resulting Act will establish a Child Maintenance and Enforcement Commission, to replace the largely discredited Child Support Agency. It will place a new emphasis on parents making and keeping voluntary maintenance arrangements. It will also remove the current requirement that parents in receipt of certain social security benefits must use the child support scheme. There are also provisions designed to help people manage their financial resources better. It is anticipated that the new scheme will come into effect sometime in 2008.

The Child Support scheme has never worked as it was intended to do. Indeed, there is evidence that, notwithstanding the efforts in other parts of the family justice system to reduce tensions between former partners, the child support system actually exacerbated the problems existing between them. The current system has also been severely criticized for damaging the new relationships that the absent parent may be trying to establish, by reducing the level of resource available for any new family. Given this track record, there remains concern that the new changes will still not be wholly effective. However, judgment on this must be suspended until the new Act has had a chance to work. At present, this is not a part of the English legal system that is currently fit for the task it should be seeking to perform.

Domestic violence

Another way in which the family justice system has been transformed over the last twenty-five years has been the recognition of the problem of domestic violence and the need for the law and legal procedures to deal with cases swiftly and effectively. There are now two principal items of legislation relevant in this context:

- Family Law Act 1996, Part IV; and
- Protection from Harassment Act 1997.

Family Law Act 1996, Part IV

This Act provides for a set of remedies in cases of domestic violence which can be sought either in the county court or the magistrates' court or (rarely) in the High

Court. Two types of order may be made:

- a *non-molestation order,* which is an order to prohibit a person from behaving in a particular way towards another or which may seek to prohibit molestation in general; and
- an *occupation order* which can define or regulate the rights of a person to occupy a home (irrespective of his ownership rights in that home).

This law is available not only to married couples, but much more widely to cohabiting couples, others who live or have lived in the same household as the person seeking the order (though not tenants, boarders, or lodgers), certain relatives (such as parents, or brothers or sisters), and those who have agreed to marry.

If the court thinks that the respondent has used or has threatened violence against either the applicant or any child of the applicant, then the court must attach a power of arrest to the order, unless satisfied that the applicant or child will be adequately protected without such a power being attached.

In addition, the court may at the same time add an *exclusion requirement* to an *emergency protection order* or *interim care order* made under the Children Act 1989 (see above, p. 183), so that the suspected abuser (rather than the abused child) may be removed from the dwelling.

There is a substantial case-load arising from these provisions. In 2005, over 17,000 applications for non-molestation orders were made, and about 10,000 applications for occupation orders—all but a handful in the county court.

Protection from Harassment Act 1997

This Act was initially introduced to combat the problem of stalking, but it applies more generally to the victims of harassment. Section 3 allows civil proceedings to be taken against anyone pursuing a course of harassment. The remedies available are an injunction—an order to prevent such behaviour in the future—and/or damages. Since September 1998, the courts have had power to make breach of an injunction enforceable by warrant of arrest. No information is available on the use of these new provisions.

The practitioners

Lawyers

Given the fact that so many aspects of family life are regulated by law, in particular the issues relating to children, relationship breakdown and other financial matters, it is inevitable that legal practitioners should be deeply involved in family law issues. This is a major area for legal specialism, with large numbers of lawyers offering family law services. A considerable part of the legal aid budget (now the Community Legal Services Fund) is devoted to family law issues.

Practitioners have given considerable thought to their proper role in assisting the resolution of family disputes. For example, should they engage in heavily adversarial forms of litigation designed to advance their clients' interests, irrespective of the interests of the other party to the marriage or relationship and the children? Or should they adopt a more conciliatory approach?

The perception that lawyers often added to the problems of separating couples rather than helping their resolution led, some years ago, to the formation of the Solicitors' Family Law Association—now called Resolution. (There is an equivalent for barristers—the Family Law Bar Association.) It aims to bring a less hostile atmosphere to the resolution of family disputes.

Research suggests that, in general, solicitors have been rather successful at not exacerbating the conflicts between couples. This is not to say that lawyers are above criticism in the area of family disputes. They are criticized for, for example:

- a desultory approach to negotiation;
- large case-loads but with little activity on each individual case;
- high costs; and
- high levels of pressure to reach final settlements, as cases approach court.

Nevertheless client demand for legal services to assist in the resolution of family disputes has remained high. Surveys of clients' responses to the legal services provided have, in general, been positive.

One of the ways in which practitioners have sought to develop the nature of their work with clients in the family law area has been through schemes of specialist training. For a number of years, the Law Society has run a *Childrens' Panel,* aimed particularly at solicitors who act for children in public law cases. Admission to the panel involves the lawyers demonstrating appropriate levels of qualifications and experience.

In addition the Law Society, during 1999, announced that it would establish a Family Law Panel. The Solicitors' Family Law Association has also established its own Family Law Panel and, in 1999, it launched a scheme for the accreditation of those lawyers who sought to join the panel.

Those who practise family law have recognized the particular character of the work they have to undertake, dealing not only with the very considerable complexities of the law but also the strong emotional context within which such work has to be carried out. As the need for special training of the judiciary has been accepted, so too the importance of special training for practitioners has also been acknowledged.

Mediation and mediators

Notwithstanding the efforts of professional lawyers to shape the nature of family law practice to the needs of clients, the view of government has been that there needed to be further changes in the ways in which family disputes are resolved, particularly those which are funded by the state. This has led to the view that a preferable way of resolving family disputes should be through *mediation* outside the courts, rather than *litigation* in the courts.

Mediation is a form of assisted negotiation. However, instead of the process taking place just between the parties to the dispute and/or their representatives, mediation involves the intervention of an impartial third party, the mediator. The mediator's function is to attempt to help the parties to a dispute reach an agreement acceptable to both sides. The mediator cannot impose a solution on the parties; nevertheless the presence of the mediator can contribute to the pressure to settle disputes.

Family mediation services are provided, broadly, by two distinct groups:

- a 'not-for-profit' largely volunteer sector of people who have received special training in the mediation process and are affiliated to specialist organizations that provide mediation services; and

- a 'for-profit' sector, principally lawyers who have received specialist training and who want to add mediation (and other forms of ADR) to the range of professional services that they are able to offer to clients.

Mediation to resolve family disputes has been used for many years. Experience suggests that it is often successful in bringing the parties to an agreement. There is also evidence that it is liked by those who have gone through the process. Nevertheless, despite the enthusiasm of those who offer mediation services, there is also clear evidence that only a small number of parties to family disputes actually ask for their disputes to be the subject of mediation.

Notwithstanding this relative lack of consumer demand, it was decided that the use of mediation in the context of family disputes should be encouraged. At least one of the reasons in the government's mind at the time was that use of mediation might save costs, particularly for those using legal aid funding to obtain a divorce or obtain other remedies from a court.

Part III of the Family Law Act 1996 amended the Legal Aid Act 1988 by providing that legal aid money could be used to pay for mediation services. These provisions were to apply in the context of all 'family matters',[11] not just divorce proceedings. The key test in the legislation was whether or not mediation might be suitable in any particular case. Those engaged in mediation were to operate under a code of practice which provided, for example, that mediation would clearly not be suitable if there was any fear of violence; nor, more generally, if either of the parties was not willing to use mediation. The teeth in the new provisions were found in section 29, which provided that, before legal aid for representation of a party before a court could be granted, the party to a family dispute who was seeking legal aid (usually the woman) had to attend a mediation meeting to determine whether or not mediation would be suitable. These provisions were introduced in September 1998, in six pilot areas.

---

[11] Defined in s. 26(1). Broadly this covers most of the issues considered in this chapter.

The impact of these provisions on costs and outcomes was researched on behalf of the Legal Aid Board. The researchers found that the number of cases deemed not suitable for mediation rose substantially, doubtless because prior to the introduction of section 29 only volunteers sought to use mediation services. Further, relatively few cases got beyond the intake appointment stage. In addition, the researchers found that the bulk of the work is provided by not-for-profit, rather than by for-profit providers. The challenge which the researchers identified was that the statutory goal of establishing a national network of specialist mediation services provided by the not-for-profit sector was unlikely to be achievable cost effectively, at least while levels of the use of mediation remained so low.

A number of more specific problems were also identified:

- solicitors remained reluctant to use mediation, and were critical of the delays inherent in the process, particularly in cases where mediation would clearly not be suitable;

- very little could be done at present to engage the second party, if he would not attend the intake appointment. Even a case deemed suitable for mediation cannot go to mediation if the second party was not willing to contemplate mediation; and

- a lot of resource was being expended on the intake appointment where no actual mediation resulted.

Notwithstanding all these difficulties, the funding code for the provision of the Community Legal Service (see further below) has retained the principles set out in the Family Law Act, Part III, which are carried into the new funding regime. The government has accepted that family mediation should remain an important form of dispute resolution for family disputes.

Box 7.4   Time for change

Case study: couple counselling: the work of Relate[12]

Relate is a national charity which offers counselling services either to couples or to individuals whose relationships are in difficulty. Counsellors undergo a lengthy period of training. The primary object of their work is not so much to save marriages (or other long-term relationships) as to assist partners to understand better the nature of the difficulties that have arisen in the relationship. This may have the effect of enabling couples to rethink their relationship and lead to the relationship continuing. Equally it may help couples to realize that the relationship is unlikely to succeed, but, by assisting

---

[12] Relate is not the only body offering counselling services; its website offers links to other counselling bodies.

Box 7.4   *Continued*

understanding of the reasons for the relationship failure, help to reduce friction after the relationship has ended. This is of particular benefit in helping the children of a relationship to adjust to the consequences of the relationship failure. Relate is not the only agency offering such services, but is perhaps the best known.

At present the provision of counselling services, whether through Relate or otherwise, is patchy. The ability of people to take advantage of the service depends on whether a service is available in any given location. In many areas long-established services are having to close for lack of resources. Furthermore, the fees payable for the service vary considerably. Many Relate centres have to charge quite high fees just to cover their overhead costs. This has the effect of preventing the less well off from using the service. Finally the service will be used only by those who wish to take advantage of it. Many of those who might benefit most from the service will not do so, as they will not see themselves as the sorts of people for whom counselling will be of assistance.

The government has been considering the extent to which the provision of such services should form part of its family policy. A report by Sir Graham Hart, published in 1999, noted that marital breakdown and divorce not only cause much damage to couples and their children, but also impose very substantial costs on the taxpayer—estimated then at around £5 billion a year.

Sir Graham was asked to consider the extent to which support for marriage might be developed and funded. He defined marriage support to include not only support when relationships were going wrong, but also the provision of help and support for people to enable them to enter and maintain long-term and stable relationships. Where marriage support can help to save marriages, there is a direct saving to the taxpayer.

While Sir Graham saw the development of marriage support as the responsibility of the voluntary sector, in partnership with local authorities, relevant statutory bodies, and the universities, he thought this would only occur with increased investment by government. In addition, he argued that the Lord Chancellor's Department, as then the department with prime responsibility for family policy, should take a positive role in the promotion of these developments. Sir Graham argued that it was important to develop service provision by assisting with the costs of running nationally provided services. He also suggested it was necessary to invest in relevant research and development projects.

The response so far has been limited. There is still a considerable way to go before the perfectly sensible objectives of the government's strategy will be achieved. A modest programme of short-term grant funding is no substitute for the regular income that can allow counselling services to become securely established. But the fact that this issue is now accepted as a responsibility of government is an important step forward. In this respect, this service may be seen as part of the family justice system, in the broad sense adopted in this book.

Funding family law cases

Family law matters were subject to special rules under the former Legal Aid scheme. Under the Access to Justice Act 1999, special rules relating to the provision of funded legal services in family law matters continue to apply. Under the Community Legal Service's *Funding Code*[13] family proceedings are defined to apply to all proceedings which arise out of family relationships, including cases in which the welfare of children is determined. Special priority is given to cases involving domestic violence.

Following amendments to the funding code in 2007, five levels of service are available in family cases. *Legal help* covers the initial meeting and any follow-up advice. Cases not resolved at this stage may be referred to *Family Mediation*. Where this is not appropriate, *Family Help (Lower)* exists to provide more substantial advice, assistance and negotiation to resolve disputes. This can also be used to support families through Family Mediation. *Family Help (Higher)* is used where is it necessary to issue proceedings with a view to securing the early resolution of a family dispute; it does not cover preparation for or representation at any final hearing. Where that is needed *Legal Representation* is available.

Children Act proceedings

Funding remains automatically available for a child in respect of whom an application for a care or supervision order, a child assessment order, an emergency protection order, or the extension or discharge of an emergency protection order has been made. In addition funding is available for any parent of or person with parental responsibility for such a child. A child against whom a secure accommodation order might be made restricting the child's liberty will also obtain legal services funding. This applies only to first instance proceedings. However, funding for any appeal is subject to a merits test—assessing the merits of the case. A limited merits test also operates in the case of adoption proceedings.

In the case of private law children disputes, legal representation may be refused unless reasonable attempts to resolve the dispute through negotiation or in other ways without recourse to proceedings have been made. A similar principle applies in cases relating to financial provision and other proceedings, such as contested divorce proceedings or nullity proceedings. Special rules apply to child abduction cases.

Total expenditure on family cases is substantial, currently over two-thirds of the Community Legal Service budget. Despite this, practitioners report that achieving profitability in legal aid practice is increasingly difficult; there are signs that the Legal Services Commission is beginning to share that concern. In March 2007 it published *Making Legal Rights a Reality for Children and Families*, setting out its view on its funding priorities for the coming years.

---

[13] Discussed in more detail, below in Chapter 10.

Conclusion

Family law disputes involve extremely difficult issues which have to be handled with particular care—especially where children are involved. This is an area both of substantive law and of legal practice which has evolved considerably in recent years, and will continue to do so. It is also an area in which the impact of research on the development of law and practice has been significant.

Looking to the future, many of the issues likely to come onto the agenda for the reform of family law will be very controversial. Although governments may claim that they are happy for individuals to make their own choices about how they should structure their lives and relationships, a desire to get 'back to basics' is one that successive Prime Ministers seem to find hard to resist.

Questions to test knowledge

1. What is the difference between public and private law children cases?
2. What is the Family Procedure Rules Committee?
3. What is the Family Justice Council?
4. What is ancillary relief?

Questions for reflection and discussion

1. What is the proper role of the state in the regulation of family relationships? What are the limits to that role?

2. Should there be a separate Family Court?

3. What are the arguments for and against family court proceedings being held in private?

4. Should all family disputes be mediated?

5. What contribution can counselling make to the resolution of family issues?

6. Is the principle of 'child support' correct? How could it be made to work so that absent parents make a proper financial contribution to the cost of their children? How can that cost be borne where the absent parent starts a new family?

7. Should decisions on contact start from the proposition that the father should see his child at least 50 per cent of the time? Should contact rights be extended to grandparents? Or is the principle of the 'welfare of the child' the only practical starting point for making decisions in contact cases?

8. How far should the law regulate the relationships of those who live together who are not married?

9. How far can the law promote good parenting? Does it have any role to play?

10. Can the law do more to prevent domestic violence and abuse?

Further reading

BARLOW, A., DUNCAN, S., GRACE, J., AND PARK, A., *Cohabitation, Marriage and the Law: Social Change and Legal Reform in the 20th Century* (Oxford, Hart, 2005)

BRIDGE, C., *The Legal Regulation of Family Relations* (Manchester, University of Manchester, Faculty of Law, 1992)

BROPHY, J., and SMART, C., *Women-in-law: Explorations in Law, Family and Sexuality* (London, Routledge & Kegan Paul, 1985)

CRETNEY, S., *Law, Law Reform and the Family* (Oxford, Clarendon Press, 1998)

—— *Same-sex Relationships: From Odious Crime to Gay Marriage* (Oxford, Oxford University Press, 2006)

—— MASSON, J.M., and BAILEY-HARRIS, R., *Principles of Family Law* (7th edn., London, Sweet & Maxwell, 2002; 8th edn. forthcoming, 2008)

DAVIES, G., *Partisans and Mediators: The Resolution of Divorce Disputes* (Oxford, Clarendon Press, 1998)

—— CRETNEY, S., and COLLINS, J., *Simple Quarrels: Negotiations and Adjudication in Divorce* (Oxford, Clarendon Press, 1994)

—— EEKELAAR, J., and MACLEAN, M. (eds), *Family Law* (Oxford, Oxford University Press, 1994)

FREEMAN, M.D.A., *Understanding Family Law* (London, Sweet & Maxwell, 2007)

HOWARD, H., *Family Mediation Handbook* (London, Butterworths Law, 2004)

MACLEAN, S., *Legal Aid and the Family Justice System: Report of the Case Profiling Study* (London, Legal Aid Board Research Unit, 1998)

ROBERTS, M., *Mediation in Family Disputes: Principles of Practice* (2nd edn., Aldershot, Ashgate Publishing, 1997)

STRANG, H., and BRAITHEWAITE, J., *Restorative Justice and Family Violence* (Cambridge, Cambridge University Press, 2004)

WESTCOTT, J.E., *Family Mediation in the UK* (Bristol, Family Law, 2004)

WIKELEY, N., *Child Support: Law and Policy* (Oxford, Hart Publishing, 2006)

Websites

http://www.dca.gov.uk/family/famfr.htm *(DCA site on family law matters still available despite the creation of the Ministry of Justice)*

http://www.justice.gov.uk/publications/cp1007.htm *(MoJ site on the Consultation Paper, Openness in family courts.)*

http://www.justice.gov.uk/whatwedo/familyprocedurerules.htm *(MoJ site on Family Procedure Rules)* http://www.dfes.gov.uk/childrenandfamilies/ *(Department for Children Schools and Families site for a range of issues on children and families)*

http://www.familyandparenting.org/ *(Family and Parenting Institute)*

http://www.everychildmatters.gov.uk/earlyyears/childcareact/ *(Site summarizing the aims and objectives of the Childcare Act 2006)*

http://www.cafcass.gov.uk/ *(Children and Family Court Advisory and Support Service)*

http://www.dca.gov.uk/family/domviol.htm *(DCA page on domestic violence still available despite creation of MoJ)*

http://www.homeoffice.gov.uk/crime-victims/reducing-crime/domestic-violence/ *(Home Office site on domestic violence)*

http://www.childcom.org.uk/ *(Children's Commissioner for Wales)*

http://www.11million.org.uk/?CFID=18718243&CFTOKEN=25034999 *(Children's Commissioner for England—the 11 million refers to the number of children)*

http://www.lawcom.gov.uk/docs/lc307.pdf *(Text of Law Commission Report, Cohabitation: The Financial Consequences of Relationship Breakdown)*

http://www.ohchr.org/english/law/crc.htm *(Text of the International Convention on the Rights of the Child)*

http://www.ohchr.org/english/bodies/crc/ *(UNHRC Committee on the Rights of the Child)*

http://www.csa.gov.uk/ *(Child Support Agency)*

http://www.family-justice-council.org.uk/ *(Family Justice Council)*

http://www.resolution.org.uk/ *(Resolution—the Solicitors' Family Law Association)*

http://www.lawsociety.org.uk/professional/accreditationpanels/familylawpanel.law *(Solicitors' Regulation Authority—family law panel)*

http://www.barcouncil.org.uk/about/specialistbarassociations/familylawbarassociation/ *(Family Law Bar Association)*

http://www.legalservices.gov.uk/docs/cls_main/FundingCodeDecisionMakingGuidance Family(Sections20)Sept07.pdf *(Detail of how CLS funding of family cases is decided)*

http://www.ukcfm.co.uk/default.asp/ *(UK College of Family Mediators)*

http://www.nfm.org.uk/index.php?page=Home *(National Family Mediation)*

http://www.relate.org.uk/ *(Relate counselling site)*

http://www.counselling4london.com/ *(Couple counselling for Londoners at the Tavistock Clinic)*

8

The civil and commercial justice system

Introduction

In this chapter, mechanisms for the resolution of all those disputes that fall outside the criminal, family, and administrative justice systems are considered. The scope of the civil and commercial justice system is huge, embracing a wide range of issues relating to legal obligations and entitlements. It is in the context of the civil and commercial justice system that many of the relationships between law and society considered in Chapter 2 are seen to operate—particularly those relating to law and economic order. This is the part of the English legal system where the protection of property and other rights may be asserted, and where questions of the ownership of land, or intellectual property, or other forms of personal property are determined. So too are the consequences of breaches of contract and acts of negligence.

Much of the conceptual framework of the civil law has been shaped by the common law. The fundamental principles of contract, negligence, trusts, and property, and the principles of the law of equity have all been created by the courts. These days, in response to considerable social pressures, most common law principles have either been supplemented or even replaced by legislation. Parliament has enacted measures, usually designed to protect the weaker party, which the common law was unable adequately to achieve. Obvious examples are consumer protection or tenant protection measures. A great deal of the work of the civil justice courts is taken up with the application of fundamental common law principles, as moderated by modern protective legislation.

There are constant pressures to add to the scope of civil justice. For example:

- as commercial interests become ever more complex and as the economy becomes more global, new demands for the protection of globalized interests arise;

- new forms of financial instrument have been created to take advantage of the internationalization of banks and other players in the capital markets, which need protection not only within English domestic law but taking European and other foreign legal regimes into account as well;

- new technologies present major challenges. For example, there is much current debate about the legal implications of the use of the internet for commercial activity on principles of the law of contract. How are consumers and suppliers of goods and services through the internet to be protected? Issues are emerging relating to how to regulate use of the internet to spread defamatory statements, or pornography; and

- the legal implications of newly emerging bio-technologies must be addressed. What can be patented? Which legal system should provide protection of the intellectual and other property rights involved? What are the legal implications of the human genome project?

While these issues may not routinely trouble the minds of district judges dealing with a list of possession cases, they emphasize the point that the civil and commercial branches of the English legal system cannot be divorced from their social and economic context. The legal system always needs to change in response to external social and economic pressures. Apart from any other consideration, if the English legal system does not respond, other legal systems will. The globalization of economic activity implies increased globalization of legal activity. If those who seek the law's protection cannot find it in England, they will take their work elsewhere.

Notwithstanding these broader considerations, the bulk of the work of the courts is devoted to more mundane matters: dealing with the consequences of people getting into debt, or breaking their contracts, or suffering personal injury (negligence). There are also more specialist areas of activity—for example relating to bankruptcy and the winding up of companies, or trade mark protection. The civil and commercial justice system plays a significant role, both in economic life and in the regulation of other social relationships, by seeking to ensure that bargains are kept, other rights are protected, and that compensation for the adverse consequences of legally unacceptable behaviour is awarded to those who have been affected.[1]

Litigation and society: a compensation culture?

One complaint that is often heard is that modern society has become too litigious.[2] It is asserted that people are too willing to rush to court when something has gone wrong. It is argued we have created a 'compensation culture'. This needs thinking about carefully.

It could be argued that, with better education, more people can now use the procedures and facilities that in the past were open only to the rich and powerful. Thus, rather than being a bad thing, an increase in the use of litigation may indicate that ordinary people are no longer willing to accept things without question, as they might

---

[1] The importance of these propositions is reinforced when one considers what happens in those countries where the rule of law to regulate social and economic behaviour is not accepted. It is extremely hard to attract investment into a country where there can be no guarantee that contracts will be enforced or property rights upheld.

[2] For current statistical information about levels of civil litigation see below, p. 208 and following.

have done before. On that basis an increase in litigation to assert rights may not only be expected, but welcomed.

Against this, it may be argued that there comes a point where the level of litigation suggests that something rather different has happened. People have acquired a willingness to complain and to put the blame on others in situations where they should be taking responsibility themselves. This in turn may lead to unacceptable levels of resource—both cash and manpower—being expended on taking or defending cases in court which could be better spent in more socially productive activity. It may also lead to the view that the ability of the citizen to take sensible risks is being undermined.

In recent years, a number of developments have encouraged the view that a 'compensation culture' is developing in the United Kingdom. Particularly noteworthy are the television advertisements encouraging those who have suffered personal injury to claim. There have also been locations, particularly hospitals, where advertisements have appeared which seem designed to encourage people to think about taking proceedings against the hospital. The government is anxious to ensure that advertisements do not appear in inappropriate locations, and—more importantly—do not create false hopes amongst those who respond to them. But a blanket ban on such advertisements seems impractical.

Indeed there is compelling empirical evidence that one of the key problems which continues to confront the civil justice system is that too many people still do not know how to assert their legal entitlements through the legal system, either through ignorance or through fear of the costs that may be involved.[3] Thus the view that *any* rise in levels of litigation is by definition a symptom of a society ill at ease with itself, as is sometimes suggested, should not be accepted uncritically. What is important is to support those with genuine and proper claims, while deterring those making claims that are wholly without foundation or merit. Achieving this goal is extremely difficult. One contribution to this would be the provision of more and better quality information about civil rights and obligations; but, if taken seriously, this would be a huge and expensive task. An alternative approach, which has been adopted elsewhere, is to limit the extent of liability, particularly for personal injury, so that claims would be admitted only where a defined percentage of injury has occurred; this is not currently on the agenda in England. The government is currently thinking of introducing a measure designed to enable people to take some risk (e.g. teachers taking pupils on a school trip) without the fear of litigation if something goes wrong.

The provision of a civil justice system

One fundamental question that needs asking is: should the state provide a system of civil justice at all? Since the disputes arising in this context are, by and large, private disputes between private parties, why should they not make arrangements for

---

[3] See Pleasance, P. and others, *Causes of Action: Civil Law and Social Justice* (Norwich, The Stationery Office, 2006).

resolving those disputes themselves? There are many answers to this provocative question, which go back to the important constitutional role of the legal system in the overall system of government.[4]

(1) As discussed in Chapter 3, our common law system requires a mechanism for the development of the principles of the common law. Fundamental legal concepts cannot develop without the existence of the courts and the authority that our constitutional arrangements give to the judges that sit in them. Although the law-making functions of Parliament and other institutions are now far more predominant than they were 100 years ago, modern statute law is still set in the common law context which has been developed by the senior courts.

(2) The very fact that statute law is now a much more significant source of law means that there is a constitutional need for a body—the court system—to provide independent interpretations of the meaning of statutory provisions. All legislation has social and political objectives. Much modern legislation is designed to reduce imbalances in power, for example between landlords and tenants or employers and employees or manufacturers and consumers. If the courts did not exist, much of this protective legislation—designed to achieve a wide range of policy objectives, including altering the nature of the relationships between parties—would be rendered even less effective than is often the case in any event.

(3) A third reason is more legalistic. Article 6 of the European Convention on Human Rights, incorporated into English law by the Human Rights Act 1998, provides that people should have a right to a fair trial for the determination of civil as well as criminal matters. A court system is necessary to satisfy this international obligation.

(4) A fourth reason for the continued existence of a civil justice system is that there would be a danger that resort to private dispute resolution procedures would, in practice, be likely to benefit more those who could afford to establish them and take advantage of them than those who could not afford them. At least the rhetoric and ambition of the courts is that all those who appear before them should be treated equally, even if this does not always happen in practice.

Problems with the civil justice system

In recent years, there has been wide recognition that the civil justice system has not been operating effectively. The main criticisms were that:

- it cost too much to bring cases to court;
- the system was too slow;
- court procedures were unnecessarily complex; and

---

[4] See above, Chapter 2.

- even if an issue was decided by a court, it might be impossible to enforce the decision.

These were not new problems. Over the last 100 years, there had been numerous reviews of and attempts to change the civil justice system. (Indeed these problems are not unique to England; they can be found in most other countries with well developed economies and justice systems.) The latest attempts at reform culminated in the introduction, on 26 April 1999, of a new set of principles as well as new rules for the operation of the civil justice system.

Access to Justice: reform of the civil justice system

The process began in 1994 when Lord Woolf was asked to undertake a review of the civil justice system. He produced first an interim and then, in 1996, a final report under the title 'Access to Justice'. He had a vision that those who wanted to bring cases to court should be able to do so efficiently, and at a cost proportionate to the amount in dispute. At the same time, the court should be the forum of last resort; every encouragement should be given to parties to settle their own disputes. At its most ambitious, Lord Woolf sought to change the culture of litigation by creating a framework within which both professional lawyers and those who wished to take their own cases to court (litigants in person) could do so with their eyes focused on the issues which needed determination by a judge and setting aside those matters which were not essential to the determination of the issue. Following a further review of the potential impact of Lord Woolf's proposals by Sir Peter Middleton, the government accepted that a programme of change to the civil justice system should be introduced. This led to the enactment of the Civil Procedure Act 1997. This created the statutory authority for the production of the Civil Procedure Rules.

Civil Procedure Rules 1999

Before 1999, procedure in civil litigation was subject to two distinct codes of practice:

- the *Rules of the Supreme Court* for cases dealt with in the High Court; and
- the *County Court Rules* for cases heard in the county court.

These two bodies of procedural law had broadly the same purpose, but there were myriad differences between them that added to the complexity of proceedings. These two codes have been replaced by a single code of procedural law, the *Civil Procedure Rules 1999*, made by the Civil Procedure Rule Committee.

Practice directions

The new procedural rules are supplemented by *practice directions* which contain directions about how the rules are to be used in practice. This has the very practical consequence that both practitioners and other potential users of the civil justice system must be as aware of the directions and the requirements they impose as of the rules themselves. The mix of rules and practice directions, and the frequency with which they were being amended following commencement of the new scheme, led to fears that it might result in the re-introduction of some of the complexity it was hoped the new system might eliminate. However, the pace of change has slackened and, in general, the new rules and directions have been widely welcomed.

Pre-action protocols

One of the most significant innovations of the post-Woolf era is that of *pre-action protocols*. These are in effect guides to good litigation practice, setting standards and timetables for the conduct of cases before court proceedings are started. They are negotiated and agreed by experienced practitioners, and approved by the Deputy Head of Civil Justice. They are designed to ensure more exchange of information and fuller investigation of claims at an earlier stage so that potential litigants may be able better to assess the merits of a case and to ensure that proper steps are taken to resolve as many of the issues in dispute as possible, prior to the parties getting anywhere near a courtroom. The protocols relate to defined classes of case. These include: personal injury, clinical negligence, construction and engineering disputes, defamation, professional negligence, and housing disrepair. Others are in contemplation. The protocols that have been agreed are also set out in the *Civil Procedure Rules*.

Key features

The new rules have, at their heart, two key features: track allocation and case management. First, potential cases are allocated to a track, the allocation depending on the size and complexity of the case:

- 'small claims track' for simpler, low value cases—currently up to £5,000 (£1,000 for personal injuries and housing);
- 'fast track' for moderately valued cases (usually between £5,000 and £15,000); and
- 'multi-track' for the most complex.

Once the track allocation has been made, the progress of the case is determined by judges managing the timetable for the case, rather than, as used to happen, the parties (or more usually their lawyers) being largely in control of progress. Both these principles—track allocation and case management—are directed to tackling delay, and trying to ensure that the process (and its cost) is proportionate to the value and complexity of what is in dispute.

Other reforms

Many other related reforms were introduced, including:

Legal language. The language of the rules has been changed to make it more easily understandable. For example, those who bring cases to court are now referred to as 'claimants' rather than 'plaintiffs'; they swear or affirm 'statements of truth' instead of 'affidavits'; the claimant may seek 'specified damages' instead of 'liquidated damages' or 'unspecified damages' instead of 'unliquidated damages'. The essential features of the case are set out in a 'statement of case' instead of 'pleadings'. There are numerous other examples. In short, the new rules seek to eliminate the Latin phrases and other old terminology which were thought to make legal proceedings more complex than they really needed to be.[5]

Forms. A related development, which continues a process begun some years ago, is that much work has been done to devise forms which can be used to start and progress potential cases. Again this is designed to make it easier for the ordinary individual to use the courts, and to reduce professional costs by ensuring that particular documents do not always have to be specially drafted by professional advisers—they simply download the relevant document and fill it in. The forms are available on the website of Her Majesty's Court Service.

Use of experts. Another change introduced by the rules relates to the use of experts. Lord Woolf had wanted to limit the use of experts to one, who would be there to assist the court, rather than to represent the interests of either side. This was felt to be too draconian a step to take. Nevertheless the *Civil Procedure Rules* provide that experts have a duty to help the court on matters within their expertise, and this duty overrides any obligation to the person by whom they have been instructed or by whom they are paid. Experts give evidence only if the court gives permission. Instructions to experts are no longer privileged, and thus their substance must be disclosed in their report. In practice, a single jointly appointed expert is becoming a common feature of civil litigation, save where the complexity of the issues warrants both sides having their own expert.

The purpose of the civil justice system: the forum of last resort

It might be thought that the primary purpose of the civil justice system was the resolution of disputes by a judge. While it would be overstating it to say that nothing could be further from the truth, the situation is much more complicated than that. The courts have long been used as a last resort in situations where the parties to a dispute cannot themselves resolve their differences without a court hearing. Even before the Woolf reforms were introduced, the 'typical' dispute was resolved by negotiation and settlement, not by a trial in court. The Woolf reforms have reinforced the view that the courts must be the forum of last resort.

---

[5] Of course, law students will still have to be aware of the former terms, as an understanding of reported decisions made before the changes came into effect will depend on that knowledge. But for the future, things should be clearer.

Latest available figures show that in 2005 over 1.87 million claims were issued in the county court. 85 per cent of these were claims for money (debts). Of the remainder, the overwhelming number (over 260,000) were claims for possession of land. However, only just over 17,000 cases were disposed of following a trial. There were also around 47,000 small claims hearings. The typical civil proceeding was thus resolved outside the courtroom, not in it. The civil justice system was much more frequently used *indirectly* as part of the process of resolution, rather than *directly* with a case being tried before a judge.

There are in fact huge incentives in the system on parties to settle. Three may be particularly noted:

- *costs.* The cost of litigation increases dramatically as the parties get closer to the courtroom door. It is at this point that the numbers of lawyers involved in a case tend to increase. Where barristers are used, their fees are significantly higher when they appear in court than when they are sitting in chambers providing written advice to clients;

- *the indemnity principle.* This provides that, in the usual case, the loser of the case pays a large proportion of the costs of the winner. Given that clear-cut cases should not be coming to court at all, and that therefore there is always some uncertainty about the outcome of a trial,[6] this rule also helps to concentrate the minds of litigants; and[7]

- *payments into court and offers to settle.* The Civil Procedure Rules (CPR) also provide that parties to proceedings may offer to settle a case or pay a sum of money into court. The formalities for making an offer or payment are set out in Part 36 of the CPR. If the offer or payment is not accepted, and the party who did not accept fails to do better at the end of any trial than the offer or payment in, then that party will be ordered to pay any costs incurred by the other side after the latest date on which such offer or payment could have been accepted without needing the permission of the court. The court has a discretion to depart from this principle where application of the rule would, in its view, be unjust.

The pre-Woolf system did little to prevent delay. Although there were incentives to settle, they did not really bite until a trial date was getting near. The speed at which a trial date approached was on the whole determined by the parties to the dispute and their advisers. There was considerable scope for delay. By giving the judges clear powers of case management to set the timetable for the litigation process,[8] the Woolf reforms are intended to ensure that settlements are reached much more speedily than before.

---

[6] The trial process has been described as a forensic lottery; see the book of that name written by Ison, T., *The Forensic Lottery: A Critique of Tort Liability as a System of Personal Injury Compensation* (London, Staples Press, 1967).

[7] The indemnity principle is now under severe attack and may well be restricted. See further Chapter 10.

[8] Each court circuit now has a special *designated judge* who ensures that judges are actively managing the case timetables.

Alternative dispute resolution (ADR)

The Woolf reforms embraced another development that has occurred over recent years—*alternative dispute resolution (see Box 8.1)* or, as it is perhaps better labelled, appropriate dispute resolution. This is an umbrella term describing a range of practices designed to assist parties achieve a resolution of their dispute without the necessity of going to court for a full trial in a courtroom. Many of these techniques were developed in the United States where they are widely used. Their use in England has been less marked,[9] but is growing slowly.

Box 8.1   Legal system explained

Forms of ADR

ADR comes in a variety of forms. The principal ones are:

- arbitration;
- mediation; and
- early neutral evaluation.

Arbitration is a process whereby the parties to a dispute choose an arbitrator to determine their dispute. It is a private process. The arbitrator is often an expert in the matter which is the subject of the dispute, say a building contract. The parties are usually bound, contractually, to accept the decision of the arbitrator. It is thus like a court decision, an imposed decision, though, unlike with the court, the whole process takes place in private, out of sight of the general public. Indeed confidentiality is one of arbitration's perceived advantages for many disputants.

Mediation is a technique whereby a third party—mediator—who is neutral so far as the parties to the dispute are concerned, attempts to explore the possibilities for the parties reaching an outcome which satisfies both of them. This is sometimes known as 'win-win', to contrast it with a court process which may be characterized as 'win-lose'. This outcome will not necessarily be one which a court would have reached (or would have had power to reach), for example because the particular remedy—e.g. saying sorry—is not a remedy available in court. It has the advantage that the decision will be one at which the parties have themselves arrived, albeit with the advice and assistance of the mediator.

Early neutral evaluation is a process where someone with legal or other relevant expertise is given a preliminary view of the case and is asked to provide a frank appraisal of the likely outcome, should the case go as far as court. This may be used as a stage in attempting to reach a settlement by negotiation, rather than going to a full trial in court.

---

[9] For the use of mediation in the family justice system see Chapter 7, p. 192.

In the case of small claims, the court system itself has long used a form of ADR, as the district judges who determine these cases do so not in a formal trial but by an informal procedure, with only the parties to the dispute present and—usually—lawyers excluded. They used to be called small claims arbitrations, although, since the introduction of the small claims track, such cases are now known as small claims hearings. Nevertheless the same procedural informality applies.

An ADR scheme has been available in the Commercial Court (see below) since 1993. An ADR scheme is also available in the Court of Appeal. The largest-scale experiment in the use of court-centred ADR has been in the Central London County Court, started in May 1996. A number of other courts have also developed ADR schemes. These have been the subject of detailed evaluation by Professor Dame Hazel Genn.[10] The common feature of all these experiments is that, to date, their use has been modest. There is evidence that those who take advantage of ADR in general find it a helpful way of resolving their disputes. But the use of ADR is not as widespread as in other countries, particularly the United States, and certainly not as widespread as those who provide ADR services would like.

The importance of ADR to the success of the Woolf reforms is not yet clear. Some initially argued that the civil procedure changes, combined with changes in the rules on the funding of litigation (see Chapter 10), would result in a substantial increase in litigation and the potential use of the courts. As this would lead to a need to divert cases from the courts, ADR would become an important means of achieving such diversion. In fact, levels of civil litigation fell quite sharply after the new rules were introduced. While there now appears to be some upturn, the particular pressures that might have resulted from substantial increases have not materialized.

A different set of arguments is based on the suggestion that the new procedural rules are changing 'litigation culture'. As the nature of litigation changes so both clients and their professional advisers will, it is argued, want to move away from the adversarial procedures of the litigation process towards less confrontational forms of ADR to resolve disputes. There is some evidence that this is happening, particularly in large commercial disputes. But, as already noted, take-up in other classes of litigation is still limited. Much depends on the extent to which lawyers and other ADR providers become entitled to receive payments for this form of dispute resolution, particularly from the Community Legal Services Fund (see below, Chapter 10).

The post-Woolf civil justice system does give power to the judge, as part of the case management strategy, to stay a case for up to twenty-eight days to give the parties a chance to use ADR where this seems to be appropriate. These powers have not been extensively used. However, the Court of Appeal has on a number of occasions stressed the importance of parties using ADR where they can. It has also indicated

---

[10] Genn, H. and others, *Twisting Arms: Court Referred and Court Linked Mediation under Judicial Pressure* (London, Ministry of Justice, 2007).

that unreasonable failure to do so may result in adverse rulings on the recovery of costs, though they have been reluctant to push too far in this direction.[11]

After a slow start, the Ministry of Justice is now much more active in promoting the use of ADR. It now sponsors a National Mediation helpline, with a central phone number which anyone engaged in civil litigation can call to ask about mediation and, if they wish, arrange a mediation. The Judicial Studies Board is also contemplating making a significant investment in judicial training on ADR, designed to give judges greater understanding of the power of ADR in resolving disputes and confidence to encourage parties to use ADR.

There are a number of difficult issues relating to the development of ADR which are currently unresolved. Among these issues are:

- *compulsion.* At present no court can *require* the use of ADR.[12] Experience in the United States suggests that use of ADR does not take off until at least an element of compulsion is introduced. But is it right for the courts to require parties to a dispute to pay for something that may not resolve the matter but only add to costs and delay? Certainly, the consensus in England and Wales is that, while ADR may be encouraged, it should not be compulsory;

- *standards.* Second there is a question of how proper standards for those who offer ADR services are to be set and monitored. This is being addressed by the ADR providers, who in 2005 formed a Civil Mediation Council. One of its first tasks is to devise principles for the accreditation of ADR providers, which is an important step towards the setting of common standards;

- *costs.* Another question relates to the costs of ADR. There is at present no intention on the part of the government to fund the provision of ADR services save for measures in the Community Legal Service (see Chapter 10). But ADR services have to be paid for. If the costs are too high and nevertheless parties are required by the courts to use a process of ADR, may this not add to the cost of dispute resolution—something the Woolf reforms were attempting to reduce?

- *outcome.* Will the fact that the parties may well be happier at the end of the ADR process than they might have been at the end of a trial compensate them for the expense of using ADR? It may well do. One of the most powerful claims for ADR is *not* that it is cheaper, but that it enables parties to disputes to retain control of the dispute resolution process, which may in turn enable them to move on with their lives more amicably than they might be able to do after a court hearing. But this will not always be the case. Indeed there will always be those who, on principle, will want to litigate and refuse to use any form of ADR.

---

[11] For the most comprehensive review of the issues see *Halsey v. Milton Keynes General NHS Trust, Steel v. Joy and another* [2004] EWCA Civ 576, CA.

[12] For the position in the family justice system see above, Chapter 7, p. 187.

The court structure: preliminary issues

Having considered the context within which the civil and commercial justice system has developed in recent years and noted the considerable changes that have occurred, the structure of the courts will now be considered. Four preliminary issues will be mentioned.

Generalist v. specialist

One of the claims made for the courts in the civil justice system is that they are, and should be, generalist rather than specialist in nature. Certainly, any type of case that does not fall into any other of the jurisdictional categories considered in this book (criminal, administrative, and family) must be disposed of in the civil courts. While the claim that the courts are generalist in nature is still to a large extent true, it should be treated with caution. There is now an increasing number of specialist courts that have been created, primarily because of the technicalities of the law and issues to be determined by those courts. This has happened particularly in areas of commercial and business law. This raises the obvious further question whether there should be more specialist courts. In recent years arguments have been made, for example, for the creation of a specialist housing court and for a specialist environment court.

There are many arguments in favour of greater specialization. Specialist judges dealing with a specific range of issues should be better informed about the relevant law; thus the quality and consistency of decision-making might be enhanced. (This was precisely one of the arguments in favour of the creation of tribunals.) Procedures could be better adapted to suit the users of the specialist courts and the types of issues to be dealt with in those courts. For example, special facilities might be available to deal with the particular types of emergency cases that might arise out of ordinary court hours. The practitioners who specialize in the areas of law concerned might be able to operate more efficiently by concentrating their resources in more specialized courts.

Against, it is argued that judges might become too narrowly focused. As a consequence judges might become bored with the tasks they were required to perform. Judicial manpower in specialist courts could not be used efficiently if the case-loads in those courts were insufficient to keep the relevant judges busy. Given recent trends, it seems likely that there will be more rather than less specialization in the years ahead.

Court fees

A second preliminary issue that needs to be borne in mind is the decision by government that the civil justice system should be—broadly—self-financing.[13] A consequence

---

[13] This has been the subject of sharp criticism by the Civil Justice Council.

of this is that Her Majesty's Court Service has to set court fees (which claimants must pay before they can get their cases started and allocated to the appropriate track) at a level that achieves this financial target. This has led to considerable controversy. One particular criticism is that the policy was introduced, in the early 1990s, without any parliamentary announcement or debate.

There are those who argue that, on principle, 'justice' should be regarded as a 'free good', which should not be subject to the principle of self-financing at all. Access to the courts for the determination of legal rights and entitlements is a constitutional right to which there should be no barriers—certainly not financial ones. Against that, others argue that the well-heeled, who may be fighting over financial matters worth thousands, perhaps millions, of pounds, should make—through the payment of fees—a relatively modest contribution towards the running of the civil justice system.

There was a chorus of complaints from judges, lawyers, and consumer groups that the combination of the fee for issuing the claim together with the fee that had to be paid when a case was allocated to a particular track was having a disproportionately adverse impact on those bringing small claims. This was deterring rather than improving access to justice. The government therefore decided to abolish the £80 allocation fee for defended civil actions worth £1,000 or less.[14] However, there has been no other relaxation in the civil justice fees regime; indeed other court fees have been regularly adjusted upwards. This issue is a source of significant conflict between the judiciary and the government.

Enforcement of judgments

A third issue which the civil justice system must address is enforcement of judgments. There can be nothing more frustrating than taking a case to court, winning it, but then finding that it is well-nigh impossible to obtain satisfaction of the judgment. In situations where the loser has the backing of an insurance company, or (either private individual or company or other legal body) is extremely resource-rich, this is not usually a problem. But where the person against whom proceedings are brought is herself of moderate means or is a company without extensive resources, enforcement may be a major problem.

The government acknowledges this. As part of the continuing programme of reform of the civil justice system, it undertook a review of the procedures available to the courts for the enforcement of judgments and, in the Tribunals, Courts and Enforcement Act 2007, has given further powers to the courts to enforce judgments. In particular, courts will find it easier to find out what the financial position of a debtor is and to track debtors if they change employment.

---

[14] This decision was effective from April 2000. New fees were introduced in April 2003. A research study, recently published by the Ministry of Justice, suggests that the level of court fees is relatively unimportant in determining whether a person will start proceedings in court: see *What's cost got to do with it? The impact of changing court fees on users* (2007).

Enforcement is an exceptionally difficult issue, particularly distinguishing between those who could pay but won't, and those who simply can't pay. There would be considerable political opposition to a return to the Dickensian days of throwing debtors into jail.[15] Yet there is no doubt that, if the civil justice system cannot force those against whom judgments are made, in particular awards of damages, to pay up, this is seen by users of the system as a serious weakness. In turn, this may encourage others not to pay.

Delivering the Court Service: local initiatives and centralized justice

The courts are managed by Her Majesty's Court Service (HMCS), an executive agency set up in April 2005. The day-to-day running of the courts is carried out on a regional basis through six *circuits*.[16] Supervision of the judicial work of each circuit is the responsibility of the *presiding judges*. These are judges of the High Court appointed—two for each circuit—by the Lord Chief Justice. They operate under a Senior Presiding Judge.

One of the issues which Lord Woolf highlighted when he was preparing his 'Access to Justice' report was that many courts had developed their own particular procedures for dealing with specific types of matter. This did not imply that the outcomes of cases would differ, but the ways in which the courts worked certainly did. Lord Woolf felt that it was important that someone appearing for trial in one town should be dealt with in essentially the same way as in any other. One of his hopes for the reform of the Civil Procedure Rules was that this would encourage greater uniformity of process. Given the not inconsiderable discretion that is given to judges to manage cases, Lord Woolf's hopes in this respect have not been fully realized.

Indeed there is an argument that a degree of procedural experiment should be encouraged to see whether the work of the courts can be made more efficient. However this should be as part of a controlled programme of pilot projects which can be properly evaluated by HMCS, rather than the result of individual courts going their own way. It is also important that when new procedures are tested and found helpful, the results of good practice should be spread throughout the court system as a whole, not kept as a 'private custom' in a particular court or circuit. This will happen only if innovations are managed by HMCS, supported by Her Majesty's Inspectorate of Court Administration.

---

[15] Even under present law, failure to pay certain taxes—a particular form of debt—can result in the imposition of a prison sentence.

[16] Midland and Oxford, run from Birmingham; North Eastern from Leeds; Northern from Manchester; South Eastern from London; Wales and Chester from Cardiff; and Western from Bristol.

The county court

The court which deals with the largest numbers of civil cases is the county court. Founded in 1846 it was designed to provide a forum for the resolution of what would these days be regarded as relatively modest consumer complaints. Over the years, its jurisdiction has expanded. Today all civil actions can be started in the county court, save for a small number of cases where there are special statutory rules which require proceedings to be started in the High Court (see below). There are 218 county courts throughout England and Wales.

County courts deal with all contract and tort cases, and all proceedings for the recovery of land, irrespective of value. They deal with certain equity and contested probate actions (e.g. arising from alleged breaches of trust obligations or questions about the administration of a will) where the value of the trust fund or the estate does not exceed £30,000, plus any case which the parties agree can be heard in the county court.

Each court is assigned at least one circuit judge and one district judge. Although circuit judges are full-time appointments, most do not spend all their time on civil matters, but also sit as trial judges in criminal cases in the Crown Court. The district judges, however, work full-time on civil issues (including some family justice matters).[17] There are about 640 circuit judges in England and Wales, compared with around 450 district judges. The former sit for a total of around 15,000 days a year on civil matters; the latter for over 72,000 days. District judges thus carry out the bulk of the work in the county court.

Recent editions of *Judicial Statistics*[18] indicated that following the introduction of the Civil Procedure Rules there was a downward trend in the activity levels of the county court (which challenged the claim that we are becoming an increasingly litigious society). The latest figures suggest that this trend has been reversed and that figures are now increasing. The reasons for this are not clear. In part, use of courts tends to reflect trends in the economy. Economic downturn leads to more mortgage possession work and increases in bankruptcy petitions. In those (rare) cases which actually go to trial, the average waiting time between the issue of the claim and the start of the trial is fifty-eight weeks. Small claims take an average of twenty-five weeks to come to trial.

In the analysis that follows, the number of cases started is compared with the number of trials conducted by the particular court. It should be noted, however, that the courts do a great deal of work that falls short of a trial. These are generically known as *interlocutory proceedings*. They deal with procedural and other issues that may relate to litigation. These proceedings often contribute to encouraging parties to litigation to settle or compromise their claims.

---

[17] They may be assisted by deputy district judges who are also judges in training who sit part-time.
[18] Published annually by The Stationery Office. They are downloadable from the Judiciary website.

The High Court

The High Court consists of three divisions. The Family Division has been considered in Chapter 7. The other two divisions are:

- the Queen's Bench Division; and
- the Chancery Division.

These two divisions handle different types of civil and commercial work.

The courts in these divisions handle cases both arising at first instance (i.e. cases being determined for the first time) and on appeal from courts lower in the hierarchical structure—the county court and a number of administrative tribunals. When sitting as an appeal court and when dealing with analogous matters such as judicial review, the High Court is known as the *Divisional Court*. Each division has a divisional court.

The Queen's Bench Division

The Queen's Bench Division is headed by the President of the Queen's Bench Division (a new post created by the Constitutional Reform Act 2005). He is supported by seventy-two full-time High Court judges.[19] It deals primarily with common law business—actions relating to contract[20] and tort. Torts (civil wrongs) embrace not only negligence and nuisance, but also other wrongs against the person, such as libel, or wrongs against property, such as trespass. Contract cases involve, for example, failure to pay for goods or services, or other alleged breaches of contract. Some fact situations give rise to actions both in tort and contract.

It is central to the philosophy of the post-Woolf era that only the most important cases should be dealt with in the High Court. As a result only personal injury claims with a value of £50,000 or more may be started there. In other cases the claim must be for £15,000 or more. In addition, three specialist jurisdictions come within the scope of the Queen's Bench Division:

- the Admiralty Court;
- the Commercial Court; and
- the Technology and Construction Court (see further below).

Cases to be tried in these courts are required to be started in the High Court, irrespective of financial amount (though in practice they will usually be substantial). There are

---

[19] They are assisted by part-time deputy High Court judges, and circuit judges sitting as High Court judges. These part-time judges deal with nearly 50 per cent of all trials.

[20] Some questions of contract are referred to the Chancery Division.

also a number of other types of proceedings which, by statute, must be started in the High Court.

Jury trial

There is a right to trial by jury in civil proceedings for fraud, libel, slander, malicious prosecution, or false imprisonment. In other cases, a judge may in her discretion allow trial by jury; but this rarely happens. Where there is a jury, the jury will decide not only liability (e.g., were the words used libellous or not) but also the amount of any damages.

Work-load

In 2005, 15,317 claims and originating summonses were issued in the Queen's Bench Division, a three per cent increase on 2004. Only about 20 per cent were issued in London, the rest in High Court District Registries around the country. In 2004, 1,963 actions were set down for trial; of these only 310 were disposed of after a full trial. As in other parts of the legal system, the full trial remains the exceptional, not the ordinary, mode of disposal. The average waiting time for a case to come to trial was ninety-seven weeks (down from 173 weeks in 2001). The average time taken for a full hearing was just over five hours.

In those cases where damages were sought, awards in excess of £15,000 were made in nearly all cases where the claimant won; most personal injury cases resulted in awards in excess of £50,000.

Divisional Court

When sitting as a Divisional Court, the Queen's Bench Division deals with judicial review cases,[21] appeals by way of 'case stated',[22] habeas corpus,[23] committal for contempt of court committed in an inferior court, or appeals and applications under a variety of statutory provisions.[24] The bulk of the work is judicial review. Nearly 4,900 applications for permission to bring judicial review proceedings were made in 2005, of which only about 14 per cent were granted. The largest single group of cases—well over half the total—relates to matters arising out of decisions relating to immigration law.[25] This area of the High Court's work has been subject to rapid increase. When dealing with judicial review, the court is known as the Administrative Court.

---

[21] Powers of judicial review are exercisable both over inferior courts and tribunals—e.g. where it is alleged that there has been a breach of proper fair procedure or an incorrect interpretation of the law—and against public bodies or government ministers or others carrying out public acts or duties. Judicial review is considered further in Chapter 6 on administrative justice.

[22] A process used, for example, by the Crown Court or a magistrates' court to obtain a ruling on a particular provision of criminal law.

[23] Where unlawful detention is alleged.

[24] E.g., under the town and country planning legislation.

[25] See Bridges, L., et al., Judicial Review in Perspective (London, Cavendish, 1995).

The Chancery Division

The Chancery Division of the High Court is presided over by the Chancellor of the High Court, supported by seventeen other High Court judges.[26]

The principal categories of business dealt with by the division relate to corporate and personal insolvency disputes; disputes relating to business, trade and industry; the enforcement of mortgages; intellectual property matters including copyright and patents; disputes relating to trust property; and disputes arising from wills and the administration of deceased people's estates (probate matters). (For uncontested probate matters, *see Box 8.2*.) The bulk of the work is handled in the Royal Courts of Justice in London, together with eight provincial centres which have High Court Chancery jurisdiction.[27]

In 2005 a total of just over 34,000 proceedings were started in the Chancery Division; during the year, only 290 cases were disposed of following a trial. In addition, 13,149 bankruptcy petitions were issued in the High Court in London. The Divisional Court of the Chancery Division also disposed of a small number of appeals from the county court. In addition to the general work of the Chancery Division, there are two specialist jurisdictions: the Companies Court and the Patent Court, considered further below.

Box 8.2   Time for change

Uncontested probate matters: the Family Division

Although the Chancery Division deals with contested probate matters, uncontested matters are dealt with in the Principal Registry of the *Family* Division of the High Court or any of the twelve district probate registries that exist in England and Wales. Grants of probate are made in cases where there was a will; grants of administration where there was not. There is a heavy workload involved. Over 299,000 grants were issued in 2005, of which nearly 75 per cent were grants of probate, the remainder grants of administration.

The government completed a review of probate work in 2004, designed to make the service more up-to-date in its administration. Among the recommendations accepted is the creation of a new Probate Service website; a telephone helpline (run as part of the Revenue's Inheritance Tax Advice Service); and the ability to download forms on-line. The government has also announced that groups, other than solicitors, should be permitted to offer probate services. Those who wished to do so would have to satisfy criteria laid down by the Lord Chancellor.

---

[26] They are assisted, as needed, by deputy High Court judges, who are either practitioners approved to act as such by the Lord Chancellor, or retired High Court or circuit judges. The extent of their use depends on the level of business before the courts.

[27] Birmingham, Bristol, Cardiff, Leeds, Liverpool, Manchester, Newcastle upon Tyne, and Preston.

Once again it can be seen that, as with other parts of the civil justice system, the court is very much the place of last resort for the resolution of disputes.

The commercial justice system

Notwithstanding the reluctance, noted above, of the judiciary to specialize, the fact is that within both the High Court and the county court systems, there now exists a range of specialist courts, established to deal with a range of (primarily) commercial and company law matters. These developments reflect the position of London in the global economy, and the need for the courts to provide appropriate levels of expertise in specialist areas. They have spread to provincial centres where there is also signifi-cant commercial activity. The specialist courts may be listed as follows:

The Companies Court

This court is part of the Chancery Division of the High Court. It deals primar-ily with the compulsory liquidation of companies and other matters arising under the Insolvency Act 1986 and the Companies Acts. For example, a registered com-pany which seeks to reduce its capital may do so only with the approval of the court. The bulk of this work is done in London, but the eight provincial district registries have the same powers.[28] Just over 15,000 originating proceedings were started in the Companies Court in 2004.

The Patents Court

This is another specialist part of the Chancery Division, dealing not only with patents, but other forms of intellectual property, including registered designs. It also hears appeals against decisions of the Comptroller General of Patents. Cases suitable for determination by a county court are heard in a specially designated county court—the Central London County Court. The work-load of this court is not high—only thirty-seven actions were listed in 2005.

The Admiralty Court

This is part of the Queen's Bench Division of the High Court, dealing—as the name suggests—with shipping matters, principally the consequences of collisions at sea and damage to cargos. As with patents, most cases are dealt with in London, but there is power to refer suitable cases to specially designated county courts. 102 actions were started in 2005; only three trials were actually heard in the court.

---

[28] See above, n. 27.

The Commercial Court

This is also part of the Queen's Bench Division of the High Court. This deals with a wide range of commercial matters, for example, banking, international credit and the purchase and sale of commodities. It also deals with shipping matters not handled by the Admiralty Court—contracts relating to ships, carriage of cargo, insurance, as well as the construction and performance of mercantile contracts more generally. The Commercial Court also deals with questions which may arise from commercial arbitrations.

The Technology and Construction Court

This is the name given in 1998 to the former Official Referees' Court. This is another section of the High Court which sits in London with seven full-time *circuit* judges, presided over by a High Court judge. Hearings are also possible outside London before specially designated or nominated judges. The court deals primarily with building and engineering disputes and also computer litigation. It can also deal with other matters such as valuation disputes and landlord and tenant matters involving dilapidations. And it handles questions arising from arbitrations in building and engineering disputes. During 2005, 340 proceedings were started; only three trials were held in London. (Figures for cases dealt with outside London are not available.)

Other courts and offices

In addition to the courts so far identified, there are also a number of other offices which form part of the Supreme Court. These include:

- *The Office of the Official Solicitor and Public Trustee.* The Official Solicitor operates under the authority of section 90 of the Supreme Court Act 1981. His primary duties are to protect the interests of children and mental patients, i.e. those who do not have full legal capacity to look after their own affairs. His department has a substantial work-load, dealing with around 4,200 new cases in 2005. Among his responsibilities are child abduction cases. In 2001, the Official Solicitor took over responsibility for the *Public Trust Office.* The Public Trustee acts as executor or administrator of deceased persons' estates or trustees of wills or settlements where he has been named and has accepted the nomination. On 1 April 2007 the Court Funds Office merged with the Offices of the Official Solicitor and Public Trustee to become the Offices of Court Funds, Official Solicitor, and Public Trustee; and

- *The Court of Protection.* The Mental Incapacity Act 2005 provides for the creation of a new Court of Protection. It is a superior court of record, able to sit anywhere in England and Wales. Welfare matters previously referred to the High Court may be referred to this court. It is intended that the Court of Protection should have a regional presence but it has a central office and registry. The court has powers to call for reports to assist in determining a case. Such reports can be commissioned from the Public Guardian (a statutory official), local authorities, NHS bodies or Court of Protection Visitors (replacing the current Lord Chancellor's Visitors). Local authority staff or NHS staff may already be providing services to the person concerned and be able to report to the court on the basis of their existing involvement. The Public Guardian or Court of Protection Visitor who is reporting to the court has access to health, social services or care records relating to the person and may interview him in private. Where a Court of Protection Visitor is a Special Visitor (e.g. a registered medical practitioner or someone with other suitable qualifications or training) he or she may, on the directions of the court, carry out medical, psychiatric, or psychological examinations. Data about the work of the court are not currently available.

The reform of civil justice—unfinished business

Despite the large number of changes that have taken place within the civil justice system over the last few years, a number of important issues remain outstanding.

A unified civil court?

First is whether the current distinction between the county court and the High Court should be retained. Many think that the creation of a unified code of civil procedure should be accompanied by a uniform court structure. Indeed, it is thought that Lord Woolf himself favoured such an idea. It would, however, have been controversial, not least amongst the judiciary. It may have been thought expedient to drop this idea in order not to prevent the procedural changes from being brought into effect. The idea has not, however, disappeared. In 2005 the government issued a consultation paper on whether or not the civil courts should be unified. It would probably not lead to a great deal of change in practice, at least not initially. High Court judges would be retained and their status as significant interpreters of the law (as well as deciders of the most difficult cases) would remain. But unification would give case managers even greater flexibility to allocate cases to the most appropriate level of court. It could also help with the distribution of judicial personnel. A summary of responses to the consultation was also published in 2005. In the light of these responses, the government has announced that unification of the civil and family courts is a long-term objective.

Costs

The second major issue is that of the cost of litigation. There is widespread recognition that the Woolf reforms have not driven down costs; indeed the emphasis on making sure that parties disclose their hands to the other side earlier has led to the front-loading of costs. The Civil Justice Council has over the last four or five years taken a leading role in trying to get agreement that there should be cost limits for certain classes of litigation. The issue of how civil litigation can be funded, particularly given pressures to reduce expenditure on legal aid, is extremely difficult and complex. It is discussed further at the end of Chapter 10.

Access to justice

Thirdly, and related to the previous point, despite the fact that Lord Woolf's reports were entitled *Access to Justice* there are concerns that his reforms have not led to the increased access he was hoping to see. This cannot all be laid at the door of the procedural reforms. Issues relating to the funding of legal services (see Chapter 10) are central to this. It must also be borne in mind that many issues on which people find themselves in dispute are now dealt with by other agencies. For example, the Financial Services Ombudsman has effectively taken over breach of contract litigation by consumers against banks and other financial services bodies; and his services are free.

Appeals and the appeal courts

We have already noted in passing that many of the courts listed above have power to hear appeals in defined circumstances. Many appeals are satisfactorily disposed of in that context.

However, a number of courts deal exclusively with appeals. They are particularly important in the English legal system, not just because they have greater authority within the hierarchical court structure, but also because it is through their reported judgments that the primary source of authority for the development of the common law and the interpretation of statutes is to be found. (See above, Chapter 3.) It can be argued that these appeal courts are the only truly generalist courts, in that they have the responsibility for dealing with whatever is presented to them by way of appeal.

Policy issues

In recent years, it has been suggested that there may be too many avenues of appeal; and that the level of court at which an appeal is determined may not always be the right one. To deal with this, important changes of principle were introduced into the law on appeals by the Access to Justice Act 1999.

Permission to appeal

It was always the case that, in order to bring an appeal in the Court of Appeal, it was necessary for the appellant to seek the permission (or—as it used to be called—the leave) of the court to bring the appeal. Under section 54 of the Access to Justice Act

1999 rules of court have been made that require permission to appeal to be obtained for all appeals to the county courts, the High Court, or the Court of Appeal (Civil Division). There are limited exceptions, for example appeals relating to court orders which affect the liberty of the individual. There is no appeal against a decision either to give or refuse permission. Where permission is refused, there remains the possibility of making a further application for permission, either in the same or another court.

Second appeals

Once a county court or the High Court has decided a matter on appeal, section 55 of the Access to Justice Act provides that there will be no possibility of a further appeal unless either the appeal would raise an important point of principle or practice, or there is some other compelling reason for the appeal to be heard. All applications for permission to bring a further appeal are dealt with by the Court of Appeal, irrespective of the court which determined the first appeal. If permission is granted, the Court of Appeal hears the appeal as well.

Destination of appeals

Section 56 of the Access to Justice Act gave the Lord Chancellor power to vary, by order, the avenues of appeal to and within the county court, the High Court and the Court of Appeal. Thus:

(1) for fast track cases heard by a district judge appeals lie to a circuit judge;

(2) for fast track cases heard by a circuit judge appeals lie to a High Court judge;

(3) in multi-track cases, appeals against interlocutory decisions by a district judge are to a circuit judge; by a master[29] or circuit judge to a High Court judge; and by a High Court judge to the Court of Appeal;

(4) in multi-track cases, appeals against final orders will be direct to the Court of Appeal, irrespective of the court making the initial decision.

The appeal courts

The particular courts of appeal to be considered here are:

- the Judicial Committee of the Privy Council;
- the House of Lords; and
- the Court of Appeal.

---

[29] Masters are judicial officers of the High Court who determine interlocutory matters.

The Judicial Committee of the Privy Council

This remains the final court of appeal for twenty-four British Commonwealth Territories[30] and six independent republics within the Commonwealth.[31] It also acts as a constitutional Supreme Court determining constitutional issues arising from those independent territories that have a written constitution. The Judicial Committee also has jurisdiction over a number of domestic matters[32] and 'pastoral' matters (which relate to the Church of England). The statutory powers of the Committee derive from the Judicial Committee Act of 1833, though the history of the Committee can be traced back to mediaeval times. The judges who sit in the Judicial Committee are (broadly) the same as those who sit in the House of Lords (below), though they are on occasion joined by a senior member of the judiciary from the country whence the appeal has come.

Many find the jurisdiction of the Judicial Committee highly anachronistic—a throw-back to a British imperial past that is long gone. Nevertheless the Judicial Committee has a steady stream of work. Seventy-one appeals were entered and thirty-eight petitions for special leave to appeal[33] were heard in 2005; and the Committee sat on 106 days. The issues it deals with are, by definition, of very considerable legal and social importance, not just for the country in question but in the common law world in general.

The House of Lords

This is currently the supreme court of appeal in Great Britain and Northern Ireland, although it cannot hear appeals in Scottish criminal cases. The House of Lords can, with permission, hear appeals from any orders or judgments of the Court of Appeal in England, the Court of Session in Scotland, or the Court of Appeal in Northern Ireland.[34] In addition, appeals may be taken, with permission, from the High Court when it has been sitting as a Divisional Court (i.e. as a court of appeal or when dealing with cases such as judicial review). In limited circumstances, an appeal may be brought direct from the High Court or the High Court in Northern Ireland, when sitting as a trial court.[35]

---

[30] This group includes both independent territories that retained this right of appeal when they achieved independence—e.g., New Zealand and Jamaica; and UK overseas territories that remain dependent on the UK, e.g., Gibraltar and the Cayman Islands.

[31] This group includes Mauritius and The Gambia.

[32] Hearing appeals from a number of professional bodies, in particular under the Medical Act 1983 and the Dentists Act 1984. The Judicial Committee has recently been given power to deal with devolution issues arising out of the passing of the Wales Act and the Scotland Act 1998.

[33] These special petitions relate to appeals in criminal cases where the Judicial Committee will not hear an appeal unless satisfied that the case raises a matter of great general importance or where there appears to be the danger of a grave miscarriage of justice.

[34] Save, in the case of Northern Ireland or Scotland, where this is prevented by statute.

[35] This is known as 'leapfrogging' and can occur where is it clear that the law in question needs clarification at the highest level, perhaps because there are inconsistent decisions from the Court of Appeal.

Permission may be granted either by the relevant Court of Appeal or, if that is not forthcoming, by the Appeal Committee of the House of Lords. (If a lower court grants permission, the House of Lords cannot overturn that decision.) In practice, permission is granted by the lower courts rather infrequently.[36] In 2005 the Appeal Committee dealt with 240 petitions for permission to appeal; only seventy-nine were allowed. The right of the citizen to 'take her case to the highest court in the land' is in reality highly contingent, subject to considerable procedural constraint. The House of Lords is a judicial resource that is sparingly used.

Appeals themselves are heard by an appellate committee of the House of Lords, consisting usually of five Lords of Appeal in Ordinary. Hearings are tightly time-controlled, lasting usually only two days. In 2005 102 appeals were presented, seventy-five of which came from the Civil Division of the Court of Appeal. They related to a wide variety of different issues.

The new Supreme Court

As a result of the passing of the Constitutional Reform Act 2005, the new Supreme Court of the United Kingdom is to be created. It will take over the appellate jurisdiction of the House of Lords and the devolution jurisdiction of the Judicial Committee of the Privy Council. The Act makes provision for the appointment of members of the court in a way that requires the participation of the judiciary and the devolved administrations throughout the United Kingdom. It also makes provision to determine the practices and procedures of the court, and makes general provision for the proceedings of the court to be broadcast in certain circumstances. As a counterpart to the creation of the Supreme Court the Act restricts the right of members of the House of Lords to sit and vote for so long as they hold full-time judicial office.

The Act makes specific provision as to the effect of decisions of the Supreme Court as judicial precedents. In essence, a decision made by the Supreme Court under a particular jurisdiction should have the same effect as a decision of the body in which the jurisdiction is currently vested (whether that is the House of Lords or the Judicial Committee of the Privy Council). So in the case of jurisdiction transferred from the House of Lords, a decision of the Supreme Court on an appeal from one jurisdiction within the United Kingdom will not have effect as a binding precedent in any other such jurisdiction, or in a subsequent appeal before the Supreme Court from another such jurisdiction. In the case of the devolution jurisdiction transferred from the Judicial Committee of the Privy Council, a decision of the Supreme Court will be binding in all legal proceedings except for subsequent proceedings before the Supreme Court itself. It will start work in October 2009.

[36] It is not uncommon for the Criminal Division of the Court of Appeal to certify that a point of law of general public importance is involved in a case, but still to refuse permission to appeal to the House of Lords.

The Court of Appeal: civil appeals[37]

The Court of Appeal is divided into two divisions: the criminal and the civil. The two senior judges are the Lord Chief Justice, who heads the Criminal Division, and the Master of the Rolls, who heads the Civil Division. They are assisted by, currently, thirty-seven Lords Justice of Appeal.[38] Both the President of the Family Division and the Chancellor of the High Court sit in the Court of Appeal for part of their time. By contrast with the House of Lords and the Privy Council, the Court of Appeal has a substantial case-load.

The Civil Division

The number of appeals coming to the Civil Division rose steadily during the early 1990s. They began to fall in 1996, and are now holding steady. During 2005, the number of applications for permission to appeal was 2,430—the same number as in the previous year. 1,103 final appeals were filed, and 1,177 were disposed of. 442 appeals were allowed. During the same period 136 interlocutory appeals—on matters that are related to the proceedings, but not finally determinative of the issues in question—were filed, and a similar number were disposed of. Nearly 50 per cent were allowed.

Comment

(1) While popular rhetoric suggests that it is the right of every English person to have his or her day in court, in practice access to the courts is surrounded by barriers. There are substantial procedural and financial pressures on litigants to settle their difference outside the courts; and appealing against the decision of a court is subject to even more restrictions.

(2) Judicial manpower is an expensive resource to be used sparingly, particularly at the most senior levels. Much of the simpler case work is in fact dealt with by part-time judges. There are also many occasions in which judges sit in a court of a higher level than the one to which they have been appointed—circuit judges in the High Court; High Court judges in the Court of Appeal, for example. There is thus considerable flexibility in how the available resource is used, though this begs the question—given the policy on court fees[39]—whether the public is actually getting the judicial service it thinks it is paying for.

(3) Delay and cost were the principal issues identified as in need of reform by Lord Woolf. Preliminary research suggests that the new Civil Procedure Rules are working well, and that there have been significant reductions in the time taken

---

[37] Information on criminal appeals is in Chapter 5 at p. 134.

[38] Other High Court judges assist, as required and as available, in the Criminal Division.

[39] See above, p. 212.

for a case to get to court. However, there are still serious complaints about the cost of taking proceedings.[40]

(4) There is also considerable frustration at the slow pace of investment in information technology in the civil justice system, that was promised at the time the Woolf reforms were introduced but which has not yet been fully delivered.

Questions for reflection and discussion

1. Has England become over-litigious?
2. Should courts be more/less specialized?
3. Should the civil courts be unified?
4. How should the civil justice system be funded? What level of state funding is justifiable?
5. Are there too many avenues of appeal?
6. Is it right that the courts should be regarded as the forum of last resort?
7. What are the arguments for and against the use of ADR to resolve disputes? Should use of ADR be made compulsory?
8. Should the Privy Council continue to hear appeals from other Commonwealth countries?

Further reading

ABEL, R.L., *The Politics of Informal Justice* (London/New York, Academic Press, 1982), 2 vols

BALDWIN, J., *Small Claims in the County Court* (Oxford, Clarendon Press, 1996)

—— *Lay and Judicial Perspectives on the Expansion of the Small Claims Regime* (LCD Research Paper 8/2002) (London, Lord Chancellor's Department, 2002)

BROWN, H., and MARRIOTT, A., *ADR: Principles and Practice* (2nd edn., London, Sweet and Maxwell, 1999)

BULLE, L., and NESIC, M., *Mediation: Principles, Process, Practice* (London, Butterworths, 2001)

CRANSTON, R., *How Law Works: The Machinery and Impact of Civil Justice* (Oxford, Oxford University Press, 2006)

DREWRY, G., BLOM-COOPER, L., and BLAKE, C., *The Court of Appeal* (Oxford, Hart Publishing, 2007)

GENN, H., *Mediation in Action—Resolving Court Disputes Without Trial* (London, Calouste Gulbenkian Foundation, 1999)

—— *Court-based ADR Initiatives For Non-Family Civil Disputes: The Commercial Court and The Court of Appeal* (LCD Research Paper 1/2002) (London, Lord Chancellor's Department, 2002)

[40] See Goriely, T., Moorhead, R., and Abrams, P., *More Civil Justice? The Impact of the Woolf Reforms on Pre-action Behaviour* (Research Study 43) (London, The Law Society and Civil Justice Council, 2002).

GENN, H., (and others) *Twisting Arms: Court Referred and Court Linked Mediation under Judicial Pressure* (London, Ministry of Justice, 2007)

JACOB, SIR JACK, *The Fabric of English Civil Justice* (London, Stevens, 1987)

JACOB, J., *Civil Litigation: Practice and Procedure in a Shifting Culture* (Welwyn Garden City, Emis Professional Publishing, 2001)

MOORHEAD, R., and SEFTON, M., *Litigants in Person: Unrepresented litigants in First Instance Proceedings* (DCA Research Series) (London, DCA, 2005)

PALMER, M., and ROBERTS, S., *Dispute Processes: ADR and the Primary Forms of Decision-Making* (London, Butterworths, 1998)

PEYSNER, J., and SENEVERATNE, M., *The Management of Civil Cases: the Courts and the post-Woolf Landscape* (DCA Research Series) (London, DCA, 2005)

PLOTNIKOFF, J., and WOOLFSON, R., *Evaluation of Appellate Work in the High Court and the County Courts* (DCA Research Series) (London, DCA, 2005)

POLDEN, P., *A History of the County Court, 1846–1971* (Cambridge, Cambridge University Press, 1999)

SHAPLAND, J., SORSBY, A., and HIBBERT, J., *A Civil Justice Audit* (LCD Research Paper 2/2002) (London, Lord Chancellor's Department, 2002)

WOOLF, LORD, *Access to Justice: Final Report to the Lord Chancellor on the Civil Justice System in England and Wales* (London, The Stationery Office, 1996)

Websites

http://www.dca.gov.uk/civil/cjustfr.htm *(Useful archive DCA website with links to material on the civil justice system)*

http://www.justice.gov.uk/whatwedo/civillawreform.htm *(Rather uninformative MoJ site)*

http://www.hmcourts-service.gov.uk/ *(Homepage for Her Majesty's Court Service)*

http://www.hmcourts-service.gov.uk/cms/publications.htm *(List of links to HM court service publications, including annual reports)*

http://www.hmcourts-service.gov.uk/onlineservices/index.htm *(Information about making claims on-line)*

http://www.justice.gov.uk/civil/procrules_fin/index.htm *(Civil Procedure Rules)*

http://www.justice.gov.uk/whatwedo/alternativedisputeresolution.htm *(MoJ site with links to information on ADR)*

http://www.dca.gov.uk/civil/adr/index.htm *(Still useful archive DCA website on alternative dispute resolution)*

https://www.nationalmediationhelpline.com/index.php *(Information about the National Mediation Helpline)*

http://www.civilmediation.org/ *(Homepage of the Civil Mediation Council)*

http://www.academy-experts.org/default.htm *(The professional body for expert witnesses)*

http://www.arbitrators.org/index.asp *(Chartered Institute of Arbitrators)* http://www.cedr.co.uk/ *(Centre for Effective Dispute Resolution)*

http://www.adrgroup.co.uk/ *(ADR group)*

http://www.adrchambers.co.uk/ *(ADR chambers UK and Europe site)*

http://www.northernmediators.co.uk/ *(Regional group of mediation providers—includes links to other regional groupings)*

http://www.dca.gov.uk/enforcement/indexfr.htm *(Website on the enforcement review)*

http://www.officialsolicitor.gov.uk/ *(Offices of Court Funds, the Official Solicitor and Public Trustee)*

http://www.hmcourts-service.gov.uk/infoabout/civil/probate/index.htm *(Probate service website)*

http://www.publicguardian.gov.uk/about/about.htm *(Office of the Public Guardian)*

http://www.publicguardian.gov.uk/about/court-of-protection.htm *(Information about the Court of Protection)*

PART III

THE DELIVERY AND FUNDING OF LEGAL SERVICES

This Part consists of two chapters. Chapter 9 looks at those who deliver legal services, including both professionally qualified lawyers and others providing legal services; it also includes consideration of the judges and legal scholars who should also be seen as groups responsible for developing and delivering the law. Chapter 10 looks at the funding of legal services, and analyses in particular the profound changes that have occurred to the funding of civil litigation following restructuring of the legal aid scheme.

9

Delivering legal services: practitioners, adjudicators, and legal scholars

Introduction

Discussions about the delivery of legal services tend to focus on the role of the legal profession and its two branches: *solicitors* and *barristers*. Here a broader approach is adopted. In the same way that we have argued that the institutional framework of the English legal system can only be understood by referring to a wide range of institutions, not simply the courts, so too thinking about the full range of those who deliver services about legal rights and entitlements involves consideration of a much greater range of actors. The purpose of this chapter is to provide an introductory account of the principal groups that provide legal services. It considers not only the professionally qualified, but also those who provide legal services without necessarily having legal professional qualifications.

The bulk of the chapter focuses on those who deliver legal services directly or indirectly to clients. The chapter also includes consideration of those who provide legal services by adjudicating disputes, whether as judges or other types of dispute resolver. Finally the role of the legal scholar is considered.

The practitioners

Three groups are considered in this part of the chapter:

- those professionally qualified as lawyers;
- those in professional groups allied to law; and
- lay legal advisers.

Professionally qualified lawyers: solicitors and barristers

There are currently over 104,500 practising solicitors in England and Wales. In addition there are another 10,500 or so barristers in private practice. A further 2,200 practise as employed lawyers working 'in-house' for a wide variety of companies, government departments, and agencies. All these totals have increased very rapidly over the last quarter of a century, though there are signs of a downturn in the numbers of barristers. They reflect increased demands for legal services resulting from economic growth, structural changes affecting the commercial world such as globalization and involvement in Europe, and numerous other social changes with greater emphasis on citizens' rights.

These global figures mask two important developments. First, there is a significantly improved gender balance of those entering the legal profession than there was twenty-five years ago. For a number of years now, more women than men have become solicitors. About a third of those in private practice at the bar are women. Secondly, the ethnic balance of entrants, though far from satisfactory, has improved. While the legal profession may still be a predominantly middle-class one, it is significantly less white and male than it used to be.[1]

What lawyers do

It is impossible to summarize the enormous variety of work that lawyers undertake. A long list could be presented, but would not be particularly enlightening. Much of the work of the large city firms relates to the commercial activities of their clients, for example the headline-grabbing financial deals or takeover bids that shape economic and commercial life. Others offer services focused on the individual client, for example defending people accused of crime, dealing with the consequences of personal injuries particularly arising from road traffic accidents, buying and selling property, handling divorces, or winding up estates after death.

The focus of this chapter is on lawyers who work in private practice. However, the work of other significant groups of qualified lawyers should also be noted. Three specific examples may be given.

Lawyers in industry. Considerable numbers of lawyers work in industry, not indirectly through the services provided for companies by those in private practice, but directly through their employment by the firms concerned. Most major companies have legal departments, staffed by professionally qualified lawyers, able to advise them on those legal issues which directly affect the company and its operations, for example matters relating to employment law, or health and safety legislation, or real estate.

---

[1] These changes are not yet reflected in the number of women and members of ethnic minority groups who have reached the highest positions in the law, e.g. judicial appointments, QCs or partners in solicitors' firms.

Lawyers in the Civil Service and local government. There are—broadly—two ways in which those professionally qualified as lawyers may be employed in central government. First they may be specifically employed for their technical legal expertise: to draft legislation (Parliamentary Counsel), or to deal with the wide range of legal issues that arise in departments (the Government Legal Service). In addition, there are many with law degrees and other legal qualifications who are not employed as lawyers, but who form part of the general Civil Service.

In local government, lawyers often hold senior positions in local authority administrations and play a very important role in ensuring that local authorities act within the scope of the powers given to them by Act of Parliament.

Lawyers in court administration. Qualified lawyers also play a very important part in the work of those courts and other dispute resolution bodies which do not use legally qualified adjudicators, for example justices' clerks in the magistrates' courts.

One of the great attractions of the law is the enormous range of employment opportunities that the law provides for those who wish to practise or work in the legal system. There are also increasing opportunities to work in international agencies of various kinds, particularly in Europe.

Preliminary issues

When thinking about what lawyers do, two preliminary distinctions should be drawn: (1) between litigious and non-litigious matters; and (2) between lawyers' services and legal services.

Litigious and non-litigious matters. It is essential to bear in mind from the outset the fundamental distinction between litigious and non-litigious matters. A great deal of the work of lawyers is directed to non-litigious work—work designed to *prevent* litigation. This includes, for example, the provision of advice or the drafting of documents designed to ensure that people's affairs run smoothly. By contrast, litigious work arises where things have gone wrong, where there are disputes that need to be resolved either between individuals or companies or between the citizen and the state. Rights to conduct litigation and to be heard in a court are subject to particular statutory rules.

Legal services and lawyers' services. A second distinction worth drawing is between *lawyers' services,* services which can only be provided by professionally qualified lawyers, and *legal services,* which may, though do not have to, be provided by professional lawyers. One of the features of the English legal system is that many people, other than those professionally qualified as lawyers, provide legal services, which are required by members of the public, and which deal with legal issues, e.g. advice about legal entitlements or the completion of legal transactions. The role of para-legal staff and lay advisers is discussed later in this chapter. (Some examples are given in *Box 9.1.*)

One example of the distinction between legal services and lawyers' services that has recently attracted considerable public attention has arisen in the context of companies providing claims management services—another example of legal services being provided by those not professionally legally qualified. Such companies advertise their willingness to take on the cases of people who have suffered harm as the result of

Box 9.1 Legal system explained

Legal services and lawyers' services

Some examples of the distinction in practice are:

- The first source of legal advice for many people faced with problems about their employment ('have I been unfairly dismissed by my employer?') is a *Citizens' Advice Bureau* or a *trade union*. The person they see is trained to give the appropriate advice; the adviser may indeed recommend that the person should see a qualified lawyer. But the initial *legal service* does not usually come from a lawyer, but from a trained lay adviser;
- Similar points may be made in relation to advice sought by a tenant in a dispute with her landlord;
- Many people anxious to obtain advice regarding their legal entitlements to social security benefits are more likely to turn to the services of a *welfare rights officer*— again a lay person, albeit specially trained, rather than to professionally qualified lawyers; and
- Those who buy or sell houses may use the services of a *licensed conveyancer* rather than a solicitor to complete their transaction.

Some legal services, in the sense set out above, are provided by other professional groups. The most obvious example is that the bulk of matters relating to individuals' legal liability to pay tax are dealt with, not by lawyers, but by *accountants*. *Legal services* are not provided exclusively by qualified lawyers.

Lawyers' services may be seen as a special sub-set of the total provision of legal services: they are services which either have to be provided by those qualified as lawyers (such as the provision of advocacy services in court—which are restricted to those who have achieved particular professional qualifications) or which, as a matter of practice, are provided by those qualified as lawyers. For example, it is inconceivable that large corporations would turn to lay advisers—however well trained—for advice on questions relating to a corporate takeover. Such clients want the expertise that professional lawyers hold themselves out as offering, and, should anything go wrong, the comfort of the insurance protection that is a part of professional responsibility.

The Legal Services Act 2007 effectively enshrines this distinction in legislation, as it provides for a number of 'reserved legal activities' (rights of audience, conduct of litigation, probate activities, notarial activities, the administration of oaths, and 'reserved instrument activities') which may only be performed by lawyers or others authorized to undertake such work. It will be a criminal offence to undertake such work without authorization.

accident on a 'no win, no fee' basis. A new regulatory regime was introduced in 2006, designed to ensure that non-lawyers who offered such services were authorized to do this work, and adhered to specified rules of conduct. (*See Box 9.2.*)

Box 9.2 Legal system explained

The regulation of claims management

Under the Compensation Act 2006, persons providing a regulated claims-management service need to be authorized. The regulation applies to claims made for compensation in relation to personal injury, criminal injuries compensation, industrial injuries disablement benefit, employment matters, housing disrepair, and financial products and services. Almost any activity in relation to claims, from simply referring claims through to representing clients, is covered.

Those who are already regulated (e.g. by being a solicitor, or under financial services legislation) are exempt from these requirements, as are certain other categories of persons or organizations including charities, not-for-profit advice agencies and some trade unions. The Act makes it an offence to operate without authorization, unless exempted.

The following services are covered: (a) advertising for, or otherwise seeking out (for example, by canvassing or direct marketing), persons who may have a cause of action; (b) advising a claimant or potential claimant in relation to his claim or cause of action; (c) referring details of a claim or claimant, or a cause of action or potential claimant, to another person, including a person having the right to conduct litigation (but not if it is not undertaken for or in expectation of a fee, gain, or reward); (d) investigating, or commissioning the investigation of, the circumstances, merits, or foundation of a claim, with a view to the use of the results in pursuing the claim; (e) representation of a claimant (whether in writing or orally, and regardless of the tribunal, body, or person to or before which or whom the representation is made).

Among the requirements of the rules of conduct are: (a) cold calling in person is prohibited; other cold calling must be in accordance with industry codes; (b) referral fees paid must be disclosed; (c) certain information must be given to clients before they sign a contract; (d) there is a fourteen-day cooling off period after a contract has been signed; (e) where a contract is cancelled any cancellation fee must be reasonable in the circumstances and reflect work done; (f) there must be an internal complaints procedure; and (g) where client money is held it must be held in client accounts that meet stipulated standards.

Regulation of the legal profession

One of the principal claims of professional bodies is that they can and should be allowed to regulate themselves. There are many arguments in favour of self-regulation, in particular that only those within the profession can set and monitor proper professional standards. Against this, it is argued that self-regulation can result in the creation of restrictive practices that work against the public interest. Over the last forty years, there has been enormous change to the ways in which the legal profession is regulated. Government has become increasingly involved in demanding regulatory change.

The attack on restrictive practices and the encouragement of competition

The attack on the restrictive practices of the legal profession began with a study by the Monopolies Commission, published in 1968. In his evidence to the Commission, Michael Zander provided a devastating critique of various professional practices, which he argued were not in the public interest.[2] Many others joined the attack. For example, during the early 1970s, Austen Mitchell, MP, led a sustained attack on the conveyancing monopoly then enjoyed by solicitors.[3]

A Royal Commission on Legal Services, under the chairmanship of Lord Benson, was established in 1976 and reported in 1979.[4] It came to the conclusion that, while a large number of detailed changes to professional practice needed to be made, many of the practices of the legal professions were in the public interest.

Further pressure to change developed when the Thatcher government came to power in 1979. Mrs Thatcher was determined to make the British economy generally much more competitive. The legal profession became caught up in a general attack on monopolistic power.[5]

Abolition of the conveyancing monopoly

The first, and probably the most symbolically significant, change to lawyers' restrictive practices occurred in 1987, when the conveyancing monopoly was broken. Until that date, only solicitors were entitled to charge for the work required to convey the title in real estate from a vendor to a purchaser. Following enactment of the Administration of Justice Act 1985, Part II, a system of licensed conveyancers, regulated by the Council for Licensed Conveyancers, was established. The first licences under the scheme were granted in 1987. In addition, the practice of using fixed-scale fees for conveyancing was stopped. There is no doubt that many solicitors had benefited very substantially from the original arrangements, though there is also evidence that there was at least some indirect social benefit, in that many solicitors used the profit from their convey-ancing work to subsidize other less profitable activity in their practices.

Right to litigate and rights of audience

Fundamental changes were also made to the rights to conduct litigation and rights of audience. Before 1990, only solicitors could prepare cases for trial; only barristers had

---

[2] Zander, M., *Lawyers and the Public Interest* (London, Weidenfeld and Nicolson, 1968).

[3] An attack joined by at least some members of the profession themselves: see Joseph, M., *The Conveyancing Fraud* (Harmondsworth, Penguin, 1975).

[4] (Cmnd 7648) (London, HMSO, 1979).

[5] There is a tendency for all professional groups to feel that they are being picked on and uniquely subjected to pressure to change. In fact all professional groups have been subject to similar pressures.

rights to argue cases in court. Under the provisions of the Courts and Legal Services Act 1990, the government began to put these rights on a statutory footing. Instead of the professional bodies simply prescribing rules relating to advocacy and litigation, as they had done in the past, the Act established a framework for authorized bodies (the Bar Council and the Law Society together with the Institute of Legal Executives) to set the rules.

The Access to Justice Act 1999 changed the rules again. It made the following provisions: all barristers and solicitors were to have the right of audience before every court in all proceedings;[6] Crown prosecutors and other employed advocates (whether solicitors or barristers) were to have the same rights of audience as if they were in private practice;[7] advocates and litigators employed by the Legal Services Commission or by bodies established by the Legal Services Commission are enabled to provide services directly to the public, without the need to receive instructions through a solicitor or other person acting for the client;[8] where a person, a barrister, had been granted the right of audience by one professional body (e.g. the Bar Council), she became entitled to retain that right if she becomes a solicitor, and thus a member of the Law Society;[9] barristers employed by firms of solicitors are able to act on the same basis as solicitors;[10] the General Council of the Bar and the Institute of Legal Executives are given power to grant their members the right to conduct litigation;[11] procedures for authorizing (and in extreme cases revoking authorizations to) new bodies to grant rights of audience and rights to conduct litigation, and for approving alterations to or the adoption of new regulations or rules of conduct were streamlined;[12] and the overriding duties of advocates and litigators to the court to act with independence in the interests of justice and to comply with their professional bodies' rules of conduct was put on a statutory footing.[13] All authorized advocates and litigators must refuse to do anything required, either by a client or an employer, that is not in the interests of justice (e.g. the suppression of evidence).

Other changes

Numerous other changes occurred as well. In particular rules on advertising were significantly relaxed so that, within the boundaries set by the Law Society's *Guide to Professional Behaviour,* firms of solicitors became entitled to advertise their services. While advertising in the United Kingdom may not have the flamboyance of lawyers'

---

[6] s. 36; these are not unqualified rights, those wishing to exercise them must obey the rules of conduct of the professional bodies and meet prescribed training requirements.

[7] s. 37. The campaign fought by the CPS to obtain rights of advocacy under the Act of 1990 was a source of very great frustration.

[8] s. 38.   [9] s. 39.

[10] s. 44; the Bar Council rules that treated barristers employed by solicitors as 'non-practising' and thus able to offer only a limited range of services are disapplied.

[11] s. 40; they are under no obligation to do so.

[12] s. 41 and Sch. 5.

[13] s. 42. This was thought to be necessary to guarantee the ability of the individual lawyer to act independently.

advertisements in the United States, nevertheless this development was also a significant break with past tradition. All significant legal practices, both solicitors' and barristers', now engage in a wide range of promotional 'practice development' activity.

Further developments

However, the changes of the 1980s and 1990s, far from being the end of the process, were
merely a foretaste of what was to come. More recent developments started in March
2001, when the Office of Fair Trading produced a report 'Competition in Professions'
which recommended that unjustified restrictions on competition should be removed.
The government responded with a consultation paper and report into competition
and regulation in the legal services market. The report concluded that 'the current
framework is out-dated, inflexible, over-complex and insufficiently accountable or
transparent... Government has therefore decided that a thorough and independent
investigation without reservation is needed'.

In July 2003, Sir David Clementi was appointed to carry out an independent review
of the regulatory framework for legal services in England and Wales. His terms of reference were: to consider what regulatory framework would best promote competition,
innovation, and the public and consumer interest in an efficient, effective, and independent legal sector; and to recommend a framework which will be independent in representing the public and consumer interest, comprehensive, accountable, consistent,
flexible, transparent, and no more restrictive or burdensome than is clearly justified.

In December 2004, Sir David published his report. The main recommendations,
which the government broadly accepted, were:

- to establish a new legal services regulator, which he called the Legal Services
  Board, to provide consistent oversight regulation of front-line bodies such as the
  Law Society and the Bar Council;

- to set statutory objectives for the Legal Services Board, including promotion of
  the public and consumer interest;

- to prescribe regulatory powers that would be vested in the Legal Services Board,
  but with powers to devolve regulatory functions to front-line bodies (i.e. professional bodies), subject to their competence and governance arrangements;

- to ensure that the front-line bodies made new governance arrangements which
  would separate their regulatory and representative functions;

- to create a new Office for Legal Complaints—a single independent body to handle consumer complaints in respect of all members of front-line bodies, subject to
  oversight by the Legal Services Board;

- to establish alternative business structures that could see different types of lawyers and non-lawyers managing and owning legal practices.[14]

---

[14] From a professional point of view, this was one of the most contentious issues. Clementi saw the
possibility of lawyers establishing multi-disciplinary partnerships (with other professional groups such

Details of the government's response were set out in the White Paper 'The Future of Legal Services: Putting the Consumer First' published in October 2005. This, in turn, led to the publication of the Legal Services Bill. It passed through Parliament in October 2007. It creates the new regulatory framework envisaged by Clementi.

Professional organization

In one important respect, Clementi's recommendations have already been brought into effect. Both the Bar Council (responsible for barristers) and the Law Society (responsible for solicitors) have re-organized themselves. Clementi thought it important that the profession's representative functions, designed to promote their members' interests to the wider public, should be separated from their regulatory functions. *Solicitors* are now professionally regulated by the Solicitors Regulation Authority, established in 2007 as the independent regulatory body of the Law Society, and *barristers* are regulated by the Bar Standards Board, the independent regulatory body of the Bar Council.

Solicitors in private practice usually come together to form partnerships, though a substantial minority practise on their own as 'sole practitioners'. One recent development is that firms of solicitors have been able to form limited liability partnerships. Barristers in private practice work in 'chambers' but they are all self-employed within those chambers. Barristers are not currently permitted to form partnerships.[15] The extent to which this will change, once the provisions of the Legal Services Act have become effective, cannot at present be predicted.

Handling complaints and ensuring quality control

In addition to changes in the regulatory framework to promote competition, another driver for change has been a concern to improve the quality of service delivery. Until the 1980s the hallmark of any profession was that those who made up the profession were regarded as the best qualified to set standards of practice and to remove miscreants from their ranks. One of the challenges that has confronted the legal professions over the last twenty years is how they should respond to the pressures to deliver a standard of service demanded by an increasingly critical client base.

---

as accountants) as a key stage towards the removal of the final unnecessary restrictive practices. He also thought that non-lawyers should be able to invest in legal practices. Clementi's views—that new forms of practice would not undermine the independence of the legal profession and would not reduce access to justice—were supported in a series of independent research papers, published in 2005 by the DCA. The proposals were, however, strongly contested by the leaders of the professions.

[15] The ability of the Bar to sustain the notion that barristers are all self-employed and are not permitted to enter into partnerships is coming under attack. The commercial pressures arising from the increased overheads which chambers must absorb suggest that the case for a more commercial approach to the organization of chambers will need addressing in the near future.

The professional bodies did take steps to ensure that lawyers kept up-to-date with developments in law and in practice management. Both the Law Society and the Bar Council introduced rules requiring practitioners to undertake regular amounts of *continuing professional development.* This is the least that can be expected of a 'learned profession'. In addition, in the specific context of legal aid, the Legal Services Commission has paid great attention to quality issues[16]—arguably doing work that the professional bodies had failed to do.

More problematic has been the question of how complaints about service delivery should be handled.

Background

The situation before 1990 was—very broadly—that while the courts were able to deal with the most serious cases of professional negligence, and while the professional bodies were able to control other forms of *gross* misconduct, the more mundane complaints—rudeness, slowness in responding to letters, general inefficiency—were not being dealt with seriously. Yet these were precisely the sorts of issues which the ordinary client, who felt she was not getting good value for the money she was being asked to pay, wanted to complain about. Both the Law Society and the Bar Council took steps to try to address these concerns.

The Law Society started the process in the mid-1980s following the long-drawn-out and very unsatisfactory handling of a complaint against one of its Council members, Mr Glanville Davies. In 1985, the Society commissioned Coopers and Lybrand to review the Society's disciplinary procedures. The consultants recommended that all these procedures be transferred to a new independent agency. The Law Society did not accept this recommendation, but it did, in 1986, establish the Solicitors' Complaints Bureau (SCB), relaunched[17] as the Office for the Supervision of Solicitors (OSS) in 1996. It has been further renamed and is currently called the Legal Complaints Service. It operates independently and has its premises in Leamington Spa.

In 1991, the Law Society also made a number of changes to its Practice Rules, most notably the introduction of Practice Rule 15, requiring all solicitors to operate a complaints-handling procedure designed to ensure that clients know who to approach in the event of a problem with the service with which they have been provided. Part of the reason for the introduction of this rule was to encourage firms to resolve complaints internally, and thus, it was hoped, reduce the pressure on the SCB.

The Bar was slower off the mark. A proposal in 1994 from its Standards Review Body[18] to set up a Barristers Complaints Bureau did not meet the approval of the membership of the Bar. Instead the post of lay Complaints Commissioner was agreed.[19] In

---

[16] See further Chapter 10.

[17] Following considerable criticism from both within the profession and outside. See, e.g., National Consumer Council, *The Solicitors' Complaints Bureau: A Consumer View* (London, National Consumer Council, 1994).

[18] Chaired by the late Lord Alexander of Weedon, QC, former Chairman of the Bar.

[19] The holder of this post is now Robert Behrens.

addition, the Bar Council in 1995 developed new practice management standards,[20] which are not mandatory but rather guidelines to good practice, and to which the Bar's Code of Conduct requires barristers to have regard. These practice management standards stated that barristers' chambers should have a written code of procedure for dealing with complaints. In 1997, changes were made to the Bar's Code of Conduct. Among other things, the code recognized for the first time the concept of 'inadequate professional service',[21] against which the Complaints Commissioner can determine complaints from barristers' clients. This went some way to addressing the gap between what clients typically wanted to complain about and the rather narrow concepts of 'negligence' and 'gross misconduct' mentioned above.

Research into these developments,[22] and in particular into the rules relating to the local office/chambers resolution of disputes, suggested that the response from practitioners was somewhat underwhelming. Heads of chambers, for example, still asserted that the 'market' will deal with the incompetent—they will not get briefed and thus go to the wall. They were not convinced that taking complaints seriously is either professionally important or commercially desirable.[23] There remained considerable pressure for the creation of a more independent complaints-handling procedure.

Statutory developments

The changes by the professional bodies were accompanied by significant statutory developments. The Courts and Legal Services Act 1990 established the office of Legal Services Ombudsman. The Access to Justice Act 1999 extended the power of the Ombudsman; and made provision for the appointment of a Legal Services Complaints Commissioner.

The Legal Services Ombudsman only took cases that could not be resolved by one of the existing professional complaints procedures.[24] The Legal Services Complaints Commissioner was to take over the handling of complaints against the legal profession, if the systems in place within the legal profession were thought by the Lord Chancellor to be inadequate. Initially the government was not minded to put these provisions into effect. But, following considerable concern about the ability of the OSS to deal with complaints, the Lord Chancellor appointed the Legal Services Ombudsman to the additional (and separate) post of Legal Services Complaints Commissioner to impose standards for the handling of complaints against solicitors.

---

[20] One way in which chambers can attest that they fall within the principles implied by the Practice Management Standards is by acquisition of the 'Barmark', a British Standards Institute accreditation.

[21] 'Conduct... or performance of professional services... which falls significantly short of that which is to be expected of a barrister in all the circumstances'.

[22] Christensen, C., *Report of an Investigation into the Operation of Complaint-handling Mechanisms Operated by Barristers' Chambers* (Bristol, University of the West of England, 2000).

[23] In the case of the Bar, which is still in theory based on the principle of the barrister being self-employed, there may be some difficulties in taking a 'corporate' approach to complaints handling. Senior clerks, however, seem much more aware of the commercial importance of chambers presenting a corporate image and learning corporate lessons from individual lapses in standards than barristers themselves.

[24] In addition to the Bar and the Law Society, the Council of the Institute of Legal Executives also runs a complaints procedure.

Under the Legal Services Act, 2007, both these posts are abolished and are replaced by the Office for Legal Complaints, as recommended by Clementi. However the work currently undertaken by the Ombudsman and the Commissioner will continue within the new framework.

The promotion of ethical standards

This is another issue that has received considerable attention in recent years, not only in relation to the work of lawyers, but in all areas of professional activity. Here is not the place to enter a detailed consideration of the need for the legal profession to adopt an ethical approach to its work, nor of the role of the professional bodies in promoting that work. It may be suggested, however, that much hostility towards lawyers is fuelled by the feeling that lawyers are not as ethical as they should be. This is certainly the basis for many anti-lawyer jokes.

It is perhaps the case that, until relatively recently, the provision of legal services by lawyers was seen by members of the legal profession themselves as a public service to which, in some rather mysterious way, commercial pressures somehow did not apply. The adoption of an ethical approach was, on this view, inherent in the provision of the service.

Whether there was ever any real justification for this belief, there can be no doubt that in the modern world the provision of legal services is quite clearly a business. If lawyers cannot make a profit at the end of the year, they go bust. Legal practice must be subject to the disciplines of financial control, quality control, and efficiency that characterize all business activity. The concern with ethical standards may have arisen from a perception that concentrating exclusively on the financial and commercial imperatives of legal practice could encourage lawyers to forget the ethical principles which should also underpin their work.

The professional regulatory bodies provide guidance on professional conduct which sets out an ethical framework for professional activity. Understanding these principles is a key feature of professional legal education, not least because failure to follow the guidance can result in the worst cases in loss of the right to practise as a barrister or solicitor. The question whether the codes of practice go far enough to incorporate an ethical dimension to legal practice is beyond the scope of this work.

Whatever the cynical view of lawyers may be, there are two particular respects in which the legal profession is able at least in part to demonstrate its ethical commitment: pro bono work; and test case litigation.

For free (pro bono) work

There has long been a tradition that lawyers offer free legal services to the poor. Before there was any legal aid, there was a history of such provision in London and other major conurbations. In recent years, there has been a renewed emphasis on pro bono work. Because the large commercial firms in the City of London and other commercial centres have been so obviously financially successful, there has been a renewed interest in the provision of free legal services by their staff in citizens' advice bureaux and other agencies. Some may regard this as little more than a token gesture. But, given the precarious funding position that many such agencies are in, it is work that makes a significant contribution to local legal service delivery. It is also true that the majority of those who offer pro bono services derive a great deal of professional interest and pleasure from the work they do.

The professional bodies have taken a great deal of trouble to promote pro bono work over the last decade. And the Attorney-General has appointed a former Law Society President, Michael Napier, QC, as his pro bono envoy. Many important new initiatives have been taken, including an annual 'pro bono' week, with events being held around the country; and the making of 'pro-bono' awards to lawyers who have developed outstanding examples of pro bono practice, both in this country and in some cases overseas.

Test case litigation

Test case litigation, or as it is sometimes called 'cause lawyering', is also often associated with lawyers being willing to take up broad general issues, particularly on behalf of more disadvantaged groups in the community. Historically, test case litigation in the United Kingdom has not had the same impact as, for example, in the United States, where legal provisions or policies were able to be tested for their constitutionality against the provisions of the US Constitution. However, with ever greater involvement in Europe, both through the European Union and, in relation to human rights, through the Council of Europe, many challenges to English law have been mounted, in some cases with dramatic success. The Human Rights Act has generated an additional amount of test case legislation, as provisions of English law are tested for their compatibility with the European Convention.

Independence of the legal professions

Independence is one of the key attributes claimed for the legal professions. This is, constitutionally, extremely important. It involves lawyers asserting their right to give advice independently of the views of the government of the day, and being protected if they do so. It also involves a professional obligation to take on cases which may be widely regarded as disagreeable or distasteful. The proposition that a person is innocent until proved guilty depends on lawyers being willing to develop and advance arguments on behalf of their clients no matter how unpleasant those clients may be. The 'cab-rank' principle which applies to the Bar, whereby barristers are professionally obliged to take on whatever case comes to them next, is perhaps the clearest example of the operation of this principle.

The assertion of independence may also imply that the professions should be free to regulate themselves in accordance with their own rules of professional conduct, without interference from government. As we have seen, there has been significant erosion of the ability of the legal profession to regulate itself. The abolition of restrictive practices, changes to legal aid, and to modes of dealing with complaints about the quality of work have all resulted in increased government intervention. The Legal Services Act 2007, takes this process further.

Each example of government engagement may be justified, particularly in contexts where the legal profession has not been willing to reform itself in ways which the public interest demands. However, the question where the boundaries should be drawn in the involvement of government in the legal profession is one that needs constant attention, if the role of the legal profession in assisting the individual, often against agencies of the state or other powerful bodies, is not to be compromised.

Trends in legal practice

As a consequence of these and other developments, the legal profession has in recent years undergone profound change. A number of trends affecting the profession are noted here.

The blurring of the distinction between solicitors and barristers

The organization of the practising legal profession in England and Wales differs markedly from that in many other countries. There is still an important distinction in professional identity between 'solicitor' and 'barrister'. However, the practical implications of the distinction are far less today than they were twenty-five years ago. Many of the services which used to be the exclusive preserve of one branch of the profession are now open to all.

There has also been concern that there should be no unnecessary restrictions on the tasks which people may perform within the legal system. The most important change in this context has been the adoption by statute of the principle that the highest judicial offices should be open to solicitors as well as to barristers (who formerly had a monopoly in relation to these appointments).[25]

Fusion? The obvious question that these developments pose is whether the time has not come when the two branches of the legal profession should fuse into a single profession, as happens in most other countries in the world. Should the long-standing distinction between solicitors and barristers continue to be defended? This has been debated on many occasions, though surprisingly not seriously in the last few years, despite the developments which have occurred and which are sketched out above. The arguments asserted by the Bar for its independence,

---

[25] The appointment of Mr Laurence Collins, QC, a very distinguished commercial solicitor, to the High Court was the first such appointment, made in 1999. The possibility of distinguished legal scholars being appointed to the highest levels of the judiciary just on the strength of their academic record has not been formally accepted. However, the appointment of Dame Brenda Hale (who prior to her appointment as a Law Commissioner had had a distinguished academic career at the University of Manchester) first to the High Court bench, then to the Court of Appeal, and most recently to the House of Lords is, perhaps, the start of a development in the direction of acknowledging the contribution legal scholars can make to the judiciary. The appointment of Professor Jack Beatson, QC, from the University of Cambridge to the High Court is another example. This certainly happens in the European Courts and the United States. Academics have long been appointed judges to the International Court of Justice.

in delivering both advocacy and other forms of legal advice, are actually very power-ful, more powerful than some of the advocates for fusion allow. But in other countries with fused professions, the independence of the advocate is still strongly asserted. Other ways could be found to protect professional independence without the reten-tion of a divided profession. It seems inconceivable that at some point in the not too distant future this issue should not again become the subject of public debate.

Growth and globalization

A second trend to be noted is the growth in the size of law firms and the increasingly global scope of their practices. These have resulted from the context within which law-yers practise, which cannot be divorced from other changes in the economy at large. The last twenty-five years have seen a major shift from an economy based on manufac-turing to one based on services. Increased globalization of the world economy has led to a growth in the need for lawyers able to advise corporations about all the national contexts within which they are required to operate. Globalization in the provision of legal services has accompanied the globalization of the economy. British lawyers have responded in a variety of ways:

- many of the large law firms in the City of London have gone through substantial programmes of merger and expansion;[26]

- significant groupings of leading firms in provincial commercial centres— e.g. Leeds, Birmingham, Bristol—have also developed, either through mergers and takeovers or the creation of networks of legal practices;

- many of these firms have established presences in other key centres of economic activity, in Europe, the Middle East, the Far East, and the Americas;

- mergers of English law firms with firms in other countries in Europe and the United States have resulted in the creation of new forms of international partnership;

- there has been a significant increase in the presence of overseas law firms, in par-ticular US law firms, in London, which has added to the competitive pressures on British-based firms; and

- there have been moves towards the creation of professional groupings that cut across traditional disciplinary boundaries—in particular, lawyers and accountants.

There is every likelihood of further developments of these kinds in the years ahead.

Specialization and niche practices

A third trend has been the increasing development of specialist/niche practices. In part this is a response to the trend towards 'mega-lawyering' noted in the previous sec-tion. Increasingly, small firms of solicitors and sets of barristers' chambers have come to specialize in particular areas—family law, criminal law, employment law, housing

---

[26] Galanter, M., and Pulay, T., *Tournament of Lawyers: The Transformation of the Big Law Firm* (Chicago, Chicago University Press, 1991).

law, to give some examples. These developments have been supported in part by the legal professional bodies themselves. For example, the Law Society has established a number of specialist panels which practitioners may join, including the Children's Panel, the Mental Health Panel, and the Medical Negligence Panel.

In addition, members of the profession themselves have taken the lead in establishing an increasing number of specialist groups, many of which cross over traditional solicitor/barrister boundaries. There are now well over forty such groups. They act in a variety of ways:

- they may be able to act collaboratively (within the competitive market) to promote the specialist services that they offer (thereby seeking to exclude non-specialists from their work);

- some, such as the Solicitors' Family Law Association, have promoted new modes of legal practice, designed to provide a different form of lawyering for their clients—in the context of family law, a less confrontational approach designed to assist those whose relationships have broken down;[27]

- others, such as the Patent Lawyers' Association, have developed specialist programmes of advanced legal education and training designed to give their members special expertise and, thus, it is hoped, a competitive edge in the legal services market place; and

- the specialist lawyer groups have also developed a very important influence in government. They are able to offer advice on how particular areas of legal practice may be affected by proposed policy changes, in ways in which the general professional bodies such as the Law Society or Bar Council may be unable to achieve.

Legal services to the poor

A fourth noteworthy trend in the shape of the legal profession has been a complete transformation in the operation of the legal aid scheme. The details of the new scheme are considered in Chapter 10. Here the principal point to note is that, whereas ten years ago in effect any firm of solicitors who wished to do legal aid work could do so, now only those firms with a contract to provide services from the Legal Services Commission are able to undertake publicly funded legal aid work. Many practitioners who used to do modest amounts of legal aid work as part of a portfolio of general legal services provided to mainly private clients have been affected by these changes. One response to these changes has been an increased emphasis on the legal profession providing services pro bono (see above, pp. 244–5).

High street practice

A consequence of these last two developments is that generalist high street practices, found in smaller towns, suburban areas and other locations, which have in the past

---

[27] See above, Chapter 7.

provided a general service to private clients, have come under increasing commercial pressure and face considerable uncertainty. The ability to make a living from a mixed practice of some criminal work, some property transactions (such as conveyancing or probate), a little bit of family and divorce work, and some personal injuries work, which even ten years ago was quite common, is now increasingly difficult. Many of the remaining sole practitioners and small firms fall into this category. The future of high street practice is under considerable threat, unless those who remain in this sector of the legal services market are prepared to rethink their commercial strategies.

Other trends

A graduate profession

A significant change over the last thirty years is that the legal profession has become a largely graduate one. The old days when professional qualifications could be obtained simply by apprenticeship in a solicitor's office or a barrister's chambers (and the passing of some not very demanding professional exams) are now long gone. Despite this, many of the graduates who enter the legal profession come with degrees other than in law. They obtain their legal qualifications through conversion courses undertaken following the obtaining of a first degree in another discipline. This has been the subject of fierce argument between the legal professional bodies and the legal academics, the latter asserting that only the grounding of a good law degree gives potential entrants to the legal profession a real understanding of how law is made and fundamental legal principles.

Information technology

Secondly, and in common with everyone else, the legal professions have been increasingly affected by the development of new information technologies.[28] Use of IT has transformed professional practice management. And as legal information from government and the legal publishers and other sources becomes increasingly available in electronic form, and as court procedures become increasingly technology-driven, the impact of IT on legal practice has intensified. Lack of IT investment, particularly in the civil courts, still limits the use of IT in civil litigation. But legal practice, including litigation, will continue to change enormously in the next decade, reflecting both increased investment and further rapid technological change.[29]

Pay and conditions

Thirdly, the expectations of those entering the profession about the pay and conditions they should receive have also changed considerably in the last quarter of a century. A real problem in this context is that the financial rewards for those in some parts

---

[28] See Susskind, R., *Transforming the Law: Essays on Technology, Justice and the Legal Marketplace* (Oxford, Oxford University Press, 2003).

[29] One of the biggest changes is likely to arise from the introduction of electronic conveyancing, to which the Land Registry is strongly committed. This should greatly speed up the process of buying and selling land.

Box 9.3   Legal system explained

Legal journalism

One consequence of the changed context of legal practice, particularly the relaxation of restrictions on advertising, is that a significant branch of journalism has developed, devoted to the telling of stories about individuals and firms in the law and their doings. Some of the broadsheet newspapers have a weekly law section, much of which is concerned with what is in effect legal gossip. In addition there are specialist papers for the profession which focus in particular on the activities of law firms and sets of chambers. The 'free' paper, the *Lawyer*—which appears weekly—is supplemented by the expensive and glossy *Legal Business* which focuses in particular on firms operating in the city and overseas.

One consequence of this new journalism is that public information about lawyers is to a large extent dominated by the stories which the PR departments of the large firms are able to place in this press. Stories about the impact and importance of the small high street firms find little place beside dramatic tales of takeovers, mergers, and other commercial/corporate activity. This creates at least three distortions:

- those thinking of entering the law as a profession are denied the opportunity to consider the full range of legal careers open to them;
- they come to assume that the only type of lawyering worth undertaking is that which pays enormous salaries; and
- the public assume that all lawyers act—and most significantly are paid—in ways suggested by the stories that appear in this press.

Much of the public hostility towards lawyers is, it may be surmised, the result of assumptions that legal services are very expensive and thus affordable only by the very rich. A more balanced picture would indicate that there are still many lawyers providing valuable services to the public for extremely modest fees.

of legal practice, particularly the corporate sector, are hugely different from those in many specialist or niche areas, particularly those offering services to the less well-off groups in society. Much of the problem is the result of a type of macho legal journalism which has developed over the last ten to fifteen years, but which arguably is not wholly in the interest of the legal profession. (See *Box 9.3*.)

Professional groups allied to the legal profession

Following the lengthy discussion of the legal profession, consideration of the professional groups allied to the legal profession is briefer. Two groups will be considered here: legal executives; and other specialist groups.

Legal executives

Many of the staff employed in solicitors' offices are not formally qualified as solicitors, but nonetheless provide a great deal of legal service to the public. These are known collectively as 'legal executives'. Many of these are members and fellows of their own professional representative body, the *Institute of Legal Executives* (ILEX). ILEX organizes its own training programmes and examinations which must be passed before a legal executive can call him- or herself a Fellow of the Institute. The Institute has its own Code of Professional Conduct, analogous to that of the Solicitors' Regulation Authority.

Legal executives play a central role in many legal practices, often being more expert in their areas of expertise that their fully professionally qualified colleagues. Legal executives who are fellows of ILEX are able, by taking additional courses and sitting additional examinations, to qualify as solicitors, and a number do so each year.

Other specialist groups

In addition to the legal executives, there are also a number of other more specialist groups providing particular kinds of legal and law-related services whose existence may be noted. These include:

- licensed conveyancers (noted in passing above) whose activities are regulated by the Council of Licensed Conveyancers;
- patent agents;
- insolvency practitioners; and
- tax advisers. This last group is not subject to the same forms of regulation as the other groups mentioned.[30]

Lay advisers and other providers of legal services

Lay advisers/advocates

In addition to the formally qualified, there are substantial numbers of people who have not obtained legal qualifications, but who nevertheless deliver legal services. These include: the lay advisers who work in advice agencies, such as the Citizens' Advice Bureaux; welfare rights workers, often employed in local authority sponsored welfare rights offices; housing-aid workers working in housing-advice centres; and many other lay advice workers working in a vast range of social, environmental, and other agencies.

---

[30] Green, S., and Leacham, K., *Tax Advice in the UK: Why Things Go Wrong and the Implications for the Tax Adviser's Profession* (London, Chartered Institute of Taxation, 1997).

Law Centres

One particular context in which the professionally qualified lawyer and the lay adviser come together is the Law Centre. The Law Centre movement started in the 1970s with the specific objective of targeting legal services to those who lived in deprived areas, principally towns and cities. Historically they have had a somewhat hand-to-mouth existence. Some have been funded by local authorities; others by private charities; one or two by central government. The rules of the Funding Code which now underpins the Community Legal Service provide that those agencies that satisfy standards set by the Legal Services Commission are able to obtain public funding for defined categories of work (see Chapter 10).

Membership services

A number of membership organizations also provide legal services to their members. These services may either be general or related to the matters which arise from membership. Examples at the more general end of provision are the legal services provided as the result of membership of trade unions or other professional groups (for example the Medical Defence Union); more specific legal services are provided to members of, e.g., the Automobile Association or the Royal Automobile Club.

Specialist agencies

In addition to the foregoing, a number of pressure groups also provide legal services. One motivation for this is to find appropriate test cases that might be brought to test the boundaries of statutory provisions. Examples include the Citizens' Rights Office, which is attached to the Child Poverty Action Group; the Public Law Project; Liberty (formerly the National Council for Civil Liberties); Shelter; and a number of environmental groups, such as Greenpeace. These agencies have been particularly successful in expanding the range of groups entitled to make representations to the courts in judicial review cases.

Adjudicators and dispute resolvers

Much has been written about judges in the English legal system. As with other topics in this book, most accounts focus on a rather narrow body of the judiciary, namely those who sit in the High Court, Court of Appeal, and the House of Lords. There can be no doubting the influence of the judges who sit in these higher courts in shaping English law. But the chances of any one individual member of the public appearing before one of these judges is remote in the extreme. Far more likely is an encounter with a district judge, a lay magistrate, a tribunal chairman, a circuit judge, or one of the army of other dispute resolvers and complaints handlers that now exist. It is these adjudicators or dispute resolvers who are, in practice, the face of the judiciary, as seen by the public at large.

Definition

For the purposes of this book, adjudicators and dispute resolvers are all those who are empowered[31] to resolve disputes that have been brought to them. This definition includes all the senior judicial figures who sit in the High Court and other courts just mentioned. But it also includes:

(1) *circuit judges* who determine civil cases in the county court, and criminal cases in the Crown Court;

(2) *district judges* who determine civil cases, including small claims hearings, in the county court;

(3) *recorders,* who are, in effect, circuit judges in training;

(4) *magistrates,* both lay and professionally qualified,[32] who determine the vast majority of criminal cases which are dealt with in magistrates' courts;

(5) *arbitrators* who determine a wide range of disputes referred to them under specially agreed arbitration agreements. Arbitrators are particularly used to resolve commercial disputes, both national and international;

(6) *tribunal members and chairmen* who deal with specific issues arising in defined legislative contexts: for example, disputes about entitlement to social security benefit, which go to Social Security Appeal Tribunals; or disputes about employment matters, which go to Employment Tribunals;

(7) *ombudsmen,* as they appear in their various guises; and

(8) *mediators, conciliators, complaints handlers,* and others who offer alternative forms of appropriate dispute resolution (ADR).

Numbers

It is not possible to give a complete picture of the total number of people holding various kinds of adjudicative office. The Ministry of Justice issues statistics of the numbers of judicial office-holders. In addition to the principal judicial office-holders—the Lord Chief Justice of England, the Master of the Rolls, the President of the Queen's Bench Division, the President of the Family Division, and the Chancellor, the number of full-time judicial office-holders at 1 January 2006 is set out in Table 9.1.

---

[31] This definition could include those who determine disputes under purely private contractual arrangements, e.g. internal employment dispute resolution procedures or student disciplinary procedures, but they are not considered here.

[32] They are called *District Judges (Magistrates' Courts); see above,* Box 5.11.

Table 9.1 Judicial appointments

	Full-time
Lords of Appeal (House of Lords)	12
Lords Justice of Appeal (Court of Appeal)	37
High Court judges	108
Circuit judges	619
District judges	419
District judges (criminal)	134
Total	1329

Source: Judicial Statistics, 2006.

There are also 1,394 Recorders, part-time judges who deal primarily with criminal trials. There are also numbers of part-time deputy district judges. In addition there are some 24,500 lay magistrates. Information about numbers of office-holders in other dispute resolution contexts is harder to establish. Figures are not always easily available. It may be estimated that there are around 20,000 part-time tribunal chairmen and members.

Judicial independence and impartiality

The importance of judicial independence was considered above. (*See Box 3.9.*) An equally important practical consideration is the importance of judges and adjudicators being impartial. There have been cases where it is suggested that there may be judicial bias, in the sense that a judge may have some direct personal interest in the outcome of a particular case.

This issue of judicial bias became the subject of much public discussion in 1999 following the revelation that Lord Hoffmann, one of the members of the House of Lords who sat in judgment in the case involving General Pinochet (the former dictator from Chile), was a member of Amnesty International, one of the parties in the proceedings involving the General. The issue having been raised, the House of Lords decided that the decision in which Lord Hoffmann had taken part could not be allowed to stand. In an unprecedented move, the original decision of the Lords was set aside, and referred for determination by another Appeal Committee from the House of Lords.[33]

Shortly thereafter a number of other cases were heard by the Court of Appeal which, though not as dramatic as that involving Pinochet, raised similar issues for consideration. In reviewing the position, the Court of Appeal laid down the following propositions:[34]

---

[33] *R v. Bow Street Metropolitan Magistrates, ex p Pinochet Ungarte* [1999] 2 WLR 272, HL.
[34] See *Locabail (UK) v. Bayfield* [2000] 1 All ER 65, CA.

(1) in general, membership of professional, political, or other organizations would not give grounds for an allegation of bias;

(2) neither would racial or ethnic origin, class, extra-judicial activities, sexual orientation, or previous judicial references to parties or witnesses, even if forthright;

(3) personal acquaintance with or antagonism towards any individuals involved in a case, especially if their credibility might be an issue, would give rise to a real danger of bias;

(4) the independent status of barristers when sitting judicially absolved them from responsibility for the interests of other members of chambers; and

(5) solicitors maintained responsibility for acts of their partners and owed a duty to their firms' clients, even if they had not acted for them personally.

Literature on the judiciary

With few exceptions, books about the judiciary have not in any strict sense been socially scientific works. Drawing inferences about how judges think and thus come to decisions simply from the skewed sample of their work represented by reported decisions in the law reports is a wholly inadequate basis for serious analysis of how judges approach the judicial task.[35] Further, it is all too easy to assume that because someone is white, male, middle-aged, and probably public school and Oxbridge educated, he (less frequently she) brings attitudes to his (or her) judicial work which affect his (or her) decisions. Such links are not provable without detailed empirical study that has only rarely been taken into the judiciary.[36]

There has, of course, been a problem, in that researchers who have sought access to the judiciary in order to conduct research into it have often found such access difficult to obtain. The stereotype of judges as white, male, of middle to late age, and from the (upper) middle class may, broadly though by no means exclusively, apply to the higher judiciary. It is far less accurate as a descriptor of the totality of judges/adjudicators/ dispute resolvers in the vast array of fora that determine the disputes brought to them by ordinary members of the public.

Comment

A number of general points about those who perform dispute resolution functions in the legal system may be made:

- they are not all professionally qualified as lawyers. Some have other professional qualifications, such as accountants, surveyors, or doctors. Many have no specific

---

[35] Griffith, J.A.G., *The Politics of the Judiciary* (5th edn., London, Fontana, 1997); cf. Hodder-Williams, R., *Judges and Politics in the Contemporary Age* (London, Bowerdean, 1996).

[36] See Paterson, A., *The Law Lords* (London, Macmillan, 1982).

professional qualification at all. In the same way that many legal services are provided by persons other than professionally qualified lawyers, so too many dispute resolution services are provided by those without legal qualifications;

- many academic lawyers are embraced by this broader definition. The notion that somehow those with an academic background have no capacity to determine disputes in a fair and proper manner is simply not borne out by the evidence;

- the total number of dispute resolvers is considerably larger than traditional definitions of the judiciary suggest;

- many appointments are full-time, but many more are part-time;

- only the highest judiciary hold office 'on good behaviour'—a concept designed to enhance the fundamental independence of the judiciary by guaranteeing their right to remain a judge until the statutory retiring age, so long as they are of good behaviour. Most other groups, particularly part-timers, hold office on terms which can result in their being required to step down before the official retirement age;

- only a limited number are able to take advantage of the attractive (non-contributory) pensions that are provided by government to full-time members of the judiciary;

- many judges sit in more than one jurisdiction. For example a full-time social security tribunal chairman may sit as a part-time district judge, thereby enabling him or her to acquire wider judicial experience. This flexible use of judges will increase when the Tribunals Courts and Enforcement Act 2007 is fully operational;

- many judges now start to sit in their early forties, some even in their thirties. They are much younger than popular images of judges may suggest;

- there are many more women holding judicial office than is often appreciated, though the numbers at the highest levels are still far too low. The numbers from the ethnic minorities are significantly less impressive;

- most judicial appointees now receive at least some training for the job, though the amount of training decreases with the seniority of the post;[37]

- there is still only a limited amount of monitoring of judicial performance. Such monitoring as does take place tends to be limited to the performance by part-timers, and is often undertaken by those in full-time office. While too heavy monitoring could compromise judicial independence, certain factors, e.g. the ability to be civil to those appearing before them or to deliver written decisions within agreed timescales, would not seem impossible targets for assessment;

---

[37] For the development of the work of the Judicial Studies Board see above, Chapter 4.

- there is a huge amount of procedural variation as between each of the adjudicative systems. The formal courts operate within a very detailed procedural framework, with a large number of rules of practice supplemented by yet more practice directions and protocols. Many other bodies have only the barest procedural outline prescribed by law, and instead operate with considerable discretion as regards procedural matters;

- not all tribunals operate on the basis that their 'typical' adjudication will involve a formal hearing of the parties. Many reach determinations on the basis of information presented in written form alone;

- while it is usual for tribunals that hold hearings to sit in public, in the sense that members of the public are entitled to attend hearings should they so wish, many do not, particularly where sensitive personal or financial information is being discussed;

- the dress of the judiciary is also much more varied than is often realized. The highly formalized process of the High Court, with impressive uniforms, dark wooden panelling, and advocates in wigs and gowns—the image of the television or film drama—is in fact a statistical rarity. The vast majority of dispute resolvers operate with none of these formal trappings; and

- dispute resolvers work in a wide variety of locations. Many sit in court buildings or other specially dedicated accommodation. But there are many examples of adjudicative bodies sitting in local authority accommodation, or in hotels, or even on occasion in people's homes.

If one takes this broader view, it is seen that there is considerably more variety and flexibility of approach to dispute resolution than is often realized. Different procedures and practices have been developed to meet the specific needs of particular bodies.

The legal scholars

Law claims to be a learned profession. Thus, a third group, delivering a rather different kind of legal service and one not usually given adequate recognition, should be noted, namely the work of the law teachers and jurists. Law teachers in the university law departments and in other locations where legal education is provided have a variety of functions.

First, law teachers provide basic education in law and legal principles, which provides new generations of lawyers with the fundamental intellectual tools to enable them to become lawyers. The leading university law schools also offer, through their law degrees, a traditional liberal university education, giving students the capacity to think critically about law and its impact on society.

Secondly, law teachers deliver a wide range of professionally focused courses which transform the recent graduate from the preliminary academic stage to a person with the skills required to enter the world of practice. Some of these courses are offered within university law departments, but other providers including the College of Law, and other private companies play a significant part in this market as well.

Thirdly, the law schools together with the private providers offer much of the further education and advanced training in new developments in the law which are needed by legal practitioners to enable them to keep abreast of developments in the law and to break into new areas of law.

Finally, law teachers—particularly those who work in the leading research universities—assist in the development of law and the legal system through the research they undertake, the books and articles they write, and the advice they give to governments and other agencies. The scope of legal scholarship has expanded enormously in recent years, again reflecting the growing complexity of the law, not only domestic law but also law coming from Europe and elsewhere. The impact of legal scholarship on practitioners is hard to gauge. Certainly the old rule that only dead authors could be cited in court has long been abandoned. Advocates now often refer to academic articles and books in their submissions, and in many reported cases the judgments adopt (or reject) the analyses of legal scholars. But this is the tip of the iceberg. Many practitioners developing a legal argument, or simply struggling to understand a particular legal doctrine, turn to the textbook writers for assistance. The importance of the work of the jurists in helping to shape legal argument should not be under-estimated. This work is also central to the work of the law reform agencies, particularly the Law Commission.

A number of areas of practice which have developed in recent years have been the result of a combination of the work of legal scholars who helped to shape the areas and the practitioners who took them into practice. Among examples that may be cited is the development of administrative law which has arisen from analysis of the principles of judicial review; many important developments in the area of family law are another; the law of restitution a third. A number of more specialist areas including private and public international law, housing law, and social welfare law have similarly been shaped by important academic contributions.

Notwithstanding these observations, there has been a surprising reluctance by the jurists to get involved in the scholarly analysis of legal practice and procedure. Thus, while endless books and articles are published offering systematic expositions and analyses of substantive law, it has been left to a very small number of legal scholars to focus on the questions of practice and procedure which are the lifeblood of most legal practice, an understanding of which is essential to understanding law and the legal system.

In addition, alongside what is sometimes described as 'black-letter' legal research, focusing on the detailed analysis of legal doctrine, there has emerged over the last twenty-five years an increasingly rich body of 'socio-legal' scholarship, in which the law is analysed in an inter-disciplinary context, employing insights and methodologies

from other social sciences, such as economics, social psychology, politics, and sociology. Much of this research is empirical in nature, and much has involved research
into the practice of law. A number of areas of government legal policy have been significantly influenced by the outcomes of socio-legal research.[38]

The university law schools have played a very significant part in opening up access
to the legal profession to people from a wider range of backgrounds (a trend noted
at the outset of this chapter). Though the extent to which people from different *class*
backgrounds have been able to take advantage of these developments may not be as
dramatic as is sometimes thought, there is no doubting that the pattern of recruitment
to universities in general and to law schools in particular has changed. This has been
of particular benefit to women, who now comprise the majority of those studying law
at university.

Further, the fact that the legal profession is now largely a graduate profession has
greatly helped to change the nature of the relationship between the legal academic and
the legal practitoner. The mutual disdain which all too often characterized the relationship twenty-five years ago has been replaced by much greater understanding and
respect.

Questions to test knowledge

1. What is the difference between a barrister and a solicitor?

2. What is the difference between lawyers' services and legal services?

3. What is the difference between the Legal Services Ombudsman and the Legal Services
Complaints Commissioner?

4. What is 'pro bono' work? Can you give any examples of such work?

Questions for reflection and discussion

1. Should the legal profession be fused?

2. What dangers arise from increased regulation by government?

3. Are any professional restrictive practices justified in the public interest? If so, which?

4. Is the independence of the legal profession important? Why?

5. What new forms of legal practice should be permitted?

6. Does legal journalism provide fair coverage of all the work of the legal profession?

7. How can ethical lawyering be encouraged?

---

[38] The importance of investing in empirical research in law was recently re-asserted in the Nuffield
Foundation's Report *Law in the Real World*.

8. How can judicial diversity best be promoted?

9. Should any limits be imposed on the types of person entitled to be appointed to the judiciary?

Further reading

ABEL, R.L., *English Lawyers Between Market and State: The Politics of Professionalism* (Oxford, Oxford University Press, 2003)

ABEL-SMITH, B., and STEVENS, R., with the assistance of Brooke, R., *Lawyers and the Courts: A Sociological Study of the English Legal System 1750–1965* (London, Heinemann, 1967)

—— ZANDER, M., and BROOKE, R., *Legal Problems and the Citizen: A Study in Three London Boroughs* (London, Heinemann Educational, 1973)

BLACKSELL, M., ECONOMIDES, K., and WATKINS, C., *Justice Outside the City: Access to Legal Services in Rural Britain* (Harlow, Longman Scientific and Technical, 1991)

BLOM-COOPER, L., and DREWRY, G., *Final Appeal: A Study of the House of Lords in its Judicial Capacity* (Oxford, Clarendon Press, 1972)

COMMITTEE ON LEGAL EDUCATION, *Report* (Cmnd 4595) (London, HMSO, 1971)

DEVLIN, BARON P., *The Judge* (Oxford, Oxford University Press, 1979)

DWORKIN, R., *Political Judges and the Rule of Law* (Oxford, Oxford University Press, 1980)

ECONOMIDES, K. (ed), *Ethical Challenges to Legal Education and Conduct* (Oxford, Hart, 1998)

GENN, H., *Hard Bargaining: Out of Court Settlement in Personal Injury Actions* (Oxford, Clarendon Press, 1987)

GRIFFITHS, J.A.G., *The Politics of the Judiciary* (5th edn., London, Fontana, 1997)

HARLOW, C., and RAWLINGS, R., *Pressure Through Law* (London, Routledge, 1992)

HODDER-WILLIAMS, R., *Judges and Politics in the Contemporary Age* (London, Bowerdean, 1996)

JUSTICE, *The Judiciary: The Report of a Justice Sub-committee* (Chairman of Subcommittee, Peter Webster) (London, Stevens, 1972)

—— *The Judiciary in England and Wales: A Report by Justice* (Chairman of Committee, Robert Stevens) (London, Justice, 1992)

LEE, S., *Judging Judges* (London, Faber, 1989)

LEWIS, P.S.C., *Assumptions about Lawyers in Policy Statements: A Survey of Relevant Research* (London, Lord Chancellor's Department, 2000)

MALLESON, K., *The New Judiciary: The Effects of Expansion and Activism* (Aldershot, Dartmouth, 1999)

MAUGHAN, C., and WEBB, J., *Lawyering Skills and the Legal Process* (2nd edn., Cambridge, Cambridge University Press, 2005)

PANNICK, D., *Judges* (Oxford, Oxford University Press, 1987)

PATERSON, A., *The Law Lords* (London, Macmillan, 1982)

ROBERTSON, D., *Judicial Discretion in the House of Lords* (Oxford, Clarendon Press, 1998)

SARAT, A., and SCHEINGOLD, S., *Cause Lawyering and Professional Responsibilities* (New York, Oxford University Press, 1998)

SHETREET, S., *Judges on Trial: A Study of the Appointment and Accountability of the English Judiciary* (Amsterdam/Oxford, North-Holland, 1976)

STEVENS, R., *Law and Politics: The House of Lords as a Judicial Body, 1800–1976* (London, Weidenfeld & Nicolson, 1979)

—— *Law School: Legal Education in America from the 1850s to the 1980s* (Chapel Hill, NC, University of North Carolina Press, c1983)

—— *The Independence of the Judiciary: The View from the Lord Chancellor's Office* (Oxford, Clarendon Press, 1997)

—— *The English Judges: Their Role in the Changing Constitution* (Oxford, Hart, 2002)

SUSSKIND, R., *Transforming the Law: Essays on Technology, Justice and the Legal Marketplace* (Oxford, Oxford University Press, 2003)

TWINING, W., *Blackstone's Tower: The English Law School* (London, Stevens & Son/ Sweet & Maxwell, 1994)

—— *Law in Context: Enlarging a Discipline* (Oxford, Oxford University Press, 1997)

WILSON, G.P. (ed), *Frontiers of Legal Scholarship: Twenty-five Years of Warwick Law School* (Chichester/New York, Wiley, 1995)

ZANDER, M., *Lawyers and the Public Interest: A Study of Restrictive Practices* (London, published for the London School of Economics and Political Science by Weidenfeld & Nicolson, 1967)

Websites

http://www.barcouncil.org.uk/ *(Bar Council site)*

http://www.barstandardsboard.org.uk/ Bar Standards Board)

http://www.barstandardsboard.org.uk/complaintsanddiscipline/ *(Links to Complaints Commissioner, Bar Council)*

http://www.lawsociety.org.uk/home.law *(Law Society home page)*

http://www.sra.org.uk/home.page *(Solicitors Regulation Authority)*

http://www.legalcomplaints.org.uk/home.page *(Solicitors Legal Complaints Service)*

http://www.olso.org/ *(Legal Services Ombudsman)*

http://www.olscc.gov.uk/index.htm *(Office of the Legal Services Complaints Commissioner)*

http://www.gls.gov.uk/ *(Government Legal Service)*

http://www.clsa.co.uk/Default.asp?page=52 *(Criminal Law Solicitors' Association)*

http://www.jc-society.com/ *(Justices' Clerks' Society)*

http://www.ilex.org.uk/ *(Institute of Legal Executives)*

http://www.cipa.org.uk/pages/home *(Chartered Institute of Patent Agents)*

http://www.itma.org.uk/intro/index.htm *(Institute of Trade Mark Attorneys)*

http://www.conveyancers.gov.uk/ *(Council for Licensed Conveyancers)* http://www.citizensadvice.org.uk/ *(The Citizens' Advice Service)*

http://www.probonouk.net/index.php?id=home *(Site of probono UK—the Attorney-General's initiative to promote pro bono work)*

http://lawworks.org.uk/ *(Solicitors' pro bono group)*

http://www.barprobono.org.uk/ *(Bar pro bono Unit)*

http://www.ncc.org.uk/ *(National Consumer Council)*

http://www.lawcentres.org.uk/ *(Law Centres' Federation)*

http://www.asauk.org.uk/ *(Home of the Advice Services Alliance)*

http://www.covlaw.org.uk/ *(Coventry Law Centre)*

http://www.equalityhumanrights.com/pages/eocdrccre.aspx *(Equality and Human Rights Commission)*

http://www.lag.org.uk/ *(Legal Action Group)*

http://www.childpoverty.org.uk/cro/CROHome.htm *(Citizens' Rights Office)*

http://www.liberty-human-rights.org.uk/ *(Liberty—civil liberties group)*

http://www.taxaid.org.uk/ *(Charity offering advice on tax matters)*

http://www.publiclawproject.org.uk/ *(Public law project)*

http://www.kent.ac.uk/nslsa/ *(Socio-legal Studies Association)*

http://www.legalscholars.ac.uk/text/index.cfm *(Homepage of the Society of Legal Scholars)*

http://www.ukcle.ac.uk/index.html *(UK Centre for Legal Education)*

http://www.lawteacher.ac.uk/ *(Association of Law Teachers)*

http://www.legalease.co.uk/ *(Site promoting journals and other literature on legal business)*

http://www.thelawyer.com/ *(Online legal information service, including job vacancies)*

http://www.oft.gov.uk/ *(Office of Fair Trading)*

http://www.dca.gov.uk/legalsys/lsreform.htm *(Archive site with information on reform of the regulation of legal services)*

10

The funding of legal services

Introduction

The final issue considered in this book is how legal services provided to the public are paid for. It is essential for the overall effectiveness of the English legal system that services required by the public are actually available to it. This chapter does not consider the funding of legal services for the corporate sector or for wealthy individuals. For present purposes it is assumed that they can afford the services they require. This chapter concentrates on the funding regimes for the delivery of legal services, in particular litigation, to the less well-off and the poor. The discussion is in two unequal sections: the first, and longer, looks at the changing shape of *publicly* funded legal services; the second considers new arrangements to assist the development of *private* funding for legal services.

Publicly funded legal services

The changing face of legal aid

When the Welfare State emerged in legislative form after the end of the Second World War, one of the measures introduced by the then Labour government was the Legal Aid Act 1949. There are many accounts of the history of this fundamentally important development, so only an outline is given here. Initially the scope of the legal aid scheme was limited to *civil legal aid*—the provision of legal representation in proceedings taken in the civil courts. It subsequently developed to embrace:

- *criminal legal aid*—funding representation in criminal cases, eventually including a scheme for the provision of legal advice in police stations;
- a *'green form scheme'* designed to permit the provision by lawyers of legal advice and assistance on any matter of English law; and
- *'assistance by way of representation'* (ABWOR) which permitted in a limited number of circumstances the lawyer to extend assistance under the green form scheme to the provision of some representation.

Despite these developments, policy on legal aid has been the subject of fierce debate and criticism over the last forty years. The issues debated included the following.

(1) Notwithstanding its potentially wide coverage, in practice civil legal aid was used primarily to fund litigation on matrimonial matters and on personal injuries/accidents. Though important, other areas of social law, for example housing or social welfare provision, were in practice largely ignored by legal aid practitioners.

(2) The provision of legal aid was subject to means-testing—it went only to those falling below certain income and capital limits.[1] When the first Legal Aid Act was passed it was estimated that nearly 70 per cent of the population was potentially entitled to legal aid. However, as the costs of legal aid increased, one of the mechanisms used by government to restrain levels of public spending was to make the means tests meaner; thus the percentage of the population covered was severely reduced.

(3) New forms of legal service delivery—in particular through law centres, which began to develop in the late 1960s—were excluded from funding by the legal aid schemes, save where such centres took on individual cases which qualified for legal aid.

(4) There were many fora in which legal aid was just not available at all. In particular, there was no legal aid for proceedings before the majority of the tribunals established to deal with disputes between the citizen and the state arising out of the social provision of the Welfare State.[2]

(5) From the government's point of view there seemed to be no way to control public expenditure on legal aid, since it was a service that was 'demand-led'—the government was committed to paying for all those cases in which the individual established an entitlement to legal aid.

(6) There were also worries about the quality of some of the work undertaken. Any legal practice could offer to do legal aid work, irrespective of the level of expertise on the issue in question in the firm. This might have the perverse effect of driving legal aid expenditure up, as it could take longer for a firm without relevant expertise to deal with a matter than a firm with such expertise.

Successive governments have tried to reform the legal aid scheme in a way that would deliver a wider range of services to the public, without public expenditure on legal aid reaching unacceptable levels.[3] The first change followed enactment of the Legal Aid

---

[1] The criminal legal aid scheme was also subject to means-testing, though the rules were not applied in practice with the rigour that applied in relation to civil law matters.

[2] See further Chapter 6. There were exceptions: e.g. legal aid was available for proceedings before the Lands Tribunal and (later) Mental Health Review Tribunals.

[3] Levels of public expenditure on legal aid rose from £1,093m in 1992–3 to £1,622m in 1998–9—a 48 per cent increase in expenditure at a time when total inflation was only 16 per cent.

Act 1988. This transferred responsibility for the administration of the scheme from the Law Society to a new government agency, the Legal Aid Board.

The Board tried to address the problem of providing a quality service by establishing a franchising scheme. Firms of solicitors could obtain a franchise only if they passed a special quality audit process. Under the scheme, solicitors were able to obtain a franchise in one or more of ten franchise categories.[4] Some 2,900 firms of solicitors obtained at least one of the available franchises. In addition, the Legal Aid Board began a series of pilot studies to test the viability of franchises being awarded to agencies other than solicitors' firms, such as advice agencies, which might provide legal advice and assistance to the same standards as solicitors' firms.

In 1997, the Legal Aid Board started to award contracts to franchised firms for the provision of defined categories of legal services. Firms with contracts were able to deliver legal services with reduced bureaucracy. Instead of having to submit claims for each item of legally aided work, they were able to deliver their services (and get paid for so doing) within the framework of the contract. A number of legal aid services had to be offered on the basis of a fixed fee, rather than the traditional method of charging by the hour. However, these measures were felt still to be inadequate to address the paradox of ever rising costs, without any significant expansion in the range of services that were funded by the legal aid scheme.[5]

The Access to Justice Act 1999, which came into effect in 2000, made further changes. The Legal Aid Board was replaced by a new body—the Legal Services Commission. Legal aid was 'rebranded' as two new services: the *Community Legal Service* (CLS) and the *Criminal Defence Service* (CDS).

Legal Services Commission

The Legal Services Commission is the body responsible for developing a network of legal services, in partnership with other funders such as local authorities and central government. In shaping the delivery of legal services, the Legal Services Commission works within a policy and financial framework prescribed by government. One of the most important of recent changes is that it is now possible for appropriately qualified 'lay advice and assistance agencies' to receive public funding for the provision of certain types of legal services, as well as lawyers working in private practice. A new uniform contract has been introduced so that all service providers operate on the same terms.

Legal aid is an extremely controversial area of government policy, particularly so far as legal practitioners are concerned. The press is full of stories about the death of legal aid. Obviously the Treasury is keen to keep a lid on public expenditure. But if

---

[4] These include: criminal, family, personal injury, housing, and social welfare. New franchise categories have been developed: e.g., a clinical negligence franchise was developed in February 1999.

[5] Although costs rose by 48 per cent in a six-year period, the numbers of people assisted rose by only 7 per cent. Indeed expenditure on civil and family legal aid rose by 42 per cent while the numbers of people assisted fell by 30 per cent.

expenditure is too restricted, there are inevitable complaints that access to justice is being denied. Despite the Treasury's best efforts, expenditure has in fact continued to rise. Current annual expenditure is well over £2.0bn. This represents a *per capita* level of expenditure significantly above that achieved in other advanced countries. One of the major problems with this figure, however, is that while expenditure on criminal legal aid has been growing, that on civil legal aid has been falling. And while costs have been rising, there do not seem to be commensurate improvements in delivery.

Over the last four years the government and the Legal Services Commission have been trying to develop strategies for the future delivery of legal services. A paper, *A fairer deal for legal aid,* was published in 2005. It argued that there was a need for more efficient and effective criminal trials; too much money was wasted on trials that did not go ahead at the last moment. It also noted how a small number of criminal cases absorbed a disproportionate share of the budget. The paper argued that it was necessary to contain expenditure on criminal legal aid to allow some rebalancing to civil legal aid.

One of the specific recommendations was that there should be a review of the ways in which the Legal Services Commission procured its legal services. Lord Carter of Coles was asked to review these issues. He reported in 2006. He recommended that there should be much greater use of funds being provided on a fixed or graduated fee basis, rather than by solicitors charging for their services on the basis of hourly rates. Carter argued that this should be the prelude to legal services being procured on the basis of market competition. Providers would eventually engage in a process of competitive tendering, in which they decide how much they can deliver for the money they are seeking. Fixed fees for most categories of civil legal aid work were introduced in October 2007.

Needless to say, these initiatives have been politically extremely hard fought, particularly by the representatives of the legal profession, and particularly in relation to criminal legal aid. Progress on reform of procurement on this side has been slower than on the civil side. One change that has been introduced is that very high cost cases can only be conducted by specially authorized providers.

One likely outcome is that the historic emphasis in the provision of funding lawyers to litigate cases in court is likely to be replaced by greater emphasis on advice and assistance to prevent cases coming to court in the first place. (Of course, this is less easy to achieve in the context of criminal cases than civil cases.) Recent annual reports from the Legal Services Commission report significant increases in the numbers of acts of assistance.

The Legal Services Commission has also been developing new models for the delivery of legal services. It now makes considerable use of information technologies to provide advice on legal problems through its CLS Direct service, which has both a website and a call centre phone advice line. It is also currently piloting new models for the delivery of legal assistance through Community Legal Advice Centres (CLACS) and Community Legal Advice Networks (CLANS). The first CLAC opened in Gateshead in 2007; the first CLAN is being set up in Cornwall. Research has shown that many people do not have single problems, but clusters of problems. The intention is that those requiring advice should be able to obtain it as far as possible from a single visit or contact, rather than being referred to a number of different advice agencies.

Community Legal Service

Introduction

Many people obtain advice on legal problems, not by going to see a solicitor in her office, but by visiting one of the over 1,500 citizens' advice bureaux, law centres, and other independent advice agencies which it is estimated exist in England and Wales. These services often have lawyers or other professionally qualified staff attached to them. Around 6,000 people with a variety of qualifications work in these agencies, supported by nearly 30,000 unpaid volunteers. They deal with over ten million inquiries each year and receive around £250 million from a wide variety of sources of public funding, from both central and local government.

The services that these agencies offer have developed haphazardly, often in response to specific local initiatives. Coverage throughout England and Wales is therefore patchy. In some areas, there is under-provision, with no effective service at all. In others there may be a number of agencies offering very similar services. Here there is over-provision and a consequent waste of scarce resources—both cash and manpower.

Funding for the Community Legal Service is provided under the terms of a *Funding Code* which sets out the detailed framework within which publicly funded legal services are delivered. The Funding Code was last revised in October 2007.

Priorities

In shaping the detail of the scheme, the Legal Services Commission is required to take into account certain priorities for funding legal services, which are set for it by the Lord Chancellor.[6] These priorities include:

- proceedings under the Children Act 1989 for which legal aid was formerly available without either a means or a merits test;[7]
- civil proceedings where the life or liberty of the client is at risk;[8]
- housing and other social welfare cases that enable people to avoid or to climb out of social exclusion;
- domestic violence cases;
- cases concerning the welfare of children; and
- cases alleging serious wrongdoing, breaches of human rights, or abuse of position or power by a public body or servant.

---

[6] Access to Justice Act 1999, s. 6(1).
[7] See below, p. 270.
[8] This was the principle that led to the more recent extension of legal aid to hearings before the Immigration Appeal Tribunal, now the Asylum and Immigration Tribunal.

Exclusions

Only legal services for individuals may be funded under the scheme. Services for firms or other types of non-individual legal persona (e.g. partnerships or clubs) cannot be provided under the scheme. In addition, certain types of legal service are excluded from the scheme altogether. These include:

- services relating to allegations of *negligently*[9] caused injury or death, though not allegations of clinical negligence (the reason for this is that it is assumed that such cases are suitable for conditional fee agreements (see below));

- cases relating to injuries caused by negligence, even where the legal claim is not cast in terms of the law of negligence (e.g. tripping cases, where the local authority is alleged to be in breach of a statutory duty to maintain the highway);

- other areas excluded because they have been judged not to have sufficient priority to justify public funding. These include allegations of negligent damage to property;[10] conveyancing; boundary disputes; matters of trust law or the making of wills; and matters arising from company or partnership law or the running of a business;[11]

- also excluded is representation in cases involving defamation and malicious falsehood.

Notwithstanding the general exclusions, help relating to making a will may be available to a person over 70, or a disabled person or a parent or guardian of such a person who wishes to provide for that person, and in certain cases involving those under the age of 16.

More generally funding of matters otherwise excluded may nonetheless be possible:

- where the matter is only incidental to an issue for which funding is permitted, or where the issue is brought into the proceedings by someone who is not being assisted by the scheme; or

- where there are two distinct claims, one of which is an excluded matter, but where it is impossible or impracticable to deal with them separately and the Commission thinks they cannot be funded by a conditional fee agreement or in some other way;

- where issues relating to boundaries, trusts, or company or partnership law arise in funded housing proceedings or funded family disputes or proceedings they may be funded even though they are more than incidental to the principal proceedings;

---

[9] The exclusion does not extend to cases of injury arising from an alleged assault or deliberate abuse.

[10] Housing disrepair cases brought by a tenant against a landlord are not excluded, as the property is not owned by the claimant.

[11] The government's view is that these risks should be covered by insurance.

- conveyancing services where they arise in the course of other funded proceedings, or to give effect to a court order or agreement to settle;

- furthermore, and notwithstanding the general exclusion of personal injury negligence claims, some help may be made available in such cases if the costs of the claim are exceptionally high (and thus likely to deter insurers or those offering conditional fee agreements);

- cases which involve a wider public interest may also exceptionally be included even though they would otherwise fall in the excluded categories;

- the broad exclusion of funding services for representation before coroners' courts and tribunals is retained.[12] However, the Lord Chancellor has stated he might on occasion fund exceptional cases before tribunals or the coroner's court where strict criteria were met.

Objectives of the Community Legal Service

Under the terms of the 1999 Act, the Community Legal Service has five broad objectives. These are the provision of:[13]

(1) general information about the law and legal system (e.g. the provision of leaflets in a supermarket or the creation of legal websites);

(2) help by giving advice about how the law applies in particular circumstances (e.g. the provision of initial advice at a Community Advice Centre or Citizens' Advice Bureau);

(3) help in preventing or settling or otherwise resolving disputes about legal rights and duties (e.g. the provision of more detailed assistance, such as telephone calls or letter writing or even some representation by a solicitor);

(4) help in enforcing decisions by which such disputes are resolved; and

(5) help in relation to legal proceedings not relating to disputes.

To ensure quality, all service providers have to obtain a quality mark relevant to the type and level of service they are offering.[14]

Service levels

There are eight service levels:[15]

- legal help;
- help at court;

---

[12] Funded legal representation before the Lands Tribunal and the Commons Commissioners, which was possible under the legal aid scheme, was withdrawn by the 1999 Act.

[13] Access to Justice Act 1999, s. 4(2).

[14] See, for details, www.legalservices.gov.uk/qmark/index.htm. A new quality mark scheme for barristers was launched in September 2002. A quality mark standard for mediation in family law was launched in January 2003.

[15] The details are set out in the Funding Code: see www.legalservices.gov.uk/civil/how/funding_code.asp.

- family help (lower);
- family help (higher);[16]
- legal representation (investigative help);[17]
- legal representation (full representation);
- family mediation; and
- such other services as are authorized by the Lord Chancellor.

Increasingly, the Legal Services Commission and the government are seeking to direct funding away from the provision of representation in court, and towards the provision of legal advice services that do not require the use of lawyers in court.

Means test

As with legal aid, clients entitled to funded services have to demonstrate that they are financially eligible—in other words they are subject to a means test.[18] Where applicants fall below a lower threshold, they pay nothing. If they fall between a lower financial threshold and a higher one, the provision of a funded service will be subject to the funded client making a financial contribution towards the cost.[19] In addition, where the proceedings are designed to obtain an award of damages or other financial provision, any award of damages is subject to a 'charge' in favour of the Community Legal Service fund.

Merits test

The general approach to the funding of cases is that funding should be available where a reasonable private paying client would be prepared to fund the case. Thus account must be taken of whether the proceedings would be cost-effective;[20] and there must be an assessment of the prospects of success.[21] Cost–benefit ratios are to be determined by relating the likely costs to the percentage prospect of success.[22] Funding is refused in cases where a conditional fee agreement (see below, p. 227) should be obtained. There are special rules for cases against public bodies that raise human rights issues. Where a court has given permission for a judicial review case to proceed to a hearing,

---

[16] This is considered in Chapter 7 on the family justice system.

[17] This will be available where the size of the claim is likely to exceed £5,000. This will be provided where the strength of a case needs to be assessed; it may lead to full representation.

[18] The provision of information and the provision of services to proceedings under the Children Act 1989 are outside this rule. For funding in family cases see above, Chapter 7, p. 196.

[19] Legal Help, Help at Court, and Family Mediation are not subject to the making of a contribution.

[20] In framing the Funding Code's provisions on these matters, the Legal Services Commission is required to take into account the *statutory factors* which are set out in s. 8(2) of the Act.

[21] This criterion does not apply to many housing cases or cases with a wider public interest. The Legal Services Commission is advised on the public interest by a Public Interest Advisory Panel.

[22] E.g., where prospects of success are 80 per cent or better, the likely damages must exceed the likely costs; where the prospects of success are 60 per cent–80 per cent, the likely damages must exceed likely costs by 2:1; where prospects of success are 50 per cent–60 per cent, likely damages must exceed likely costs by 4:1.

there is a presumption that legal services funding will be granted, so long as the client is within the financial threshold.

Very expensive cases

To prevent a large proportion of the Community Legal Services fund being expended on a relatively small number of very expensive cases, a Special Cases Unit controls the costs of such cases. Cases likely to exceed £25,000 in costs are referred to the Unit. Special arrangements also apply to multi-party actions, where a large number of claimants are claiming loss from a single event or cause.

Alternative dispute resolution

ADR is funded where this may be more effective than court proceedings. Where complaints procedures or ombudsman schemes are available which might be appropriate to resolve the problem in question, funding is not considered until these have been exhausted.

Comment

The basic concept of the Community Legal Service is not new. The case for the creation of a national legal service or a community legal service has been made by many pressure groups and other social activists on numerous occasions over many years. The importance of the recent developments and current ideas for further reform is that the government acknowledges that the provision of legal services is an important component in the achievement of broader social goals. Effective legal services have the potential to empower the powerless and to enable them to take advantage of the protective provisions of social legislation. But to be cost-effective, the provision of legal services must be planned, so that it meets clear social needs, rather than just springing up in piecemeal fashion. It is also clear that there can never be a truly national provision of legal services—particularly for the less well-off—provided exclusively by professionally qualified lawyers; other agencies must be involved as well.

Other very important features of the new scheme should also be recognized. First, most of the research on legal services argues that the provision of good quality information and advice at an early stage can save costs later on. The increasing emphasis on these early stages seems in principle to be correct. Secondly, the ability of the Community Legal Service to fund the provision of electronic[23] and telephone services[24]—not possible under legal aid—may alleviate problems of physical access, though there are concerns that the primary client groups for the Community Legal Service may not have the same access to these facilities as other groups in the population.

---

[23] The *Community Legal Advice (formerly CLSDirect)* website is an important source of information for the citizen. See www.communitylegaladvice.org.uk.

[24] Provision of a telephone advice line CLS Direct was launched in 2004, and has recently been expanded. The telephone number is 0845 345 4 345.

Much has been made of the fact that, unlike legal aid, the Community Legal Service is subject to cash limits. As with all public spending, there is a need for financial discipline. The existence of cash limits does not *necessarily* mean that services needed by the public cannot be delivered. Much depends on the level at which those limits are set and the effectiveness of the use of available resources to deliver cost-effective legal services. Indeed, as noted above, expenditure on legal aid has continued to rise significantly. The problem is that the bulk of that rise has been on the criminal side; expenditure on the civil side has fallen.

There are signs that the Community Legal Service is under stress. There are areas of law for which there is still little legal aid funding. There are areas of the country where it is hard, if not impossible, to get legal advice. Yet research, from the Legal Services Commission's own research unit, points to the fact that many people who might have rights that they could assert through the legal system in fact fail to do so. And for some time, the Commission has reported its concern about the number of firms that have left the scheme,[25] and that a significant number of other providers are seriously considering giving up doing work for the Community Legal Service. They say that the primary reason for this is the difficulty providers face in making legal aid work profitable. There are few young practitioners willing to take up legal aid practice. In response to this, the Legal Services Commission provides funding for about 100 training contracts, designed to give opportunities for new entrants to train in legal aid practices.

Nevertheless, the battle for an appropriate level of resources for the funding of legal services remains intense. Such a socially important service cannot depend simply on the public-spiritedness of individuals wanting to provide assistance to the ordinary citizen. As with all cash-limited public services there will always be argument about the extent to which further funding should or should not be made available. And there will never be public acknowledgement by those who provide the services that the service is adequately funded.

Reports of the death of legal aid are premature and exaggerated. Indeed it can be argued that the Community Legal Service offers an imaginative framework for the delivery of legal services which goes a considerable way to addressing many of the criticisms that were raised over the previous twenty-five years in relation to legal aid. But those responsible for running and delivering the service must continue to ensure that there is a realistic level of funds available to them if gloomier predictions are not to become reality.

Criminal Defence Service

The Criminal Defence Service is the other legal service introduced by the Access to Justice Act 1999. The Legal Services Commission has power to secure the provision of legal advice, assistance, and representation for those suspected of committing a

---

[25] The Commission is particularly worried at the decline in the number of firms doing family work.

criminal offence and thus under investigations, or actually facing criminal proceed-ings[26] in court.

There are four principal components of the CDS:

(1) the provision of criminal defence services in police stations and magistrates' courts through contracts with private-practice solicitors' firms;

(2) the provision of a national network of police station and magistrates' court duty solicitor schemes;[27]

(3) the management of individual case contracts with defence teams for very high cost criminal cases; and

(4) the provision of services directly to the public through the Public Defender Service (PDS).[28]

A key difference from the Community Legal Service is that the Criminal Defence Service remains a demand-led, rather than a cash-limited, service.[29]

The bulk of legal services provided under the Criminal Defence Service are pro-vided by solicitors in private practice. All such firms have to have a contract to provide such services with the Legal Services Commission. At 31 March 2007 2,510 firms of solicitors held such contracts. As with the Community Legal Service, the Commission is concerned about a downward drift in the numbers of firms with contracts; the 2007 figure was 3.7 per cent down on 2006. In addition, the Commission has noted that the average age of solicitors doing criminal work is increasing, and that few young people are entering this sector of the legal profession. They anticipate significant problems of supply in small towns and rural areas.

During 2001–2, the Commission launched on a pilot basis a new service, the Public Defender Service (PDS). The aims of the service, as seen by the Commission, were to:

- provide independent, high quality, value-for-money criminal defence services to the public;

- provide examples of excellence in the provision of criminal defence services nationally and locally;

- provide the Commission with benchmarking information to be used to improve the performance of the contracting regime for private practice suppliers;

---

[26] 'Criminal proceedings' are defined to include not only criminal trials, appeals, and sentencing hear-ings, but also extradition hearings, binding-over proceedings, appeals on behalf of a convicted person who has died, and proceedings for contempt in the face of any court: Access to Justice Act 1999, s. 12. The Lord Chancellor has power to add to this.

[27] The Legal Services Commission has started a pilot call centre project, CDS Direct, to see if part of this service can be delivered by telephone advice. Initial evaluation suggested this has been a success so the pilot has been extended for a further 18 months.

[28] The salaried providers employed in the PDS are subject to a Code of Conduct published by the Commission and approved by Parliament: Access to Justice Act 1999, s. 16.

[29] Access to Justice Act 1999, s. 18. It is this principle that leads to loss of resources for the Community Legal Service while the costs of the Criminal Defence Service rise substantially.

- raise the level of understanding within government, including the Lord Chancellor's Department and all levels and areas of the Commission, of the issues facing criminal defence lawyers in providing high quality services to the public;

- provide the Commission with an additional option for ensuring the provision of quality criminal defence services in geographical areas where existing provision is low or of a poor standard;

- recruit, train, and develop people to provide high quality criminal defence services, in accordance with the PDS's own business needs, which will add to the body of such people available to provide criminal defence services generally; and

- share with private-practice suppliers best practice in terms of forms, systems, etc., developed within the PDS to assist in the overall improvement of Criminal Defence Service provision.

Originally, eight offices were opened, which in 2004–5 dealt with 4,500 cases. They operate on the basis that the PDS must attract and retain clients as a result of the quality of service that it provides. Clients are not compelled to use the PDS in areas where it exists; they can choose between the PDS and solicitors with contracts from the Legal Services Commission. The initial development of the PDS was designed to take place over four years; during that time, it was the subject of a specially commissioned research report. The PDS was reviewed in the light of experience, and from 2007, the number of offices was reduced to four.

Creation of the Criminal Defence Scheme was the subject of fierce debate in Parliament. Critics argued that:

(1) it meant that the better off, who do not rely on publicly funded legal aid, still had complete freedom of choice over who should represent them. This would lead to an unacceptable distinction between what the better off and the less well off were able to receive by way of legal assistance. However, there was an opposing argument, that those providing legal services paid for out of public funds should be able to demonstrate basic levels of professional competence—which limiting provision to those with contracts is designed to achieve—so that there will be some guarantee that public money is not wasted on the incompetent or inexperienced; and

(2) there was some evidence from the United States[30] that public defender schemes do not work as well as they should in defending the interests of the accused or suspect. There were therefore considerable worries that if the predominant form of provision in England were to become the public defender system, this would lead to a less competent mode of delivering criminal legal services. This could well become a problem were the publicly funded service to become the sole mode of delivering this form of legal service. However, this is certainly not going to be the situation in the short term.

---

[30] See McConville, M., and Mirsky, C.L., 'Criminal Defence of the Poor in New York City' (1986–7) 15 *New York University Review of Law and Social Change* 581–964.

The new arrangements were more streamlined than the former, often highly frag-mented, provision in which a person might get advice in the police station under one funding scheme, advice in the solicitor's office or in prison under another, and representation in court under yet a third. The new criminal law contracts provide for a single service from arrest until completion of the case. Nevertheless, the CDS has continued to attract criticism.

First, it is criticized by the legal profession, who argue that it does not offer a suf-ficient level of remuneration to enable practitioners to remain in business. The gov-ernment responded to this concern by establishing the review of the procurement of legal services, under the chairmanship of Lord Carter of Coles (see above, p. 266). He recommended substantial changes to the procurement system for criminal legal services which achieves maximum value for money and control over spending, whilst ensuring quality and fairness in the criminal justice system. Here too Carter recom-mended greater use of fixed fees. The Legal Services Commission has also developed a Preferred Supplier scheme, designed to offer benefits to providers who provide signifi-cant amounts of high quality legal services. Adoption of the Preferred Supplier scheme is currently being taken forward.

Second, there was criticism that criminal defence services were being provided without a means-test. There were a number of high-profile cases where apparently very wealthy individuals received substantial aid from the scheme. Means-testing had been used before but had led to two problems. First, it was wasteful of money; means-testing is an expensive process. Secondly, it added to delay, in that a trial could not proceed until the issue of representation had been sorted out. Notwithstanding these criticisms, the government has decided to re-introduce means-testing. The Criminal Defence Service Act 2006 provides for means-testing, which it is hoped will save about £35m a year.

Third, decisions on funding criminal defence in magistrates' courts were taken by magistrates, not the CDS. It was felt this hampered the ability of the LSC to control the costs of the CDS. The Criminal Defence Service Act 2006 also provides for these decisions to come under the control of the CDS.

Private funding mechanisms[31]

The changes to legal aid cannot be seen in isolation. Other means to promote the pri-vate funding of the cost of taking legal proceedings have also been introduced in recent years. Behind these developments has been a desire to increase access to justice, while maintaining control of public expenditure. The challenge has been to devise ways of

---

[31] The emphasis in this section is on the funding of litigation, not the funding of non-contentious busi-ness, such as the drafting of wills, the administration of estates after a person has died, or the buying or selling of property.

enabling those who might want to litigate to do so without incurring disproportionate costs.

Three developments are considered here:

- the Civil Procedure Rules;
- conditional fee agreements; and
- fixed fees.

The Civil Procedure Rules

As noted in Chapter 8, Lord Woolf saw reduction in the costs of taking a case to court as a key objective in the reforms that he was proposing. There were two principal ways in which he envisaged that this objective might be achieved.

Making costs proportionate

Before the Woolf reforms were introduced, the basic principle used to determine disputes about costs was that those charging the costs had to demonstrate that the costs they incurred were reasonable. Following the introduction of the CPR, this principle has been amended. The costs must be both reasonable *and* proportionate to the issue in dispute.[32] In cases where relatively small sums of money are involved, it might well be reasonable for a number of legal steps to be taken in preparing the case, but if the cost of taking those steps was substantial, the total costs, while reasonable, might still not be proportionate. A judge would therefore be required to disallow costs which, though reasonable, were not proportionate. The difficulty with this principle is the obvious one: what is reasonable? and what is proportionate?

Case management

The emphasis in the CPR on judicial case management was designed to ensure that cases were dealt with more quickly. By preventing proceedings from dragging on, it was thought that the cost of litigation could be reduced. The problem here is that this objective is, to a significant extent, in conflict with other changes introduced in the CPR. There is now an emphasis in the post-Woolf era on the need for parties to put their cards on the negotiating table earlier than they used to. This means that cases which, prior to the introduction of the Woolf reforms, would have settled well before any trial was likely to take place, now require more work to be done at an early stage. This leads to a 'front-loading' of expense, which increases the costs of such cases.

While there has been very broad support in general for the Woolf reforms, there is considerable anecdotal evidence and some harder empirical evidence that the goal of cost reduction has yet to be achieved.[33]

---

[32] The details are set out in CPR Part 44—general rules about costs.

[33] See Goriely, T., *et al., More Civil Justice? The Impact of the Woolf Reforms on Pre-action Behaviour* (London, Law Society and Civil Justice Council, 2002).

Conditional fee agreements

The concept of the conditional fee agreement (CFAs) was introduced by the Conservative government in 1990. CFA is defined in section 58 of the Courts and Legal Services Act 1990, as amended by section 27(1) of the Access to Justice Act 1999, as 'an agreement... which provides for...fees and expenses, or any part of them, to be payable only in specified circumstances'. The importance of CFAs in the funding of litigation was significantly increased by the Access to Justice Act 1999. It became a principle that public funding of litigation through the Community Legal Service should not be provided in cases where alternative funding (including CFAs) is available.[34] (CFAs cannot be entered into in relation to criminal and most family proceedings.)

CFAs, also known as 'no win-no fee' agreements, allow solicitors to agree to take a case on the understanding that, if the case is lost, they will not charge their clients for all or any of the work undertaken. The client also agrees that if the case is successful, the solicitor can charge a *success fee* on top of the normal fees, to compensate for the risk the solicitor has run of not being paid all or some of her fees. The success fee is calculated as a percentage of the normal fees and the level at which the success fee is set reflects the risk involved. Regulations provide that the 'uplift' of the success fee should be no more than 100 per cent of the normal fee.

Until 1999, the success fee was paid out of damages recovered. The Law Society advised[35] solicitors that the uplift should not exceed 25 per cent of any damages recovered, where that figure would be less than the figure agreed in the CFA. Since 1999, the law was amended so that the success fee has to be paid by the party against whom a costs order has been made (in essence the losing party) in addition to any damages that may have been awarded. The same party also has to pay the costs of any After the Event Insurance (ATE) premium.

The party who loses an action faces the prospect of considerable costs. Since most of those represented under CFA agreements do not have the resources to pay those costs, ATE insurance is designed to cover them. This change to the funding of litigation meant that where a person covered by insurance lost, the insurance company was liable not only to meet the costs of the other side, but also the 'success' fee.

The law provided that CFAs that did not strictly comply with detailed statutory requirements were not enforceable. There thus arose an enormous 'satellite' litigation about whether or not CFAs complied with regulations. (It has been estimated that between 150,000 and 180,000 technical challenges were brought raising this issue.)

The government eventually responded by repealing all the statutory requirements, and instead saying that CFAs would be enforceable so long as they conformed to the Law Society's practice rules on CFAs. In addition, some additional certainty regarding

---

[34] See the *statutory factors* in the Access to Justice Act 1999, s. 8(2). This criterion does not apply in all cases, e.g. housing cases.

[35] Despite this link with damages, it should be stressed that CFAs are related only to the professional fees charged, *not* to damages. Any arrangements to recover costs by taking a percentage of damages recovered—contingency fees—are not lawful in England and Wales.

costs was introduced by a number of agreements fixing the fees to be charged in certain types of circumstance (see below).

Despite these changes, the ATE Insurance market remains fragile. The premiums paid for insurance cover are determined by the provider and are dependent on a number of factors, including the strength of the case, the likely measure of damages involved in the case, and the legal representative's experience of undertaking such cases. Premiums may range from relatively modest sums to many millions of pounds depending on the case insured. There has been a sharp increase in premiums for more run-of-the-mill cases, as the insurers who provide this form of cover initially underestimated the cost of meeting claims under the policies and so lost money in the early years. There are currently few companies offering ATE insurance, with those that do indicating limited if any profitability.

The ATE market is also being weakened by increasing use of Before the Event (BTE) insurance, usually purchased as an 'add-on' to household or motor insurance premiums. Where these are used, CFAs are not available. The future of CFAs remains uncertain.

In addition to CFAs, section 28 of the Access to Justice Act 1999 introduced a new concept, the *litigation funding agreement*. This allows a party to be funded by a third party (rather than the solicitor), e.g. a trade union or other prescribed group. In these cases the funder pays the solicitor's normal fees. However, where the case is won, the funder is entitled to be paid the success fee by the losing side and is able to retain that element of the fee to cover losses on cases which are not won.

Fixed fees

In order to try to bring some certainty to the market, the Civil Justice Council, which advises the government on issues relating to the civil justice system, lead a series of discussions with practitioners and the insurance industry to try and make some of the costs of litigation more predictable. In 2003, this resulted in the creation of a scheme for the use of fixed fees in relation to claims arising out of road traffic accidents for less than £10,000. These apply where liability for the accident was admitted, and where the only issue was the exact amount to be paid to settle the claim. The principle of predictable costs has been extended to the success fees to be applied in employer liability cases and Road Traffic Act accident cases. Further work is being done in other areas where there is scope to agree more predictable costs.

Conclusion

Access to justice is essential if the claim to have an efficient legal system is to be sustained. We have seen in this Chapter that the availability of legal aid, particularly in civil matters, is currently being seriously squeezed.

Debate on legal aid was, in the past, dominated to a large extent by the legal profession. The legal aid scheme was largely designed and developed by the Law Society. While there should be no doubt that those who undertook this work were determined to create a scheme that delivered a needed service to the public, it is also the case that the legal profession was the principal beneficiary of it. The injection of over £2 billion of public money into the legal profession—the total amount of current public expenditure on legal services—is not trivial. It was obvious that the rate of growth of public expenditure in this area—despite rhetorical claims that 'justice is without price'— could not be sustained.

Put another way, if policy-makers had started the legal aid scheme from scratch with a budget of over £2 billion, would they have devised the legal aid scheme that eventually developed? Those who accept that the answer to this question must be 'no' must then think what the shape of any alternative might be.

The Access to Justice Act 1999 provided the opportunity for a new scheme to emerge. It is inevitably built upon its historical legacy. There is still a chance that the Community Legal Service will ultimately prove to be more fit for its purpose than the civil legal aid scheme it replaced. A range of important initiatives in service delivery have been introduced, many of which are extremely imaginative. The challenge for the Community Legal Service is to ensure that there continues to be sufficient funding to ensure that an adequate supply of well-qualified lawyers remains committed to the delivery of high quality services, particularly in relation to the difficult and unusual case. The desire of the service to fund those other than professionally qualified lawyers to provide legal services for the straightforward case must not destroy the ability of the service to provide lawyer's services for the difficult and demanding case. (An important recent development is the requirement that, in presenting proposals for new legislation to Parliament, ministers must offer an estimate of the impact of the Bill on the demand for legal services.)

The jury is still out on the Criminal Defence Service. Since it was created, the CDS has been successful in increasing the level of funds it has received. Practitioners argue that this is only a response to the additional work that has come to court resulting from the government's drive to reduce criminality and bring more people to trial. The government will face a real challenge if the provision of criminal defence services is not made a sufficiently attractive career option to attract the young, able lawyer.

The potential relationship between the public funding of legal services and new incentives to encourage the private funding of litigation is less clear. Lawyers do have a considerable track record of turning new opportunities for earning a living to their advantage. In so doing, there is at least a reasonable prospect that the individual will have greater access to justice. However, while CFAs arguably provided a means for increasing access to justice, they too are subject to the availability of an ATE insurance market that does not appear to be particularly robust. In any event, CFAs are open to a number of forms of abuse.[36]

---

[36] These were identified by Lord Bingham in his judgment in *Callery v. Gray* [2002] 1 WLR 2000 at 2003, HL.

(1) Lawyers may charge excessive costs knowing that their own client will not have to pay them.

(2) Lawyers may set the success fee at a level that is grossly disproportionate to any fair assessment of the risk involved in the case.

(3) Insurers may charge premiums grossly disproportionate to the risk being underwritten.

If the difficulties with legal and conditional fee agreements persist, alternative sources of funding of civil litigation need to be explored. The Civil Justice Council has recently published an important advice to the Lord Chancellor urging that consideration be given to a number of additional funding avenues.

The first is a *Supplementary Legal Aid scheme*, based on a model developed in Hong Kong, which provides legal aid to a wider group of people than the current scheme, but then requires them to pay a levy into the scheme either from the damages they recover or the costs they recover.

The second is to move from conditional fees to *contingency fees*. This is the principle used not only in the United States, but also every Canadian province save Ontario. The key feature of contingency fees is that lawyers get their fees by taking a percentage out of the damages recovered by their own clients. The Civil Justice Council argues that initially this should only be used in multi-party claims arising out of a single set of events. Experience might lead to consideration of extending contingency fees to other cases.

The third is *third party funding* where an investor buys the right to conduct litigation on behalf of a claimant or, more usually, a group of claimants. The funder recovers the cost of the investment by taking a percentage of damages or costs recovered, as agreed at the start of the outset. This process, sometimes called 'claim-farming', has been developing in a number of other jurisdictions notably in Australia.

There has as yet been no government response to these ideas.

Questions for reflection and discussion

1. What should be the balance between the role of the state and the responsibility of the individual in funding litigation? Is the current balance correct?

2. Will a Public Defender Service weaken or enhance the criminal justice system?

3. Should the legal aid budget be 'cash-limited'?

4. Can access to civil justice be improved through new arrangements for the funding of litigation?

5. Could there be greater use of fixed fees?

6. What are the arguments for and against contingency fees?

7. How far can advice be delivered by telephone or the internet?

8. How can the gap between those who might benefit from legal advice and those who actually receive legal advice services be bridged?

Further reading

Davis, G., Donkor, K., and Morgan, R., *Ethnic Minorities' Legal Needs and Perceptions of Legal Services: Report of a Pilot Investigation for the Law Society* (London, The Law Society, 1993)

Department for Constitutional Affairs and the Law Centres Federation, *Legal and Advice Services: A Pathway to Regeneration* (London, Department for Constitutional Affairs, 2004)

Genn, H., *Paths to Justice* (Oxford, Hart, 1999)

Goriely, T., and Das Gupta, P. (with Bowles, R.), *Breaking the Code: The Impact of Legal Aid Reforms on General Civil Litigation* (London, Institute of Advanced Legal Studies, 2001)

—— Moorhead, R., and Abrams, P., *More Civil Justice? The Impact of the Woolf Reforms on Pre-action Behaviour* (Research Study 43) (London, Law Society (and the Civil Justice Council), 2002)

Kempson, E., *Legal Advice and Assistance* (London, Policy Studies Institute, 1989)

Legal Action Group, *A Strategy for Justice: Publicly Funded Legal Services in the 1990s* (London, Legal Action Group, 1992)

Legal Services Commission, *Making Legal Rights a Reality* (London, Legal Services Commission, 2005)

Legal Services Research Centre, *Causes of Action: civil law and social justice. The final report of the first LSRC survey of justiciable problems* (2nd edn., London, Legal Services Commission, 2006)

Lord Chancellor's Advisory Committee on Legal Education and Conduct, *Setting Standards for Community Legal Services* (London, Lord Chancellor's Department, 1999)

Regan, F., *et al., The Transformation of Legal Aid: Comparative and Historical Studies* (Oxford, Clarendon Press, 1999)

Steele, J., and Seargeant, J., *Access to Legal Services: The Contribution of Alternative Approaches* (London, Policy Studies Institute, 1999)

Websites

http://www.lapg.co.uk/ *(Legal Aid Practitioners' Group)*

http://www.lag.org.uk/ / *(Legal Action Group)*

http://www.clsa.co.uk/Default.asp?page=52 *(Criminal Law Solicitors' Association)*

http://www.legalservices.gov.uk/ *(Legal Services Commission)*

http://www.legalservices.gov.uk/civil/guidance/funding_code.asp *(Community Legal Service Funding Code)* http://www.clsdirect.org.uk/index.jsp?lang=en *(CLS Direct)*

http://www.civiljusticecouncil.gov.uk/ *(Homepage of the civil justice council)*

http://www.civiljusticecouncil.gov.uk/files/future_funding_litigation_paper_v117_final.pdf *(CJC paper on options for the funding of civil litigation)*

http://www.lawsociety.org.uk/home.law *(Law Society homepage)*

http://www.das.co.uk/main.asp *(Legal expense insurance company)*

http://www.national-accident.co.uk/index.html *(Site advertising services relating to personal injury litigation)*

http://www.foil.org.uk/ *(Forum of Insurance Lawyers)*

http://www.apil.com/ *(Association of Personal Injury Lawyers)*

http://www.claimscouncil.org/ *(Organization setting standards for claims management companies)*

http://www.citizensadvice.org.uk/ *(Primary site for information about Citizens' Advice Bureaux)*

http://www.adviceguide.org.uk/ *(Online advice service provided by Citizens' Advice)*

http://www.asauk.org.uk/ *(Homepage of the Advice Services Alliance, with links to legal advice, and also ADR)*

CONCLUSION

11

Is the English legal system
fit for purpose?

Introduction

At the start of this book, the question was posed: is the English legal system currently fit to meet the demands placed upon it? In subsequent pages, many issues have been considered: what are law's functions? how is law made? what are the contexts in which it is practised? who are the different actors in the legal system? how are legal services funded? A number of specific issues about the fitness of the legal system to achieve its apparent purposes have been raised in context above.[1]

In this final chapter I return to that initial question. This chapter does not provide definitive answers but raises matters not specifically considered earlier, and encourages readers to think critically about the issues that have been raised.

Law plays a variety of key roles, not necessarily consistent with each other, in the organization of modern society. Countries where the rule of law is less well established than in the United Kingdom may be seen to be at something of a disadvantage. However, the world is going through a period of rapid and considerable change. Is the English legal system able adequately to respond to this changing world?

Images of law

Chapter 1 suggested that those without direct experience of law or lawyers might come to the study of law with pre-conceptions about the legal system that were at best limited, at worst seriously distorted. Subsequent chapters have demonstrated that there is much more to the legal system than crime; that those providing legal services are far more varied in character than the fat-cat lawyers sometimes portrayed in the press; that both the institutions of the legal system and those who deliver legal services are undergoing profound change; that problems of inefficiency and delay, particularly in the litigation process, are increasingly acknowledged and are being addressed.

---

[1] Just by way of example note the comments on Child Support, above, at Chapter 7, p. 190.

Institutional innovation is driven in part by the government's modernization agenda, and its response to current social pressures—particularly those arising out of anti-social behaviour. But innovation is also a response to the needs of an increasingly global economy which contribute substantially to the pressure for institutional change. In the past, the leaders of the legal profession may, on occasion, have appeared resistant to change as they sought to defend the interests of practitioners who feared an uncertain future and were unwilling to embrace change. Today, they seem more open to the need for change and to respond to the consumers of legal services. Indeed, many individual practitioners and firms of lawyers have shown considerable dynamism and imagination in shaping their practices to respond to clients' needs and wider pressures.

Many other indicators suggest that negative images of law and the legal system are unfair. There is still a great desire on the part both of professionally qualified lawyers and other lay legal advisers to deliver legal services to all sections of the public, not just the well-heeled and powerful. Standards of education and training of lawyers and other advisers have increased greatly in recent years. The judiciary are notably free of corruption.

But to stop at this point would risk the complacent conclusion that the English legal system *is* the best in the world, requiring at most only modest further adjustment. The fact is that there are many other issues on which one can be more critical. It is important that those coming to the legal system for the first time think about those features which can be criticized. The future development of robust legal institutions lies at least in part in the hands of those now entering the legal system.

One key problem is the treatment of legal issues in the mass media. Apart from the drama of the big criminal trial or a scandal involving a miscarriage of justice, discussion about law in the mass media is not well-rounded. With notable exceptions such as the BBC Radio programme, *Law In Action,* or the weekly law pages in some of the broadsheet newspapers, together with a number of consumer programmes which touch on aspects of the law, there is little rounded discussion about law making, the practice of law, or the impact of law on the citizen. Unlike other aspects of our intellectual life, such as history or science or medicine, law is not regularly the subject of mainstream media programming.

Yet the centrality of law to different social orders suggests that the media neglect of law and legal issues is unsatisfactory. Programme makers may feel that law is too complex a subject to make it attractive for mass programming. It is almost inconceivable that a UK television channel would made a four hour documentary on the House of Lords, as the Public Broadcasting System in the USA did on the US Supreme Court.[2] But this simply contributes to the mystique of law and enhances the power of the lawyer in society, at a time when arguably opportunities for greater general understanding of and access to law should be growing.[3]

---

[2] See: http://www.pbs.org/wnet/supremecourt/index.html

[3] See Government Taskforce on Public Legal Education, at http://www.pleas.org.uk/

Part of the reason public discussion of legal issues is so limited may be that those who operate within the legal system themselves have shown only limited interest in presenting their work to a wider audience. Much professional legal activity is conducted on the basis of secrecy and confidentiality, which may result in a lack of individual enthusiasm to enter the public eye. Furthermore, there are those in the legal profession who think that it goes against the professional grain to seek publicity for their work. However, a consequence of such attitudes is that the law and its practitioners tend to hit the headlines only when things have gone wrong.

Considerable effort is these days spent placing stories in the media which form part of the public relations activity of promoting the work of individual legal firms or practices. Lawyers and other practitioners should also be willing to shape a more educational public information agenda, and to work with the media to develop opportunities for a fuller understanding of law and the legal system in all our lives. The difficulties of making a wider range of programmes about law may be substantial; nevertheless the challenge ahead remains to provide a new, more informed, treatment of legal issues in the mass media. This would play an important part in the shaping of public perceptions about the legal system and those who work in it, which could in turn contribute to making the legal system function more effectively.

One particular idea is whether trials should be televised. This happens a great deal in the United States; there was a notable recent experiment in the United Kingdom when a number of trials in Scotland were shown in edited form on television. While such a step might give the appearance of greater openness of the legal system to the public, it should be remembered that televising trials may merely serve to exacerbate current images of law—that the typical legal process is a criminal one, in which there is a lengthy trial of the case for and against the accused. There is little discussion about televising cases in the administrative justice, family justice, or civil justice arenas; or programmes dealing with the vast majority of cases that are resolved without a full-scale trial.

In addition to the treatment of law in the media, other issues also need consideration. First, there are important questions to be resolved about patterns of recruitment to and career development in the legal profession. Although there are now greater opportunities for women to become lawyers than was the case some years ago, they have not yet achieved their full potential to rise to the most senior positions. In addition, the improvement in the opportunities for women to enter law does not appear to have been matched by comparable increases in the opportunities for those coming from working-class backgrounds or ethnic minority backgrounds. Given the importance of equality of treatment and evenhandedness in the delivery of legal services, it is important that those running the profession and the institutions of the law take issues of recruitment and advancement seriously.

Secondly, are current modes of dress appropriate in the twenty-first century? As noted in Chapter 9, a large number of actors in the legal system do not put on any kind of formal clothing before they undertake the services required of them by the public.

And the Lord Chief Justice has announced that judicial dress in civil cases should be less formal. The question still arises: should other aspects of legal dress remain unchanged?

Law's functions

A wide range of issues about the social functions of law were considered in Chapter 2. In relation to many of these, readers have their own views, not all of which can be canvassed in an introductory work. The tension between the use of law to control and regulate behaviour and the use of law to protect people by giving them rights and entitlements was particularly emphasized.

The issue that arises out of that discussion, which bears most fundamentally on the question whether the English legal system is fit for purpose, is whether there is now too ready a recourse to the use of law to try to deal with the issues facing modern society. There are occasions on which politicians and others pay lip-service to the proposition that law should not be used to regulate human activity more than absolutely necessary. But there are few incentives *not* to make law. Politicians' and civil servants' reputations are based on the laws they create, not those that they prevent. And the reputation of practitioners is enhanced by their pushing at the boundaries of law, as they try to establish new areas of legal liability, not by seeking to limit the scope of law. The Human Rights Act 1998 has added to these pressures. Certainly the amount and complexity of the law that emerges from government and the courts are constantly increasing.

In this context, the proposition that ordinary citizens can in any real sense be assumed to know the law that governs their lives is just not sustainable. While it may not be realistic to complain that there is too much law, the implications for lawmakers and others involved in the working of the legal system in providing better information about law are clear. The Legal Services Commission has started to invest in the provision of useful information about the law and its procedures. Other agencies are also increasingly using this as a source of information. But lack of usable information remains a weakness in the current institutional arrangements of the legal system. As with the challenge of providing better general information about law through the mass media, there is still a considerable challenge to be faced, particularly within government, about the use of new information and communication technologies to make information about citizens' rights available to a much wider public than is presently the case. This is an area of activity in which there has already been much change and where it may be anticipated that there will be rapid progress in the years ahead.

Law making—legitimacy and authority

The primary law-making bodies today are the legislative institutions of the European Union and the United Kingdom. Both claim to derive legitimacy for the exercise of legislative powers from political theories of democracy. However, the extent to which ordinary people understand the nature of such assertions of legitimacy must be open to doubt. The processes of Parliament are poorly understood; those of the institutions of the European Union are shrouded in even greater mystery. There is great ignorance about the links between institutional assertions of legitimacy and the democratic will of the people. Even less clear is the relationship between majority opinion and the protection of minorities—a key issue in modern pluralist societies.

There is evidence that this is beginning to be taken seriously. Many of the institutional and constitutional reforms, both in the United Kingdom and in Europe, are influenced by an increasing acknowledgement that voter apathy is not a satisfactory basis on which to claim legitimacy for the exercise of law-making power. At some point, unless more is done to encourage people to understand that, for example, elections are important, there will be a danger that those theoretically governed on the basis of consent may come to deny the legitimacy of their governors to govern. The decision to introduce instruction on citizenship into the school curriculum (in England, but not Wales) is a recognition of the importance of this issue.

A likely trend in the next decade is much greater effort by government institutions to explain what they are doing and to encourage input into the law-making process.[4] Many of the recent procedural innovations to the law-making machinery in the United Kingdom—considered in Chapter 3—reflect this need. Questions remain, though: do these changes go far enough? Should recent procedural changes in both the UK and European Parliaments be taken further? Should there be further changes to the electoral system? To what extent is there a 'democratic deficit'? If there is such a deficit, what measures are needed to reduce it? Should there be greater opportunities for lobbyists and other groups to influence the shape and content of legislation?

The law-making functions of the judges are also under intense scrutiny, particularly with the coming into force of the Human Rights Act 1998. Initial indications are that English judges have been very restrained and have not sought to use the Human Rights Act to usurp the essentially political functions of Parliament and the executive to deliver its legislative agenda. But voices are being heard that the judges have been too timid. It is impossible to predict how the judges will respond to such pressure, though it may be guessed that they will continue to take a cautious line for some time yet.

In any event, most governments would claim that they already operate within both the spirit and the letter of the European Convention on Human Rights. But a

---

[4] In fact, a vast amount of consultation already goes on between government and groups in society; indeed, some complain of 'consultation fatigue' as yet another consultation exercise arrives in the post or e-mail. But it is important that, whatever the problems, governments continue this trend.

moment's reflection indicates that, in difficult cases, there is potential for considerable tension to develop between the legislative and executive branches of government and the judicial branch. If a significant political/legislative objective is declared incompatible with the European Convention on Human Rights by the courts, whether in the United Kingdom or in Strasbourg, this may at best result in embarrassment for the government, at worst in considerable frustration. There is a powerful argument that adherence to human rights standards by government should be in general a political responsibility, not a judicial one.

Experience in the United States, where the Supreme Court has long asserted a power to review legislation in the context of the US Constitution and the Bill of Rights, may suggest that the impact of the courts on the legislative process has been limited. Experience in other countries—for example, Canada—suggests that such a view may be too sanguine. Whichever way the British judiciary goes, it seems inevitable that the constitutional role of the judiciary will become the focus of sharp debate in the years ahead.

This leads to a broader question: has the time come for the creation of a written constitution, which seeks to provide specific legitimacy for the different branches of government, and the systems of checks and balances that they should operate to preserve the rule of law and prevent abuse of power? At present, this seems to be unlikely, but is an issue that will not disappear.

Notwithstanding all the procedural changes, there remain many practical questions about the law-making process which still need addressing. For example, where there is agreement that a particular rule of law needs changing, the problem of parliamentary time means that this cannot easily be achieved. A significant number of Law Commission reports remain unimplemented. Where the common law lacks clarity or certainty, the ability of the judiciary to develop legal principle is dependent on the right case being brought before it. Should special procedures, either in Parliament or before the courts, be made more readily available where the state of the law is clearly unsatisfactory?

A different issue relates to styles of legislative drafting. One of the reasons legislation, in particular, is so hard to understand is that legislative draftsmen seek to define everything in legislation—whether primary, secondary, or tertiary—with a very high degree of linguistic precision. This leads to very considerable complexity. In turn this raises the question whether a more 'plain English' approach to the drafting of statutes might be appropriate. Certainly, the new Civil Procedure Rules were drafted on the basis that they should be easier to read and understand. And there are lawyers who have signed up to the Plain English Campaign's[5] initiative for clearer drafting of legal documents. The question of the extent to which such initiatives should spread more widely into legislative drafting practice is being considered.

In fact, legislative drafting styles change. An Act or a Bill drafted today is very different from one drafted twenty-five, fifty, or 100 years ago. Currently the focus is on getting the architecture of an Act right so that the reader can acquire more easily a

---

[5] See www.plainenglish.co.uk/index.html.

sense of what the legislation is seeking to achieve. This is supported by the new practice of publishing explanatory notes. A particular difficulty is to know whether new drafting practices would lead to more or less legislative uncertainty. It is likely that, to be fully effective, radically new legislative drafting practices would have to be supported by the senior judiciary.

Justice and efficiency

The chapters in Part II of the book reveal a number of common themes. Most prominent is the pressure in all justice systems to deal with cases as expeditiously and as economically as possible. These are perfectly proper aims, but nevertheless raise the question of the extent to which the shaping of the legal system should be driven by demands for efficiency and value for money, as opposed to other demands, such as the need for the justice system to be just. While unnecessary delay and expense must be deplored, it should still be asked whether current trends to dispose of cases rapidly or even to divert them completely from courts and other dispute-resolution fora always operate in the interests of justice.

These issues cannot be addressed by vague assertions that 'justice has no price'. Justice clearly does have a price, which has to be paid for either by the citizen or by the state (whose resources come from the taxpayer). At the same time important principles relating to the need for fairness of the trial process must be borne in mind. There must be some doubt, especially in the context of criminal justice, whether the apparently increasing focus on the 'crime control' model of criminal justice is compatible with a 'due process' model. If taken too far, the question will arise whether the system will be compliant with the human rights standards set down in the European Convention on Human Rights.

Another set of issues relates to avenues of appeal. In the context of the criminal justice system, for example, some of the recent serious cases of miscarriage of justice seem to have been exacerbated, at least in part, by the rather restrictive bases on which the Court of Criminal Appeal may determine criminal appeals. The creation of the Criminal Cases Review Commission was designed in part to assist. Will this be enough to prevent further serious miscarriages of justice? What other mechanisms are needed to ensure both that the innocent are not convicted and sentenced, and that those who have committed offences are brought to trial?

In relation to administrative justice and civil justice, the question was raised whether there were too many avenues of appeal and complaint for the individual to pursue. Changes to appeal routes in the civil justice system have reduced the number of appeals that can be brought in that context. The reform of the tribunal system may be the first step in a more fundamental review of the administrative justice system. It may be asked whether the current sharp distinctions between courts and tribunals will exist in ten years' time.

One issue that affects the whole of the institutional framework of the English legal system is whether all citizens, and particularly members of ethnic minorities, feel that they are dealt with fairly. Following the Stephen Lawrence case, a major programme of research on the experience of those from the minority groups in all parts of the legal system was undertaken. On the whole, little overt discrimination was found. But the issue needs to be kept under review. If the legal system is revealed as being unable to deliver equal treatment to all those who come into contact with it, this will be a concern of the utmost importance which will have to be dealt with urgently.

One pressure for change not considered in the main text is a set of ideas currently being developed within the policy-making bodies in Europe which might lead towards the development of a more European-wide court system. There could be some merit in these ideas. If the EU encourages greater freedom of movement of its citizens around the different countries of Europe, should it not also enable those citizens to enforce their rights in the country of their choice? However, for many the very idea of such integration would be anathema. This is not an idea that is currently well-developed and has certainly not been widely discussed. It is not pursued further here. But it is an issue to which attention needs to be drawn. Were such moves to be seriously contemplated, the major distinctions between the British common law approach to law and the Continental European civil law approach would be likely to prove a major hurdle to the integration of judicial systems. It is in this context that the suggestion of the need for closer legal integration between the common law countries of Europe, principally the United Kingdom and Ireland, might gain more significance.

Professional organization

Chapter 9 considered a number of questions relating to professional organization. It considered the increasing part played by government in seeking to regulate standards of professional activity. It was suggested that this could prove a worrying trend. Although there is no suggestion that government will seek to limit the proper independence of the professionally qualified lawyer to take up controversial or unpopular cases, this does not mean that this could not happen at some future time if the trend towards greater government intervention accelerates further.

The funding of legal services

The final issue addressed in the book is whether the new arrangements for the funding of legal services will—in some general sense—'work'. Here there is considerable uncertainty. The new arrangements for the state-funded Community Legal Service and Criminal Defence Service and the related arrangements for alternative ways of funding other forms of litigation are still too recent for a definitive conclusion to be reached.

Those who predicted a complete breakdown in the provision of quality legal services to the public have so far been confounded. However, the changes are having a big impact on the legal profession, particularly small firms or sole practitioners in small towns or rural areas, where it is hard for them to generate the levels of business needed to stay afloat financially. It is likely that there will have to be more mergers and consolidations to increase business efficiency that have already taken place at the more commercial end of the legal professional market.

More generally, whether all the promises offered by government for the effectiveness and impact of the new structure will be delivered must also be open to doubt. What is needed is agreement on a reasonable level of government expenditure on the delivery of legal services, accompanied by an acceptance by legal practitioners that they must justify the £2.0 billion of public money that is paid to them. At the same time, it does seem inevitable that the line between legal services and lawyers' services will become even more blurred, with more legal services being delivered by those without formal professional legal qualifications.

Conclusion

Much of the English legal system is pretty fit for purpose, but it is not perfect. There is always room for change and improvement. Those coming new to law should seek to support what is good, but not seek to defend the indefensible. The discussion in these pages is designed to encourage the thought, reflection, and action needed to bring about change that is necessary, while preventing change that is undesirable.

Table of References

Index